Sport Governance and Operations

Governance is at the centre of the work of all sport organizations, from small sport clubs to international sport federations. This book explores sport governance in today's globalized marketplace.

It adopts a broad, modern definition of 'governance' that includes the operational process of organizing resources and the implementation of standing policies and plans, as well as regulation, direction, control and evaluation. This book presents a series of cutting-edge case studies that shine important new light on key themes in contemporary sport management, including sustainability, human resource management, cross-cultural management and labour markets, across a wide range of sporting contexts, from Formula One and the Commonwealth Games to the NCAA. Bringing together researchers and practitioners from five continents, it represents an important platform for the international exchange of ideas, best practices and scholarly enquiry.

This is fascinating reading for any student, researcher or practitioner with an interest in sport business and management, event management or international business.

Euisoo Kim is Visiting Assistant Professor of Sport Management in the Department of Kinesiology and Health at Georgia State University, USA.

James J. Zhang is Professor of Sport Management and Director of the International Center for Sport Management (ICSM) at the University of Georgia, USA.

World Association for Sport Management Series

Series Editors:
Brenda G. Pitts, Georgia State University, USA
James J. Zhang, University of Georgia, USA

The World Association for Sport Management (WASM) was founded to facilitate sport management research, teaching and learning excellence, and professional practice, across every continent. The WASM book series is designed to support those aims by presenting current research and scholarship, from well-established and emerging scholars and practitioners, on sport management theory, policy, and practice. Books in the series will explore contemporary issues and key challenges in sport management, and identify important new directions for research and professional practice. Above all, the series aims to encourage and highlight the development of international perspectives, international partnerships, and international best practice in sport management, recognizing the globalised nature of the contemporary sport industry.

Available in this series:

Sport Business in the United States
Contemporary Perspectives
Edited by Brenda G. Pitts and James J. Zhang

International Sport Business Management
Issues and New Ideas
Edited by James J. Zhang, Brenda G. Pitts and Lauren M. Johnson

Sport Governance and Operations
Global Perspectives
Edited by Euisoo Kim and James J. Zhang

For more information about this series, please visit: https://www.routledge.com/World-Association-for-Sport-Management-Series/book-series/WASM

Sport Governance and Operations
Global Perspectives

Edited by
Euisoo Kim and
James J. Zhang

LONDON AND NEW YORK

First published 2022
by Routledge
2 Park Square, Milton Park, Abingdon, Oxon OX14 4RN

and by Routledge
605 Third Avenue, New York, NY 10158

Routledge is an imprint of the Taylor & Francis Group, an informa business

© 2022 selection and editorial matter, World Association of Sport Management (WASM); individual chapters, the contributors

The right of World Association of Sport Management (WASM) to be identified as the author of this Work has been asserted by them in accordance with sections 77 and 78 of the Copyright, Designs and Patents Act 1988.

All rights reserved. No part of this book may be reprinted or reproduced or utilised in any form or by any electronic, mechanical, or other means, now known or hereafter invented, including photocopying and recording, or in any information storage or retrieval system, without permission in writing from the publishers.

Trademark notice: Product or corporate names may be trademarks or registered trademarks, and are used only for identification and explanation without intent to infringe.

British Library Cataloguing-in-Publication Data
A catalogue record for this book is available from the British Library

Library of Congress Cataloging-in-Publication Data
Names: Zhang, James J., editor. | Kim, Euisoo, 1946– editor.
Title: Sport governance and operations : global perspectives | edited by James J. Zhang and Euisoo Kim.
Description: First Edition. | New York : Routledge, 2022. | Series: World association for sport management series | Includes bibliographical references and index. |
Subjects: LCSH: Sports administration. | Sports and globalization.
Classification: LCC GV713 .S6753 2022 | DDC 796.06/9—dc23
LC record available at https://lccn.loc.gov/2021020392

ISBN: 978-1-032-10104-0 (hbk)
ISBN: 978-1-032-10107-1 (pbk)
ISBN: 978-1-003-21367-3 (ebk)

DOI: 10.4324/9781003213673

Typeset in Goudy
by codeMantra

Contents

List of contributors   vii

1   **Sport governance defined: an introduction**   1
EUISOO KIM, YUNDUK JEONG AND JAMES J. ZHANG

2   **Governance of sport for the 21st century: contemporary perspectives**   9
DARLENE A. KLUKA

3   **Sport policies and their sociocultural impacts**   21
JEPKORIR ROSE CHEPYATOR-THOMSON, SEAN SEILER,
KATJA SONKENG AND SEHWAN KIM

4   **Effective governance through human resources: international experience in career development of football administrators in Poland**   39
KAROLINA NESSEL

5   **Cultural frame switching: bicultural-bilingual vs. monocultural-monolingual coaches**   60
GARETH WINSLOW AND GEOFF DICKSON

6   **Governing sport organizations: significance and determinants of innovations**   77
YUNDUK JEONG, EUISOO KIM, AND JAMES J. ZHANG

7   **Governing economic flows in European professional football clubs**   103
JAN ŠÍMA AND TOMÁŠ RUDA

vi Contents

8 Efficiency of financial investment in Formula One racing: a new era in motor sport   115
WILLIAM OSTER AND BRANDON MASTROMARTINO

9 Policy implications in rhythmic gymnastics judging: a case analysis   132
ROSA LÓPEZ DE D'AMICO AND MAYERLITH CANELÓN

10 Restructuring CUBA and Chinese collegiate sports: learning from the governing success of NCAA   146
RUNTAO MAO

11 Impact of athletic talents on team structure: marquee players in Major League Soccer   165
ANDREW MACUGA AND EUISOO KIM

12 Endorsing public diplomacy through international sport events: impact of sport fan engagement   192
KEVIN K. BYON, SUNG-UN YANG, WOOYOUNG (WILLIAM) JANG, AND TAEYOUNG KIM

13 Transcending ball and ballin': connecting the Jordan Brand and college football fans   210
C. KEITH HARRISON, KATHY BABIAK, JACOB TINGLE, JESSIE DICKENS, WHITNEY GRIFFIN, AND SCOTT BUKSTEIN

14 Structuring sustainable sport events and achieving desirable impact on urban development   225
CRISTIANA BUSCARINI, FABIO CERRONI, AND SARA FRANZINI GABRIELLI

15 New directions for professional preparation: a competency-based model for training sport management personnel   244
JANA NOVÁ

Index   269

Contributors

Kathy Babiak, University of Michigan, USA.

Scott Bukstein, University of Central Florida, USA.

Cristiana Buscarini, University of Rome "Foro Italico", Italy.

Kevin K. Byon, Indiana University, USA.

Mayerlith Canelón, Universidad de Carabobo, Venezuela.

Fabio Cerroni, Sapienza University of Rome, Italy.

Jepkorir Rose Chepyator-Thomson, University of Georgia, USA.

Rosa López de D'Amico, Universidad Pedagógica Experimental Libertador, Venezuela.

Jessie Dickens, Duke University, USA.

Geoff Dickson, La Trobe University, Australia.

Sara Franzini Gabrielli, University of Rome "Foro Italico", Italy.

Whitney Griffin, Cerritos College, USA.

C. Keith Harrison, University of Central Florida, USA.

Wooyoung (William) Jang, University of West Georgia, USA.

Yunduk Jeong, Kookmin University, South Korea.

Sehwan Kim, University of Georgia, USA.

Taeyoung Kim, Loyola University Chicago, USA.

Darlene A. Kluka, University of Pretoria, South Africa.

Andrew Macuga, Major League Soccer (MLS), USA.

Runtao Mao, University of Shanghai, China.

Brandon Mastromartino, Southern Methodist University, USA.

Karolina Nessel, Jagiellonian University, Poland.

Jana Nová, Masaryk University, Czech Republic.

William Oster, University of Georgia, USA.

Tomáš Ruda, Charles University in Prague, Czech Republic.

Sean Seiler, University of Georgia, USA.

Jan Šíma, Charles University in Prague, Czech Republic.

Katja Sonkeng, Western Illinois University, USA.

Jacob Tingle, Trinity University, USA.

Gareth Winslow, New Zealand Professional Golfers Association, New Zealand.

Sung-Un Yang, Indiana University, USA.

Chapter 1

Sport governance defined
An introduction

*Euisoo Kim, Yunduk Jeong and
James J. Zhang*

Introduction

In recent years, governance has gained increased research interest among scholars in various areas of social science, such as public administration, business, social work, and sports. The origin of the word "governance" can be traced back to the Greek word *kubernanan*, then Latin word *Gubernare*, both of which mean "to steer" (Abubakar et al., 2020). Although the term governance is widely used in numerous ways, no universally agreed definition of governance exists. Bevir (2012) suggested that the process of governing is the core concept of governance that is based on rules and practices in which accountability, fairness, and transparency have to be embedded, whether a sovereign state governs its citizen, a corporation does to its employees, or an organization manages its members. Studies of corporate governance initially began with a series of failures among corporations in the United Kingdom in the early 1980s; thereafter, similar failures were witnessed in other regions of the globe, making scholars and practitioners rethink the meaning, role, and importance of governance, its process, and its influence on the success of a corporation (Bevir, 2012; Clifford & Evans, 1996). To respond to these inquires, one of the main areas of research in corporate governance has been focused on conformance of management and board members, and their influence on the enhancement of organizational performance (Hoye & Cuskelly, 2007).

There are generally two schools of defining and conceptualizing the term "governance". Traditionally, this term is used to describe policies, regulations, directions, and control and evaluation. Thus, governance is the way rules, norms, and actions are structured, sustained, regulated, and held accountable (Kooiman, 2003). The traditional view of governance is focused on the governing body and policies, regulations, and structures set by the governing body. More contemporary application of the term also includes governing actions, namely the operational process of organizing resources, implementing standing policies and plans, achieving goals, and sustaining the organization. Governance encompasses the system by which an organization is both controlled and operated. It is a theoretical concept referring to the actions and processes by which stable practices and

DOI: 10.4324/9781003213673-1

organizations arise and persist (Empter & Janning, 2009; Governance Institute of Australia, 2021).

In a similar fashion, traditionally the most common factors that constitute the concept of sport governance include directions, policies, regulations, and control (Hoye & Cuskelly, 2007). More recent conceptualizations and practice of sport governance also emphasize the process of effective carrying out of set directions and enforcement of stated policies (Hums & MacLean, 2018). Setting a clear direction for a sport organization, controlling activities of organization including staff members to align with strategies, and establishing rules and policies that regulate members in an organization are critical elements of good sport governance, which would enhance performance of sport organizations while effectively supervising organizational activities. In other words, main responsibilities of sport governance include overseeing the setting up of overall directions of an organization and ensuring proper organizational functions (Kikulis, 2000). Therefore, governance is an essential element that should be institutionalized in all sport organizations, from small sport clubs to international sport organizations, in order to achieve the best interests of an organization and all its related stakeholders (Hoye & Cuskelly, 2007; Hums & MacLean, 2018).

Sport governance at different levels (e.g. local, national, and international organizations) would focus on different agendas. For instance, while the leading topics of National Collegiate Athletic Association (NCAA), the governing organization of college sports in the U.S., deal with sport rules, championships, health and safety, and matters impacting women in athletics and opportunities for minorities (NCAA, 2020), the main focus of sport governance among international sport organizations such as the International Olympic Committee is to come up with the most effective sport policy among diverse alternatives by analyzing three major issues: ideology, political risk, and stakeholders (Thoma & Chalip, 1996). Moreover, although similarities in the structure of sport governance across borders exist within the same level (e.g., professional sport league organizations), many differences exist. A good example could be found in the governance structure of soccer. While the administrative structures of soccer leagues in almost all countries employ a promotion and relegation system, the same system is not applicable to the Major League Soccer (MLS) in North America, making it the only first-division professional soccer league in the globe without movement between divisions (Galarcep, 2019).

External and internal environments influence sport organizations to a great extent as they belong to the greater society; therefore, one of the important roles of sport governance is to react properly to the expected environmental changes (Hums & MacLean, 2018). For instance, sport participation of female athletes in American colleges has increased sharply with the establishment of Title IX in 1972, which legally forces federally funded institutions to provide equitable sport participation opportunities between men and women (WSF, 2016). This external environmental change has brought significant policy changes among athletic departments in the U.S. Another example is the governing board of the NCAA, which has been dealing with potential changes of its bylaws and policies to allow student athletes to gain financial compensation on commercial use of their name, image, and likeness (NIL) (Osburn, 2019). The proposed policy change is the result of a series of lawsuits against NCAA from student athletes on NIL compensation, which was initially brought up by O'Bannon who filed a lawsuit in 2009 and followed by several other student athletes later on (Berkowitz, 2020). This example shows how internal members of an organization, namely student athletes, in this case could affect rules and policy changes of sport organizations.

Common practices of governance in sport industry

Having regulatory power over its members would be one of the most influential aspects of sport governance. By setting up rules and regulations, sport organizations are able to enforce members to follow these rules necessary to ensure effective work process, while imposing punishments for those who break these regulations (Hoye & Cuskelly, 2007; Hums & MacLean, 2018). For instance, a salary cap is a regulation that limits the amount of overall payroll of a team, which is adopted by all four major professional sport leagues in the U.S. However, specific rules differ from sport to sport. In case of National Football League (NFL), the organization imposes a hard salary cap, meaning every team in the NFL cannot exceed the salary cap on any occasion. On the other hand, the National Basketball Association (NBA) and the Major League Baseball (MLB) employ a soft cap that allows each team to exceed the cap; however, when the aggregate payroll of any team exceeds the cap amount, a luxury tax is going to be imposed. While the MLS also imposes salary cap, the organization employs a "designated player rule", which allows each MLS team to recruit up to three exceptional players (i.e., designated players) whose payrolls and transfer fees are not counted toward the salary cap for the team (MLS, 2017). By setting up this unique rule, teams in MLS are able to sign star players of football clubs in other continents to the league, such as David Beckham, Ricardo Kaka, and Zlatan Ibrahimović. Different governing organizations would have different rules. In the case of European soccer leagues, they have to follow the *Union of European Football Associations'* (UEFA) financial fair play principle, which limits the total amount of spending by each club based on their revenue; otherwise, teams will be suspended during the transfer period (UEFA, 2015).

Analyzing the external and internal environments that a sport organization faces and making a decision on governance issues that is based on the long-term goal of an organization are other crucial tasks of a governing body in order to be competitive and successful (Kim et al., 2021). For example, various football clubs within UEFA Leagues would have different goals to achieve. Big clubs such as Liverpool FC in the English Premier League (EPL) are going after winning league championship and UEFA Champions League, whereas the priority of small clubs that are at the bottom of league standings is not to be relegated to the English Football League (EFL), which is the second division in the English football league system. It is obvious that the decisions of governing bodies on club operations would differ among clubs.

In professional sport leagues in the U.S., one of the strategies that some teams have taken to was tanking; instead of competing to win, these teams would choose to lose in order to get a better draft position to recruit a highly talented young player for the future of the team as well as to save operating costs by having less expensive players on the roster (Calcaterra, 2019). There have been a few success stories for this strategy, such as the Houston Rockets that won the NBA title twice by drafting Hakeem Olajuwon, and the Chicago Cubs and the Houston Astros in the MLB winning the World Series. Although it is debatable whether the unsportsmanlike strategy of tanking should be adopted by giving up the present performance, it is the decision of the governing body that has considered diverse elements of a team such as its financial status and talent pool.

Governance of sport in globalized market place

Globalization has significantly impacted the sport industry. Development of technology in broadcasting and transportation has contributed to the popularization, production, and dissemination of sports in a global scale (Zhang et al., 2017). There are several issues that the governing body of a sport organization has to deal with in the era of globalization, including freer movement of athletes across boarder and increased competitions among sport teams and leagues. Recruiting international talent has become a common practice for sport organizations in both advanced and emerging economies. Several benefits are expected by signing on international athletes. Not only can these players enhance on-pitch performance, they also attract foreign fans and media from the countries of these athletes (Zhang et al., 2018). For instance, quite a few football clubs in European leagues actively recruit players from Asian countries, which are markets with huge growth potential. While most of the recruited soccer players from Asia make significant contribution in terms of performance and promotion of a team, some are doubted to have been recruited only for marketing purposes. Benefits of having "marketing players" as a member of a team exceed the cost in many cases.

However, recruiting talented international athletes may not always bring positive outcomes. In case of the Ladies Professional Golf Association (LPGA), the organization had to deal with the superb performance of international golfers in its tours. With its open policy adopted in the late 1990s, gradually an increasing number of foreign golfers were presented in the tours. By the late 2000s, more international golfers filled the leaderboard of the tours. The governing body of the LPGA is concerned about losing popularity of the tours in the U.S.; its initial reaction was to attempt to impose an English language proficiency regulation, requiring international players to demonstrate ability to communicate in English for pro-am contestants, acceptance speeches, and media interviews (Shipnuck, 2008). Due to much negative press responses and the probability of violating anti-discrimination laws, the policy was not implemented. It was suspected that the policy was targeted to prevent the tour leading foreign golfer group of 45 Korean players from competing in the tournaments (Dorman, 2008). The strategic movement of the organization had shifted with the arrival of a new commissioner in 2010. Confronting the changed competitive landscape, its marketing strategy was to promote cultural and ethnic diversity, and its global presence while welcoming golfers from around the globe (Kim et al., 2020). The implementation of this changed strategy seems to be successful in the expansion of the tours as LPGA attracts an increased number of overseas corporate sponsors, media viewers, and spectators (Alvarez, 2018) while it also secured 500 television hours globally in 2020, which is the most media coverage hours in the organization's history (Levins, 2019). This case shows the importance of strategic direction and decision making of the governing body of a sport organization: sport governance should act for the best interests of an organization.

Another important aspect that the governing body of sport organizations, specifically for professional teams and leagues, should be aware of is its increasing competition in the globalized sport industry. More specifically, globalization has provided sports fans enormous opportunities to follow clubs on a global scale. In many cases, diverse media outlets such as television and social media provide live broadcasting as well as highlights of sport matches globally. On one hand, the changing environments provide internationally renowned sport teams more opportunities to attract fans globally; on the other hand, sport teams in less developed sport leagues would have more difficulty in securing domestic fans as some fans would watch and follow more exciting and higher quality performance of foreign teams (Zhang et al., 2018). For instance, it was reported that about 80% of Chinese Super League (CSL) fans were willing to watch EPL matches over its domestic soccer games (Gratton & Solberg, 2007). In a similar vein, most watched soccer matches in Thailand, Malaysia, and Singapore were those of the EPL although all these countries have their own domestic soccer leagues and teams (Solberg & Haugen, 2008). Furthermore, due to the quality of performance, it is likely that star players in the emerging leagues would be recruited by foreign teams, which makes the league less attractive to some fans who would begin following foreign teams that their favorite star players are transferred to. For instance, after losing several top talents to the MLB in recent years, the Korean Baseball League began losing spectators after it reported record-high 8.4 million spectators in 2017. It took less than two years for the number of stadium spectators to fall below 8 million after the record attendance (Jeong, 2019). These examples suggest that competitors also exist overseas; thus, the governing bodies of professional sport leagues and teams in emerging economies have to prepare counter-measures to secure fans in a globalized competitive landscape.

As the competition to attract global fans becomes intense among sport leagues in developed economies, an important issue that governing bodies of teams and leagues should consider is how to maintain a balance in serving both domestic and global fans. As La Liga, the top division of the Spanish football league, has been competing with the EPL in the Asian market, its governing body decided to change the kick-off time of El Clásico a few times in recent years (e.g. 2017, 2019), which attracts the highest number of audiences in the globe for a soccer match between Real Madrid and FC Barcelona, in order to be broadcast during prime time in the Asian region (McMahon, 2017; Smith, 2019). When La Liga changed its kick-off time for the first time in 2017, criticism was raised among supporters of both clubs that the league worked in favor of international audiences and did not care adequately for the convenience of fans in Spain who had difficulties attending and watching the match with the time change (Turrell, 2017). In spite of this criticism, the league once again changed the kick-off time in 2019. The president of La Liga explained that Spanish football is for a global audience beyond Spanish people (Smith, 2019). This strategic movement may attract additional audiences and fans to Spanish football; yet, it may also send a wrong signal that domestic fans and audiences are less important. The governing body should be cautious in addressing these kind of issues when considering global expansion. In spite of such negative feedback, tapping into a new market is not unusual among many professional leagues. A few regular season games of the NBA and the MLB were held in other continents such as Asia and Europe to serve international fans (Zhang et al., 2018). In brief, sport governance should pay extra attention to maintain a balance between domestic and international fans. A professional sport league cannot sustain over time if local fans turn their back on the organization.

Necessity of inquires into sport governance in global context

This chapter has shown the major roles and related stakeholders regarding sport governance and organizations such as regulatory power and development of strategies. At the same time, as the sport industry is becoming increasingly globalized, more issues would emerge and should be considered by the governing bodies of sport organizations, such as maintaining balance in serving local and global fans, both of whom are stakeholders. Considering these characteristics, scholars have investigated sport governance phenomenon by employing several theories; among them, the most frequently used include constituency theory, agency theory, stewardship theory, institutional theory, managerial hegemony theory, institutional theory, and stakeholder theory (Ferkins et al., 2009; Hoye & Cuskelly, 2007). When it comes to the theme of exploration within the sport governance field, a significant number of studies have explored the diverse aspects of sport governance such as the role of the board in sport organizations, executive committee cohesion and decision-making, board performance and structure, the shared leadership dynamic between the board and CEO, and board strategic capability (Shilbury et al., 2013). Although these studies provide meaningful insights, little attention has been paid to the role and impact of governing bodies of sport organizations that operate in a global marketplace. Moreover, previous research findings were mainly derived from organizations in developed economies. Therefore, more balanced views that represent diverse regions of the globe are necessary. To this end, this book provides global perspectives of sport governance from scholars belonging to diverse countries.

About this book

The co-editors of this book have selected research papers relevant to the issues at hand. In addition to this introductory chapter, this book contains a total of 15 chapters. These chapters are contributed by a total of 29 scholars representing ten countries or territories around the world, including Australia, China, Czech Republic, Italy, New Zealand, Poland, South Africa, South Korea, United States of America, and Venezuela. Co-editors Euisoo Kim and James J. Zhang would like to take this opportunity to thank these eminent scholars for their remarkable contributions to the completion of this book project. This book is commissioned by the World Association for Sport Management (WASM) Executive Board, representing this organization's leadership and commitment to develop, summarize, synthesize, and analyze knowledge that can help enhance the global sport industry. It covers a range of key research and practical issues in globalized sport management governance in diverse cultural contexts of both global and local settings. The book combines scholarly output derived from diverse inquiry protocols such as review of literature, documentary analysis, qualitative research, and quantitative investigations.

References

Abubakar, Y. I., Mustapha, R. A., & Ajiboye, E. S. (2020). Impact of governance on financial development: Evidence from West Africa. *Hasanuddin Economics and Business Review, 3*(3), 103–111.

Alvarez, A. (2018, January 23). While some are saying golf is on the decline, the LPGA Tour is enjoying an upswing. *ESPN.* www.espn.com

Berkowitz, S. (2020, June 15). New name, images, likeness lawsuit against NCAA could put hundreds of millions of dollars at stake. *USA TODAY.* https://www.usatoday.com/

Bevir, M. (2012). *Governance: A very short introduction.* Oxford, UK: Oxford University.

Calcaterra, C. (2019, December 30). Top 25 baseball stories of the decade—No. 5: Tanking epidemic. *NBC Sports.* https://mlb.nbcsports.com/

Clifford, P. W., & Evans, R. T. (1996). The state of corporate governance practices in Australia. *Corporate Governance: An International Review, 4*(2), 60–70.

Dorman, L. (2008, August 26). Golf Tour's rule: Speak English to stay in play. *The New York Times.* http://www.nytimes.com/

Empter, S., & Janning, J. (2009). Sustainable governance indicators 2009 – An introduction. In B. Stiftung (Ed.), *Sustainable governance indicators 2009, policy performance and executive capacity in the OECD* (pp. 1–15). Gütersloh, Germany: Verlag Bertelsmann Stiftung.

Ferkins, L., Shilbury, D., & McDonald, G. (2009). Board involvement in strategy: Advancing the governance of sport organizations. *Journal of Sport Management, 23*(3), 245–277.

Galarcep, I. (2019, April 3). Explained: Why US soccer doesn't have relegation and promotion – And will MLS ever change? *Goal.* https://www.goal.com/

Governance Institute of Australia. (2021). *What is governance?* Retrieved on February 5, 2021 from https://www.governanceinstitute.com.au/resources/what-is-governance/

Gratton, C., & Solberg, H. A. (2007). *The economics of sports broadcasting.* Abingdon: Routledge.

Hoye, R., & Cuskelly, G. (2007). *Sport governance*. Amsterdam, Netherlands: Elsevier.

Hums, M. A., & MacLean, J. C. (2018). *Governance and policy in sport organizations*. London, UK: Routledge.

Jeong, H. (2019, December 12). Reasonable rush to the foreign leagues and the commercial dilema KBO faces. *SportsChosun*. https://sports.chosun.com/

Kikulis, L. M. (2000). Continuity and change in governance and decision making in national sport organizations: Institutional explanations. *Journal of Sport Management, 14*(4), 293–320.

Kim, E., Chung, K.-S., Chepyator-Thomson, J. R., Lu, Z., & Zhang, J. J. (2020). The LPGA's global tour and domestic audience: Factors influencing viewer's intention to watch in the United States. *Sport in Society, 23*(11), 1793–1810.

Kim, E., Qian, T. Y., & Zhang, J. J. (2021). Strategic visionary management as enabler of commercial sport management. In R. L. de D' Amico, K. Danylchuk, A. Goslin, & D. Kluka (Eds.), *Managing sports across borders* (pp. 41–63). Berlin, Germany: International Council on Sport Science and Physical Education.

Kooiman, J. (2003). *Governing as governance*. Thousand Oaks, CA: Sage.

Levins, K. (2019, November 22). LPGA Tour announces 2020 schedule, with record prize money and television hours. *GolfDigest*. https://www.golfdigest.com/

McMahon, B. (2017, December 21). El Clásico is a must-see game, but is its global audience overstated? *Forbes*. https://www.forbes.com/

MLS. (2017, January 1). MLS designated players. *Major League Soccer*. https://www.mlssoccer.com

NCAA. (2020). Governance. *National Collegiate Athletic Association*. http://www.ncaa.org

Osburn, S. (2019). Board of Governors starts process to enhance name, image and likeness opportunities. *National Collegiate Athletic Association*. http://www.ncaa.org/

Shilbury, D., Ferkins, L., & Smythe, L. (2013). Sport governance encounters: Insights from lived experiences. *Sport Management Review, 16*(3), 349–363.

Shipnuck, A. (2008, August 28). Legal questions surround LPGA's new rule requiring players to speak English. *Golf*. http://www.golf.com/

Smith, J. (2019, October 5). Barcelona vs Real Madrid: Tebas defends early Clasico kick-off time. *Sportstar*. https://sportstar.thehindu.com/

Solberg, H. A., & Haugen, K. K. (2008). The international trade of players in European club football: Consequences for national teams. *International Journal of Sports Marketing & Sponsorship, 10*(1), 73–87.

Thoma, J. E., & Chalip, L. H. (1996). *Sport governance in the global community*. Morgantown, WV: Fitness Information Technology.

Turrell, R. (2017, December 22). El Clasico: Why Real Madrid vs Barcelona is kicking off at early time of 12 pm. *Dailystar*. https://www.dailystar.co.uk/

UEFA. (2015, June 30). Financial fair play: All you need to know. *Union of European Football Associations*. https://www.uefa.com/

WSF. (2016, September 2). Title IX and the rise of female athletes in America. *Women's Sports Foundation*. https://www.womenssportsfoundation.org/

Zhang, J. J., Kim, E., Marstromartino, B., Qian, T. Y., & Nauright, J. (2018). The sport industry in growing economies: critical issues and challenges. *International Journal of Sports Marketing and Sponsorship, 19*(2), 110–126.

Zhang, J. J., Pitts, B. G., & Kim, E. (2017). Introduction: Sport marketing in a globalized marketplace. In J. J. Zhang & B. G. Pitts (Eds.), *Contemporary sport marketing: Global perspectives* (pp. 3–20). London, UK: Routledge.

Chapter 2

Governance of sport for the 21st century
Contemporary perspectives

Darlene A. Kluka

Introduction

There continues to be a growing base of knowledge determined by experience and research involving fields dedicated to sport and its governance. There is an abundance of scientific journals and publications investigating sport through a variety of different lenses including, but not limited to, biomechanics, economics, ethics, history, law, management, medicine, motor behavior, psychology, and sociology. Because sport management investigations and textbooks have historically been based upon administrative principles in physical education and sport, management and governance had been virtually absent from the literature (Doherty, 1998). Over the past four decades, governance of sport has, however, emerged as a viable topic that warrants investigation and specialization (Hindley, 2003). In recent years, the governance of sport has become a centerpiece for discussion and concern (Lam, 2014). Interest has developed from recent social scandals and global economic crises (e.g. Enron and Worldcom scandals; impeachments of former US President Donald Trump; global COVID-19 pandemic; FIFA scandal; USA Gymnastics vs. Dr. Larry Nassar scandal).

Failures within the sporting context include the Federation Internationale de Football Association (FIFA) and the Russian Olympic doping scandal. At times, sport governance capacity has been impeded by governments and organizations that are not forthcoming and by intellectuals who are unable to find common ground to communicate across disciplines to present paradigms appropriate for the governance of sport. This has frequently been the case when scholars have attempted to make comparisons across the globe. The concept of governance is also linked to the dynamic of power, where power lies within sport organizations systems and how power serves as a dynamic in the concept of governance. To better understand the nature of sport governance, understanding the characteristics of organizational structure is helpful.

Gomez, Kase, and Urrutia (2007) have shown that the structure of national sport organizations can be characterized by sport national governing bodies (NGBs), with primary responsibilities for promotion and development of specific sporting codes at all levels and geographical regions. These include being the

DOI: 10.4324/9781003213673-2

official national organization of a specific sport (e.g. volleyball, skiing, swimming, boxing) that is promoted by the Olympic Movement and related agencies. These also consist of management and control of a sport, recurring competitions at national and international levels, amateur and professional, as well as grassroots to senior participation. NGBs also determine rules of the game and safeguard values that have been identified as inherent in sport (Parry, 2006). Sport promotion entities are responsible for the production of sport events that include sport as entertainment (e.g. leagues, circuits, tours, championships). These organizations are secondary to the rules and regulations of NGBs and professional teams. They are designed for creating competition systems that are appealing to spectators and fans. This category includes those who develop commercial pursuits and bridge the divide between sport participation and entertainment (e.g. licensing, merchandising, ticketing, marketing, sponsorship, and television broadcast rights). Sport as entertainment entities involve groups that design and deliver sport programs for specific communities (e.g. clubs, community recreational centers, fitness centers, pubs/bars, and academies).

Governance has been recognized as a "paradigm-generating concept" (Bellamy & Palumbo, 2010, p. xii), yet there has been little systematic attempt to capture the extent by either public administration, management, or sport management scholars. Definitional agreement within the broader public administration and management literature remains problematic as well. It is important, then to set the groundwork for a discussion of the governance landscape of sport by presenting historical development, national policies, non-profit sport organizations, and professional sport.

Systems of sport governance

Governance can be broadly defined as a way in which societies or groups within them are organized to make decisions. This concept extends beyond politics and power and encompasses groups of people of any size working together to achieve collective goals. To understand how these systems work, it is important to learn about these systems and functions within them. Systems of governance include several key elements: mechanisms for establishing authority, processes for decision making, and a means of enforcing accountability to ensure that the collective decisions are adhered to. In western democratic nations, the way that votes in elections are aggregated at local, state, regional, and national levels, the rules by which elected representatives make laws, and different ways that laws are enforced, are examples. These are critical factors in determining outcomes. Expertise in governance, then, allows individuals to anticipate how the structure and members of boards of directors can determine the course and development of organizations (Goslin & Kluka, 2020).

Bayle and Robinson (2007) postulated that the key to National Governing Body (NGB) success lies with the permanence and position of the main unpaid executives (volunteer leaders). For example, the professional background, personality, charisma, and career of those on boards within the governance system explained numerous performance-related factors of board governance. Decisions made, such as strategic direction, political functioning, relations with volunteers and paid staff, and recruitment policies for the organization as well as in personal contacts, networking, and relationship building within systems have played critical roles (Cuskelly, 1999; Welch & Costa, 1994).

Systems of governance are usually associated with context. Through findings by Bayle and Robinson (2007), there appear to have been four main systems of governing NGBs. These systems are not yet, however, generalized to other for-profit and/or private sport organizations but have been noted here for additional investigation. The first system identified was the *strong presidency*. The president makes major decisions affecting the governance of the NGB. This can be structured according to staff positions that support this type of leadership. The second system involved a *tandem presidency*, where decision making is determined by two or more people, particularly the president and the executive director and/or vice presidents. The third was *dispersed presidency* where the president serves to coordinate the board of directors' work. The final system, the *managerial system*, involves a paid director who controls decision making, whether formal or informal. In general, strong and tandem presidential systems of governance have been characterized as dependent upon the complexity of the structure. It was found that, when there were less than 20 paid staff and inactive board of director members, complexity lacks; therefore, strong and tandem appeared to be the systems of governance used in these contexts. Dispersed governance and managerial systems were found in more complex systems like organizations with more than 50 paid staff (Bayle and Robinson, 2007). It seems, then, that a fundamental component of NGB sport governance involves systems of governance in context, thereby making theoretical concepts highly supple.

Systems of sport governance have been identified as early as the Ancient Olympic Games (Robertson, 1988). When the secular tradition of Homeric athletics (love of perfection and beauty in body and mind) fused with the religious traditions of Olympia, the Olympic Festival became one of the centerpieces of the Greek world. The governance system revolved around the gods and was couched in physical and mental prowess. As the Ancient Games declined, Rome became the cultural heir to Greece. Roman-era competition included chariot races and contested pseudo-combat events that became increasingly secular. Governance of the era was determined mostly by legion commanders and reigning emperors. As the Middle Ages approached, pseudo-combat and competition were viewed as preparation for war by regions that participated. As a result, governmental leaders viewed sport as under their purview and readily determined that a primary purpose for sport was to identify and display prowess for war. When the Protestant Reformation emerged, some leaders dissuaded participation in sport. Throughout these times, competition between villages and other groups required rules for fair play as well as governance of sport locally. Many sports had their beginnings in Europe, specifically in England (e.g. cricket, rugby, football/soccer, tennis, badminton, netball, and rowing), from where systems of sport governance were spread to other regions of the world through colonial expansionism (Krotee, 1988).

By the early 19th century, England and its established colonies had organized sport within school systems as well. Although England conceptualized and initiated several sports that have continued worldwide, other countries have substantively contributed to the present potpourri. The USA, for example, is credited with the initiation of American football, baseball, basketball, billiards, racquetball, softball, snowboarding, volleyball, and wind surfing. Athletics – track and field, Greco-Roman wrestling, and boxing (Greece) – were and continue to be mainstays in Ancient and Modern Olympic Games. By the early 20th century, several European members of aristocracy met together and formed the International Olympic Committee (IOC) to administer an international sport festival once every four years. Pierre Fredy, Baron of Coubertin, is considered the Father of the Modern Olympic Games (Zeigler, 1988), and was instrumental in the promotion and organization of this international sport festival. Because international sport events necessitated national systems of governance to manage teams, and international governance systems to determine rules, eligibility, and governance aligned with international involvement, the need for specific international sport organizations [also known as international federations (IFs)] and NGBs [also known as National Sport Federations (NSF) or National Sport Organizations (NSO), and National Olympic Committees (NOC)] became apparent.

To enhance communicative efficiency and effectiveness, the Association of National Olympic Committees (ANOC), the General Association of International Sports Federations (GAISF), and the International University Sports Federation were constituted. International Paralympic Committee (IPC), Special Olympics International (SOI), and the International Committee of Sports for the Deaf (ICSD) were established to govern sport for those with disabilities. By the mid-20th century, national governments became interested in the governance of sport, particularly after 1950. Many national governments created ministries of sport to oversee sport and its development, thereby setting up those countries for governmental funding and control. The United Nations (UN) International School Sport Federation (ISSF) was established. Founding members represented European countries that are presently recognized by the IOC and GAIFS.

Generally, corporate governance models have been analyzed over the years. Three models appear to have dominated sport organizations: UK-US model, German model, and Japanese model. The differences between them lie in their foci. The UK-US (also referred to as the Anglo-Saxon) model was oriented toward the stock market at the professional sport level, while the German and Japanese models have been focused on banking and credit markets. The Japanese model has been the most rigid, while the Anglo-US, most flexible. In July 2002, the US Congress passed the Sarbanes-Oxley Act (SOX), a result of Enron and Worldcom scandals, which was designed to make corporations more transparent and accountable to stakeholders. This Act was instituted to prevent corporate fraud

Governance of sport for the 21st century   13

in businesses while exemplifying good practice in financial reporting, accounting services, and improving corporate responsibility. Professional sport governance has been based on this Act in the USA.

In brief, governance matters. The UK-US model holds the board of directors and shareholders as controlling parties. Managers and chief officers have secondary authority. Managers gain their authority from the board, which is tied to the voting shareholders' approval. The German (European or continental) model is characterized by two groups: the *supervisory council* and the *executive board*. The executive board has been responsible for corporate management, while the supervisory council has controlled the executive board. The council is chosen by employees and shareholders. Government and national interest strongly influence governance and thus, much attention is paid to corporate responsibility to submit to the government's objectives and the betterment of society. Banks have played a huge role financially and in decision making. The Japanese model appears to be one that has lacked transparency because of the conservative nature where the hereditary caste system has been important, while business entities, the government, and union groups play leading roles in policies and have implicit control over negotiations (Ross, 2020). After World War II, a new culture was built in Japanese business. The government ensured mass privatization of most companies that were owned by prominent Japanese families. The growth of Japanese industry is now a mix of private and state capitalism. Professional sport organizations today use the Japanese model with its mix of private and state capitalism.

Governance is a combination of systems, structures, and policies along with strategic and operational frameworks that align organizational leadership to act so that they can make effective and efficient decisions with accountability (Barlow, 2016). A model specifically for sport governance, then, can reflect how policies, systems, structures, and frameworks interface with one another and who has responsibility for them. For example, is the entire board responsible for policies, systems, structures, and frameworks or does the responsibility lie with individual board members? (Barlow, 2016). Board governance models for non-profit and for-profit sport organizations can be quite different. Non-profit sport organizations generally serve humanity through the provision of sport programs, projects, and initiatives that fulfill a need. For-profit organizations generate income for employees, owners, and shareholders. Certain models can be amenable to non-profit, while others can be more appropriate to for-profit groups. It is also possible for a board to adopt a combination of board governance models that can be in line with organizational values and mission as well as the composition of the board. Non-profit sport governance board models hold organizational mission and funding to support organizational work at the forefront. Those who serve on boards because of their commitment to the mission can also be an important component to the model. Frequently, these can be considered as "working boards" where board members are actively involved in the oversight of organizational responsibilities on fiduciary matters as well as other matters of vision, mission, values, and goals, focusing upon the positive directionality of each sport.

For the most part, governance of sport models was parceled into five areas: advisory board, patron, cooperative, management team, and policy board (Burger, 2004). The *Advisory Board* model involves a chief executive officer (CEO) who founds the organization and recognizes the need for an advisory board that serves to supplement advice. Members offer their professional skills free of charge and may also serve to provide advice to the board. They have expertise in a non-profit context and can increase the organization's credibility, fundraising, and/or public relations initiatives. A *Patron Governance* mode, although akin to an Advisory Board model, provides board members with opportunities related to fundraising. Board members typically hold personal wealth or weight in the field. By using their networks to secure additional contributions for the organization, board members possess less authority over the CEO or the board than in the Advisory Board model. A *Cooperative Governance* model operates without a CEO. The board tends to reach consensus and appears to be the most democratic model of governance. With a limited hierarchy, no one person holds power. Each member is perceived to have an equal obligation to the organization and is prepared to be accountable for board actions. Apparently one of the most popular board models, the *Management Team* model formulates committees to perform various duties that other models may hire for (e.g. human resources, fund raising, planning, and programs). The fifth model, the *Policy Board* model, provides a high level of trust and confidence in the CEO. Regular meetings are held, with updates by the CEO to the board on organizational activity. Few standing committees exist, board members have a displayed commitment to the organization and to the group, and are willing to grow in competencies and expertise in the organization.

The governance of sport as leadership comprises three approaches to governance: fiduciary, strategic, and generative modes. The *fiduciary* approach is basic and fundamental to good sport governance, which includes protection of assets, deployment of resources for all, and acting with the best interests of the organization in mind. The *strategic* approach is one whereby the board and management work together to determine strategic importance and outcomes. The final approach, *generative*, requires boards to provide leadership in framing issues and development of strategic plans and solution-making (Chait, Ryan & Taylor, 2004). The generative approach, presently, appears to be the most uncomfortable, particularly for non-profit sport organizations because it presents challenges that require different ways of thought, ability, and competence by its leadership. These challenges may at this point be too much of a stretch for those who serve on boards, but it is an approach that can bring governance and leadership into a collective system designed to weave them into *collaborative governance* for sport in the 21st century.

The present system approaches to governance of sport, however, may not be the most appropriate to governance that is inclusive, diverse, safe, and equitable for the 21st century. The basic principles of governance now include accountability, transparency, fairness, and responsibility that, despite their disparities across the world, provide relevance for the future. Ethical behavior, environmental awareness, transparency, values, risk management, and professionalism appear to be some of the current critical issues that are pertinent now. Governance that contains checks and balances as well as separation of powers appears to lack adjudication for individual cases, enforcement of penalties, and law making. Today, whether boards of directors represent youth sports or international sports, they must incorporate ethical practices with professionalism, strategic planning, risk management, responsibility, accountability, and transparency, all interwoven between theory and practice. Sport organizations must be able to evolve and adapt, as has recently been illustrated from the COVID-19 pandemic. Generative governance that is collaborative will require new approaches from old governance systems involving vertical control.

Here is a question: how will those in sport management education programs across the world be prepared to govern when present systems appear to be losing their relevance in providing sustainable growth with purpose? Competent people are key to governing complex strategies and organizations operating in environments that are inclusive, diverse, safe, and equitable globally. According to the World Economic Forum (WEF) (2020), work skills for the future have been placed into five categories: physical and manual; basic cognitive; higher cognitive; social and emotional; and technological. WEF also predicts that those who seek to gain readiness to thrive in the 21st century after success in the formal educational system by 2030 will need the following skills in addition to traditional academic learning content: (a) complex problem solving, (b) critical thinking, (c) creativity, (d) people management, (e) coordinating with others, (f) emotional intelligence, (g) judgement and decision making, (h) service orientation, (i) negotiation, and (j) cognitive flexibility.

Challenges and opportunities

Based on the WEF's life-long learning paradigm (2015), proficient entrance into the sport management industry and specifically, sport governance requires collaborative, communicative, and problem-solving skills developed through social and emotional learning. These, linked with traditional academic skills, can permeate gaps in the following literacies: numeracy and scientific literacy, information and communications technology literacy, financial literacy, and cultural and civic literacy. Further, competencies related to how complex challenges are approached involves the skills of critical thinking, problem solving, creativity, communication, and collaboration. How the changing environment is approached includes skills of curiosity, initiative, persistence/grit, adaptability, leadership, and social and cultural awareness. It has been estimated that 65% of those entering primary schools will work in areas that do not even presently exist (Leopold, Trehan & Zahidi, 2017). Obviously, creativity, initiative, and adaptability will be skills that the next generation will need to continue contributing in meaningful ways in societies throughout the world.

Additionally, the Global Mindset Project (GMP), driven by the Thunderbird School of Global Management (2010), concluded that a global mindset is a vital characteristic of global citizenship. It appears that in multicultural sport working environments a global mindset is also necessary for successful governance of board members. It is multi-dimensional and consists of intellectual, social, and psychological capital. Intellectual capital reflects intellectual curiosity and centers around knowledge of sport in a broad sense across borders, diverse values, complex issues in sport, and possession of cultural intelligence. Social capital revolves around the ability to establish networks, relationships, norms, trust, and goodwill in social relationships across cultures and borders. Psychological capital reflects the disposition towards contact with diverse cultures, an eagerness in learning and exploring other cultures as well as improving resiliency. There is also a willingness to extract the best behavior from people (Carvalho & Kluka, 2017). Those who demonstrate a global mindset are externally oriented and tend to operate across personal and national boundaries, continuously gaining insight into linkages between dimensions and synthesizing them into best practices. This paradigm of global mindset needs to be infused into sport management/governance education in higher education curricula.

A technological revolution (the Fourth Industrial Revolution) that has begun to alter life, work, and human relations, will be unlike anything that has been experienced before. Responses to this life transformation must be wide-ranging and amalgamated, involving those stakeholders who care for governance of sport. This will include public and private entities as well as academic and public citizenry. This Fourth Industrial Revolution has begun to realize rising global income levels that can improve the quality of life globally. Technological development, particularly in sport with new products and services, has begun to increase efficiency and effectiveness in the governance of sport by means of ease and reduced expenses of travel, making payments, game play opportunities, and fan demand that can be done remotely. Further, the Fourth Industrial Revolution has brought economic successes as well as concerns, one of which is inequality. Those who possess intellectual and physical capital can continue to be successful, while those dependent on providing labor will continue to struggle. The chasm between those in sport administrative and leadership positions and those who labor to prepare fields, stadia, and athletes can easily continue to grow, as digital technologies and dynamics of information can cause great disparities.

Boards of directors have a responsibility to continuously create value and reinvent sport organizations to ensure that they are fit for purpose relative to the changing landscape that includes shifting user demands, social expectations, and unexpected tragedies. Technological innovation continues to be at the core of the Fourth Industrial Revolution and is rapidly changing work-leisure-life balance across borders. The UN has emphasized the necessity for innovation through the Sustainable Development Goals (2019), which are designed to enable a more sustainable economy, including sport, by 2030. Sport organizations would be wise to provide programs, projects, and initiatives that better serve societies socially, politically, environmentally, and guide decision making and establish priorities aligned to the UN goals. This can facilitate the alignment of goals and objectives that are beneficial for overall global development, with sport as the tool.

One of the most recent skill sets used in change management that can be appropriate for governance of sport involves Appreciative Inquiry (AI). AI can be a process that assists sport governance students in learning to lead change through collaboration, owning, and appreciating everything that gives life to organizations, communities, and larger human systems when they are most alive, effective, creative, and healthy in their interconnected ecology of relationships. To recognize and value that which has value can assist in a way of knowing and valuing the best. AI can provide a fresh understanding of dynamics that are described by excellence, thriving, abundance, resilience, or as exceptional and life-giving. It is a generative process (Figure 2.1) as it produces generative images like ideas, metaphors, and visual representations. This process allows people to think differently about something in a way that opens new possibilities for making decisions and actions. Images are attractive to people and can act in the new ways opened for consideration.

There are core principles behind the practice of AI. The following core principles about human systems and organizing are derived from applications of AI, positive psychology, positive organizational scholarship, and neuroscience:

1 *Constructionist principle*: Human systems move and grow in the direction of what they most talk about. Words create our world. This shifts the way we think about language and places emphasis on conversation as an organizing force. Words are potent tools that do something, as navigation tools that allow members of a culture to move about and coordinate ongoing relations with one another. How and what we converse about is fateful.
2 *Poetic principle*: As we choose topics of inquiry, so we open new horizons of action. Sport organizations are open-ended, evolving networks of possibilities

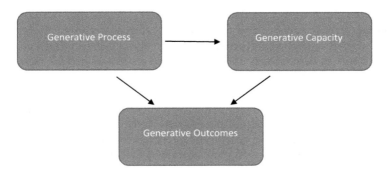

Figure 2.1 Illustration of Appreciative Inquiry as a Generative Process. Adapted from Fry (2014).

open to an endless variety of interpretive perspectives. We can study anything in any organization, at any time. We can choose to notice dynamics of stress, conflict, competition, or study the dynamics of hope, cooperation, competence, or joy. In AI, the change agent is more like a poet who is providing a difference in perspective. Choosing positive topics can lead to transformation of the sport organization's governance.

3 *Simultaneity principle*: As all ask positive questions, so we transform. Inquiry is intervention. There is no such thing as a neutral question. Every question into a social topic begins a conversation that creates, maintains, or transforms a way of being and doing.

4 *Anticipatory principle*: As we imagine, so we create. If you want to change a human system, change the future. People anticipate the future, project likely maps, and proceed to live as if it were already happening. Deep and lasting change comes from changing or anticipating images of the future. Positive images can change us at the cellular level (healing, recovery, resilience).

5 *Positive principle*: As we express hope, joy, and caring, so we create new relations. Sport organizations are affirmative and responsive to positive images and positive language. The more positive questions, the more opportunities to create and sustain positive discourse. Board members and sport organizations are heliotropic. They tend to grow in the direction of the helios or life source. Conversations of hope, joy, and inspiration are key to lasting change and enduring health of the sport organization.

6 *Narrative principle*: Stories weave a connectedness that bridges the past with the future. The power of stories is a catalyst for change. Positive stories about best past experiences can provide commonalities from which to build upon.

The AI process is an important one for proficiency in governance of sport, to guide groups through change. Students who learn this process can greatly influence the governance of sport. Its platform supports a shared roadmap that provides change as well as what remains constant. Tools are needed to create at least a 4:1 ratio of hope and inspiration to despair and deficit in interactions (Fry, 2014). AI involves altering thought processes to (a) discover what gives life when we are at our best. Stories are shared about core success factors on what worked well in the organization by sharing best past experiences; (b) dream of shared images about the positive future by describing possible images that go deeper into the most attractive future vision; (c) actionable ways provide the development of an opportunity map about ideas that would make important prioritization. Action plans, process mapping, creating rapid prototypes of the intended change effort are included; (d) destiny engages change initiatives that are ready to be implemented (Fry, 2020).

Because the sporting environment and global environment continue to move at lightning speed, alterations in sport consumer behavior force sport organizations to adapt the way they design, market, and deliver products and services. From a sport governance perspective, leadership must make decisions and plan accordingly. Presently, there appears to be four main effects that are prominent with the challenge of the Fourth Industrial Revolution and sport, and are poised to intersect: fan expectations, product enrichment, collaborative improvement, and organizational procedures and practices. Fans and consumers of sport can be centrally placed in future governance, which will lead to a continuance of service. To increase value, products and services can be enhanced by digital capacity that increase value. Data and analytics have begun to transform the way in which new technologies become more sturdy and supple. To continue to adjust to happenings in the Fourth Industrial Revolution, sport governance ability, ethos, and organizational governance systems will need to be rethought. The use of AI to adjust governance decisions can facilitate these types of changes. There needs to be a comprehensive and globally shared view of how technology will affect lives and reshape economic, social, cultural, and human environments. Those who are in higher education sport management programs cannot afford to be trapped in traditional linear thinking, as strategic thinking about the forces of disruption and innovation are part of shaping the future of sport.

Conclusion

Governance of sport will ultimately revolve around people and values. A future that works for all by putting people first and empowering them to become leaders through their sport experiences can supersede the notion of robotizing humanity and depriving hearts and souls. Governance of sport, in the future, will need systems that lift humanity through sport into collective and moral consciousness based on a shared sense of destiny and processes to manage change.

References

Barlow, J. (2016, April 19). Board governance models: A comprehensive list. Retrieved from https://www.boardeffect.com/blog/board-governance-models-a-comprehensive-list/

Bayle, E., & Robinson, L. (2007). A framework for understanding the performance of national governing bodies of sport. *European Sport Management Quarterly, 7*(3), 249–268.

Bellamy, R. P., & Palumbo, A. (Eds.). (2010). *Government to governance*. Farnham, UK: Ashgate.

Burger, S. (2004). Compliance with best practice governance systems by National Sports Federation of South Africa. Retrieved from http://hdl.handle.net/2263/41806

Carvalho, P., & Kluka, D. (2017). Globalization of sport management education programs. In M. Dodds, K. Heisey, & A. Ahonen (Eds.), *Handbook of international sport business management* (pp. 65–76). Abingdon, UK: Routledge.

Chait, R., Ryan, W., & Taylor, B (2008). *Governance as leadership: Reframing the work of non-profit boards*. Hoboken, NJ: Wiley.

Cuskelly, G. (1999). Differences in organizational commitment between paid and volunteer administrators in sport. *European Journal for Sport, 6*, 39–61. Retrieved from https://scholar.google.com/scholar?q=related:7tqkDJxGUCcJ:scholar.google.com/&scioq=cuskelly+1999+organisational+commitment&hl=en&as_sdt=0,19

Doherty, A. (1998). It takes a village: Interdisciplinary research for sport management. *Journal of Sport Management, 27*(1), 1–10.

Fry, R. (2014). Appreciative Inquiry. *The SAGE Encyclopedia of Action Research, 1,* 44–48.

Gomez, S., Kase, K., & Urrutia, I. (2010). *Value creation and sport management.* Cambridge, UK: Cambridge University.

Goslin, A., & Kluka, D. A. (2020). Integrative framework for international sport business management and its macroenvironment. In A. Goslin, D. Kluka, R. Lopez-D'Amico, & K. Danylchuk (Eds.), *Managing sport across borders* (pp. 1–36). Abingdon, UK: Routledge.

Hindley, D. (2003). Resource guide in governance and sport. Retrieved from https://www.advance-he.ac.uk/knowledge-hub/tags/hospitality-leisure-sport-and-tourism

Krotee, M. (1988). An organizational analysis of the International Olympic Committee. In J. O. Seagrave & D. Chu (Eds.), *The Olympic Games in transition* (pp. 113–148). Champaign, IL: Human Kinetics.

Lam, E. T. C. (2014). The role of governance in sport organizations. *Journal of Power Politics and Governance, 2*(2), 19–31.

Leopold, T. A., Trehan, A., & Zahidi, S. (2017). White Paper – Realizing human potential in the Fourth Industrial Revolution: An agenda for leaders to shape the future of education, gender, and work. Retrieved from https://learning-evolution.com/2018/03/26/65-of-children-entering-primary-school-will-find-themselves-in-occupations-that-today-do-not-exist-the-role-of-technology-in-the-education-of-the-future/

Parry, J. (2006). Sport and Olympics: Universals and multiculturalism. *Journal of Philosophy of Sport, 33*(22), 188–204.

Robertson, N. (1988). The Ancient Olympics: Sport, spectacle, and ritual. In J. O. Seagrave & D. Chu (Eds.), *The Olympic Games in transition* (pp. 11–26). Champaign, IL: Human Kinetics.

Ross, S. (2020, March 24). What are some examples of different corporate governance systems? Retrieved from https://www.investopedia.com/ask/answers/051115/what-are-some-examples-different-corporate-governance-systems-across-world.asp

Sarbanes, P., & Oxley, M. (2002). *Sarbanes-Oxley Act.* Retrieved from http://citeseerx.ist.psu.edu/viewdoc/download?doi=10.1.1.474.2105&rep=rep1&type=pdf

Thunderbird School of Global Management. (2010). Global mindset inventory. Retrieved from https://thunderbird.asu.edu/faculty-and-research/global-mindset-inventory

United Nations Sustainable Development Goals 2030. (2019). UNSDG and the 2030 Agenda. Retrieved from https://unsdg.un.org/2030-agenda

Welch, P., & Costa, D. M. (1994). A century of Olympic competition. In D. M. Costa & S. R. Guthrie (Eds.), *Women and Sport: Interdisciplinary Perspectives* (pp. 123–138). Champaign, IL: Human Kinetics.

World Economic Forum. (2015). Life-long learning paradigm. Retrieved from http://www.unesco.org/new/fileadmin/MULTIMEDIA/HQ/ED/ED_new/pdf/WEF_report_E.pdf

World Economic Forum. (2020). World Education Forum 2015: Final report. Retrieved from http://www3.weforum.org/docs/WEF_Schools_of_the_Future_Report_2019.pdf

Zeigler, E. F. (1988). *History of physical education and sport.* Reston, VA: AAHPER.

Chapter 3

Sport policies and their sociocultural impacts

Jepkorir Rose Chepyator-Thomson, Sean Seiler, Katja Sonkeng and Sehwan Kim

Introduction

Sport is a multidimensional global phenomenon. People of all works of life embrace it not only because it revitalizes communities economically and socially but also because it unifies and challenges individuals and societies to appraise and problematize social and cultural conditions for the betterment of all people living within locales, whether small-towns or districts, metropolitan cities or large societies or nations. It purports universality of a language (Annan, 2004) that all individuals regardless of nationality, culture, and social class can understand and participate in various forms of sporting competition. During the 1995 Rugby World Cup, Mandela enthusiastically demonstrated sport's potential to unify and make changes where other societal institutions had failed to bring a spectrum of diverse people to work together towards a common goal (Daley, 2013; Hughes, 2010). As such, sport has created spaces for the development of human interaction that promoted competitions between nations and communities as a way of soft diplomacy and bringing out positive changes in communities and nations (Sage, 2010). The purpose of this paper is, therefore, to explore the socio-cultural impact of sport policies on centralized sports governance structures. To accomplish this, the first section of this chapter encompasses ways in which public policy is defined, and how regulations help shape the way sport is governed in post-colonial contexts, drawing specific examples from various continents, including Africa, Asia, North America, and Europe. Upon this understanding, the chapter centers on how sport managers navigate the ever-changing landscapes of political institutions, sport organizations, and sport communities to meet individual, social, and economic needs through sport competitiveness, efficacy, and leadership.

Fast forward to 2021 and many social and liberation movements later (e.g., Civil Rights Movement and Women's Liberation Movement), public policy has proven to be a powerful weapon in the quest for social and human justice, as it serves as a way to understand societal issues, social control, and authority in social institutions. Just like a goal without a plan is only a wish, and "an organization without policy is an organization without control" (Isaac, 2019, p. 1). Regardless of the nature and purpose of an entity, formal policies and procedures are

DOI: 10.4324/9781003213673-3

therefore essential and fundamental components of successful organizations, as such they provide guidance and ensure fairness, consistency in decision-making, and adherence to acceptable norms and behaviors. Accordingly, as explained in the Merriam-Webster dictionary, policy can be defined varyingly:

> 1a: prudence or wisdom in the management of affairs, 1b: management or procedure based primarily on material interest, 2a: a definite course or method of action selected from among alternatives and in light of given conditions to guide and determine present and future decisions, 2b: a high-level overall plan embracing the general goals and acceptable procedures especially of a governmental body.
>
> (Merriam-Webster, 2019, p. 1)

Essentially sport policy as used in this chapter follows Byron's (2014) understanding. According to Byron (2014), sport policy is a living document that is instrumental in enabling contemporary sport to function in a way that promotes achievement of national and global goals and objectives. Other scholars further regard sport policy to be one of many public policies utilized in a broader government agenda that is intended to address multiple socio-cultural and technically non-sport-related policy objectives, such as youth crime reduction, social inclusion, anti-social behavior, as well as obesity and health issues in society (Bergsgard, Houlihan, Mangset, Nodland & Rommetvedt, 2007; Coalter, 2007; O'Boyle & Bradbury, 2013; Palmer, 2013). Sport used as a tool for the advancement of social policy and development is strongly underpinned by the widely accepted power of sports as a unifier, character builder, making it, according to Bergsgard et al. (2007), "a distinctive public service, and, in many countries, an important aspect of overall welfare provision, but it is also an important element of the economy in terms of job creation, capital investment and balance of payments" (p. 3). Additionally, Palmer (2013) contends that sport policy and policymaking are critical to the understanding of the current rapidly evolving global sport landscape, citing "tensions between exogenous and domestic sport as well as the events that are staged, sponsored and mediated on a global scale" (p. 8). Sports policy, thus, forms an integral part of the broader field of social or public policy study. Hence, scholars need to understand sports policy as a key component of a "network of networks [that point to] an interconnected, inhabited world" (Palmer, 2013, p. 14), considering sport policy is a "product of considerable cultural work on the part of a whole range of individuals and organizations, and this has significant implications for the management, administration and governance of sport and sports policy" (Palmer, 2013, p. 8). To this end, Byron (2014) determines the role of policy to be "sacrosanct within the confines of social justice in a globalized world where sports are becoming, hugely, symbols of corporate neoliberalism" (p. 19) and an instrument of social change worldwide.

Sport policies in diverse countries

Essentially, sport policies guide development goals in regions worldwide, communities, and nations. In the African continent, sport policies are patterned along the lines of triple heritage: European, Arab, and African. In each country there are sport policies in operation that are influenced by the diverse heritage. While indigenous and Arab sport policies are responsive to cultural and social aspects of life and to the preservation of the ways of sport competitions and interactions across many age- and ethnic- groupings in pre-colonial Africa, sport policies in post-colonial Africa are part and parcel of globalization. Sport policies regardless of nation or locality in the continent are used to advance each nation's visibility worldwide and to help meet welfare needs of communities, hence a two-pronged policy is practiced. While elite sport policies spearhead internationalization and visibility of nation states at mega-sport events like the Olympic and commonwealth games, sport for all policies emphasize mass participation and involvement in recreational and leisure sport activities, while helping promote unification of ethnic and social groups within a nation and enhancing the quality of life for youth and young adults, among others, in society.

In South Africa, mass sport was used as a means for people to pursue participation in recreation activities and elite sport focused on development of high-performance sport, with athletes training to compete at the highest level of competition, the Olympic Games (Jacobs, De Bosscher, Venter & Scheerder, 2019). According to these authors, sport policy is used "as a tool to achieve national and global priorities" (p. 178.). School sport policy is used to reach large numbers of youth, meeting mass and recreational participation in the national development goals and objectives of South Africa, with recreational and mass sport participation relying on government-run agencies to change quality of life in communities (Mogajane, Meyer, Toriola, Amusa & Monyeki, 2014). According to Chepyator-Thomson (2014), "school sport has been used to promote nation's prestige, social engineering, and economic development" (p. 512).

Across many countries in Africa, specific ministries are responsible for formulating and implementing sport policies, offered through departments of sport. In contemporary Ghana, for instance, the Ministry of Youth and Sport develops sport policies intended to achieve "national integration and international recognition [as well as] promote empowerment and self-development and [enable] an environment conducive to sport development, organization and promotion" (Charway & Houlihan, 2020, p. 504). In Kenya, the Ministry of Sports, Culture and Heritage and the Ministry of Education are charged with implementing sport policies. Specifically, the Ministry of Education typically enacts school sport programs, while the Ministry of Sports, Culture and Heritage is primarily responsible for carrying out after-school sport activities (Byron & Chepyator-Thomson, 2015). Sport policies in Kenya are operationalized through Olympic and non-Olympic sport divisions, with sport programs being implemented and managed through national sport federations, with the National Olympic Committee responsible for the selection of Olympic athletes in cooperation with each sport federation (Byron & Chepyator-Thomson, 2015).

Meanwhile on the North American continent, in Canada, policy operates at all levels of sport engagement from national to the provincial and territorial locations (Krahn, 2019). In the Caribbean region, Jamaica's national sport policy was created to provide guidelines for the development of sport with one objective – to promote competitive involvement in local and global contexts across diverse sport disciplines (Jamaica White Paper on the National Sport Policy, 2013), with the country's national sport policy "fully aligned with the key goals of Vision 2030 Jamaica," aiming to "promote the integration of sport in the national economy with the creation of globally competitive products and services, and [with] enhanced earnings of [their] athletes and associated industries" (Jamaica White Paper on the National Sport Policy, 2013, p. 9).

In Southeast Asia, the country of Malaysia employs sport policy to reinvigorate urban development, as recommended in the 2005 UN report. Malaysia's efforts to utilize sports policies to stimulate urban areas is, according to Barghchi and Omar (2014) a direct outcome of the changing role of sport in the country. In more specific terms, the importance of sport and its facilities in urban areas and metropolitan cities has reportedly increased due to globalization and urbanization (Barghchi & Omar, 2014) with sport facilities now considered and built for the purpose of stimulating urban areas – as can be observed in Malaysia, especially after the country hosted the 16th Commonwealth Games in 1998 (Megat Daud, 2007). The National Urbanization Policy (2006–2020), for instance, refers to sports complexes as "provided for urban hierarchies at national growth conurbation, regional growth conurbation, sub-regional growth conurbation, state growth conurbation, and district growth conurbation" (Barghchi & Omar, 2014, p. 26). In fact, the development of sports facilities to host international sporting events such as the Commonwealth Games was the initial reason for the Ministry of Youth and Sports to add the required sport facilities to the National Sports Policy. Against this backdrop, Barghchi and Omar (2014) conducted a quantitative research study to examine town planners' perceptions of sport facilities and urban development at the state level in Malaysia with specific focus on the amount of public money spent on sport facilities.

Sports policy in South Korea primarily focuses on the development of elite athletes for the purpose of guaranteeing remarkable performances at international games such as the Olympic Games (Choi, Jo & Ok, 2019). This policy direction has led the country to the successful hosting of major multi-sport events, such as the Asian Games and the Olympics, resulting in a drastic change of the public's perception of sport. In March 2016, the Korean Sport and Olympic Committee and the National Sports for All Association merged to become the Korean Sports & Olympic Committee, which allowed for the development of sports for all policies aimed at improving people's health and quality of life through participation in sports activities in South Korea (Won & Hong, 2015; Park & Lim, 2015).

According to Choi et al (2019), sports for all can be defined as "sporting or physical activities voluntarily performed by people of all ages in various environments, whose goal is to enjoy improved quality of life" (p. 877). As such, the core of sports for all policies includes facilities (expansion and efficient use), programs (diversification and equal dissemination), instructors (cultivation, efficient use, stronger follow-up management), organizations (cultivation of a central organization for sports for all and reinforcement of its function), public relations, and budget (securing state subsidies, local government expenses, funds, and private capital). In recent years, the Korean government's sports for all policies have shown both quantitative and qualitative growth that focused on participation rates, member organizations, facilities, programs, and instructors (Hong, 2010; Lee, 2013). As a result, sports policy in South Korea played a significant role in changing the value of sports. Using a two-pronged approach to sport policies – elite athletes and enhancement of health and fitness of the public – both leisure and recreational activities were used effectively, promoting and improving the welfare of the public (Skille, 2015). This two-pronged policy in South Korea exemplifies the use of sports as an instrument not only for enhancing the country's performance at the international sports competition stage but also to improve the quality of life for the majority of the population (Fahlén & Skille, 2017; Smith & Waddington, 2004).

In Europe, the United Kingdom perceives sports policy as a practical tool to address and tackle broader governmental public policy issues, such as social exclusion, obesity, and health, while diminishing anti-social behavior and youth crime through the creation of more education and sport participation opportunities. Walters and Tacon (2013) thoroughly examined the countries complex sport system, highlighting the involvement of the numerous governmental and non-governmental organizations in the development and implementation of sport policy. The result is a "crowded and sometimes confusing policy space" (Walters & Tacon, 2013, p. 108), located within the Department for Culture, Media and Sport in England, and equivalent administrations in Scotland, Wales, and Northern Ireland. The bulk of the sports funding comes from the National Lottery and the central government. Beneficiaries are key non-departmental public bodies, UK Sport, and the home country sport councils (Sport England, Sport Scotland, Sport Wales, and Sport Northern Ireland).

In other European countries such as Denmark, Germany, and Spain, sport policies have been applied at the municipal level. Examples include Denmark's and Germany's capitals Copenhagen and Berlin, as well as the city of Valencia in Spain. City officials there have increasingly turned to sport policies as a means to actively engage and integrate disadvantaged groups, especially refugees, girls, and ethnic minorities. Combining sports and exercise with recreation, leisure, and culture both on active and spectator levels has proven to be an effective method to bring people together. In Valencia, for instance, this approach led to a significant growth in sports participation by all residents. In Berlin, furthermore, *Tentaja*, a non-profit organization organized by and for refugees has successfully promoted the social integration of Syrian refugees by offering free sports activities to both refugees and local residents in the hangar of the former Tempelhof airport – the very same location that once sheltered 3,000 refugees at the peak of the European migrant crisis (Ginzel, 2018).

Sport policies function at all levels of participation locally and globally. It is therefore critical that country governments work hand in hand with sports federations to develop and implement sport policies that effectively address any potentially negative impacts of sporting practices resulting from globalization while nurturing and fostering ways to enhance the creation of economic, socio-cultural, physical, and mental health benefits emanating from professional and recreational sports (Byron, 2014), which are linked to global sport associations.

Sport policies in indigenous communities

Community leaders are increasingly recognizing sport as a practical tool to achieve much needed changes in their areas, with sport for development (SFD) being positioned as an instrument of social change, and an emergent area of research worldwide. Within the past five years, literature on sport policy and social development and change has been conducted throughout the Americas, ranging from Belize (Wright, Jacobs, Howell & Ressler, 2019), Guatemala (Mandigo et al., 2018), and Jamacia (Mwaanga & Adeosun, 2017) to Colombia (Hills, Gómez Velásquez & Walker, 2018). Indigenous communities, moreover, have received considerable attention within the critical paradigm of SFD policy for positive social change. A critical, often post-colonial, paradigm reviewing and appraising approach has been the common approach in the extant literature, revealing the positive effects of sport policy to generate positive social change, especially for the youth (e.g. positive youth development). Ultimately, this is underpinned by the core tenets of SFD to promote social change prioritizing low income or disadvantaged communities mostly in the Global South.

Sport policy and development research in indigenous communities has also occurred amongst the Sami communities in Sweden and Norway (Skille, Fahlén, Stenling & Strittmatter, 2021; Fahlén & Skille, 2017) and Aboriginal communities in Australia (Lucas, Jeanes & Diamond, 2020; Ross & Rynne, 2013). In the Americas, most of the research pertaining to sport policy for social change has been situated in Canada amongst First Nations communities. Specifically, sport has been used as an extension of a colonialist project for assimilation and development of First Nation communities by Euro-Canadians. Because of this historicity, it is imperative to critically evaluate the role and impact of sport policies among First Nation communities within neoliberal forms of governance and policy to not only challenge the previous hegemonic associations between sport and positive change, but also problematize current policy development and implementation.

Canadian sport policies continuously encourage the promotion of sport as a connector between individual and community development. For First Nation populations, particularly, this view is reflected in various sport-centric policies, such as Right to Play and Sport for Life. The latter regards sport as a panacea for healthier people, communities, and persevering life. Upon this notion, public and private sport-centric policies seemingly play a vital role in future First Nation peoples' involvement in sport (Gardam, Giles & Hayhurst, 2017). However, sport as a panacea for First Nation communities is not an apolitical and ahistorical utopian policy. Rather, it might be more of a nostrum for a neoliberal political economy.

Nevertheless, sport has been always leveraged as an instrument for policy by Euro-Canadians towards assimilation and development of First Nation groups (Gardam et al., 2017; Hayhurst, Giles & Wight, 2016). Based on current research, this narrative may not have changed. For example, a transnational postcolonial feminist participatory action research study (TPFPAR) conducted by Hayhurst et al. (2016) found that Sport for Development (SFD) programs may target young, urban First Nation women and girls to preserve the neoliberal hegemony. They showcased how biopedagogies of neoliberalism contribute to the specific education and employment skills of young, urban First Nation women and girls, as a requisite for participation in a neoliberal capitalist society. As such, Millington, Giles, Hayhurst, van Luijk and McSweeney (2019) argued that the extraction industries of oil, gas, and mining and their companies fund First Nation SFD programs merely to 'red wash': representing good corporate citizens concerned with social equity and responsible members of the community while obfuscating harmful impacts of exploitative industries practices, and histories of colonialism. In addition, Arellano and Downey (2018), Gardam et al. (2017), Millington et al. (2019), and van Luijk, Giles, Millington and Hayhurst (2019) discussed the various organizations involved in SFD initiatives with First Nation communities of Canada: Right to Play, Nike, and resource (mining, oil, gas) extraction companies. In particular, Right to Play partners with Aboriginal communities in northern Ontario through its Promoting Life-Skills in Aboriginal Youth (PLAY) program "to enhance education outcomes, improve peer-to-peer relationships, increase employability and improve physical and mental health amongst Aboriginal children and youth" (Gardam et al., 2017, p. 34).

Sport policy implementation and challenges

Since the early 2000s, various corporate, governmental, and non-governmental organizations throughout the world have pursued development and social change sport policy. However, Millington et al. (2019) noted a similar policy trend in Canada. Specifically, the Canadian Government hosted a discussion on SFD in 2005, concluding that scholars needed to examine examples in international contexts focusing on the ways SFD could be adapted domestically and augmented by non-profit SFD entities in partnership with the private sector (Millington et al., 2019). As the public sector encourages investments from the private sector to fund SFD projects, van Luijk et al. (2019) posits that the private sector, namely the resource extractive industry has had an important role in the colonial oppression of First Nation communities in Canada. With support from the federal government, corporations had moved into First Nation lands and removed natural resources from community-based collaborations (Barsh, 1994; van Luijk et al., 2019).

Amid the emergence of corporate social responsibility (CSR), pressure has been put on resource extraction companies to assess their part in promoting the well-being of communities and lands that they impact (van Luijk et al., 2019). Essentially, this is the centuries-long neoliberal corporatist practice which understands accountability for adverse social or environmental consequences as negligible (Harvey, 2005), and as a result has contributed to the decline of the general welfare and well-being of First Nation communities van Luijk et al., 2019). It is thus imperative for corporations to be mindful of three important aspects when implementing policy. First, a general lack of deference for local First Nation cultures. For example, Arellano and Downey (2018) revealed how reports and activities of PLAY do not specify nor mention any localized cultural knowledge and epistemologies of the First Nation communities. Arellano and Downey (2018) further noted that measurable outcomes in annual reports are not based on First Nation cultural and governance fluency.

Aspects related to elder engagement, kinship knowledge, language recovery, ecological renewal, self-determination, or ceremonial knowledge acquisition are not the measurable goals of the program (Arellano & Downey, 2018). Second, programming is based on a neoliberal assumption that the specific cultural knowledge are non-transferable skills and do not enhance integration and employment into a neoliberal marketplace (Arellano & Downey, 2018). This certainly stems from the long history of colonialism and its generated binary discourses that perpetuated the notion of First Nation as inferior, lazy, worthless, unintelligent, and dirty (Adams, 1999; Hayhurst et al., 2016). Consequently, the colonialist discourse is deeply rooted and embedded in neoliberal paradigms of employment and the marketplace, and further perpetuated through sport development programs (Hayhurst et al., 2016). Indeed, Forsyth and Wamsley (2006) and Hayhurst et al. (2016) argued that public, private, or administrative policy designs implemented strict guidelines and programs – including in sport – with the intent to integrate First Nation beliefs and customs into the dominant culture.

According to Nicholls, Giles, and Sethna (2011), social development and sport program policies are still permeated by underlying Eurocentric views, ultimately preserving the marginalization and suppression of local knowledge and epistemologies. The third and final point refers to the general 'flattening of Indigeneity' in the prior two points that turned SFD policies into dangerous implicit weapons to simultaneously silence or understate the diversity and specificity of First Nation knowledge and nationhood (Arellano & Downey, 2018). Up to this point, Right to Play and programs such as PLAY have embraced such a neoliberalist, institutional subjectification of First nation communities (Arellano & Downey, 2018), and its emphasis of a 'pan-First Nation' identity in local and national policy implementation within communities may be the key reason for the continued suppression of First Nation identities, cultures, knowledge, and epistemologies as self-determining nations (Arellano & Downey, 2018).

Sport policies in context of global sport bodies

Global sport bodies that lead policy development and implementation include international sport federations such as such as the International Federation of Association Football (FIFA), International Volleyball Association (FIVB), International Basketball Federation (FIBA), and the International Olympic Committee (IOC). In addition, professional sport leagues, teams and other professional sport franchises are all governed through policy enactments and implementation strategies occurring via their regulatory bodies located at their core and peripheral global locations. Major global sport bodies are located in northern country regions, namely Europe. FIFA, housed in Switzerland, is a European founded body of sport that uses its rules and regulations as well as policy directives to govern and to "confront national governments and defend its autonomy to regulate football" (Meier & Garcia, 2015, p. 901). Additionally, countries' national governments change sport policies and legislation as per FIFA's requests, which can include "defined deadlines for governments to comply" (Meier & Garcia, 2015, p. 901) and thus it is critical that country governments work in consensus with sports federations to articulate and implement sport policies that address negative impacts of sporting practices resulting from globalization and nurture ways that enhance creation of economic benefits emanating from professional sports (Byron, 2014).

The laws of FIFA, as crafted by International Football Association Board (IFAB) have been adopted "throughout the world from the FIFA World Cup final through to a game between young children in a remote village" and can only be modified with permission from IFAB (FIFA.com, 2021, p. 1). For instance, FIFA stipulates what types of equipment to be worn in game plays, for example, Law #4 indicates that, for safety reasons, "a player must not use equipment or wear anything that is dangerous" (FIFA.com, p. 1). Football federations in each country abide by FIFA rules and regulations. In Kenya, for instance, the government of Kenya and Kenya Football Federation had a conflict with a FIFA rule that states: "governments should not interfere" with the affairs of football federations [with the disagreement] subjected to arbitration at the Court of Arbitration of Sports because of this government interference (Byron & Chepyator-Thomson, 2015, pp. 306–307). It is known that FIFA gains enormous benefits from its global popularity. According to Meier and Garcia (2015) FIFA has expanded generation of revenues, among other benefits but lacks "societal corrective forces" to challenge the power of FIFA in global context.

The International Basketball Federation (FIBA), which was founded in France in 1904 and moved to Geneva (Switzerland) in 1932 serves as the governing body of basketball, including international competitions of basketball in association with national federations located in each country that has basketball as a national sport (FIBA, 2021). Like FIFA, FIBA has been accused of discrimination based on equipment. FIBA's discriminatory policy came under public scrutiny during the 2014 Asian Cup when two Sikh players were ejected by officials on the grounds of having violated FIBA rules on the equipment that states: "All equipment used by players must be appropriate for the game. Any equipment that is designed to increase a player's height or reach or in any other way give an unfair advantage is

30 Jepkorir Rose Chepyator-Thomson et al.

not permitted" (Rule 4.4.1) and that "players shall not wear equipment (objects) that may cause injury to other players" (Rule 4.4.2). The following not permitted: "Finger, hand, wrist, elbow or forearm guards, helmets, casts or braces made of leather, plastic, pliable(soft) plastics, metal or any other hard substance, even if covered with soft padding)" (FIBA, 2020, p. 1). In 2016, some members of United States Congress led by Ami Bera and Joe Crowley sent a letter to FIBA requesting the change of this policy, which was granted with effect from the 2016 Olympic Games (States News Service, 2016, August 23).

Olympics is the world's number one mega-sport event that draws diverse sport participants from across the globe, and is intertwined with each country's sport entities, particularly Olympic committees. For instance, Ghana was about to have its country's athletes compete in the 2012 London Olympics but failed to do so because the government of Ghana interfered with the Ghana Olympic Committee resulting in suspension of the sports body by the International Olympic Committee (IOC), mainly because the act of interference undermined the "autonomy of the National Olympic Committee" (Charway & Houlihan, 2020, p. 503) in the country. Consequently, the National Sport Federation of Ghana (NSF) became autonomous and the government curbed its involvement in making decisions that impacted this Olympic entity. The top-down sport policy Ghana is carried by the National Sport Authority (NSA) whose aims are to enable achievement of national goals and objectives through policy implementation. The Authority implements its goals "through collaboration with relevant stakeholders such as Ghana Olympic Committee, National Paralympic Committee, NSFs, sport for development agencies, tertiary schools" (Charway & Houlihan, 2020, p. 504).

Glocalization-localization of sport policies

Connecting the global with the local through effective sport policies has characterized landscapes of human interaction in sport. While at the global level there is a macro-level of understanding of sport policy encompassing participation, performance, and competition in particular communities within nations (Houlihan, 2005), at the micro-level sport policy points to lesser focused sport policies in specific communities and regions. This involves not only policies of compromise in local-global connections but also cross-cultural adjustments that bring positive changes at the regional country level which reverberates across the spectrum of sport competitions. For instance, women wearing *Muslimat* – head and neck covers – in national and global competitions have been subject to what a global sport body – FIFA – wants in enforcement of rules and regulations that were operational earlier in the 2010s, but now have been modified in the following decade to allow these women to fully take part in elite sport competitions (Hamzeh, 2015). As Hamzeh (2015) explains, this did not happen without players and supporters fighting for the inclusion of *Muslimat* use in worldwide sporting competitions. This change occurred, to the credit of the Jordanian women's national football team which fought for the inclusion of *Muslimat* in global sport participations.

There are non-Anglocentric sport policies that impact sport labor migration and participation. Bosman's 1995 ruling permitted professional football aka soccer players to transfer between leagues after contract completion without any fee payment (Hamil, Morrow, Idle, Rossi & Faccendini, 2010) became a revolutionary policy that changed the landscape of sport, specifically football and other professional sports in Europe and elsewhere forever – ultimately revealing the power and influence of sports policies and governance as well as its utilization in the context of sport labor migration.

Bosman-Ruling

The 1995 Bosman-Ruling significantly impacted sport labor migration as an academic field, while being resoundingly felt worldwide as a practical outcome of globalization. Set into motion by a relatively unknown then 25-year old Belgian midfielder, this revolutionary change in the sporting world ultimately turned into a watershed moment in global sports history. The minor professional football player filed a lawsuit when his former club RFC Liege refused to let him transfer to second division club USL Dunkirk in France without a mandatory fee after his contract expiration. After five years of court battles, the European Court of Justice (ECJ) granted Bosman's case approval on 15 December 1995, changing the face of modern football and sports as a whole forever, in the process. Upon "citing the 1957 Treaty of Rome, which guaranteed the freedom of movement for players anywhere in Europe" (Brand, 2015, p. 1), the mandatory transfer fee that clubs had to pay even after the expiration of a player's contract was completely eliminated (Brand, 2015; Frick, 2009) – creating free agency for players across the continent and beyond, while also removing any legal restrictions on the number of foreigners in a team in Europe which essentially violated the European Union's (EU) regulations according to Article 58 of the Treaty of Rome that granted absolute freedom of movement for the Union's workforce and professionals – and that surely includes sport labor migrants. Specifically, the pre-Bosman foreign player eligibility quota was a so-called 'three-plus-two' rule, meaning no more than three foreign layers were allowed to be on the court or field at the same, with an additional two who had been 'home-grown' in the club's academy (Riach, 2015).

Ironically, more than 20 years later, the foreign eligibility quotas are a continuous subject of heated controversies in European leagues with the home-grown player rule serving as preferred homegrown rule. One of the major arguments from opponents of sport labor migration in academia and policymaking is two-fold: On the one hand is the concern over the decreased competiveness of the sport system of the sending country – the so-called 'brain drain' phenomenon, "which refers to the migration of educated, especially young individuals, from poorer to wealthier regions and countries" (Hall, 2017, p. 336; Orlowski, Wicker & Breuer, 2018) and thus a form of neo-colonialism that could be blamed for the "underdevelopment of the African football game with player agents and European clubs being the main profit makers" (Darby 2000; Lanfranchi & Taylor, 2001; Scherrens, 2007, p. 9).

As further noted by Darby (2000) and Lanfranchi and Taylor (2001), professional European football clubs (predominantly in France, Portugal, and Belgium) have recruited African players since the colonial era, indicating a long historical presence of sport labor migration (Darby, 2000; Lanfranchi & Taylor, 2001). This sport development accelerated significantly since the Bosman-Ruling despite the gradual independence of African countries (Darby, Akindes & Kirwin, 2007).

The Bosman-Ruling is a striking example of how sport policies are utilized in sport labor migration, as for example in basketball. The National Basketball Association (NBA) crowned the Canadian team Toronto Raptors as the first non-American team to be NBA champions, and made Milwaukee Bucks star Giannis Antetokounmpo aka the 'Greek Freak' its Most Valuable Player (MVP) of the 2018–2019 season. Fittingly, NBC News opted for the following headline "NBA MVP Giannis Antetokounmpo's success is a victory over anti-immigrant populist" (Smith, 2019, p. 1). This would not have been possible without the Bosman-Ruling that paved the way for international players to take their talents overseas or elsewhere. However, this is just one of many sport policies that have had a transformative, sustainable impact on the sports industry and therefore, society, considering the intertwined relationship between the two.

Fundamentally, thus, by ruling in favor of Bosman, the European Union acted as a supranational organization (Douvis & Billonis, 2005; Hargrave, 2019), imposing a sports policy rule that undeniably had an immense impact not only on the international migration of professional athletes but also the sports industry as a whole. Prior to this landmark ruling in 1995, the European Union had limited direct influence on sports policies and regulations in Europe, leaving it mostly to the member states of the European Union to govern and regulate their sports and recreation systems, while serving in a more advisory role. However, this changed with the introduction of a European Sports Policy as part of the ratification of the Treaty of Lisbon in 2009 (Euractiv, 2010). Nevertheless, despite the EU officially being powerless in shaping the sports landscape in Europe, it still yielded legislative control in the form of many rules, policies, and programs that may not have been directed at sports, but still affected it to some extent, considering its nature of being interwoven in all walks of life, including local and global politics (Palmer, 2013). This is particularly true for the common market regulations in Europe, which is a free trade zone with no tariffs for goods and free movement of capital, commodities, and services. Simply put: it allows EU citizens to move and work freely in another member state (Suranovic, 1998).

Applying this policy to sport labor migration, the result was effectively the elimination of nationality quotas in sports leagues – which is precisely what the Bosman ruling effectively and unapologetically confirmed and adopted when first passed in 1995. Add to this a free market after eliminating the mandatory transfer fee, and the landscape of professional sports in the EU changed once and for all, with internationally known football teams like FC Barcelona, Real Madrid or Bavaria Munich gathering talent from all over Europe to the extent that teams were fielded with no domestic players at all. Amid the subsequent high influx of foreign players to European football and basketball clubs, the ongoing controversy of foreign player eligibility quotas emerged, with policymakers' attempting to curb the influx of non-European players through restrictive regulations and sports policies. Almost simultaneously, circumvention methods quickly developed, such as home-grown player rules or the acquisition of dual citizenship and naturalisation (Hall, 2017). This has become particularly visible in European football due to its high profile and status as the most popular and globalized sport in the world. For instance, in 2011 the "premier leagues of UEFA (the Union of European Football Associations) members were home to representatives of 157 countries" (Hall, 2017, p. 336). Similarly, Frick (2009) found the percentage of domestic players in the German Bundesliga "decreased from about 70% in 1995 to less than 50% in just 5 years" (p. 90). Agreeing with Falcous and Maguire (2005) and building upon studies from other economic historians and sociologists, Frick (2009) particularly draws attention to the "socially embedded" (p. 90) nature of the international migration of football players, highlighting it as a direct result of well-established and deep social, cultural, economic, and historical roots and relationships (Frick, 2009; McGovern, 2002; Taylor, 2006).

Way forward for policy development and implementation

While Hayhurst et al (2016) have stated that sport and physical activity programs are committed to increasing the participation of First Nation youth, there is a need for a more grounded understanding of what exactly social development and change means for First Nation communities, and how a program is implemented within a First Nation cultural and epistemological paradigm. In fact, as Strachan, McHugh, and Mason (2018) highlighted, the role that participants' knowledge, particularly First Nation knowledge and pedagogies, play or could play in SDP programs has received scant attention in research. Sport-centric social and development programs led by Indigenous peoples concerned with and shaped by Indigenous voices, epistemologies, and paradigms could provide better opportunities to challenge current biopedagogical and often, colonialist beliefs (Hayhurst et al., 2016). However, a cautious approach is required. Programs and policy that encourage First Nation self-determination and rupture dominant relations of power may find it difficult to secure similar funding to counter the centrality of current corporations and the SDP paradigm (Hayhurst et al., 2016). Also, there is a latent possibility that programs, despite the ubiquity of neoliberal logic and biopedagogies, could prepare the participants to successfully negotiate Eurocentric institutions and assist them in promoting social change (Hayhurst et al., 2016).

Within the programs, Gardam et al.'s (2017) review of academic literature on sport-related programming with First Nation communities identified a need for cross-cultural mentorship between mentors and/or staff, and a program participation framework that highlights integrating First Nation persons into the program itself towards self-determination. Further, sport cannot be a mutually exclusive objective for social change or development but must be part of broad social and economic objectives of the community (Gardam et al., 2017). Van Luijk et al (2019) also called for more First Nation-led programming and projects across Canada. For example, Mason, McHugh, Strachan, and Boule (2018) and Skinner, Hanning, and Tsuji (2005) discussed barriers to active lifestyles in urban and rural socio-cultural contexts, respectively. Policies aimed at improving community health outcomes around sport and physical activity need to address issues related to accessibility (Mason et al., 2018).

In terms of programming itself, Arellano and Downey (2018) have stated the sport of Lacrosse may be a fitting pathway to structure First Nation language, history and tradition, ritual, and ceremonial epistemologies into sport policy. While various local forms of Lacrosse historically existed within First nation communities, it was appropriated and secularized in the beginning of the mid-19th century by Euro-Canadians in the pursuit of forming a national identity (Arellano & Downey, 2018). Presently, sport policies such as PLAY contain a focus on Lacrosse that reduced the complexity of First Nations to 'Aboriginal', and continues to undermine empowerment, self-determination, and nationhood. Contemporary identification of a colonized sport (e.g. lacrosse) self-proclaimed as the national game of Canada exists under an apolitical frame (Arellano & Downey, 2018). Such an understanding leaves First Nation communities devoid of localized interconnections between physical, spiritual, intellectual, and emotional epistemologies within different First Nation communities, and preserves the ongoing colonization of the game (Arellano & Downey, 2018). Hence, the 'de-colonizing' course of sport-centric development and social change is authorizing colonialist structures to continue (Arellano & Downey, 2018). Sport policy design and implementation must resolve the short- and long-term effects of exposing First Nation youth to an appropriated, compartmentalized, portrayed as secular and commodified as 'Aboriginal' as it operates under a presupposed universality of 'Aboriginal culture and identities' with games like Lacrosse being a part of this narrative. (Arellano & Downey 2018).

In brief, as demonstrated by the discussed examples drawn from varied regions of the world, understanding and defining the impact of policies is paramount as they play a key role in the development of sport policy which informs governance structures in the sport landscape and beyond. Sport at macro, micro, and meso levels are operationalized through policies and governance structures that are felt globally and have implications for the preservation of indigenous cultural frameworks of human life. Indigenous communities have historically used sport to positively engage the youth and adults alike in the essence of cultural preservation and community revitalization. However, sport polices facilitated through corporations have brought challenges to the preservation and revitalization of local culture and community. In addition, sport has served as an instrument of unification and social change across the spectrum of ethnic and racial diversification and has also provided ways for new articulations in the use of cultural equipment in global mega-sports events like the Olympics and FIFA World Cup championships.

Sport policies and sociocultural impacts   35

Global sport bodies headquartered in Europe have enforced rules and regulations that govern all sport competitions in local and global communities. Countries' governments are not permitted to interfere with the affairs of local sport federations that are governed internationally through global sport associations. Sport policies at the country level often follow a two-pronged approach – sport for all and for elite sport – in spite of challenges faced at varying levels of implementation (e.g. in South Korea). Glocalization-localization of sport policies has been effective in sport labor migration as it allowed for smooth interracial and interethnic participation in global sport competitions and permitted border-crossings without conflict, and restored harmony in societies.

References

Annan, K. (2004). *Universal language of sport brings people together, teaches teamwork, tolerance, secretary-general says at launch of international year.* Retrieved from https://www.un.org/press/en/2004/sgsm9579.doc.htm

Arellano, A., & Downey, A. (2018). Sport-for-development and the failure of aboriginal subjecthood: Re-imagining lacrosse as resurgence in indigenous communities. *Settler Colonial Studies, 9*(4), 457–478.

Barghchi, M., & Omar, D. (2014). Town planners' perceptions of sports facilities an urban development: A case study of 13 states' main sports facilities in Malaysia. *Journal of the Malaysian Institute of Planners, XII,* 19–34.

Bergsgard, N. A., Houlihan, B., Mangset, P., Nodland, S. I., & Rommetvedt, H. (2007). *Sport policy: A comparative analysis of stability and change.* Oxford, UK: Elsevier.

Barsh, R. L. (1994). Canada's Aboriginal Peoples: Social Integration or Dis-integration? *Canadian Journal of Native Studies, 14*(1), 1–46.

Brand, G. (2015). *How the Bosman rule changed football -20 years on.* Retrieved from https://www.skysports.com/football/news/11095/10100134/how-the-bosman-rule-changed-football-20-years-on

Byron, K. C. (2014). *Global-local examination of athletics in Kenya: A case study of "Kaptuiyoot" community.* Unpublished doctoral dissertation, University of Georgia. Athens, GA.

Byron, K. C., & Chepyator-Thomson, J. R. (2015). Sports policy in Kenya: Deconstruction of colonial and postcolonial conditions. *International Journal of Sport Poicy and Politics, 7*(2), 301–313.

Charway, D., & Houlihan, B. (2020). Country profile of Ghana: Sport, politics and nation-building. *International Journal of Sport Policy and Politics, 12*(3), 497–512.

Choi, Y.-d., Jo, S.-h., & Ok, G. (2019). Evolution of the sports for all policy in National Sports Promotion Plan in South Korea, 1962–2017. *The International Journal of the History of Sport, 36*(9–10), 876–891.

Chepyator-Thomson, J. R. (2014). Public polibcy, physical education and sport in English-speaking Africa. *Physical Education and Sport Pedagogy, 19*(5), 512–521.

Coalter, F. (2007). *A wider role for sport: Who's keeping the score?* London, UK: Routledge.

Daley, B. (2013). *Mandela saw sport as a way to bring South Africans together.* Retrieved from https://theconversation.com/mandela-saw-sport-as-a-way-to-bring-south-africans-together-21244.

Darby, P. (2000). The new scramble for Africa: African football labour migration in Europe. *European Sports History Review, 3,* 217–44.

Darby, P., Akindes, G., & Kirwin, M. (2007). Football academies and the mgiration of African footblal labor to Europe. *Journal of Sport & Social Issues*, *31*(2), 143–161.

Douvis, J., & Billonis, T. (2005). Implications and consequences of the Bosman Ruling: The case of the Greek Basketball League. *Spor Hekimligi Dergisi Cilt*, *40*(4), 157–164.

Euractiv.com. (2010). *Sports, a promising tool in reinforcing European identity*. Retrieved from https://www.euractiv.com/section/sports/opinion/sports-a-promising-tool-in-reinforcing-european-identity/

Fahlén, J., & Skille, E. (2017). State sport policy for indigenous sport: Inclusive ambitions and exclusive coalitions. *International Journal of Sport Policy and Politics*, *9*(1), 173–187.

Falcous, M., & Maguire, J. (2005). Globetrotters and local heroes? Labor migration, basketball, and local identities. *Sociology of Sport Journal*, *22*(2), 137–157.

FIBA.com. (2020). Official basketball rules. Retrieved from http://www.fiba.basketball/documents/official-basketball-rules-yellow/2020.pdf.

FIFA.com. (2021). Laws of the Game 20/21/. Retrieved from https://resources.fifa.com/image/upload/ifab-laws-of-the-game-2020-21.pdf?cloudid=d6g1medsi8jrrd3e4imp<

Forsyth, J., & Wamsley, K. B. (2006). "Native to native . . . we'll recapture our spirits": The World Indigenous Nations Games and North American Indigenous games as cultural resistance. *International Journal of the History of Sport*, *23*(2), 294–314.

Frick, B. (2009). Globalization and factor mobility. The impact of the "Bosman-Ruling" on player migration in professional soccer. *Journal of Sports Economics*, *10*(1), 88–106.

Gardam, K., Giles, A., & Hayhurst, L. (2017). Sport for development for Aboriginal youth in Canada: A scoping review. *Journal of Sport for Development*, *5*(8), 30–40.

Ginzel, L. (2018). *Get in the game – Social integration through football-based programmes*. Retrieved from www.streetfootballworld.org

Government of Jamaica. (2013). *White paper on the National Sport Policy* (Ministry Paper No# 29/13). Retrieved from https://jis.gov.jm/media/National-Sports-Policy-March-25-2013-FINAL-6.pdf

Hamil, S., Morrow, S., Idle, C., Rossi, G., & Faccendini, S. (2010). The governance and regulation of Italian football. *Soccer & Society*, *11*(4), 373–413.

Hamzeh, M. (2015). Jordanian national football Muslimat players: Interrupting Islamophobia in FIFA's hijab ban. *Physical Education and Sport Pedagogy*, *20*(5), 517–531.

Hall, D. (2017). *Tourism and geopolitics. Issues and concept from Central and Eastern Europe*. Ayrshire, UK: CABI.

Hargrave, M. (2019). *Supranational*. Retrieved from https://www.investopedia.com/terms/s/supranational.asp

Harvey, D. (2005). *A brief history of neoliberalism*. New York, NY: Oxford University.

Hayhurst, L., Giles, A., & Wight, J. (2016). Biopedagogies and Indigenous knowledge: Examining sport for development and peace for urban Indigenous young women in Canada and Australia Sport. *Education and Society*, *21*(4), 549–569.

Hills, S., Gómez Velásquez, A., & Walker, M. (2018). Sport as an analogy to teach life skills and redefine moral values: A case study of the 'Seedbeds of Peace' sport-for-development programme in Medellin, Colombia. *Journal of Sport for Development*, *6*(10), 19–31.

Hong, E. (2010). *An analysis of the sport policy process in the Republic of Korea: The cases of elite sport development and sport for all*. Loughborough, UK: Loughborough University.

Houlihan, B. (2005). Public sector sport policy: Developing a framework for analysis. *International Review for the Sociology of Sport*, *40*(2), 163–185.

Hughes, R. (2010). Its host success, change triumphs. Retrieved from http://www.nytimes.com/2010/07/12/sports/soccer/12iht-wcsoccer.html

Krahn, A. N. (2019). Sport policy praxis: Examining how Canadian sport policy practically advances the careers of nascent female coaches. *Women in Sport and Physically Activity Journal, 27*, 118–127.

Lanfranchi, P., & Taylor, M. (2001). *Moving with the ball. The migration of professional football*. Oxford, UK: Berg.

Lee, Y. S. (2013). A study on effectiveness evaluation of sport for all policy. *Journal of Korean Society of Sport Policy, 11*, 15–28.

Lucas, R., Jeanes, R., & Diamond, Z. (2020). Sport for development and Indigenous Australians: A critical research agenda for policy and practice. *Leisure Studies*. http://doi/abs/10.1080/02614367.2020.1808050?journalCode=rlst20

Jacobs, S., De Bosscher, V., Venter, R., & Scheerder, J. (2019). *Country profile: Sport in South Africa. International Journal Sport Policy and Politics, 11*(1), 175–191.

Isaac, L. (2019). *Online learning for sports management*. Retrieved from http://www.leoisaac.com/policy/top126.htm

Mandigo, J., Corlett, J., Holt, N., van Ingen, C., Geisler, G., MacDonald, D., & Higgs, C. (2018). The impact of the Hoodlinks Programme on developing life skills and preventing youth violence in Guatemala City. *Journal of Sport for Development, 6*(11), 21–37.

Mason, C. W., McHugh, T. L. F., Strachan, L., & Boule, K. (2018). Urban indigenous youth perspectives on access to physical activity programmes in Canada. *Qualitative Research in Sport, Exercise and Health, 11*(4), 543–558.

McGovern, P. (2002). Globalisation or internationalization? Foreign footballers in the English League, 1946–95. *Sociology, 36*, 23–42.

Megat Daud, M. A. (2007). Sport management movement in Malaysia. *Asian Sport Management Review, 1*(1), 21–31.

Meier, H. E., & Garcia, B. (2015). Protecting private transnational authority against public intervention: FIFA's power over national governments. *Public Administration, 93*(4), 890–906.

Merriam-Webster.com (2019). *Policy*. Retrieved from https://www.merriam-webster.com/dictionary/policy

Millington, R., Giles, A., Hayhurst, L., van Luijk, N., & McSweeney, M. (2019) 'Calling out' corporate redwashing: The extractives industry, corporate social responsibility and sport for development in indigenous communities in Canada. *Sport in Society, 22*(12), 2122–2140.

Mogajane, V. S., Meyer, C., Toriola, A. L., Amusa, L. O., & Monyeki, M. A. (2014). The availability of recreation policies and strategies for the provision of recreation services delivery in the North West Province, South Africa. *African Journal for Physical, Health Education, Recreation and Dance, 20*(1), 24–39.

Mwaanga, O., & Adeosun, K. (2017). Decolonisation in practice: A case study of the Kicking AIDS Out programme in Jamaica. *Journal of Sport for Development, 5*(9), 58–69.

Nicholls, S., Giles, A. R., & Sethna, C. (2011). Perpetuating the 'lack of evidence' discourse in sport for development: Privileged voices, unheard stories and subjugated knowledge. *International Review for the Sociology of Sport, 46*(3), 249–264.

O'Boyle, I., & Bradbury, T. (2013). *Sport governance. International case studies*. New York, NY: Routledge.

Orlowski, J., Wicker, P., & Breuer, C. (2018). Labor migration among elite sport coaches: An exploratory study. *International Review for the Sociology of Sport, 53*(3), 335–349.

38 Jepkorir Rose Chepyator-Thomson et al.

Palmer, C. (2013). *Global sports policy*. London, UK: Sage.

Park, J.-W., & Lim, S. (2015). A chronological review of the development of elite sport policy in South Korea. *Asia Pacific Journal of Sport and Social Science, 4*(3), 198–210.

Riach, J. (2015). *Jean-Marc Bosman: 'I think I did something good – I gave players rights'.* Retrieved from https://www.theguardian.com/football/2015/dec/12/jean-marc-bosman-players-rights-20-years

Rossi, T., & Rynne, S. (2014) Sport development programmes for Indigenous Australians: Innovation, inclusion and development, or a product of 'white guilt'? *Sport in Society, 17*(8), 1030–1045.

Sage, G. (2010). *Globalization and sport: How organization, corporations, media and politics are changing sports*. Boulder, CO: Paradigm.

Scherrens, J. (2007). *The muscle drain of African football players to Europe: Trade or trafficking?* Karl-Franzens University of Graz: A European master's in human rights and democratisation 2006–2007.

Skille, E. A. (2015). Community and sport in Norway: Between state sport policy and local sport clubs. *International Journal of Sport Policy and Politics, 7*(4), 505–518.

Skille, E. Å., Fahlén, J., Stenling, C., & Strittmatter, A. M. (2021). (Lack of) government policy for indigenous (Sámi) sport: A chain of legitimating and de-legitimating acts. *International Review for the Sociology of Sport*. https://doi.org/10.1177/1012690220988650

Skinner, K., Hanning, R., & Tsuji, L. (2005). Barriers and supports for healthy eating and physical activity for first nation youths in northern Canada. *International Journal of Circumpolar Health, 65*(2), 147–161.

Smith, C. (2019). *NBA MVP Giannis Antetokounmpo's success is victory over anti-immigrant populist forces*. Retrieved from https://www.nbcnews.com/think/opinion/nba-mvp-giannis-antetokounmpo-s-success-victory-over-anti-immigrant-ncna1021406

Smith, A., & Waddington, I. (2004). Using 'sport in the community schemes' to tackle crime and drug use among young people: some policy issues and problems. *European Physical Education Review, 10*(3), 279–298.

States News Service. (2016, August 23). Ahead of expected decision, Bera and Crowley lead members of congress to press international basketball federation to change discrimination policy against Sikh players. Gale OneFile: http://www.link.gale.com/apps/doc/A461870106/STND?u=uga&sid=STND&xid=7c14bdb9

Strachan, L., McHugh, T. L., & Mason, C. (2018). Understanding positive youth development in sport through the voices of indigenous youth. *Journal of Sport and Exercise Psychology, 40*(6), 293–302.

Suranovic, S. M. (1998). *International trade theory and policy*. Retrieved from http://internationalecon.com/Trade/Tch110/T110-2.php

Taylor, M. (2006). Global players? Football, migration and globalization, c. 1930–2000. *Historical Social Research, 31*(1), 7–30.

van Luijk, N., Giles, A., Millington, R., & Hayhurst, L. (2019). The extractives industry: (Un)likely and (un)welcome partners in regenerating Indigenous cultures in Canada? *Annals of Leisure Research*. https://doi.org/10.1080/11745398.2020.1768877

Walters, G., & Tacon, R. (2013). United Kingdom. In I. O. Bradbury (Ed.), *Sport governance: International case studies* (pp. 107–124). New York, NY: Routledge.

Won, H.-J., & Hong, E. (2015). The development of sport policy and management in South Korea. *International Journal of Sport Policy and Politics, 7*(1), 141–152.

Wright, P., Jacobs, J., Howell, S., & Ressler, J. (2018). Immediate outcomes and implementation of a sport for development coach education programme in Belize. *Journal of Sport for Development, 6*(10), 45–59.

Chapter 4

Effective governance through human resources

International experience in career development of football administrators in Poland

Karolina Nessel

Introduction

One of the pillars of economic integration within the European Union (EU) is the liberty of free movement of workers across borders. Its introduction in 1968 led to important migratory movements within the EU, and intensified internationalisation of the European workforce. The internationalisation also entered universities, where within the Erasmus Programme alone about 300,000 students leave for a semester to study abroad each year. In the sporting field, international mobility was additionally strengthened with the Bosman ruling in 1995 explicitly banning restrictions on footballers' movement between clubs within the EU. Consequently, today, the European sport labour market is highly internationalised, at least in regard to athletes and coaches. The phenomenon also makes it the object of a large body of multidisciplinary research exploring issues of motivations, migratory patterns, adjustment experiences, or sporting outcomes of the migrating sportspersons (see Agergaard & Ryba, 2014; Bale & Maguire, 1994; Elliott & Harris, 2011; Horowitz & McDaniel, 2015; Maderer et al., 2014; Maguire & Falcous, 2011).

In contrast, there is hardly anything known about the internationalisation of sport administrators in the EU, which is surprising considering the ongoing commercialisation, professionalisation, and global expansion of many sports today. And, although there is rich research in the field of international human resources on the internationalisation of business people, one may not be sure of a direct application of its results for the sports business. In fact, it is known that the effects of employees' internationalisation on their careers or the development of their organisations are dependent, *inter alia*, on the characteristics of their home organisations, which relates also to the specificity of the industry (Potts, 2015; Suutari et al., 2018).

The goal of this study is, therefore, to explore the internationalisation of careers of sport administrators. Given the exploratory character of the study, its scope is limited to football administrators in Poland. The choice of football is due to its high international popularity, commercialisation and, thus, management professionalisation. The choice of Poland, on the other hand, results from

DOI: 10.4324/9781003213673-4

its specific economic and political history. In fact, despite almost 30 years of Polish political and economic transformation, the transition of the sports system has not been accomplished and the emergence of the sport administrators profession is only progressive (Gulan, 2012). One could, thus, expect that international experience may be an advantage for career development in football in Poland, as it may enable a valuable knowledge and skills transfer from more developed football markets.

In particular, this research is guided by two main research questions:

- RQ1. What are the scale and forms of international experience of football administrators in Poland?
- RQ2. What is the impact of their international experience on their career capital and career success upon return to Poland?

The results of this investigation may help complete our understanding of the internationalisation of the football industry. They may also be of interest for sport management educators in their pursuit to prepare a next generation of sport administrators for the European and global markets. Finally, the current and potential sport administrators themselves could be helped in their decisions about internationalisation possibilities.

Theoretical framework

The research on outcomes of international experience (IE), defined as experience gained through factual time spend abroad in different contexts (Schworm et al., 2017) in international human resource management, is focused mainly on expatriates deciding to go abroad for work in forms of either international assignments within the same organisation, or self-initiated expatriations (Dickmann et al., 2018; Inkson et al., 1997; Suutari & Brewster, 2003). The main conceptual framework used in this strand of research is career capital. Its development through IE is supposed to positively impact expatriates' career success, especially upon returning back home (Eby et al., 2003). The other stream of research in this field concentrates on study abroad programmes and their impact on students' and young graduates' development. Also, in this case, the capital career framework is used, even if not as the dominant perspective (Felker & Gianecchini, 2015).

International experience and career capital

According to the career capital model by DeFillippi and Arthur (1994), the competencies developed by individuals over their careers can be classified as three ways of *knowing*. *Knowing-how* refers to career-related skills and work-related knowledge, as well as understanding that is needed for performance. *Knowing-why* capabilities allow the owner to understand oneself, explore new possibilities, and to adapt to changing work situations thanks to personal meaning, career motivation, and work identity. Finally, *knowing-whom* relates to intra- and inter-firm professional and social networks and contacts, which are helpful in career development (Jones & DeFillippi, 1996; Parker & Arthur, 2000). All three kinds of knowing are built up over time and transferable across organisational boundaries (Dickmann & Doherty, 2008).

Although the impact of an international experience on an individual's career capital is generally seen as positive, both for expatriates (Gregersen et al., 1998; Jokinen et al., 2008) and students (Felker & Gianecchini, 2015), it is not evident, especially for the former group (Dickmann & Harris, 2005). In fact, it is positive mainly in the case of *knowing-how* capabilities, which may get enriched through an improvement in cross-cultural competencies and cultural intelligence, adaptability, foreign language proficiency, and ability to solve problems in a multicultural context (Ang et al., 2007; Bracht et al., 2006; Franklin, 2010; Potts, 2015). Yet, these conclusions hold only if these skills are transferable to the domestic context, which implies, *inter alia*, an applicability of the skills in a home country organisation (Bonache et al., 2001; Dickmann & Harris, 2005). Concerning *knowing-why*, an IE has been usually found to influence personal identity and international aspirations in an enriching way (Franklin, 2010; Kohonen, 2005; Tharenou, 2003). The most debatable issue is the impact of IE on *knowing-whom*. Whereas, in the case of students, the research finds mainly neutral or positive outcomes for the development of a professionally useful network (Dickmann & Harris, 2005; Norris & Gillespie, 2009), in the case of expatriate workers, especially those on internal assignments, there are risks of losing relations with the hierarchy in the home headquarters, which may be more important for their career development than increased professional and social contacts abroad (Georgakakis et al., 2016).

International experience and career success

Career success may be defined as achievements accumulated by individuals in the course of their professional experience (Hughes, 1937). These achievements may be both real (i.e. measured with objective criteria such as pay, promotions, and occupational status [Arthur et al., 2005]) and perceived (based on such subjective criteria such as career or job satisfaction, work-life balance, sense of identity, and personal comparisons of one's own achievements with those of professional peers [Dries et al., 2008; Felker & Gianecchini, 2015; Heslin, 2005]). The way international experience impacts both categories of career success is the subject of an intense debate (Biemann & Braakmann 2013; Schworm et al., 2017). According to human capital theory, an international assignment may be considered as an individual's rational investment in own human capital and, as such, should have a positive impact on individuals' long term careers: a rise in individual productivity because of an improved career capital is supposed to be recognised and rewarded by labour markets (Benson & Pattie, 2008; Kraimer et al., 2009; Ng et al., 2005).

In the case of students, this positive outcome is often confirmed in the literature (see the review by Roy et al., 2018), even if there is more evidence on short-term and subjective measures of career success (like perceived employability), than on longer term objective ones (e.g. in terms of wages). In relation to professionals, however, the empirical evidence in this area is less explicit, as it concerns mostly short-term effects of an IE and provides mixed findings (Baruch et al., 2013). In fact, as well as the earlier research in the 1990s, many recent studies in a more globalised reality also point to disappointing career outcomes or risks of international work experiences (see Derr & Oddou, 1991; Forster, 1994; Harvey, 1989; Inkson et al., 2012; Richardson & Zikic, 2007). These negative effects come around when the organisations in the home country fails to value the skills acquired at an international level, the repatriates suffer from the loss of status or from reverse culture shocks on their return, as well as from the losses in professional domestic networks due to repeat and long absences from the headquarters in the event of international assignments (Georgakakis et al., 2016; Hamori & Koyuncu, 2011; Suutari & Brewster, 2003; Suutari & Välimaa, 2002). On the other hand, the evaluation of perceived marketability or other measures of subjective success by the repatriates upon their return is usually positive (Benson & Pattie, 2008; Feldman, 1991; Stahl et al., 2002; Suutari & Brewster, 2003).

In parallel, the long-term evaluations of top managers' careers supply some empirical evidence of improved opportunities, better salaries, or faster job promotion (Bolino, 2007; Carpenter et al., 2001; Daily et al., 2000; Hamori & Koyuncu, 2011; Magnusson & Boggs, 2006; Ng et al., 2005). Furthermore, recently, Suutari et al (2018) reported the results of one of the first studies to examine the long-term effects of international work experience on career success (both subjective and objective) of other expatriates than top managers. Having worked on a sample of 134 Finnish engineers, they found that the outcomes are generally positive and mainly unrelated to whether the work experience was acquired as an assigned or self-initiated expatriate. Suutari et al. (2018) also consider that the contradictions of the empirical evidence on the impact of IE on career success in various studies may stem not only from the different time-frames of evaluation (results of an IE in short vs. long term) or definitions of career success (objective vs. subjective), but also from the heterogeneity of the contexts in which an IE is used back in the home country. Actually, the necessity to investigate the role of the organisation's internal and external contingencies in the relationship between IE and career advancement is a repeated call in international career literature (see Hamori & Koyuncu, 2011).

Research context

Undoubtedly, football is the most popular sport played and watched in Poland – in 2018 almost 500,000 people played it in clubs, while more than 1 million observed each round of competitions in the top league. It is also the sport attracting the majority of sponsors' funding. However, in terms of clubs' revenue, with €124 million in 2017/2018 the Polish top league (called Ekstraklasa) falls into the category of middle leagues (just behind Sweden). The financial underperformance of the league is matched by the disappointing sporting results of its clubs in international competitions in the recent seasons. On the other hand, the men's national team ranked 19th in the FIFA World Ranking at the end of 2019.

The competition system is based on five leagues operating according to promotion and relegation rules. It is governed by a national football federation (Polski Związek Piłki Nożnej – PZPN) helped by league governing bodies (in case of the first and second league) and regional federations (for the lower leagues). Football clubs and football academies employ almost 30,000 coaches and trainers – half of all training staff in Poland. Regrettably, there are no statistics or academic research about the administrative employment in the discipline. Nonetheless, football is believed to be the most professionalised sport in Poland, which is assumed on the basis of its high commercialisation. Also PZPN is said to be the most effective among Polish sport federations.

Besides international competitions of Polish football clubs and representations, the most intensive internationalisation of the sport is observed in the domain of sporting talent. In 2018/2019 foreign players comprised, on average, one third of the football teams in the top league, while six out of 16 teams were managed by a foreign coach. There are also a considerable number of international transfers of footballers from Poland each year. In contrast, only one Ekstraklasa football club has a foreign owner (and only since autumn 2018).

Method

A mixed method approach was applied in this study. In the first stage, a quantitative content analysis of football administrators' profiles available on LinkedIn was conducted to estimate the scale and forms of international experience in the profession, and to identify individuals with such an experience. In the second stage, semi-structured interviews were conducted with 12 of them to investigate the possible outcomes of IE on their careers.

The first stage of data collection and analysis took place in June and July 2018. LinkedIn platform (a global business social network) was used to find people working in the administration of football in Poland (in clubs of first to fifth league, national and regional football federations, and football academies). The search yielded 320 profiles, which make the initial research sample (Table 4.1). The data publicly available in these LinkedIn profiles were manually coded by a research assistant and the author, and subsequently analysed with basic statistical tools.

The second stage of data collection and analysis involved semi-structured interviews consisting of four key parts: (1) career path and forms of the IE, (2) impact of the IE on career capital, (3) impact of the IE on career success, and (4) applicability of the IE in football organisations. With the advancement of the data collection and initial analysis, new questions were introduced into the

44 Karolina Nessel

Table 4.1 Sample Composition by Organisation Type and Sex (Number of Persons)

Sex	National Football Federation	Regional Football Federations	Leagues' Governing Bodies	I League Football Clubs	II League Football Clubs	Other Football Clubs	Football Academies	Total
Women	11	3	1	41	8	2	1	67
Men	38	27	18	103	30	19	18	253
Total	49	30	19	144	38	21	19	320

Table 4.2 Interview Sample Characteristics

Interviewee	Age	Sex	Organisation	Job level	International Experience
Interviewee #1	25–30	M	I league club	Specialist	sE, sW
Interviewee #2	20–25	M	I league club	Specialist	sE, Sw
Interviewee #3	30–35	M	I league club	Senior manager	oE, sI
Interviewee #4	30–35	M	II league club	Senior manager	sE, sI
Interviewee #5	35–40	W	National football federation (PZPN)	Senior manager	sE, oE
Interviewee #6	30–35	M	I league governing body (Ekstraklasa)	Manager	sE
Interviewee #7	30–35	M	Regional football association	Senior specialist	oE
Interviewee #8	35–40	M	II league club	Manager	oE, oW
Interviewee #9	30–35	M	National football federation (PZPN)	Specialist	oE, oW
Interviewee #10	20–25	M	Football academy	Specialist	oI
Interviewee #11	30–35	M	National football federation (PZPN)	Specialist	oW
Interviewee #12	35–40	M	I league club	Specialist	oW

Notes: sE = sport education; oE = other education; sI = sport internships; oI = other internships; sW = sport work; oW = other work.

interview guide to explore in more detail the mediating impact of business culture on the utility and applicability of IE in Polish football.

To identify prospective interviewees, judgemental sampling was employed. It ensured that interviewees represented different forms of international experience and current employment, as well as both sexes. It was not possible to interview two of the chosen persons. The interviewees' identification, contact, interviews, and initial data analysis were performed in rounds. The process stopped after the second round, when data saturation was observed, resulting in the interview sample of 12 persons (Table 4.2).

The interviews were conducted by phone in August and September 2018 and lasted 30 to 90 minutes (about 670 minutes in total). All interviewees were informed about the study's purpose and their right to remain anonymous. They all agreed to the recording of the interviews. The interviews were transcribed verbatim into Word documents, where thematic analysis through emerging coding in relation to the a priori research themes of capital career, career success, and IE application was employed. The thematic analysis was guided by both deductive and inductive reasoning, balancing prior knowledge from the literature on the outcomes of the international experience with the elasticity needed to incorporate novel information from the interviews concerning a new, not yet researched, sport context (Gibbs, 2018). Interviews, their transcription and analysis, as well as translation of the quotes from Polish into English were performed by the author.

Results

Scale and forms of international experience

The analysis of scale and forms of career internationalisation among the LinkedIn sample of sport managers shows that only 19% of them have any kind of international experience, and 9% any kind of sport-related international experience. Importantly, in the sample there are no foreigners working in football administration in Poland. Among the forms of the internationalisation (Figure 4.1), the dominant one is foreign education (including Erasmus exchange), followed by work, and the smallest group including all kinds of internships, projects, trainings, and volunteering. The work and education are mostly non-sport oriented and roughly more than half of them last for more than one year. On the other hand, internships etc. reported by the sample are clearly focused on sport and rather short-term.

The education in sport involves master and bachelor programmes run fully abroad, and MBA programmes offered as periodical sessions, mostly in the UK, Spain, and internationally, besides the UEFA Certificate in Football Management (CFM) being run in Poland. The non-sport related education (other than Erasmus exchange) is likewise most often realised in the UK and Spain, but also in the USA. It comprises MBA, master, and bachelor studies, as well as shorter programmes. Considering sport work experience abroad, in 33% of cases it takes the form of short-term student jobs in the sport industry (e.g. steward) done during education abroad. The rest of the cases are longer in term and concentrated in coaching and scouting. In the sample, there are no cases of managerial positions in sport business abroad. Among the more numerous non-sport jobs abroad, there is even a higher proportion of student jobs, but also there are more managerial positions. In both kinds of professional experiences, the dominant host country is the UK, followed by the USA and Ireland. Among other international experiences reported by the sport administrators, there are only two cases (less than 1% of the sample) of internships in foreign sport clubs, while three persons reported

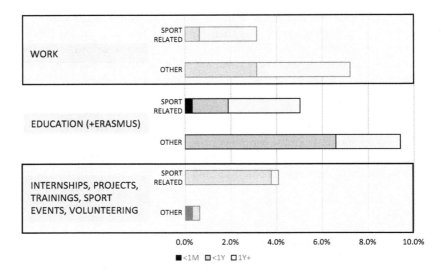

Figure 4.1 International Experience of Sport Administrators in Poland (% of the Sample).

volunteering at international sport events, and also three of them volunteered as youth coaches during their studies abroad. Another two persons took part in a foreign sport-related camp or forum.

Overall, the international experience of managers working in Polish football is rather limited, even more when only sport-related experience is considered. The administrative sport internships or volunteering are rather isolated cases. Somehow more common is international education in sport, which, moreover, is often accompanied by coaching or students jobs, and volunteering (often not in the sport industry) while abroad. On the other hand, the non-sport experience is more frequent, and takes the form of higher level jobs. The leading host countries are the UK, the USA, Ireland, and Spain. The latter observation correlates with foreign language knowledge declared by the sample administrators: English is declared or used in the LinkedIn profile by 60% of them, German by 20%, Spanish by 10%, Italian by 8%, and French by 4%.

Impact of international experience

The presentation of the findings is structured as follows: (1) impact on career capital, (2) impact on career development, (3) applicability of the IE in the football context in Poland. Where appropriate in the analyses, a difference is made between sport and non-sport IE.

Impact on career capital

The main benefits of the sport IE evoked by interviewees correspond very well to the career capital framework, as stated by Interviewee #5, who summarised them this way:

> The main benefits? Knowledge, contacts, and reinforced professional value. [Interviewee #5: oE, sE]

- *Knowing-what*

For all the interviews, an improvement in foreign language skills is an important and evident benefit of their IE. It goes along with a perceived rise in communication abilities and relation building, which is assigned not only to improvement in language skills, but also to a greater assertiveness and openness to different communication styles. The openness is also a valuable benefit in a more general meaning – as a realisation of and sensitivity to differences in culture, opinions, ways of thinking, mentality, business culture, work styles etc. Even if it is often a benefit that took time to be fully realised:

> It is the ability to function with people who are different than me, the ability to build relations with people of completely different backgrounds, experiences, culture, ways of thinking. It was like throwing myself into deep water. Now I can see it. [Interviewee #2: sE, sW]

Additionally, in the context of sport-related IE, the benefit of a greater openness means an awareness of the heterogeneity of sport models and sport management practices across countries. It is also described by interviewees as a deeper knowledge of the sport/football industry, marketing, finance, communication, and current trends. The interviewees find it inspiring for problem solving in actual and potential professional challenges. Some of them even deliberately used their training or studying experiences to work on Polish cases in hope of their future implementation, or kept notes with good ideas:

> These clubs are very active in marketing, they have well developed structures. I came back with the head full of new ideas, with plenty of notes, with some reports. I wanted to implement these ideas in practice on my return. [Interviewee #4: sE, sI]

- *Knowing-why*

Almost all the interviewees report an increased self-esteem, which they link to improved competencies. In fact, they see their IE as a successful learning experience and a proof of their capacities to manage in challenging situations. In some cases, it was a demystification of other people met during the IE that led to a change in the perception of own professional value:

> It has opened my mind for one more thing, a very subjective one. I have realised that I'm not different from the rest of the group, and candidates or people who work there. And, in some points, I even have some advantages over them. [Interviewee #5: oE, sE]

The interviewees usually find their IEs beneficial for their autonomy in professional development and inspiring for future professional plans. During their IEs, most of them considered new options for their further careers. In the cases of two interviewees, these were the study programmes they had undertaken abroad that redirected them into their present specialisations.

- *Knowing-whom*

When asked about the evaluation of contacts made during their IEs, interviewees' spontaneous answers were usually concentrated on the enrichment and inspiration they got from the people they had met. In the case of sport-related IEs, some of these contacts are also found to be a valuable part of their professional network, which is already used or may be used in future to exchange knowledge, work on common projects, or as social capital:

> Indeed, these people have different competencies, different experience, but nevertheless they work in sports. So, first, we could learn a lot from each other. Second, these contacts make relationships in the international structures easier as we support each other. [Interviewee #5: oE, sE]
>
> These are contacts from all over the world, these people work in high positions in sports. We stay in touch. I'm convinced these contacts will pay off throughout life, as football becomes a global business. We may start an interesting project together in Poland soon. [Interviewee #6: sE]

The non-sport related IEs are also reported to have led to interesting and valuable social contacts. And, even if the interviewees have not used them for professional purposes, they do not exclude this possibility in future. Simultaneously, however, they declare to continue their professional work in football, so these declarations may be treated more as a proof of overall satisfaction of their IEs than as an improvement of *knowing-whom* career capital.

None of the interviewees regrets a deterioration in the home professional network during their IE. This observation, however, may be due to the characteristics of the sample, where there are no cases of typical international assignments within a multinational organisation. Moreover, the majority of the sample consists of people who had no rich contacts in Polish football before their IEs. One of the few interviewees, who could have suffered from a loosening of ties to the

Polish football network when leaving for three years for a non-sport related work abroad, believes to have stayed in the network, as it is very small and the information travels fast:

> The football world is very hermetic. In reality, it is hardly possible to get there from outside. I don't know if there is someone who entered this world from outside just on the basis of his fantastic education. In general, you have to know someone to be treated as one of them (...). This is specific to this world. So, even if you are not physically present and you don't work with these people on the daily basis, if only you keep in touch with people you know, people with whom you have played football, worked together, you will not lose anything. [Interviewee #11: oW]

Impact on career success

Considering the short term impact of the IEs, those related to sport are generally found to have a positive influence on interviewees' further career and may be helpful in getting a job in football:

> Yes, it has changed my situation on the labour market. No doubt about it. I saw the reaction of the marketing director who was interviewing me when I described my studies and work I had been doing in the UK. And finally I got the job. [Interviewee #2: sE, sW]
>
> This diploma opened some doors for me. At least for initial conversations. No one has told me directly that it was this diploma that made us talk, but nevertheless the interlocutors were stressing my rich experience at such a young age, so it must have been a reason. [Interviewee #4: sE, sI]

Nevertheless, this positive outcome was not always immediate and granted:

> I wanted to return to Poland as soon as possible. I believed that, with a good foreign diploma, I would be able to get an interesting job in a big football club. However, upon the return, I must admit it was not so easy. (...). Hardly any football club announces job openings. I followed the market for two years – there was only one internship offer in club X (...), and club Y made two public offers, but they were restricted to people from the region, to the clubs' fans (...). So I worked first in a corporation in Cracow, then one and a half years in Warsaw in a big hospital. Simultaneously, I was working also as a referee, I was invited to a football conference (...) so I kept in touch with football, mostly at local level. Then, I decided to accept an internship in a local club in a small town (...). And only later there was this job announcement in club Z; I got two interviews, the club presented itself very well. They gave a chance to young people from all over the country, they were searching for competencies, not a fan's attachment to the club (...). Later, I learned that

there were 300 applications for this job (…). I was also told that it was my CV that made the difference. And that, during the interviews, I had been very enthusiastic, open, direct, assertive – I think I have built it abroad. [Interviewee #1: sE, sW]

The biggest disappointment in this regard is in fact reported by interviewees with non-sport related experience and with no strong contacts in the football world. But, for interviewees already active in the football business, their sport-related IEs (internships, MBA programmes) are found to bring about advancement in their careers, greater autonomy of decisions, working on better projects, and improvement in economic status. Moreover, in two cases, an international MBA in football/sport management was used as a pivotal element in a strategy of career reorientation.

When asked about the persistence of the IEs' impact on their careers, the interviewees have mixed judgements. Some of them, especially those with short and non-sport related IEs (e.g. Erasmus study or internship programmes) consider it rather short-lived – an interesting element in one's CV at the beginning of the career that will fade away with the accumulation of further work experiences. Nevertheless, even they believe that these IEs have a long lasting effect on their personality, which will continue to impact their professional development:

I don't believe it has a very strong impact on my career any more – the Erasmus exchange is very popular now. It is surely a nice supplement on one's CV, maybe at the beginning of the career it may help somehow. Later, it becomes only an interesting fact (…). I think it has had an impact on my career; this experience has shaped me in a way, it has opened my mind. But on the other hand, I'm not sure it is a bonus. [Interviewee #7: oE]

Maybe now the impact is not great, but considerable. This experience enriches personality, adds self-confidence. As a supplement to other personality traits, such as diligence, conscientiousness. It pays off all the time in my job. [Interviewee #9: oE, oW]

It doesn't have an impact now, but I think it will. However, it is not so much about a specific stay abroad. This is rather about the openness and shift of perspective on some things; they can make that one day I will get to this professional level I'm thinking about. [Interviewee #11: oW]

What is more, the belief in positive long-term impacts of their IEs is expressed also by interviewees for whom finding a football job after their expatriation was difficult and not helped by their IEs, as in the case of Interviewee #8:

Also, thanks to the very good command of English, I got accepted to the UEFA football management course that is going to be organised in Poland, but with international enrolment. I think the benefits are coming progressively (…). These hard and soft skills are getting more and more visible now (…). They have an impact on my position and salary. [Interviewee #8: oE, oW]

This long-term impact on their career capital, the interviewees' subjective marketability is in most cases improved, even if they are very conscious that employment opportunities in Polish football are not always related to their career capital.

The subjective positive evaluation of their IEs is confirmed by interviewees' attitude to possibilities of future expatriation – some of them have already undertaken or tried to get another IE, and all of them report ready to accept one, even if under some conditions (it would have to fit into their careers in football, not collide with actual work obligations, be acceptable for their family, and – for most of them – of temporary character).

The final proof of interviewees' satisfaction with their IEs is the comments summarising the whole experience:

> This student loan is an investment that I pay back with serenity, with no remorse. Only, only benefits... [Interviewee #1: sE, sW]
>
> This was a powerful experience, I learnt a lot (…). I would have taken this decision once again (…). The whole adventure gets a great 'plus'. [Interviewee #2: sE, sW]
>
> It was really cool! [Interviewee #9: oE, oW]

Importantly, these positive evaluations are given also by interviewees whose careers have not developed according to their initial plans and the immediate positive impact of IEs was absent (e.g. they failed to find a sport-related job abroad or have struggled to find such job upon their return).

Applicability of international experience in the football context in Poland

Clearly, the most used skill acquired during IEs is a foreign language (mainly English or Spanish) combined with improved general communication capacities. According to the specificity of a job, these capacities are used in contacts with foreign players, coaches and their families, football managers, as well as with journalists, foreign clubs' and international federations' representatives, fans, interns, sponsors, for preparation of international conferences, tournaments, or training camps. Internally, some interviewees use a foreign language to research international football marketing practices or other information online. Moreover, the good knowledge of English is a prerequisite for participation in UEFA CFM Programmes offered in cooperation with PZNP – which are considered by two of the interviewees.

The use of other skills resulting from non-sport IEs is not evident for the interviewees. In particular, many of them do not see a direct application of their increased sensitivity to multicultural differences, as their work is primarily in the national environment. Only in some rare cases, some general business skills (e.g. in marketing communication in the case of Interviewee #10) are applied.

On the other hand, some sport and football-specific knowledge and skills may be practised, albeit under some conditions. In particular, the marketing knowledge and practices learnt during sport management courses or internships are reported to be potentially applicable. However, it depends whether the organisation is elastic enough to accept them, and whether the interviewee has enough decision liberty to apply them. And in both respects the interviewees' experiences are mixed. On the positive side, interviewees working in PZPN are able to apply them and even to transfer them to their teams, as are marketing directors of two football clubs from the first and second leagues, or a junior specialist in a first league football club:

- Interviewee #5 (oE, sE) actively makes use of her IE network, prepares new projects with UEFA, transfers knowledge and skills on her team;
- Interviewee #6 (sE) implements his study projects (intentionally prepared for the Polish context);
- Interviewee #3 (oE, sI) makes use of the work techniques learned during his IE (e.g. research on marketing activities of other clubs, team management);
- Interviewee #4 (sE, sI) applies inspirations gained through his IE in marketing activities, which is important, as in this club "we are building the marketing from scratch";
- Interviewee #2 (sE, sW) benefits of his language proficiency and knowledge of football marketing to do research on football trends, translations, business presentations.

This application nevertheless requires some adaptation and acceptance of the teams:

> We are talking about certain practices that were successful in club X. But we always have to consider the specificity of the market. And back in Poland I had to learn some things again, as not everything works as in Spain. Some corrections were needed, but, in the end, the framework is similar (…). I'm lucky to work with open-minded people. [Interviewee #6: sE]

In contrast, other interviewees often feel blocked in their innovativeness, and frustrated with the low openness to change on the part of their bosses or colleagues:

> Unfortunately, there are a lot people in Polish football who think to know everything, but in fact their perspective is very narrow (…). They are not capable of accepting a different point of view. [Interviewee #12: oW]

The interviewees' opinions are also mixed when asked whether Polish football would benefit from more people with international experience. Those who see the international connections of Polish football and those who are critical of business culture in football organisations tend to support this thesis:

> I think an international experience is very important. Because of the fact, for example, that most of the decisions about football development are taken

Football administrators in Poland 53

in Switzerland (...) and you have to have a network there to try to lobby for your interests (...). Second, there are the issues of international transfers and, what is even more important – the system of dispute settlements based on CSA, FIFA, UEFA, it requires a perfect knowledge of French, English. [Interviewee #7: oE]

Surely an international experience would be useful. Certainly, the world view, the capacity to see the things from other perspectives. Undoubtedly, it helps in each job. In Poland, we are often sure to be right, and that others are not. And it is so difficult to convince us that we are not right. All of us are like this. But I think that, when abroad, facing different challenges, you learn to accept others' point of view, you learn humility. [Interviewee #11: oW]

Other interviewees, however, point out that most of competencies needed in Polish football administration may be acquired at home, not necessarily through an expatriation:

I don't think an international experience is a key. Maybe it would help the development of football in Poland, but in my opinion it is not fundamental. I would rather say that the key is open-mindedness. It doesn't matter if it comes through an international experience or other ways. [Interviewee #6: sE]

Of course, Polish football would benefit from more people with international experience, but it is already very international. When I look at my colleagues, I can see that they are already very international, even without having stayed abroad (...), in the sense that they have a lot of contacts at international level (other federations, coaches etc.), they speak foreign languages, they have relations with people of other cultures (...). I think you can internationalise your mind without going abroad (...). But it would be great to have more international assignments through PZPN, as happens in many multinational corporations. [Interviewee #9: oE, oW]

Discussion and conclusions

The main conclusion to emerge from the data analysis is that an IE is highly valued by football administrators themselves and has potential to advance both their careers and the football industry. However, in the Polish context, first, the phenomenon is limited in scale and forms, and secondly, its positive impact is hampered by the specific business culture prevailing in the sport.

In terms of a universal impact of IE on career capital in football management, the results of this research are largely in line with the previous studies in other industries, especially in relation to the improvement in the *knowing-why* capital, which seems the least industry-dependent and is considered to pay off in the long-term. Considering the *knowing-what* capital, the research shows that the sector-specific knowledge and skills (in particular in sport/football marketing) acquired abroad are not only of subjective value for the football administrators, but also may be successfully applied and, thus, contribute to the development of a football industry in another national context (although with some adaptation, which is indicative of the glocal dimensions of football). Importantly however, also generic, non-sport career capital accumulated during an IE (related to open-mindedness, change management, cross-cultural competencies, as well as language proficiency) may be an advantage for a career in football management. In fact, football organisations, in order to compete for fans, sponsors, media, and players' attention in the national market alone, need employers who are proactive, open-minded, capable learners, innovative and risk-takers, able to cope with new situations and different-minded partners. And clearly these attitudes are strengthened during an international experience.

The most industry-specific result of this research in terms of career capital relates to *knowing-whom*. Whereas the literature on international assignments highlights the danger of losing ties to home networks, which often turns out detrimental for a further career (Georgakakis et al., 2016), the data in this research does not show this phenomenon. While it may be due to the characteristics of the sample (with no cases of typical internal international assignments), the data also reveal that, at least in the case of Poland, the world of football administration is quite small and, often, hermetic. This creates entry barriers to the profession, but, on the other hand, seems to build strong ties among the insiders, which are not easily lost, even with an international expatriation of a few years. In contrast, the contacts made during an IE, especially those in the sport business, are highly valued, at least by the individuals themselves. There are two reasons advanced for this: actual or potential professional use of these contacts, as well as a personal and professional enrichment through them.

Regarding the Polish context, the applicability of career capital acquired during an IE and subsequent career development are clearly dependent on the business culture of football organisations. According to the interviewees' experience and opinions, most of the organisations (clubs, regional federations) are not only closed to open recruitment, but also to new ideas. Apparently, it is due to issues of limited human capital resources (in their quantity and quality) and their suboptimal management subsisting since the socialist era. These findings suggest that most football in Poland is still far away from full management professionalisation (and confirm the earlier observations by Gulan, 2012, and the more recent ones by Nessel & Drewniak, 2020). There are, however, a few important exceptions to this general observation. First, few of the biggest first league clubs seem to have advanced their transformation towards more openness and effectiveness. Second, football academies, having mostly operated in a free market since their beginnings, are evidently more business-like organisations. Third, the first league governing body, Ekstraklasa S.A., clearly invests in professional, open-minded, and innovative employees. But it is PZPN that makes the most important difference in Polish football. Today, it is an effective, market-oriented, innovative, and financially prosperous corporate-like organisation. It recruits new employers through public job announcements in search for specific management competencies for its developing structures, not necessarily from the football world. And this is in a sharp contrast not only to other national sport federations in Poland, but also to PZPN itself ten years ago. In fact, the transformation of PZPN started in 2012 with the arrival of its new president, Zbigniew Boniek. And, interestingly, Boniek is a former world class footballer having played not only for Polish clubs, but also for Juventus F.C. and A.S. Roma, with a successful business career in Italy. The transformation of PZPN under his presidency also has an impact on the professionalisation of other football organisations, albeit a limited one as football clubs are independent from the federation – e.g. PZPN hosts UEFA CFM Programme, which is open for participants from national and regional football associations and football clubs in Poland, as well as external participants from Eastern Europe.

Importantly, regardless of their experience in this bipolar football world in Poland and short-term career outcomes upon return, all football administrators taking part in this research expressed their overall satisfaction with their IE, and the confidence about its beneficial impact on their personal and professional development and, thus, on their long-term careers. This observation is consistent the findings of previous research on the IEs of students and employers in other business (see Potts, 2015; Suutari et al., 2018).

Taken together, the above conclusions point to both subjective as well as potential objective utility of international experience for football administrators themselves and the football organisations. The utility of an IE is, nevertheless, dependent on the characteristics of the experience (whether it is sport-related or not), of the organisation (whether it is open for new people and ideas), and of the job's characteristics and level (whether there are opportunities of international communication and hierarchical liberty to implement own ideas).

These findings provide some practical implications. For current and aspiring football administrators, the main one is the incentive for international study or work experiences, as they will not be regretted, even if it may take time to see their positive outcomes. Moreover, to be fully used as a career development factor in Poland, these experiences should be accompanied by an early network building in Polish football. Importantly, this implication is probably also valid for other national contexts, while the importance of a professional network to get into the sport world was also observed, e.g. in the US (Pedersen & Thibault, 2014) and Germany (Horch & Schütte, 2003). From the perspective of football organisations in Poland, the research findings encourage advancing their management professionalisation through changes in business culture, human resources development and management. In this endeavour, there seems to be a role for PZPN as a change facilitator. Only with a greater openness of clubs and their readiness to innovate, one may think about an effective transfer of foreign knowledge and practices into Polish football – be it through individual international experiences of football administrators, international contacts of clubs (built by clubs themselves, league governing bodies, or clubs' sponsors), or opportunities created by PZPN (like the UEFA CFM Programme).

The research implication of the study relates to the application of the chosen research method. It seems fruitful for further studies exploring the internationalisation of football administration to proceed with this mixed method design in other national contexts. In particular, the quantitative analysis would allow for comparison of scale of human capital internationalisation in the management of the industry across countries, while the qualitative research would verify the universality of current conclusions for other countries and other forms of international experience (not present among football administrators in Poland, such as managerial positions in sport abroad).

The implications of this study should, however, be nuanced by some limitations of the research design. The first one is due to its exploratory character – clearly more research in other national contexts, and probably also in other sports is needed to better understand the internationalisation of sport administrators. The second limitation to be borne in mind is the sampling method that took into account only people currently working in football administration, and, thus, excluded those whom the international experience had not helped get a football job as excepted.

To conclude, there are two main contributions of this research. First, the analysis shows how an international experience of sport and non-sport character may impact a football administrator's career capital and their career development in a domestic football organisation. Second, the research highlights how these outcomes are moderated by the business culture of football organisations, in this case – in Poland.

References

Agergaard, S., & Ryba, T. V. (2014). Migration and career transitions in professional sports: Transnational athletic careers in a psychological and sociological perspective. *Sociology of Sport Journal, 31*(2), 228–247.

Ang, S., Van Dyne, L., Koh, C., Ng, K. Y., Templer, K. J., Tay, C., & Chandrasekar, N. A. (2007). Cultural intelligence: Its measurement and effects on cultural judgment and decision making, cultural adaptation and task performance. *Management and Organization Review, 3*(3), 335–371.

Arthur, M. B., Khapova, S. N., & Wilderom, C. P. M. (2005). Career success in a boundaryless career world. *Journal of Organizational Behavior: The International Journal of Industrial, Occupational and Organizational Psychology and Behavior, 26*(2), 177–202.

Bale, J., & Maguire, J. (1994). Introduction. In *The Global Sports Arena: Athletic Talent Migration in an Interdependent World* (pp. 1–22). London: Cass.

Baruch, Y., Dickmann, M., Altman, Y., & Bournois, F. (2013). Exploring international work: Types and dimensions of global careers. *The International Journal of Human Resource Management, 24*(12), 2369–2393.

Benson, G. S., & Pattie, M. (2008). Is expatriation good for my career? The impact of expatriate assignments on perceived and actual career outcomes. *International Journal of Human Resource Management, 19*(9), 1636–1653.

Biemann, T., & Braakmann, N. (2013). The impact of international experience on objective and subjective career success in early careers. *The International Journal of Human Resource Management, 24*(18), 3438–3456.

Bolino, M. C. (2007). Expatriate assignments and intra-organizational career success: Implications for individuals and organizations. *Journal of International Business Studies*, 38(5), 819–835.

Bonache, J., Brewster, C., & Suutari, V. (2001). Expatriation: A developing research agenda. *Thunderbird International Business Review*, 43(1), 3–20.

Bracht, O., Engel, C., Janson, K., Over, A., Schomburg, H., & Teichler, U. (2006). *The professional value of ERASMUS mobility*. Kassel: Final Report, International Centre for Higher Education Research, INCHER.

Carpenter, M. A., Sanders, W. G., & Gregersen, H. B. (2001). Bundling human capital with organizational context: The impact of international assignment experience on multinational firm performance and CEO pay. *Academy of Management Journal*, 44(3), 493–511.

Daily, C. M., Certo, S. T., & Dalton, D. R. (2000). International experience in the executive suite: the path to prosperity? *Strategic Management Journal*, 21(4), 515–523.

DeFillippi, R. J., & Arthur, M. B. (1994). The boundaryless career: A competency-based perspective. *Journal of Organizational Behavior*, 15(4), 307–324.

Derr, C. B., & Oddou, G. R. (1991). Are US multinationals adequately preparing future American leaders for global. *International Journal of Human Resource Management*, 2(2), 227–244.

Dickmann, M., & Doherty, N. (2008). Exploring the career capital impact of international assignments within distinct organizational contexts. *British Journal of Management*, 19(2), 145–161.

Dickmann, M., & Harris, H. (2005). Developing career capital for global careers: The role of international assignments. *Journal of World Business*, 40(4), 399–408.

Dickmann, M., Suutari, V., Brewster, C., Mäkelä, L., Tanskanen, J., & Tornikoski, C. (2018). The career competencies of self-initiated and assigned expatriates: assessing the development of career capital over time. *International Journal of Human Resource Management*, 29(16), 2353–2371.

Dries, N., Pepermans, R., & Carlier, O. (2008). Career success: Constructing a multidimensional model. *Journal of Vocational Behavior*, 73(2), 254–267.

Eby, L. T., Butts, M., & Lockwood, A. (2003). Predictors of success in the era of the boundaryless career. *Journal of Organizational Behavior*, 24(6), 689–708.

Elliott, R., & Harris, J. (2011). Crossing the Atlantic from football to soccer: Preliminary observations on the migrations of English players and the internationalization of major league soccer. *WorkingUSA: Journal of Labour and Societyur and Society*, 14(4), 557–570.

Feldman, D. C. (1991). Repatriate moves as career transitions. *Human Resource Management Review*, 1(3), 163–178.

Felker, J., & Gianecchini, M. (2015). Influence of pre-graduation international experiences on early career internationalization: The mediation effect of career capital. *European Management Journal*, 33(1), 60–70.

Forster, N. (1994). The forgotten employees? The experiences of expatriate staff returning to the UK. *International Journal of Human Resource Management*, 5(2), 405–425.

Franklin, K. (2010). Long-term career impact and professional applicability of the study abroad experience. *Frontiers: The Interdisciplinary Journal of Study Abroad*, 19, 169–190.

Georgakakis, D., Dauth, T., & Ruigrok, W. (2016). Too much of a good thing: Does international experience variety accelerate or delay executives' career advancement? *Journal of World Business*, 51(3), 425–437.

Gibbs, G. R. (2018). *Analyzing qualitative data* (U. Flick (ed.)). London: Sage.

Gregersen, H. B., Morrison, A. J., & Black, J. S. (1998). Developing leaders for the global frontier. *Sloan Management Review, 40*(1), 21–33.

Gulan, U. (2012). *Uwarunkowania tworzenia profesji menedżerów sportowych w Polsce.* Warszawa: Uniwersytet Warszawski.

Hamori, M., & Koyuncu, B. (2011). Career advancement in large organizations in Europe and the United States: Do international assignments add value? *International Journal of Human Resource Management, 22*(4), 843–862.

Harvey, M. G. (1989). Repatriation of corporate executives: An empirical study. *Journal of International Business Studies, 20*(1), 131–144.

Heslin, P. A. (2005). Conceptualizing and evaluating career success. *Journal of Organizational Behavior: The International Journal of Industrial, Occupational and Organizational Psychology and Behavior, 26*(2), 113–136.

Horch, H.-D., & Schütte, N. (2003). Competencies of sport managers in German sport clubs and sport federations. *Managing Leisure, 8*(2), 70–84.

Horowitz, J., & McDaniel, S. R. (2015). Investigating the global productivity effects of highly skilled labour migration: How immigrant athletes impact Olympic medal counts. *International Journal of Sport Policy and Politics, 7*(1), 19–42.

Hughes, E. C. (1937). Institutional office and the person. *American Journal of Sociology, 43*(3), 404–413.

Inkson, K., Arthur, M. B., Pringle, J., & Barry, S. (1997). Expatriate assignment versus overseas experience: Contrasting models of international human resource development. *Journal of World Business, 32*(4), 351–368.

Inkson, K., Gunz, H., Ganesh, S., & Roper, J. (2012). Boundaryless careers: Bringing back boundaries. *Organization Studies, 33*(3), 323–340.

Jokinen, T., Brewster, C., & Suutari, V. (2008). Career capital during international work experiences: Contrasting self-initiated expatriate experiences and assigned expatriation. *The International Journal of Human Resource Management, 19*(6), 979–998.

Jones, C., & DeFillippi, R. J. (1996). Back to the future in film: Combining industry and self-knowledge to meet the career challenges of the 21st century. *Academy of Management Perspectives, 10*(4), 89–103.

Kohonen, E. (2005). Developing global leaders through international assignments: An identity construction perspective. *Personnel Review, 34*(1), 22–36.

Kraimer, M. L., Shaffer, M. A., & Bolino, M. C. (2009). The influence of expatriate and repatriate experiences on career advancement and repatriate retention. *Human Resource Management, 48*(1), 27–47.

Maderer, D., Holtbrügge, D., & Schuster, T. (2014). Professional football squads as multicultural teams: Cultural diversity, intercultural experience, and team performance. *International Journal of Cross Cultural Management, 14*(2), 215–238.

Magnusson, P., & Boggs, D. J. (2006). International experience and CEO selection: An empirical study. *Journal of International Management, 12*(1), 107–125.

Maguire, J., & Falcous, M. (2011). Introduction. In J. Maguire & M. Falcous (Eds.), *Sport and migration: Borders, boundaries and crossings* (pp. 1–12). Oxon: Routledge.

Nessel, K., & Drewniak, D. (2020). Motivation (for) and outcomes of a continuing professional education in football management: an exploratory study. *Polish Journal of Sport and Tourism, 27*(2), 3–7.

Ng, T. W. H., Eby, L. T., Sorensen, K. L., & Feldman, D. C. (2005). Predictors of objective and subjective career success: A meta-analysis. *Personnel Psychology, 58*(2), 367–408.

Norris, E., & Gillespie, J. (2009). How study abroad shapes global careers: Evidence from the United States. *Journal of Studies in International Education, 13*(3), 382–397.

Parker, P., & Arthur, M. B. (2000). Careers, organizing, and community. In M. A. Peiperl, M. B. Arthur, R. Goffee, & T. Morris (Eds.), *Career frontiers: New conceptions of working lives* (pp. 99–121). New York: Oxford University Press.

Pedersen, P. M., & Thibault, L. (2014). Managing sport. In P. M. Pedersen & L. Thibault (Eds.), *Contemporary sport management* (5th ed., pp. 1–31). Champaign: Human Kinetics.

Potts, D. (2015). Understanding the early career benefits of learning abroad programs. *Journal of Studies in International Education, 19*(5), 441–459.

Richardson, J., & Zikic, J. (2007). The darker side of an international academic career. *Career Development International, 12*(2), 164–186.

Roy, A., Newman, A., Ellenberger, T., & Pyman, A. (2019). Outcomes of international student mobility programs: A systematic review and agenda for future research. *Studies in Higher Education, 44*(9), 1630–1644.

Schworm, S. K., Cadin, L., Carbone, V., Festing, M., Leon, E., & Muratbekova-Touron, M. (2017). The impact of international business education on career success—Evidence from Europe. *European Management Journal, 35*(4), 493–504.

Stahl, G. K., Miller, E. L., & Tung, R. L. (2002). Toward the boundaryless career: A closer look at the expatriate career concept and the perceived implications of an international assignment. *Journal of World Business, 37*(3), 216–227.

Suutari, V., & Brewster, C. (2003). Repatriation: Empirical evidence from a longitudinal study of careers and expectations among Finnish expatriates. *The International Journal of Human Resource Management, 14*(7), 1132–1151.

Suutari, V., Brewster, C., Makela, L., Dickmann, M., & Tornikoski, C. (2018). The effect of international work experienceo nt the career success of expatriates: a comparison of assigned and self-initiated expatriates. *Human Resource Management, 57*(1), 37–54.

Suutari, V., & Välimaa, K. (2002). Antecedents of repatriation adjustment: New evidence from Finnish repatriates. *International Journal of Manpower, 23*(7), 617–634.

Tharenou, P. (2003). The initial development of receptivity to working abroad: Self-initiated international work opportunities in young graduate employees. *Journal of Occupational and Organizational Psychology, 76*(4), 489–515.

Chapter 5

Cultural frame switching
Bicultural-bilingual vs. monocultural-monolingual coaches

Gareth Winslow and Geoff Dickson

Introduction

Globalization highlights "...the need to use language as a source of competitive advantage. Individuals and organizations that dominate foreign languages will have an advantage in terms of being able to participate in trade and exchange on a world-wide level" (Li & Kalyanaraman, 2012; Molinsky, 2007). Therefore, the ability to communicate in a second language creates the opportunity for professionals to access more of the available labour market. Golf is one of the world's most popular sports, played by approximately 80 million people in more than 100 countries. With its origins in Scotland in the 15th century, and initial diffusion across the United Kingdom and into the United States, golf began predominantly as an English-language sport. Consequently, the majority of golf's expansion in more recent times has been into non-English speaking nations, or at least where English is a second language. This global propagation of golf has, in the past few decades, created a high demand for bilingual coaches in non-English speaking regions.

This situation brings into question how a coach can best communicate in a foreign language. Problematically, there is a limited understanding as to how communicating in a second language impacts coaching in any sport. Furthermore, in golf, bilingualism is not part of any accreditation process. Therefore, this study seeks to understand how multilingual coaches feel when coaching in different languages. We explore the challenges of coaching in a second language and how coaches overcome these challenges. Additionally, the study also addresses the issue of cultural diversity. Coaches are not only coaching in a second language but also in another culture. According to Kreitler and Dyson (2016, p. 95), "With the ever-increasing globalization within society, it becomes essential to understand the complexities of all cultures." The study is limited to the golf instruction dimension of golf coaching. Golf instruction focuses on skill acquisition and motor control, whereas golf coaching will also include course management, effective practice routines and programs, strength and conditioning, psychology and nutrition.

DOI: 10.4324/9781003213673-5

Conceptual framework

The relationship between language, personality, and culture is complex. Personality impacts an individual's ability to integrate into another culture and communicate effectively in a second language (Ożańska-Ponikwia, 2012). According to Kim (2001, p. 85), "...personality traits such as openness, strength and positivity play an important role in successful cross-cultural adaptation." Furthermore, research on personality traits shows that knowledge of other languages, their usage outside the classroom and the acculturation process might influence personality (Dewaele & Van Oudenhoven, 2009; Kim, 2001; Ożańska-Ponikwia, 2012). This suggests that not only does the personality of the individual influence their ability to integrate themselves into a new culture, but also that acculturation may play a role in influencing one's personality.

Biculturalism is defined as an immersion into two distinct cultures, where the individual exhibits characteristics of behaviours and beliefs from both cultures, while participating in cultural customs such as cuisine and attire. In terms of bilingualism, according to Grosjean (2015, p. 576) "...bilinguals are those who use two or more languages in their everyday lives." However, use of two languages by a bilingual individual seldom means an equal degree of ability in both languages. Native speaker fluency in both languages is quite rare, meaning that a "dominant language" often exists. In the case of the bicultural-bilingual, such individuals possess not only the qualities of biculturalism, but also the ability to communicate bilingually in both languages. According to Kreitler (2016), cultural frame switching occurs when "...bicultural individuals shift between interpretive frames rooted in different cultures in response to cues encountered in a given situation." Bicultural-bilinguals may exhibit different verbal behaviours in their two languages and may be perceived differently by their interlocutors, depending on the language they use in a particular context (Ożańska-Ponikwia, 2012; Pavlenko 2006). According to Qiu, Lin and Leung (2013, p. 1), a bicultural individual "can flexibly change their behaviours in response to different cultural contexts."

However, Grosjean (2015, p. 573) states "...individuals can be not only bicultural and bilingual, but also bicultural and monolingual, monocultural and bilingual, as well as monocultural and monolingual. Thus, contrary to a widely held belief, biculturalism and bilingualism are not necessarily coextensive." In addition, biculturalism and bilingualism may not be at the same level. According to Grosjean (2015, p. 574), "...many bilinguals are dominant in a language (globally or by domain), as opposed to 'balanced'. Dominance is difficult to define and is based not only on language fluency and on language use, but also on how the languages are distributed across domains of life." Therefore, the primary aim of this study is to explore the cultural frame switching experiences of bicultural-bilingual golf coaches.

The use of a foreign language is likely to impact personality. Bilingualism influences personality, self-perception, and perception of the world whenever there is a language switch (Hull, 1990; Koven, 1998; Ożańska-Ponikwia, 2012; Ramírez-Esparza et al., 2006). The term 'bicultural-bilingual' emphasizes the point that the frame switching phenomenon entailed far more than merely switching languages. This is because biculturals possess distinct cognitive frameworks associated with each language and underlying culture (Briley, Morris & Simonson, 2005; Luna, Ringberg & Peracchio, 2008; Phinney & Devich-Navarro, 1997). Studies demonstrate this cultural frame switching. This is reflected in the following statement by one of the participants: "I find when I'm speaking Russian I feel like a much more gentle, 'softer' person. In English, I feel more 'harsh,' 'businesslike'" (Dewaele & Nakano, 2013). The same sentiments were evident in a study of multilinguals. A multilingual participant noted, "I feel more at ease speaking in my mother tongue. It's like being at home with all the usual familiar worn and comfortable clutter around you. Speaking the second language is like being you but in someone else's house" (Dewaele & Pavlenko, 2001/2003, p. 19). A second participant in the same study revealed, "I tend to be more polite and self-conscious when speaking L2 to L5 I don't tend to consider as much what I say when speaking L1" (Dewaele & Pavlenko, 2001/2003, p. 18).

Method

Participants

Interviews were conducted with six golf coaches with Professional Golf Association (PGA) accreditations, living and teaching golf in China. The participants were all male and represented three different nationalities (Canada, the United Kingdom, and the United States). They ranged in age from 28 to 46 years (M = 37.5; SD = 5.5), and all had worked as golf coaches in China for a meaningful amount of time (M = 12.5; SD = 10.9), as part of a longer career in golf instruction (M = 17.3; SD = 15.4). Please see Appendices 5.1 and 5.2 for a summary of participant characteristics. The criteria for being bicultural-bilingual was having lived for a minimum of five years in China, and the ability to communicate fluently in Chinese both within the workplace as well as in everyday situations. In Study 2 and 3, interviews were conducted with an additional six PGA accredited coaches, and six of their students. The Study 2 sample were also teaching golf and living in China. However, in contrast to Study 1, these participants were monocultural-monolinguals, teaching golf via a translator. Please see Appendix 5.3 for a full list of interview questions.

Procedures

Identifying bicultural-bilingual golf coaches was somewhat challenging. A 'judgmental sampling'(Blaikie, 2010, p. 178) approach ensured that prospective interviewees were capable of providing substantial first-hand and in-depth information. The initial participants were recruited from personal contacts. However, it was necessary to also use a snowball sampling technique (Taylor & Bogdan, 1998) to identify potential participants. Interviews were conducted via Skype, as the interviewer and participants resided in distant cities. Digitally recorded, the formal interviews ranged in length between 37 and 64 minutes. The interview guide contained questions that reflected theoretical sensitivity (Strauss & Corbin, 1990), the theoretical framework, as well as personal and professional experiences in coaching golf in China as a bicultural-bilingual. The integration of such approaches is a feature of other qualitative research in sport (Kauer & Krane, 2006; Krane & Barber, 2003; Melton & Cunningham, 2014). Example questions included (1) What do you recall about your earliest experiences teaching golf in China? (2) What can you remember about the first lessons you conducted solely in Chinese? (3) What differences (if any) do you feel when teaching in Chinese, as opposed to English? To improve credibility and trustworthiness, the researcher's personal observations and perceptions were recorded in a personal journal (Glesne, 2006). The process of reflexive journaling allows researchers to understand the influence of their own biases towards the research process (Malacrida, 2015). To confirm their thoughts and experiences were correctly portrayed in the study, participants reviewed the researcher's interpretations and conclusions drawn.

Data analysis

Each interview was transcribed verbatim. The first stage of data analysis was about familiarization and involved reading each interview several times. Next, in a process of open coding (Berg, 2001), the researcher identified common patterns and categories. A number of categories initially emerged during this process, including (1) A greater need for clarification; (2) Frequent misinterpretations, and (3) An increase in non-verbal communication. In the next stage, broader connections were made among all open coding categories – a process known as axial coding (Strauss & Corbin, 1990). Integrating the categories and experiences of all the participants allowed higher order themes to emerge. In the final stage, the higher order themes were compared to concepts found in the theoretical framework. Such an approach ensures that the findings and interpretations relate to the theoretical framework (Melton & Cunningham, 2014).

Findings

Study 1

Unsurprisingly, the bicultural-bilingual golf coaches acknowledged an increased level of nervousness when speaking in their second language, compared to their mother-tongue. "In terms of teaching in a different culture, you definitely do change; more serious, more nervous," was a comment from one coach, while another coach mentioned "...nervousness, high stress, worry about messing up." This stress of teaching in a second language was not the only kind of stress experienced by participants. Stress was also associated with the high expectations of the Chinese golf students. Within Chinese culture, Chinese golfers typically employ a much more serious and determined approach towards learning, which in turn creates a more stressful learning environment and a much larger degree of pressure on the coach to perform. One participant commented "You tend to become a little bit more nervous", while another stated "You're totally more under pressure…their expectation is a lot higher than teaching in the West."

Such a working environment also created the situation where coaches felt anxiety during their lessons, making them susceptible to trying too hard to help their students improve. "A little bit anxious sometimes when speaking in Chinese, then starting to rush things too much," was a comment made by one coach. When coaching a group of golfers, coaches experienced the additional stress of having students fight for their attention. One coach commented "When you're teaching a group…they all expect 100% of your time, which you don't possibly have." These issues combined with the inherent difficulties of speaking in a second language, often caused coaches to lack assurance – "To get up on stage or something…that's where I kind of lose some confidence." Coaches subsequently found themselves to be far less relaxed when teaching, and much less patient. "Frustration level or anger level is much faster triggered in Chinese than in English," was one coach's remark, while another participant stated, "More serious, more abrupt…less easy going." However, along with these frequent frustrations, also came a great sense of satisfaction when being able to directly communicate with a student in his/her mother tongue. "There's a different feeling in interaction with your client when you can walk over and greet them in their own language," one interviewee remarked, while another coach commented that he was able to "connect with someone on their level."

Such observations about personality changes when speaking in Chinese, also made coaches more aware that within the Chinese language, dialogue can often be interpreted to contain a certain degree of negativity. "They don't ever seem to be very supportive or positive towards each other…they don't really provide any encouragement," was one comment. This prompted coaches to pay extra attention to their own attitudes that they wished to project onto their students – "I try to keep it really positive," was remarked by one coach, while another commented, "I think you need to be more encouraging and sensitive." In terms of noticeable changes that occurred for coaches when teaching in their second language, one of the key messages that came through very strongly was that communication had to be kept very simple. One of the major reasons for this was that when speaking in a foreign tongue, coaches were typically unable to explain things in as much detail as they could in their native language. "Verbal communication became a lot simpler, because you can't go into as much depth as you would do in English, because of your limited vocabulary," was one statement reflecting this. Additionally, given that golf is a relatively new sport in China and that the majority of Chinese golfers are not particularly familiar with the game, it was imperative to keep the vocabulary simple. This would avoid using a lot of technical terms and jargon which would often be misunderstood. "You talk about concepts much less because they have no idea," was a comment from one participant; and as the Chinese language itself also tends to be fairly concise, lacking many of the more expressive terms that exist within the English language, an inclination towards simpler dialogue was often a common theme. "[There are a] reduced [amount of] descriptive words in the Chinese language," was an observation made by one coach.

Besides limited golfing knowledge, coaches also noted that their clients were quite passive when compared to non-Chinese students. This compelled coaches to employ a more authoritative role. "The culture is no one makes a conversation at all. Not really a flow to the conversation, it's either a command or a statement," was one comment, along with another participant adding "Lack of reaction, lack of wanting to communicate". It was also mentioned that students are "Less likely to ask questions...asking questions is disrespectful," while another coach remarked "They're not used to being as involved in the lesson process as opposed to just receiving information." Given these differences in communication style, coaches found it essential to frequently seek clarification from their students, with one coach commenting that it is essential to "ask them if they understand".

Participants also commented that the ability to speak Chinese perfectly was not essential. For example, one commented that "[I could] speak pretty averagely with a lot of mistakes and still communicate", suggesting that the need to speak flawlessly was not necessary to convey one's meaning. The use of consistent vocabulary was another key to communication raised by participants. Coaches were inclined to utilize tried and tested terms to facilitate comprehension. "I kind of stick more to consistent vocabulary...stick to what you know the students can understand...a blanket vocabulary...I stick to the words where I know this gets the highest level of understanding," was one coach's comment.

The coaches' limited ability to communicate in their second language also encouraged them to be far more creative in their teaching approach, often discovering new ways to communicate with their students, other than just verbally. "Verbal diarrhoea...overwhelming for the student," said one coach, while another coach stated, "Waffling in a second language...it'll just make things more confusing." Such observations also led to the conclusion by coaches that there are noticeable benefits to having a reduced ability to converse in a second language. One participant remarked, "Talking non-stop [you] miss out on the other forms of communication. So, having a slightly limited vocabulary is actually an advantage." Another commented that the "times when (you're) not understood (are) greatly reduced when it's less reliant on verbal commands."

A reduced vocabulary was also the catalyst for a natural progression towards a greater use of non-verbal communication. "It probably increases your use of the other areas of learning vs. just auditory, which is almost always going to be useful in any culture," was one coach's comment, with another coach adding, "It widens your thinking for getting a message across, it makes you think a little bit outside the box." An increase in the use of visual learning aids was also mentioned – "More hands-on, more using pictures, video...more balanced way of getting things across as it's not just verbal." Another coach commented that what came as somewhat of a surprise to him was "How little I can say and still get my point across", while another participant summarized quite succinctly the overall importance of non-verbal communication thus, "We receive a lot more information from non-verbal communication than we do from verbal communication."

Coaches also raised the issue that native English speakers tend to speak far more directly, getting right to the point in most cases: "English is much more direct, you say what you mean." Coaches also commented that Chinese often do not say exactly what they mean, and tend to speak very indirectly. This approach is often a strategy employed to 'give face', and avoid a situation where there is potential to cause offence. "Protect face by telling you one thing and actually feeling another thing" was the feedback of one coach. Given this tendency for Chinese to communicate in a less direct manner, coaches would often struggle to follow what was happening, and experience frequent misunderstandings. "More confusing in terms of reading a situation" was mentioned, along with "You have to read between the lines to analyse what they mean." Coaches further went on to discuss this point by commenting, "Listening to what someone says and watching what they do and assuming that means one thing when it can often mean something completely different." Another coach stated "Nodding doesn't necessarily mean they agree with you, they might just be giving you face and avoiding a confrontation." A further example of this is that in situations where the student may fear creating offence or embarrassment, he/she is unlikely to speak directly to their coach, instead opting to discuss their issues with one of the coach's colleagues. A coach explained, "They'll actually avoid speaking to you on occasions, and they'll speak through a third party quite often because they don't want to speak directly to you."

However, the more familiar the coaches became with Chinese language and culture, the more they were able to decipher what was being communicated. One coach commented that "Subtle comments kind of take on a different meaning… pick up on more hidden meanings." As there are obvious differences between Eastern and Western cultures, coaches also found themselves far more aware of the need to respect the culture of their adopted homeland, learning to become more sensitive to cultural diversities, and to not cross cultural lines. "Trying my hardest not to upset someone or say the wrong thing" was mentioned, as was "Talk a bit more diplomatically, not so straight to someone…more careful, like to not upset someone or to say something that comes across in the wrong way."

Study 2

For the monocultural-monolingual participants in Study 2, despite their inability to communicate in a second language, their responses and feedback shared a number of similarities to the bicultural-bilinguals in Study 1. Given that the coaches in Study 2 were non-Chinese speaking and had to communicate with their students via a translator, the need to keep the dialogue both simple and concise became even more of a priority. "Work on one point at a time" was remarked by one coach, while another coach commented "Shorter, simpler sentences". The native-English speakers hail from a variety of countries, each with their own accent. This was a challenge for many translators. One coach commented about the need to "speak really slowly and clearly…basic language, repeating a lot." Another coach was inclined to "ask the translator if they understand (then) repeat it back to me." This approach made it much easier for the coach to ascertain whether or not the original instruction was understood by the translator, a likely prerequisite of the coach being understood by the student. With the inclusion of a translator in the lesson, one coach made clear his preference to coach in a "quiet environment". Moreover, "Good rapport with both translator and student" was regarded by almost all coaches as being a critical element. This meant not only developing a good relationship with the translator within the workplace, but also maintaining a strong friendship away from the golf course. One coach also insisted that his translator project a "Friendly, happy, receptive and good mood" during lessons. Another coach went further, by saying "The translator is the most important person for us, because (otherwise) we have no voice."

For some participants, besides the translator providing them with a verbal link to their students, translators were also found to be adept at performing a variety of other tasks. For one coach, the translator was frequently utilized to supervise students when practising, with the coach remarking "Use your translator as a supervising coach." Because the translator was present during all lessons, their understanding of the training content enabled them to assist the students during practice, ensuring that they continued to train according to the coach's instructions. Additionally, another coach would "use the translator to demonstrate to the student", which freed up the coach to step in at any time and adjust the student's movements.

Beyond the relationship with the translator, it was also emphasized by the coaches that no matter how proficient the translator was in 'everyday English', no assumption should be made about their proficiency to comprehend technical terms. This meant that in most cases, coaches had to first spend time educating their translators to an acceptable standard before they could work together as an effective team. "Teach them basic golf terminology," was suggested by many a coach, along with the advice to "Teach them golf, take them on the course… invest time in their development". Further to improving their overall golf knowledge and technical vocabulary, it was also pointed out that the degree of interest the translator had in the game would also affect their passion and commitment towards learning to become more skilled at their profession. "Spend some time trying to cultivate their interest," was one coach's remark. An interesting phenomenon that occurs during a translated lesson is the inevitable delay or lag in the translation process. However, some coaches saw this as a potential advantage, with one participant remarking, "During the pause, you can think about what you're going to say next." Having to stop briefly after every few sentences also made coaches more aware of how much they actually said, with one coach commenting, "The lag can stop you from over-talking."

The non-Chinese speaking participants of Study 2, as with the Chinese-speaking coaches of Study 1, emphasized the importance of non-verbal communication. One coach remarked "Say less, demonstrate more", while another went into much greater detail, stating

> I found that a lot of the time I'd get really good results from body language… and I really felt that in some cases they learned better, because they were really focusing on my body movements and they seemed to visualize what they needed to do better…therefore they seemed to learn more quickly.

The role of training aids and other visual aids was also raised, and their effectiveness in reducing the coach's habitual tendency towards verbal explanations. "As much as possible on training aids…find a training aid and be more visual, things can become very self-explanatory," was remarked by one coach, while another added "Use video all the time…video and Trackman."

Study 3

In the final phase, we sought the opinion of the student; arguably the definitive litmus test of effective coach/player communication, when relying on a translator. From the students' perspective, because they were conversing directly with another native-Chinese speaker, it was not necessary for them to make any noticeable adjustments or alterations to the way in which they communicated. However, they did face a challenge in that they were required to grasp the meaning of what was being translated to them, while at the same time endeavouring to calibrate these auditory instructions with what the coach was demonstrating. Despite this potential conflict, one student remarked, "Most of what I learn from my coach is by watching what he does." Such feedback from students suggests that although they experienced no major difficulties in communicating through a translator, when it came down to clarification of the coach's meaning, they appeared to place far more trust in non-verbal communication than in verbal communication, with one student commenting, "I focus less on the words, and more on what my coach is doing…easier to understand what he wants me to do." This further illustrates the point that an increase in dialogue is by no means commensurate with an increase in comprehension. On the contrary, despite less dialogue, students felt there was far more structure and order to their lessons, when learning from a non-Chinese speaking coach, with one golfer commenting, "My foreign coach teaches me in a much more systematic way…makes things easier to follow."

Discussion

These three studies attempted to further understand the effects of cultural frame switching on bicultural-bilingual golf coaches. Data were collected via interviews with bicultural-bilingual golf coaches, monocultural-monolingual coaches who

Cultural frame switching 69

utilized translators, and a selection of their students. The setting for the research was China.

During Study 1, when switching to their second language/culture, participants experienced a number of different emotions and feelings. Students generally possessed a minimal understanding about golf, offering little in the way of communication or discussion. Simple dialogue was adopted by coaches, with an increase in non-verbal communication. Language mistakes were inconsequential, provided the vocabulary was kept consistent. Cultural differences in communication frequently led to misunderstandings, but decreased with experience. Study 1 participants generally felt more nervous, anxious, and under pressure to perform in their second language/culture; this resulted in them feeling less relaxed, less patient, more serious, and more easily frustrated. Similar comments were noted in a previous study "In English, my speech is very polite, with a relaxed tone, always saying 'please' and 'excuse me.' When I speak Greek, I start talking more rapidly, with a tone of anxiety and in a kind of rude way…" (Dewaele & Nakano, 2013). Many of these personality changes were found to be more noticeable in a group coaching situation, producing a loss of confidence. However, participants still felt a sense of satisfaction by being able to communicate with their students in their native language.

Participants agreed that overall, there was a greater sense of negativity felt within the Chinese language, and a general lack of support or encouragement. This prompted coaches to employ a more positive approach. It was noted that the subject matter was very foreign to most Chinese golfers; this combined with a cultural tendency towards minimal communication/feedback with a coach/teacher, created a noticeable lack of interaction. Additionally, as coaches felt their second language vocabulary was somewhat limited, dialogue was kept very short and simple, resulting in a shift towards an increased use of non-verbal communication. Coaches became aware that less than perfect communication in their second language was still capable of getting their main point across, providing they maintained a consistent use of vocabulary. According to a previous study, a similar approach was adopted by a participant, who made the following comment with regard to English as his second language: "When I'm speaking in English, I tend to rely on 'ready made phrases'… [I] use phrases that I heard from other people" (Dewaele & Nakano, 2013). Given that the Chinese language adopts more of an indirect style of communicating, versus a more direct style present in the English language, coaches were prone to misunderstanding situations. A well-known and controversial case of cross-cultural miscommunication in professional football, also highlights this point "…it was a misunderstanding based on failures of communication across languages" (Baines, 2013). However, with more experience and a better understanding of cultural nuances, coaches were able to pick up on hidden meanings, and develop a greater cultural sensitivity.

During Study 2, for the monocultural-monolingual coaches, a number of strategies were used to noticeably improve communication quality. Slow, simple dialogue, with frequent repetition and clarification was employed, as was an emphasis on training the translator well, and creating a good rapport. The lag during translation was found to help avoid over-talking, and a greater use of demonstration and visual training aids were found to be very effective communication tools.

To ensure that communication through the translator delivered the right message to the student, coaches maintained a very basic vocabulary, delivered slowly and clearly, while constantly confirming with the translator what had been said. A similar approach was noted in a previous study that when speaking in a second language, a participant commented that "I think before I speak in Spanish and am slow and thoughtful" (Dewaele, 2016). The delay during translation was found to prevent coaches from talking excessively; this combined with language limitations, encouraged coaches to increase their use of non-verbal communication, allowing them to present a much clearer and less ambiguous picture to the student. It was remarked in a 2016 study that "I feel totally different when I speak Spanish. Because I have to use facial expressions and body language to communicate effectively..." (Dewaele, 2016), again emphasizing this logical shift in strategy when verbal communication is somewhat limited.

For the students who participated in Study 3 that were being trained by their coach via a translator, their key task was to piece together the translated verbal instruction with the coach's demonstrations. Participants remarked that visual cues gave them a better understanding of necessary movements, and that this was a much more systematic way to learn. As this may well be the first time that the flow of communication during translated sports instruction from the perspective of the student has been examined, there is currently little data to compare our results with. Students received verbal translated dialogue while at the same time processing non-verbal demonstrations from their coach. Feedback indicated that demonstration provided a clearer message when compared with verbal instruction. It was also remarked by participants that a greater use of visual examples with less dialogue was found to be a more systematic way of learning. This was because there was a tendency to focus on a single issue.

Practical implications

The findings of this study have a number of practical findings: (1) due to golf's rapid globalization, familiarity with cultural frame switching, and its effects on coaching will likely become increasingly important, particularly in high-performance environments; (2) the knowledge and insight that can be obtained from coaches who are well versed at working within a multicultural/multilingual environment, should be harnessed to add to the existing research on communication strategies within the sports coaching industry; (3) second-language coaches should utilize simple words, shorter sentences, speak slowly, clarify understanding, use a blanket (basic) vocabulary, and repetition; (4) second-language coaches should focus on delivering key messages rather than speaking flawlessly; (5) second-language coaches should increase non-verbal communication, increase use of visual aids; (6) coaches should expect nerves, stress, anxiety, frustration, and a loss of confidence when teaching in a second language; and (7) second-language coaches should monitor and reflect how communicating in a second language impacts their personality. To provide the most effective and efficient training environment, golf coaches should look beyond their understanding of technical skills, and critically examine their communication methods and strategies.

Limitations

With respect to data collection, there were certain limitations to these studies that should be noted. Although all of our Study 1 participants have spent many years in China and can confidently demonstrate themselves to be bicultural-bilinguals, their individual levels of comprehension towards their second language/culture are extremely difficult to quantify. This resulted in our participants responding to the interview questions not only from the perspective of their experiences in China, but also in accordance with their degree of cultural and linguistic understanding. Furthermore, as our sample was collected solely from native English-speaking coaches based in China, the data gathered is limited predominantly to the cultures of East and West and to the Chinese and English languages.

Future research

This study is, to the best of our knowledge the first time that cultural frame switching has been researched with respect to its effects on sports coaching. Given that golf is not alone when it comes to global diffusion, understanding coaching language barriers in new markets will remain a salient topic for future research. The obvious starting point for future research is to investigate cultural frame switching in countries other than China and in sports other than golf. Another is to pursue how golf technologies (i.e. pressure plates, launch monitors) may ameliorate second-language coaching barriers. Given the evident ambiguity and unreliability of verbal communication within the sports coaching setting that this study reveals, the traditional paradigm of visual, auditory, and kinesthetic (VAK) learning styles within a sporting environment require further research and understanding, as although individual students may well exhibit personal preferences towards these styles, the question of overall learning effectiveness still remains.

Conclusion

As the world is increasingly becoming a melting pot of cultures and languages, the need for understanding and respect towards others that come from backgrounds vastly different to our own, continues to grow. Nowadays, it has almost become a requirement for large companies hiring employees that candidates have experience working in diverse environments, and with the ability to speak more than one language; communicating only with people who share a similar background is almost a thing of the past. Furthermore, when placed into a multilingual/

multicultural environment, such as our study participants were, communicating effectively becomes the number one priority. Subsequently, their responses have provided us with a deeper insight into an area of coaching that often receives little attention.

Understanding exactly how much is learned visually needs further research, but what has become clear from this study is that regardless of how much knowledge or expertise a coach has, the ability to communicate a message clearly should not be overlooked, nor should the method(s) by which it is communicated. The results indicate that golf coaching is impacted by language use and the use of interpreters. Identifying a recipe for such an undertaking is fraught with difficulties given the nuanced nature of the coach, the student, and their relationships with each other. The secret formula for golf coaching in a second language is not yet evident, but to borrow a phrase from golf legend Ben Hogan, the secret is probably in the dirt.

References

Baines, R. (2013). Translation, globalization and the elite migrant athlete. *Translator, 19*(2), 207–228.

Berg, B. L. (2001). *Qualitative Research Methods for the Social Sciences.* Boston, MA: Allyn and Bacon.

Blaikie, N. (2010). *Designing Social Research.* Cambridge: Polity.

Briley, D. A., Morris, M. W., & Simonson, I. (2005). Cultural chameleons: Biculturals, conformity motives, and decision making. *Journal of Consumer Psychology, 15*(4), 351–362.

Dewaele, J. M. (2016). Why do so many bi- and multilinguals feel different when switching languages? *International Journal of Multilingualism, 13*(1), 92–105.

Dewaele, J.-M., & Nakano, S. (2013). Multilinguals' perceptions of feeling different when switching languages. *Journal of Multilingual and Multicultural Development, 34*(2), 107–120.

Dewaele, J.-M., & Pavlenko, A. (2001/2003) *Web questionnaire on bilingualism and emotion.* Unpublished manuscript, University of London.

Dewaele, J.-M., & Van Oudenhoven, J. P. (2009). The effect of multilingualism/multiculturalism on personality: No gain without pain for third culture kids? *International Journal of Multilingualism, 6*, 443–459.

Glesne, C. (2006). *Becoming Qualitative Researchers: An Introduction* (3rd ed.). New York: Pearson Education.

Grosjean, F. (2015). Bicultural bilinguals. *International Journal of Bilingualism, 19*(5), 572–586.

Hull, P. V. (1990). *Two languages, two personalities?* Unpublished doctoral dissertation, University of California, Berkeley.

Kauer, K., & Krane, V. (2006). "Scary dykes" and "feminine queens": Stereotypes and female collegiate athletes. *Women in Sport and Physical Activity Journal, 15*, 42–55.

Kim, Y. Y. (2001). *Becoming Intercultural: An Integrative Theory of Communication and Cross-Cultural Adaptation.* Thousand Oaks, CA: Sage Publications.

Koven, M. (1998). Two languages in the self/the self in two languages: French Portuguese bilinguals' verbal enactments and experiences of self in narrative discourse. *Ethos*, 26(4), 410–455.

Krane, V., & Barber, H. (2003). Lesbian experience in sport: A social identity theory perspective. *Quest*, 55, 328–346.

Kreitler, C. M., & Dyson, K. S. (2016). Cultural frame switching and emotion among Mexican Americans. *Journal of Latinos and Education*, 15(2), 91–96.

Li, C., & Kalyanaraman, S. (2012). What if Web site editorial content and ads are in two different languages? A study of bilingual consumers' online information processing. *Journal of Consumer Behaviour*, 11, 198–206.

Luna, D., Ringberg, T., & Peracchio, L. (2008). One individual, two identities: Frame switching among biculturals. *Journal of Consumer Research*, 35(2), 279–293.

Malacrida, C. (2015). Reflexive journaling on emotional research: Ethical issues for team researchers. *Qualitative Health Research*, 17(10), 1329–1339.

Melton, N., & Cunningham, G. (2014). Who are the champions? Using a multilevel model to examine perceptions of employee support for LGBT inclusion in sport organizations. *Journal of Sport Management*, 28(2), 189–206.

Molinsky, A. (2007). Cross-cultural code-switching: The psychological challenges of adapting behavior in foreign cultural interactions. *Academy of Management Review*, 32(2), 622–640.

Ożańska-Ponikwia, K. (2012). What has personality and emotional intelligence to do with 'feeling different' while using a foreign language? *International Journal of Bilingual Education and Bilingualism*, 15(2), 217–234.

Pavlenko, A. (ed.) (2006). *Bilingual Minds: Emotional Experience, Expression, and Representation*. Clevedon: Multilingual Matters.

Phinney, J. S., & Devich-Navarro, M. (1997). Variations in bicultural identification among African American and Mexican American adolescents. *Journal of Research on Adolescence*, 7, 3–32.

Qiu, L., Lin, H., & Leung, A. K.-y. (2013). Cultural differences and switching of in-group sharing behavior between an American (Facebook) and a Chinese (Renren) social networking site. *Journal of Cross-Cultural Psychology*, 44(1), 106–121.

Ramírez-Esparza, N., Gosling, S. D., Benet-Martínez, V., Potter, J. P., & Pennebaker, J. W. (2006). Do bilinguals have two personalities? A special case of cultural frame switching. *Journal of Research in Personality*, 40(2), 99–120.

Strauss, A., & Corbin, J. M. (1990). *Basics of Qualitative Research: Grounded Theory Procedures and Techniques*. Thousand Oaks, CA: Sage Publications

Taylor, S. J., & Bogdan, R. (1998). *Introduction to Qualitative Research Methods: A Guidebook and Resource* (3rd ed.). Hoboken, NJ: John Wiley & Sons.

Appendix 5.1 Participant Information – Study 1 and Study 2

	Interviewees	Age	PGA Affiliation	PGA Membership Class	Coaching Experience (Years)	China Coaching Experience (Years)
Study 1	A	46	British PGA	AAA	27	20
	B	28	British PGA	Advanced	8	5
	C	39	British PGA	AAA	19	12
	D	33	PGA of America	A	11	11
	E	39	British PGA	Advanced	19	14
	F	39	PGA of Canada	A	21	13
Study 2	G	44	PGA of S. Africa	AAA	17	10 Months
	H	28	British PGA	A	6	3
	I	34	NZPGA	AAA	10	6
	J	31	PGA of S. Africa	AAA	7	3 Months
	K	60	British PGA	A	38	13
	L	53	PGA of Aus.	AAA	22	5

Appendix 5.2 Participant Information – Study 3

Interviewees	Age	Average Score (18 Holes)	Playing Experience (Years)	Training Time with Coach (Years)
M	19	90–95	3	1
N	22	85–90	4	2
O	23	100–110	2	1
P	28	85–95	4	2
Q	43	90–100	8	2
R	34	Unknown	2	1

Cultural frame switching **75**

Appendix 5.3 Interview Questions

Study 1:
1. How long have you been a Golf Professional for?
2. What was your initial motivation to come to China?
3. What do you recall about your earliest experiences teaching golf in China?
4. How long have you lived in China for and when did you first begin to study Chinese?
5. When compared with English, what was your first impression of the Chinese language?
6. How did you go about developing your Chinese language skills?
7. How and when did you first begin to integrate the Chinese language into your lessons?
8. What can you remember about the first lessons you conducted solely in Chinese?
9. When considering Chinese culture, what differences in verbal communication style have you noticed when compared with your own native culture?
10. Given the cultural differences, have you ever found yourself taking on a different persona when teaching in Chinese as opposed to English?
11. Do you recall experiencing different feelings or emotions when teaching in Chinese, which seem somewhat unusual or foreign to you when compared with teaching in English?
12. Have you ever noticed yourself saying or doing things when giving lessons in Chinese that you may not normally say or do when teaching in English?
13. When translating certain phrases from English to Chinese in your mind, besides the literal translation, do you often find yourself considering how the phrase would be communicated from a Chinese cultural perspective?
14. Are there any other changes you have noticed about your character or behavior when teaching in Chinese?
15. As you have become more and more deeply integrated into Chinese culture, how do you feel your use of the Chinese language has evolved over time?
16. When considering the different ways in which people communicate across cultures, what do you prefer about teaching golf in a second language, and what do you dislike about teaching golf in a second language?
17. What specific techniques would you recommend to other coaches to optimize the quality of their communication when teaching/coaching in a second language?
18. Do you have any other comments that you would like to add?

Study 2:
1. How long have you been a Golf Professional for?
2. What was your initial motivation to come to China?
3. How long have you lived in China for?
4. What do you recall about your earliest experiences teaching golf in China?

(Continued)

5. When compared with English, what was your first impression of the Chinese language?
6. What can you remember about the first lessons you conducted with Chinese-speaking students via a translator?
7. Do you feel there are changes in the way you communicate verbally when using a translator?
8. How do you view the role of non-verbal communication when using a translator?
9. When working with your translator, under what conditions do you find communication to be most effective?
10. What specific techniques would you recommend to other coaches to optimize the quality of their communication when teaching/coaching via a translator?
11. Are there any additional strategies that you employ to improve communication?
12. What do you see as an advantage about teaching golf via a translator, and what do you see as a disadvantage teaching golf via a translator?
13. Do you have any other comments that you would like to add?

Study 3:
1. How did you get into golf?
2. What do you enjoy about playing golf?
3. How long have you played golf for?
4. What is your average score for 18 holes?
5. How long have you been taking lessons with your non-Chinese speaking coach for?
6. Do you feel you've had to change the way you normally communicate when taking lessons with your non-Chinese speaking coach?
7. Have you found anything difficult or challenging about communicating through a translator?
8. Have you previously had lessons with local (Chinese) coaches? If so, what differences have you noticed when taking lessons from a local coach vs. lessons with your non-Chinese speaking coach via a translator?
9. What do you see as an advantage about taking golf lessons via a translator, and what do you see as a disadvantage about taking golf lessons via a translator?
10. Do you have any other comments that you would like to add?

Chapter 6

Governing sport organizations
Significance and determinants of innovations

Yunduk Jeong, Euisoo Kim, and James J. Zhang

Introduction

Unlike in Western countries, where professional sports have grown through private sector support, South Korean (hereafter Korean) professional sports development has been overseen by the government. In the early 1980s, the military government planned to launch professional sports leagues as a means of reducing public interest in politics (Jeong & Kim, 2019). In the process, the Korean government strongly urged some of the country's largest corporations to participate in the league. For such large corporations, involvement in these leagues via the founding and running of their professional sports teams served as a means of promoting their corporation's image and brand (Jeong, Kim, Kim & Zhang, 2019). Accordingly, the first professional sport league in Korea, the Korea Baseball Organization (KBO), was launched in 1982, and was followed by soccer and *Ssireum* (Traditional Korean wrestling) in 1983 (Kim, 2008). Since then, attending and watching professional sports has become a popular leisure activity (Jeong, 2017). After the 2002 Korea/Japan World Cup, municipal governments, in addition to large corporations, became primary stakeholders of soccer teams, coinciding with a quantitative expansion of professional soccer in the country (Jeong, 2017). Professional basketball was launched in 1997, with professional volleyball following shortly thereafter in 2004, both of which have become representative winter professional sports in Korea. As of 2020, Korea's four major sport leagues are: soccer, baseball, basketball, and volleyball. The men's leagues consist of 12 professional soccer teams in the K1 league, 10 teams in the K2 league, 10 teams in professional baseball and basketball, and 7 teams in professional volleyball.

Today, professional sports teams in Korea are operated with different systems than those seen in the West. While western professional sport teams make profits through various marketing activities, most Korean teams spend more revenue than they are generating, relying largely on their parent companies and local governments to help subsidize a portion of their operating expenses (Jeong, 2017). Since the inception of most teams, it is reported that subsidies received usually account for about 60–80% of the club's finances through the mid-2010s (Jeong et al., 2019). Therefore, these sports teams did not have to worry about financial deficits

DOI: 10.4324/9781003213673-6

due to the support they have received from parent companies and municipal governments. In other words, these teams did not get incentives to actively engage in financial self-reliance or aggressive marketing activities. Meanwhile, the corporate culture of many East Asian companies emphasizes hierarchy in the workplace (Zhang, Lin, Nonaka & Beom, 2005). According to one survey, more than half of employees (57.2%) in Korea agree that there is a hierarchy in the workplace and that supervisors and subordinates collectively engage in a top-down relationship. Many researchers point out that organizations with strong hierarchical cultures are likely to lower employees' creativity and potential (Arkani-Hamed, Dimopoulos & Dvali, 1998).

This unique financial structure and Korea's hierarchical corporate culture are undergoing a gradual change (Fort, 2017; Lee & Fort, 2014). Many large corporations such as Samsung and Hyundai are reducing subsidies by recognizing that professional sports teams' operations are not the same effective promotional tools that they once were (Lee, 2015). Many teams have since experienced tighter budgets and, in some cases, financial difficulties. Two professional soccer teams even went bankrupt. As such, professional soccer and basketball teams are suffering from reduced subsidies and declining attendance (Jeong & Kim, 2019). Many young Korean sport consumers follow foreign professional leagues such as the Major League Baseball (MLB) and English Premier League (EPL) over domestic professional sports leagues (Lee, 2006). Korean broadcasting stations have broadcast the English Premier League more frequently than they have domestic professional soccer leagues. Consequently, an evolving internal/external financial environment and increased competition have forced professional sport teams to reconsider their business models (Jafri, 2010). Therefore, employees of professional sports teams in Korea are required to become more innovative as a means of enhancing the performance of their respective organizations (Yuan & Woodman, 2010). In many cases, innovation has been used interchangeably with creativity. However, the two concepts are distinct. Creativity has to do with the production of new and original ideas (Mumford & Gustafson, 1988), while innovation has to do with the production or adoption of effective ideas as well as idea implementation (Kanter, 1988). Innovation has long been regarded as a key component of an organization's survival and growth, and has become commonplace in the daily language of today's corporate environment (Pieterse, Van Knippenberg, Schippers & Stam, 2010). Without innovation, corporations are likely to fall behind in competition, as explained by the Red Queen effect (Derfus, Maggitti, Grimm & Smith, 2008).

Federations and teams of each professional sport league are searching for diverse ways to enhance employee innovation in the interest of securing external sponsorship and attracting spectators via diverse marketing activities (Jeong, 2018). In doing so, the quality of human resources has gained much attention and various training programs, specifically those focused on marketing, have been offered to enhance organizational performance. However, researchers argue that companies should focus more on the development of employee potential rather than system and program operations. Kim and Mauborgne (2014) affirmed that only about 30% of employees in the United States work voluntarily and actively, with the majority working passively. Utilizing the "Blue Ocean/ Red Ocean" concept, researchers proposed that the underdeveloped potential of employees is a blue ocean that would generate tremendous benefits to organizations (see Pfeffer, 2010). In this regard, Pfeffer (2010) emphasized the role of leaders in the development of potential of employees. He proposed the importance of the relationship between leaders and subordinates of an organization in that established mutual trust between the two would lead subordinates to be more focused on their work and come up with innovative solutions.

Given the importance of the relationship between leaders and subordinates in an organization, the leader–member exchange (LMX), proposed by Dansereau, Graen, and Haga (1975), has garnered the most attention in the leadership field and is becoming one of the main theories that stands in contrast to existing leadership theories. Many traditional leadership theories argue that leadership styles and the characteristics of a leader are consistent, causing subordinates to perceive the leader's behaviors as reflective of their intentions. LMX, on the other hand, concentrates on the differentiated relationships between leaders and subordinates. As such, LMX is based on the principle that each leader–follower relationship within an organization is unique and varies in quality (Anand, Hu, Liden & Vidyarthi, 2011). Many researchers have reported that the formation of a high LMX through sustained interactions between leaders and subordinates is characterized by mutual influence, trust, and respect (Dansereau et al., 1975; Liden & Maslyn, 1998). On the contrary, low-quality relationships are bound by terms of a contract of employment and tend to result in a perfunctory relationship (Anand et al., 2011). Many scholars have proposed that the differentiation of subordinates allows leaders to make efficient and productive use of their limited time and resources (Wayne, Shore & Liden, 1997).

As was noted earlier, the external environment surrounding the sports organizations is changing rapidly, and the influence of the leaders as well as the voluntary efforts of individuals within an organization are becoming increasingly important. This indicates that apart from following instructions of supervisors, members of organizations are required to actively perform tasks autonomously. Ghosh (2015) mentioned that it is important for employees to develop their creativity and be innovative by adapting their own thoughts and behaviors. In this regard, self-leadership is an important research topic that has continually attracted the attention of scholars (Müller & Niessen, 2018). A simple definition of self-leadership is the process through which organizational members derive their voluntary efforts and enthusiasm from potential abilities (Manz, 1986). Contrary to what is argued in existing leadership theories, the most important characteristic of self-leadership is that internal rather than external factors be the main drivers of job performance. Many scholars have noted that self-leadership allows members to seek innovative solutions, since members strive to set and achieve their own goals (Carmeli, Meitar & Weisberg, 2006).

An increasing number of companies and clubs recognize the importance of their employees and are constantly striving to develop the potential of these individuals through their behaviors (Jeong, 2017). Many researchers argue that various means of support should be provided to motivate employees at the organization level. Among them, a representative concept is "empowerment," which allows employees to work with confidence and autonomy (Menon, 2001). Thomas and Velthouse (1990) maintained that empowered employees showed improved job performance, such as increased productivity and enhanced business processes. In other words, employees who recognize high empowerment will take on a sense of ownership within the organization, and will ultimately work proactively and autonomously to drive innovation. Many scholars argue that LMX and self-leadership should be the premise to maximize the effectiveness of empowerment (Harris, Wheeler & Kacmar, 2009; Thomas & Velthouse, 1990). Consequently, we can infer that LMX, self-leadership, and empowerment can enhance the innovative behaviors of employees. In contrast to the exhaustive scholarship on each of the four variables, there have been few studies that investigate integration. In other words, despite the rise of LMX, self-leadership, and empowerment as important factors that can affect innovation, few have attempted to address the process by which these elements can be integrated into an organization. Accordingly, in this study, our aim is to add a new perspective in managing human resources and the governance of professional sports teams by analyzing the structural relationship among LMX, self-leadership, empowerment, and innovative behavior, and by deriving theoretical and practical implications that can be put into practice. The results and discussions of this study can be used as useful data for human and organizational management of professional sports clubs that emphasize innovation.

Review of literature

LMX is a leadership theory that was first proposed and developed by George Graen and his colleagues in the 1970s to identify differentiated relationships between leaders and their subordinates (Dansereau, Cashman & Graen, 1973; Dansereau et al., 1975). According to the vertical dyad linkage (VDL), which is the starting point of the LMX theory, leaders differentiate the relationships that exist among different subordinates. With the passage of time, leaders made a clear distinction in the quality of each subordinate's relationship (Dansereau et al., 1975; Graen & Schiemann, 1978). That is, when a leader performs his or her duties with subordinates, they do not apply a consistent approach to all of the subordinates, instead utilizing different approaches on a case-by-case basis.

LMX provides the theoretical basis for this by applying the role theory (Graen & Uhl-Bien, 1995). According to Graen (1976), leaders make subordinates perform various tasks as a means to evaluate their abilities and prescribe their roles and duties within the organization. Graen and his team argued that such roles and duties of subordinates were developed by continuous interactions with leaders. In the same vein, Graen, Orris, and Johnson (1973) mentioned that the tasks performed by organizational members are ultimately determined by the roles assigned by leaders. In other words, leaders give subordinates the expectation of performance and assign an appropriate level of duties to each of them according to their unique abilities (Graen, Dansereau, Minami & Cashman, 1973). Thus, LMX is unique in that it proposes a form of leadership that is simultaneously different from existing leadership styles and performs various functions within the organization (Northouse, 2015).

Building on VDL theory, many scholars sought to further develop LMX theory throughout the 1970s and 1980s. The first study was a longitudinal study of 60 leader–subordinate dyads in the housing division of a large public university. The differentiated relationships between leaders and subordinates range from types of employment contracts to goodwill, respect, and trust (Dansereau et al., 1975). In this way, according to the quality of the exchange relations formed between leaders and subordinates, Graen and Cashman (1975) categorized the individuals as members of an "in group" or "out group." The researchers argued that members of the "in group" had high confidence, mutual communication, and support over leaders, while members of the "out group" exhibited opposing characteristics.

In the 1980s, Dienesch and Liden (1986) raised issues with existing research. They indicated that scholars had not obtained any conceptual or empirical justification regarding the process of establishing LMX as a singular dimension based on role theory. Accordingly, Dienesch and Liden (1986) asserted the multidimensional nature of LMX and said that LMX consists of three attributes: attachment, loyalty, and contribution. In the 1990s, Graen and Uhl-Bien (1995), contrary to previous studies, explored the attributes of LMX based on the levels perspective not addressed by VDL. To apply the levels perspective, they classified leadership theories into three areas according to the domain perspective. In other words, they classified LMX into three types of research: what constitutes proper leadership, the ability of leaders to motivate subordinates, and examining leadership based on the relationship between leaders and subordinates. In this way, they identified the attributes of the LMX on a step-by-step basis in terms of leadership based on the third leader–member relationship described above. In other words, they identified trust, respect, and obligation as core areas of leadership capable of influencing one another while also describing the development process of each in detail. Liden and Maslyn (1998) tried to complement the multidimensional nature of LMX identified by Dienesch and Liden (1986) via in-depth study. In addition to role theory, which explains the process of job or role formation, Liden and Maslyn (1998) asserted that social exchange theory also has a significant correlation with LMX. They argued that social exchange theory can provide a theoretical basis for LMX because the various attributes related to the job between leaders and subordinates in LMX is similar to various attributes, such as information and advice, outlined in social exchange theory.

In sum, LMX theory started from the exploration of VDL theory in the early 1970s, with many researchers conducting empirical studies until the publication of Liden and Maslyn's (1998) work. Their research established LMX theory as a multidimensional concept based on social exchange theory. In this process, several studies have made important achievements in concept exploration,

82 Yunduk Jeong et al.

multidimensional identification, and development of scale. The current status is shown in Table 6.1. Attempts to measure the quality of LMX have continued for more than 20 years since the 1970s, and various measures have been developed during that time. Dienesch and Liden (1986) classified LMX as affect, loyalty, and contribution through research. Phillips, Duran, and Howell (1993) proved that all of the three dimensions of LMX presented by Dienesch and Liden (1986) were identified as independent areas. After that, Liden and Maslyn (1998) examined the factor analysis and content validity of 31 items for 302 working students and 249 employees based on social exchange theory. Liden and Maslyn (1998) developed a new LMX scale in four dimensions that added "professional respect," denoting respect for the expertise and abilities of a leader. The conceptual definition and characteristics of the four areas identified by Dienesch and Liden (1986) and Liden and Maslyn (1998) are provided in Table 6.2.

Table 6.1 Theorizing the Process of Leader–Member Exchange (LMX)

Division	Year	Rationale	Contents
VDL (Dansereau, Cashman & Graen)	1973	Role theory	Exchange relationship [Differentiation]
Uni-dimensional LMX-7 (Scandura & Graen)	1984	Role theory	Uni-dimensional [Scale development]
3 Multidimensional LMX	1986	Role theory	Multidimensional [affect, loyalty, contribution]
LMX Development in Stage 4 (Graen & Uhl-Bien)	1995	Levels perspective	Theoretical evolution
4 Multidimensional LMX (Liden & Maslyn)	1998	Social exchange	Add multidimensional factor [professional respect]

Table 6.2 Definitions of LMX Dimensions

Dimension	Definitions
Affect	The mutual affection members of the dyad have for each other based primarily on interpersonal attraction rather than work or professional values.
Loyalty	The expression of public support for the goals and the personal character of the other member of the LMX dyad.
Contribution	Perception of the amount, direction, and quality of work-oriented activity each member puts forth toward the mutual goals (explicit or implicit) of the dyad
Professional respect	Perception of the degree to which each member of the dyad has built a reputation, within and/or outside the organization, of excelling at his or her line of work.

Self-leadership

Self-leadership began with the acknowledgment that the traditional leadership could no longer achieve the goals of the organization due to the rapid changes in the organizational environment and changes in the values of members in the 1980s (Neck & Manz, 2010). In accordance with this trend, Manz (1986) proposed self-leadership for the first time in terms of expanding self-management. In the definition of self-leadership, Manz (1986) described self-leadership as 'a comprehensive self-influence perspective that concerns leading oneself toward performance of naturally motivating tasks as well as managing oneself to do work that must be done but is not naturally motivating.' Also, Neck and Manz (2010) broadly define self-leadership as 'the process of influencing oneself.' Alternatively, Manz (1991) described self-leadership as

> a self-influence process and set of strategies that address *what* is to be done (e.g., standards and objectives) and *why* (e.g., strategic analysis) as well as *how* it is to be done . . . [it] incorporates intrinsic motivation and has an increased focus on cognitive processes.
>
> (p. 17)

The first empirical study of self-leadership in the field of organizational management is 'Leading workers to lead themselves: The external leadership of self-managing work teams' by Manz and Sims (1987). They examined the role of self-leadership in the context of both empowering leadership and self-managing teams. Since then, many self-leadership researchers have begun to apply a variety of variables, such as the nature of spirituality in organizations (Neck & Milliman, 1994), performance of performance appraisers (Neck, Stewart & Manz, 1995), organizational change (Neck, 1996), entrepreneurship (Neck, Neck & Manz, 1997), job satisfaction (Houghton & Jinkerson, 2007; Roberts & Foti, 1998), self-efficacy (Prussia, Anderson & Manz, 1998), team performance (Stewart & Barrick, 2000), empowerment (Lee & Koh, 2001), ethics (VanSandt & Neck, 2003), organizational commitment (Bligh, Pearce & Kohles, 2006), and innovation and creativity (DiLiello & Houghton, 2006). In addition, over the last 20 years, many popular books on self-leadership have been published, with considerable success (Neck & Manz, 2010). As such, self-leadership has been actively researched and is recognized as a factor that enhances the effectiveness of individuals and organizations in academia and practice.

Self-leadership strategies can be broadly divided into behavior-focused strategies for effective behavior and cognitive strategies that deal with effective thinking and attitudes. The cognitive strategies are divided into natural reward strategies that deal with internal rewards and constructive-thought-pattern strategies that promote effective thinking and emotion (Manz & Sims, 2001). Behavior-focused strategies, based on Bandura's social learning theory, address the notion that people behave within the confines of certain criteria as they act and try to eliminate inconsistencies in their behavior when they do not meet this criteria. In doing this, they control themselves by setting higher standards and goals (Bandura, 1971). These strategies include self-observation, self-reward, self-correcting feedback, self-goal setting, and practice or rehearsal (Houghton & Neck, 2002). Self-observation is the act of collecting information related to specific behaviors and acting according to goal setting, thereby eliminating past behavior that is ineffective (Neck, Neck, Manz & Godwin, 1999). Self-reward is simply a reward for oneself. For example, after a person has completed a difficult problem, he or she may reward himself/herself by eating at a good restaurant or watching a movie (Houghton & Neck, 2002). Like self-reward, self-correcting feedback is designed to effectively form desirable behaviors (Houghton & Neck, 2002). Setting self-goals is a strategy whereby one sets challenging and specific goals to improve their individual performance (Locke & Latham, 1990). Finally, practice is used to rehearse tasks physically and mentally before actually performing them (Houghton & Neck, 2002). These can lead to increases in the success rate and effectiveness of job performance (Manz & Sims, 1980).

Natural reward strategy suggests that people enjoy their tasks and are thus motivated intrinsically. In other words, natural reward strategies emphasize the pleasant aspects of a given task or activity (Houghton & Neck, 2002). Through natural reward activities, members feel that their abilities are improved, which empowers them while performing a task. Therefore, it is important for members to intentionally focus on the aspects of a task that feel most rewarding. Constructive-thought-pattern strategies can be seen as strategies that allow members to set their own thoughts in a desirable direction (Houghton & Neck, 2002). These strategies were further expanded in the mid and late 1990s under the name of thought self-leadership (TSL). TSL is designed for employees in an organization to establish constructive thought patterns for themselves, using cognitive strategies such as positive self-talk, mental imagery of successful future performance, beliefs, and assumptions (Neck, Smith & Godwin, 1997). Thus, the application of the TSL has implications for an employee's job satisfaction, mental performance, and self-efficacy, consequently contributing to improved organizational performance (Neck & Milliman, 1994).

Empowerment

Empowerment has been recognized as an important concept in various fields, including psychology (Bolton & Brookings, 1998; Rappaport, 1981; Zimmerman, 2000), social work (Gutierrez, GlenMaye & DeLois, 1995; Saleebey, 1992), business administration (Conger & Kanungo, 1988; Thomas & Velthouse, 1990), public health (Wallerstein, 2002) and sociology (Jennings, Parra-Medina, Hilfinger-Messias & McLoughlin, 2006). On the other hand, when reviewing various literatures on empowerment, there is no agreed-upon definition, and the term is used interchangeably in various socio-cultural environments and political contexts. Self-strength, control, mastery, self-power, self-reliance, own choice, own decision making, being free, independence, awakening, and capability are some of the frequently appearing terms in empowerment discourse (Oladipo, 2009). For example, the Swiss Agency for Development and Cooperation (SDC) conceptualizes empowerment as 'an emancipation process in which the disadvantaged are empowered to exercise their rights, obtain access to resources and participate actively in the process of shaping society and making decisions' (Luttrell, Quiroz, Scrutton & Bird, 2009, p. 2). This definition is closely related to the concept of empowerment in the fields of practical disciplines such as social work, public health, and psychology. In the field of business administration, empowerment has been defined as the process of helping to improve self-efficacy and to exercise internal motivation (Conger & Kanungo, 1988; Thomas & Velthouse, 1990). In other words, empowerment was defined in terms of the relationship between managers and subordinates.

Empowerment begins with the behavioral science concept of motivation, which dating back to literature from the 1950s and 1960s, has suggested ways to utilize human psychology. Until the early 1970s, research on empowerment was centered on individual motivation, potential, and value, as human potential and individual development tended to be most important. From the mid-1980s onward, empowerment has gradually been introduced into the field of business administration and has attracted attention as a tool for maximizing organizational performance by making organizational members more engaged at work. Since the 1990s, the *Academy of Management Journal* has served as a conduit for empowerment research, and empowerment has been emphasized as part of its efforts to innovate management in the United States.

If we summarize empowerment research, it can be said that empowerment consists of four dimensions: meaning, competence, self-determination, and impact (Thomas & Velthouse, 1990). Meaning is a form of human perception that deals with the suitability between desire, value, and belief in one's role (Spreitzer, 1995). In other words, when an individual feels that their work is desirable and conforms to a given belief system, the members judge that it is meaningful. Conceptually, meaning is closely related to competence. Competence is the belief that an individual has the skills and abilities necessary to perform their duties well (Bandura, 1977). Self-determination is the ability of an individual to determine the path of his or her own life, which translates to autonomy in and control over their work (Fetterman, 1996). To better understand the meaning of self-determination, the following four things must be considered: consistency and persistence in behavior, the courage to take risks, initiative and proactivity, and the ability to voice one's own opinion. Impact is the degree to which an individual can influence strategic, administrative, or operative outcomes at work (Ashforth, 1989). Impact is distinct from self-determination. It is self-determination that dictates the degree to which an individual has control over their own work, while impact dictates the extent to which an individual has control over the performance of the organization.

Research questions

Regarding the relationship between LMX and empowerment, employees who have formed a high level of exchange with a leader will gain more information than employees who have formed a low-level exchange relationship (Kanter, 1988). Kim, Won, and Kwak (2016) examined the relationships between LMX, empowerment, and job performance of fitness center instructors and revealed that LMX plays a key role in building empowerment. Moon and Kang (2010) analyzed the relationships between LMX, empowerment, and organizational commitment of workers in sports centers and confirmed that LMX is a direct antecedent of empowerment. Concerning the relationship between self-leadership and empowerment, employees with a lot of information enjoy a greater degree of responsibility, and by better understanding the meaning and purpose of work through information, they can make active decisions (Conger & Kanungo, 1988). In addition, Blanchard (1995) noted that employees who practice self-leadership have confidence that they can perform their jobs well, and Thomas and Velthouse (1990) insisted that these employees are more cognizant of the meaning, impact, and autonomy in their work environment. Houghton and Yoho (2005) proposed empowerment as a dependent variable of self-leadership and the interplay between the two variables ultimately improved organizational performance. Ahn (2012) investigated the relationships of soccer coaches' self-leadership, empowerment, organizational satisfaction, and demonstrated that self-leadership is a critical factor in improving empowerment.

With respect to the relationships between LMX and innovative behavior, Graen and Scandura (1987) stated that if the quality of LMX between leaders and subordinates is high, leaders will provide generous support for the innovative behavior of subordinates while carrying out unstructured tasks with them. Through these partnerships, leaders can have a positive impact on subordinates' innovation and creativity by transferring their business know-how to them, thereby boosting subordinate confidence and enthusiasm (Schermuly, Meyer & Dämmer, 2013). Kyoung and Huh (2018) tested the relationship between LMX, work engagement, and innovation behavior in fitness centers and indicated that LMX boosts innovation. In addition, with respect to the relationship between self-leadership and innovative behavior, employees who practice self-leadership within an organization can help drive innovation by popularizing the belief that they can perform their task and achieve their goals (Neck & Manz, 1996). Likewise, employees who practice self-leadership tend to pursue pleasure rather than express dissatisfaction from work when performing their duties, while also taking on challenging new jobs as potential outlets for innovation (DiLiello & Houghton, 2006). Seo (2018) examined the effect of self-leadership on innovative behavior of sports center instructors, and suggested there is a significant relation between self-leadership on innovative behavior. Jeong and Yun (2016) investigated the effects self-leadership and procedural justice on innovation among organizational members and revealed that a member with higher level of self-leadership is more likely to exhibit innovative traits.

Regarding the relationships between empowerment and innovation, Drucker (1985) emphasized empowerment as the most appropriate way for employees to lead innovation in today's competitive landscape. Amabile (1988) insisted that employees who are empowered exhibit innovative rather than passive behavior within their organizations because they believe that they have autonomy and influence. Lee, Lee, and Kim (2009) analyzed the effects of self-leadership and empowerment on innovative behavior in the field of sports and showed that empowerment has a positive influence on innovative behavior. Hong and Ahn (2016) challenged the relationship between empowerment and innovative behavior in small business and demonstrated that empowerment (meaning, autonomy, self-efficacy, and impact) appeared to be positively related with innovative behavior (idea development and idea implementation). As we have seen, based on the results of many researchers, it can be assumed that there are positive relationships between LMX, self-leadership, empowerment, and innovative behavior. Therefore, based on the theoretical basis, it can be inferred that empowerment plays a mediating role between LMX and innovation, as well as between innovation and self-leadership. As such, we set the following research hypotheses:

Hypothesis 1: LMX positively influences empowerment.
Hypothesis 2: LMX positively influences innovative behavior.
Hypothesis 3: Self-leadership positively influences empowerment.
Hypothesis 4: Self-leadership positively influences innovative behavior.
Hypothesis 5: Empowerment positively influences innovation.

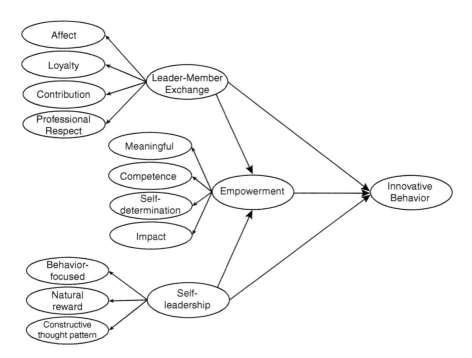

Figure 6.1 Proposed Research Model for Testing.

88 Yunduk Jeong et al.

Hypothesis 6: Empowerment mediates the relationship between LMX and innovative behavior.

Hypothesis 7: Empowerment mediates the relationship between self-leadership and innovative behavior.

Method

Participants and procedure

The target population of this study were the front office employees of 30 professional sports clubs in South Korea. The survey was conducted through a visiting survey and a mail survey after the author and assistant researchers thoroughly explained the purpose of the research to middle managers of each club from 1 May to 30 July, 2017. In the case of visiting surveys, the purpose of the questionnaire was explained to participants and the questionnaire was answered by participants via self-administration. In the mail survey, 300 questionnaires were returned from 15 clubs. A total of 650 questionnaires were ultimately gathered and 38 were discarded because of missing values. Therefore, 612 surveys were analyzed for this study. As shown in Table 6.3, demographic characteristics included basic personal information, such as gender (72.9% male and 27.1% female); age (32.8% were in their 20s, 48.9% were in their 30s, and 18.3% were in their 40s or older); department (40.4% public relations & marketing, 32.4% management support, 14.3% team support, and 12.9% other departments); and level of education (7% high school, 82% university, 11% graduate school).

Table 6.3 Demographic Characteristics of Participants

Variable	Category	N	%
Gender	Male	446	72.9
	Female	116	27.1
Age	20–29	201	32.8
	30–39	299	48.9
	<40	112	18.3
Education	High School	43	7
	University	502	82
	Graduate School	67	11
Position	Ordinary employee	231	37.8
	Assistant Manager	214	35
	Manager	108	17.6
	General Manager	59	9.6
Department	Public relations and marketing	247	40.4
	Management support	198	32.4
	Team support	88	14.3
	Miscellaneous	79	12.9

Measurement

We formulated a survey that contained four sections to assess LMX, self-leadership, empowerment, and innovation. Based on the study of Liden and Maslyn (1998), we revised the LMX items to be more applicable within the context of Korean professional sports. LMX measures consisted of 3 items of affect, 3 items of loyalty, 3 items of contribution, and 4 items of professional respect, for a total of 12 items. Based on Houghton and Neck's (2002) research, we modified self-leadership to suit the Korean organizational environment and then applied it as a factor. The items measured three self-leadership dimensions: behavior-focused strategies (five items), natural reward strategies (four items), and constructive-thought-pattern strategies (five items). In the case of empowerment, Spreitzer's (1995) research was utilized. Meaning, competence, self-determination, and impact comprised four items each, for a total of 16 items. Scott and Bruce (1994) developed a measurement tool capable of measuring innovation. Based on this measurement tool, we made some modifications and built a framework composed of six items. Elements of the survey instrument for this study were modified from existing scales, and a panel of experts, including sport management professors ($n = 2$), a doctor of statistics ($n = 1$), and middle managers of professional sports teams ($n = 2$), examined the questionnaires for content validity. Respondents were asked to indicate their level of agreement with each of the 48 items on a Likert scale ranging from 1 (strongly disagree) to 5 (strongly agree). To investigate the applicability of the written questionnaire, a preliminary survey was conducted with 61 employees. They answered that they did not have any difficulty with the questionnaire items, so we composed the final questionnaire and conducted the survey (Table 6.4).

Date analyses

After the data were collected, frequency analysis, reliability analysis, and correlation analysis were performed using SPSS. Confirmatory factor analysis for the validity test was conducted using AMOS, and the structural equation model (SEM) was analyzed for the research hypothesis test. Based on the theoretical background, confirmatory factor analysis was performed to statistically confirm the relationship between manifest variables and latent variables. To carry out confirmatory factor analysis, the maximum likelihood method, which assumed multivariate normal distribution, was used. The fit index was calculated using CMIN/DF, NFI, TLI, CFI, and RMSEA.

A confirmatory factor analysis was employed to assess the dimensionality of the measurement model by using the maximum likelihood estimation. The second order measurement model displayed satisfactory fit with data ($x/df = 2.381$, NFI = 0.907, TLI = 0.922, CFI = 0.901, and RMSEA = 0.054). All model fit indices were within the recommended thresholds (Hooper, Coughlan &Mullen, 2008). Construct validity was assessed by using convergent and discriminant validity. To examine convergent validity, factor loadings, construct reliability (CR), and average

90 Yunduk Jeong et al.

Table 6.4 Questionnaire Items

Constructs		Items
LMX	Affect	I want to be on good terms with my leader, like a friend. I like my leader very much. I find it enjoyable when I work with my leader.
	Loyalty	My leader stands up for me in front of others even when I lack task knowledge. My leader protects me from unreasonable things. My leader defends me from other people even if I make business mistakes.
	Contribution	I will be willing to work beyond my job description for my leader. I will devote my time and effort to meeting my leader's business goals. I will gladly accept difficult tasks for my leader.
	Professional respect	I was impressed with the task knowledge of my leader. I respect my leader's knowledge and abilities. I respect the professionalism of my leader.
Self-leadership	Behavior-focused strategies	I carry out tasks by considering the short- and long-term goals. I establish detailed goals to increase the likelihood of achievement. I benchmark and check so that I can track my progress. I record errors that occurred during the performance of a task. I often check whether I am doing well in the course of my work.
	Natural reward strategies	I motivate myself in a pleasant way to achieve my goals. I am satisfied with and motivated by my job. I think that my decisions are important in carrying out a task. I focus on the positive side rather than the negative side of my organization.
	Constructive-thought-pattern strategies	I encourage myself when the results of the task are satisfactory. I am satisfied with the results and speak proudly to my colleagues. I reflect and criticize myself for unsatisfactory results. I imagine a successful task. I try to communicate to myself that I can overcome problems I encounter.

Empowerment	Meaningful	My job performance is personally meaningful.
		I am confident of achieving my business goals.
		I have autonomy in deciding how to do business.
		I exert an influence on what happens in our department.
	Competence	I feel rewarded for what I do.
		I want to achieve higher goals than others.
		I do my work freely and in my own way.
		I can control what happens in my department.
	Self-determination	What I do is important within the organization.
		I have the ability to achieve my business goals.
		I tend to assert my opinion in the course of my work.
		I have an influence over what happens in my department.
	Impact	My job is important for me to develop in my career.
		I am confident in my organization to pursue what I have planned.
		I can make important decisions about how I work.
		What I do affects my department.
Innovative behavior		I develop new ideas to solve difficult problems related to work.

variance extracted (AVE) were calculated. From Table 6.5, all factor loadings were greater than 0.55 (Tabachnick & Fidell, 2007), CR values all exceeded the recommended value of 0.7, and AVE values all exceeded the minimum requirement of 0.5, establishing the scale's convergent validity (Fornell & Larcker, 1981). For discriminant validity, we verified that the AVE of the latent variable was greater than the square of the correlation between latent variables (Fornell & Larcker, 1981). Since it is difficult to verify all variables, the pair with the highest correlation between variables was selected and verified. If the AVE value was higher than the square of the correlation coefficient between the latent variables, the discriminant validity was deemed to be present and vice versa. Table 6.6 shows that the highest correlation was 0.497 (LMX – self-leadership) and the square of 0.497 is 0.247. LMX AVE is 0.754, and self-leadership AVE is 0.750. Since the AVE values are all greater than the square of the correlation coefficient, discriminant validity is established.

The reliability estimates (Cronbach's alpha) are valid for the four bases of LMX, the three bases of self-leadership, four bases of empowerment, and lone base of innovative behavior. The results revealed that Cronbach's alpha coefficients ranged from 0.820 to 0.870 for LMX scales, 0.880 to 0.918 for self-leadership scales, 0.896 to 0.938 for empowerment scales, and 0.893 for innovative behavior scales (see Table 6.5). The reliability test indicated that the items are internally

Table 6.5 Convergent Validity and Reliability

Variable	Dimension	Item	β	CR	AVE	α
LMX	Affect	1	0.822	0.864	0.681	0.820
		2	0.831			
		3	0.707			
	Loyalty	1	0.831	0.870	0.692	0.870
		2	0.777			
		3	0.873			
	Contribution	1	0.716	0.861	0.675	0.847
		2	0.886			
		3	0.841			
	Professional respect	1	0.765	0.861	0.675	0.841
		2	0.766			
		3	0.910			
Self-leadership	Behavior-focused strategies	1	0.823	0.922	0.703	0.918
		2	0.800			
		3	0.892			
		4	0.858			
		5	0.784			
	Natural reward strategies	1	0.910	0.893	0.682	0.880
		2	0.908			
		3	0.850			
		4	0.580			
	Constructive-thought-pattern strategies	1	0.790	0.897	0.636	0.905
		2	0.886			
		3	0.783			
		4	0.792			
		5	0.812			
Empowerment	Meaningful	1	0.932	0.946	0.814	0.933
		2	0.935			
		3	0.857			
		4	0.802			
	Competence	1	0.930	0.907	0.714	0.896
		2	0.918			
		3	0.856			
		4	0.602			
	Self-determination	1	0.830	0.919	0.739	0.910
		2	0.853			
		3	0.876			
		4	0.837			
	Impact	1	0.943	0.944	0.809	0.938
		2	0.907			
		3	0.823			
		4	0.881			
Innovative behavior		1	0.677	0.899	0.599	0.893
		2	0.743			
		3	0.706			
		4	0.837			
		5	0.824			
		6	0.790			

Table 6.6 Inter-factor Correlation Analyses

Variable	LMX	Self-leadership	Empowerment	Innovative Behavior
LMX				
Self-leadership	0.497**			
Empowerment	0.446**	0.462**		
Innovative behavior	0.448**	0.413**	0.340**	

Note: ** $p < 0.01$.

consistent since the items are considered to be reliable when a Cronbach's alpha coefficient is more than 0.70 (Nunnally & Bernstein, 1994).

Results

Structural model and hypothesis testing

The overall structural model showed good fit to the sample data (x^2/df = 2.727, NFI = 0.916, TLI = 0.917, CFI = 0.931, and RMSEA = 0.054). To analyze the positive relationships, the influences between variables were verified and the following conclusions were drawn. First, as shown in Table 6.7, as a result of checking the path coefficient between LMX and empowerment, LMX had a significant, positive influence on empowerment (0.370, $p < 0.001$). Therefore, Hypothesis 1 was supported. Second, as a result of checking the path coefficient between LMX and innovative behavior, LMX had a significant, positive effect on empowerment (0.413, $p < 0.001$). Therefore, Hypothesis 2 was supported. Third, as a result of checking the path coefficient between self-leadership and empowerment, self-leadership had a significant, positive influence on empowerment (0.370, $p < 0.001$). Therefore, Hypothesis 3 was supported. Fourth, as a result of checking the path coefficient between self-leadership and innovative behavior, self-leadership had a significant, positive effect on innovation (0.246, $p < 0.001$). Therefore, Hypothesis 4 was supported. Fifth, the path coefficient value between empowerment and innovation was statistically significant (0.106 $p < 0.05$). Therefore, Hypothesis 5 was supported.

Mediating effect of empowerment

In examining the mediating effect of empowerment, the present study abided by Baron and Kenny's (1986) general guideline and investigated the significance of

94 Yunduk Jeong et al.

the indirect effects using Preacher and Hayes' (2008) bootstrap procedure. Some
conditions are required to establish the mediating effect (Baron & Kenny, 1986).
First, the independent variable must have an effect on the dependent variable
without the mediating variable. Second, the independent variable must be related
to the mediating variable. Third, the mediating variable must be associated with
the dependent variable. Partial mediation is established when the relationship between the independent variable and the dependent variable is significant, while
the mediating variable and the relationship coefficient must be reduced when
controlling for the mediating variable. Complete mediation is established when
the path between the independent variable and dependent variable is not significant with the mediating variable.

As shown in Table 6.8, concerning Hypothesis 6, the independent variable
(LMX) had an effect on the dependent variable (innovation) without the mediating

Table 6.7 Results of Structural Equation Modeling Analysis and Hypothesis
Tests

Hypothesis	Path	Standardized Estimate	SE	CR	Test/ Result
1	LMX → Empowerment	0.370	0.087	7.586***	Accepted
2	LMX → Innovation	0.413	0.073	5.640***	Accepted
3	Self-Leadership → Empowerment	0.370	0.055	6.789***	Accepted
4	Self-Leadership → Innovative Behavior	0.246	0.046	4.751***	Accepted
5	Empowerment → Innovative Behavior	0.106	0.073	2.145*	Accepted

Note: ***$p < 0.001$, *$p < 0.05$.

Table 6.8 Mediating Effect of Empowerment

Relationships	Direct Effects without Mediator	Direct Effect with Mediator (CI)	Indirect Effects (CI)	Mediation Hypotheses
LMX – empowerment – innovative behavior	0.337***	0.306** (0.173 to 0.425)	0.039 (−0.004 to 0.094)	Not supported
Self-leadership – empowerment – innovative behavior	0.288***	0.246** (0.121 to 0.394)	0.034 (−.001 to 0.098)	Not supported

Note: ***$p < 0.001$, **$p < 0.01$; bootstrap confidence in parentheses, CI = confidence
interval.

variable (empowerment). Once the mediating variable was included in the model, findings showed the independent variable still had an effect on the dependent variable and the relationship coefficient was reduced from 0.337 to 0.306. However, since the indirect effect was not significant and the confidence interval included zero, mediation was not supported. Regarding Hypothesis 7, the independent variable (self-leadership) had an effect on the dependent variable (innovative behavior) without the mediating variable (empowerment). Once the mediating variable was included in the model, findings indicated the independent variable still had an effect on the dependent variable and the relationship coefficient was reduced from 0.288 to 0.246. However, since the indirect effect was not significant and the confidence interval included zero, mediation was not supported.

Discussion and conclusion

The main objective of this study was to investigate the relationship between LMX, self-leadership, empowerment, and innovation. The proposed integrative framework allows the identification of relationships between (1) LMX and empowerment; (2) LMX and innovation; (3) self-leadership and empowerment; (4) self-leadership and innovation; and (5) empowerment and innovation. From a theoretical point of view, the current study offers several contributions to research in sport-focused organizational behavior and human resource management. Our study emphasizes the importance and necessity of developing LMX as a means of nurturing empowerment and innovative behavior. Traditionally, previous studies have concentrated on transformational leadership, organizational culture, justice, and support as antecedents of empowerment and innovation in management literature (Afsar, Badir & Saeed, 2014; Choi, Kim, Ullah & Kang, 2016; Kim & Kim, 2014; Jeong, 2017; Young, 2012). However, in advancing knowledge, findings reveal that LMX has a favorable influence on empowerment and innovation. If an organization concentrates on the differentiated relation between leaders and subordinates, employees are encouraged to foster empowerment and innovation.

The result of the positive relationship between LMX and empowerment is in line with past research. For instance, Byun and Ko (2012) analyzed the effects of LMX quality as recognized by hotel F&B employees on empowerment, job satisfaction, and organizational commitment and found that LMX relationships of super deluxe hotel employees have a significant, positive effect on competence, self-determination, and empowerment impact. In the context of sport-focused organizational behavior, Moon and Kang (2010) closely analyzed the positive relationship among LMX, empowerment, and the organizational commitment of workers in sports centers and indicated that LMX plays a key role in fostering empowerment. The result of the positive relationship between LMX and innovation is in alignment with the work of Kyoung and Huh (2018), and Schermuly et al (2013), who highlighted the importance of LMX in enhancing employee innovation and overall effort. Therefore, generating and managing LMX in an organization is important in developing and sustaining an organization.

The current study heeds the argument of existing researchers by seeking to understand the role of self-leadership in the prediction of empowerment and innovation. If an organization assists its employees to actively perform their tasks with autonomy, the employees are more likely to have fresh and innovative ideas. More specifically, Kim and Kim (2012) explored the link between self-leadership, empowerment, and organizational innovation in private security guards and found that employee self-leadership plays a key role in stimulating empowerment and innovation. Likewise, Yang, Kim, and Jang (2015) examined the effect of self-leadership on psychological empowerment and innovative behavior of taekwondo preliminary instructors, confirming that there exists a positive relationship between self-leadership and innovation. In other words, when employees possess high levels of self-leadership, they are more likely to bring a fresh outlook and innovative ideas to the table, thus crystallizing the importance of self-leadership in encouraging employees to continually innovate. Therefore, strengthening self-leadership among employees should be top priority in the vein of organizational innovation.

By concentrating on the relationship between empowerment and innovation, we highlight the need to include empowerment in an innovation model. Evidence of the path is captured by Fernandez and Moldogaziev's (2012) study that empirically explored the relationship between empowerment and innovation in the public sector, demonstrating that empowered employees are more likely to enhance performance largely by finding innovative ways of reducing errors and redesigning work processes. Thus, the authors emphasized that organizations should grant employees rich opportunities to boost discretion and acquire job-related knowledge. In a sports context, Lee et al (2009) indicated a direct relationship between empowerment and innovation, proposing that empowerment of soccer leaders contributes to innovation. Thus, it is advised that managers in sport organizations make the most of their time and effort by motivating team members to become fully immersed in their work.

The major findings of this study offer to sport organization managers, organizational behavior and human resource management implications for their organizations. First, to develop LMX, the fundamental solution of an "out group" should be mutual understanding and respect. It is widely acknowledged that our group is devoid of mutual trust between leaders and subordinates compared to that observed in an "in group." For organizational development, it is imperative to build a long-term relationship characterized by firm trust. Thus, desirable organizational culture, such as clan culture that emphasizes a family-like atmosphere, cooperation, and cohesion, should be formed. When friendly feelings develop, mutual trust will replace discord and suspicion. Next, to embody self-leadership, employees must establish work goals. If employees do not have clear, specific plans regarding their work, they cannot foment self-leadership. For goal achievement, employees should divide major tasks into small steps. In other words, employees have to start with realistic and achievable goals in order to achieve bigger goals. These goals will help employees stay focused and monitor their progress, thus reinforcing skills associated with self-leadership.

The substantive findings of our study should be considered in light of their limitations. First, it would be of value for future studies to explore other possible variables affecting empowerment and innovative behavior. For example, emotional intelligence, transactional leadership, transformational leadership, servant leadership, organizational culture, and organizational support may be assessed as possible contributing factors. Second, it would be worthwhile for future studies to consider other mediating variables. This study employs empowerment as a mediator of the relationship between LMX and innovation, as well as innovation and self-leadership. Nonetheless, grounded in the work of previous studies, we believe that there are other mediating variables, such as job satisfaction and organizational commitment. Third, given the lack of official data about sport organizations, it is difficult to establish a representative sample. Future research should investigate the model in other organizations of differing sizes.

References

Afsar, B., Badir, Y. F., & Saeed, B. B. (2014). Transformational leadership and innovative work behavior. *Industrial Management & Data Systems*, 114(8), 1270–1300.

Ahn, C. (2012). The causal relationship of soccer coach's self-leadership and empowerment, organizational satisfaction. *The Korean Society of Sports Science*, 21(1), 347–359.

Amabile, T. M. (1988). A model of creativity and innovation in organizations. *Research in Organizational Behavior*, 10(1), 123–167.

Anand, S., Hu, J., Liden, R. C., & Vidyarthi, P. R. (2011). Leader-member exchange: Recent research findings and prospects for the future. In A. Bryman (Ed.), *The sage handbook of leadership* (pp. 311–325). London: Sage.

Arkani-Hamed, N., Dimopoulos, S., & Dvali, G. (1998). The hierarchy problem and new dimensions at a millimeter. *Physics Letters B*, 429(3–4), 263–272.

Ashforth, B. E. (1989). The experience of powerlessness in organizations. *Organizational Behavior and Human Decision Processes*, 43(2), 207–242.

Bandura, A. (1971). *Social learning theory*. Morristown, NJ: General Learning Press.

Bandura, A. (1977). Self-efficacy: Toward a unifying theory of behavioral change. *Psychological Review*, 84(2), 191.

Baron, R. M., & Kenny, D. A. (1986). The moderator–mediator variable distinction in social psychological research: Conceptual, strategic, and statistical considerations. *Journal of Personality and Social Psychology*, 51(6), 1173–1182.

Blanchard, K. (1995). Point of power can help self-leadership. *Manage*, 46, 12–13.

Bligh, M. C., Pearce, C. L., & Kohles, J. C. (2006). The importance of self-and shared leadership in team based knowledge work: A meso-level model of leadership dynamics. *Journal of managerial Psychology*, 21(4), 296–318.

Bolton, B., & Brookings, J. (1998). Development of a measure of intrapersonal empowerment. *Rehabilitation Psychology*, 43(2), 131.

Byun, J., & Ko, J. (2012). The effects of the LMX quality of super deluxe hotel F&B employees on the empowerment, job satisfaction and organizational commitment. *Korean Journal of Hospitality & Tourism*, 21(6), 39–60.

Carmeli, A., Meitar, R., & Weisberg, J. (2006). Self-leadership skills and innovative behavior at work. *International Journal of Manpower*, 27(1), 75–90.

Choi, S. B., Kim, K., Ullah, S. E., & Kang, S. W. (2016). How transformational leadership facilitates innovative behavior of Korean workers. *Personnel Review, 45*, 459–479.

Conger, J. A., & Kanungo, R. N. (1988). The empowerment process: Integrating theory and practice. *Academy of Management Review, 13*(3), 471–482.

Dansereau, F., Cashman, J., & Graen, G. (1973). Instrumentality theory and equity theory as complementary approaches in predicting the relationship of leadership and turnover among managers. *Organizational Behavior and Human Performance, 10*(2), 184–200.

Dansereau Jr, F., Graen, G., & Haga, W. J. (1975). A vertical dyad linkage approach to leadership within formal organizations: A longitudinal investigation of the role making process. *Organizational Behavior and Human Performance, 13*(1), 46–78.

Derfus, P. J., Maggitti, P. G., Grimm, C. M., & Smith, K. G. (2008). The Red Queen effect: Competitive actions and firm performance. *Academy of Management Journal, 51*(1), 61–80.

Dienesch, R. M., & Liden, R. C. (1986). Leader-member exchange model of leadership: A critique and further development. *Academy of Management Review, 11*(3), 618–634.

DiLiello, T. C., & Houghton, J. D. (2006). Maximizing organizational leadership capacity for the future: Toward a model of self-leadership, innovation and creativity. *Journal of Managerial Psychology, 21*(4), 319–337.

Drucker, P. F. (1985). The discipline of innovation. *Harvard Business Review, 63*(3), 67–72.

Fernandez, S., & Moldogaziev, T. (2012). Using employee empowerment to encourage innovative behavior in the public sector. *Journal of Public Administration Research and Theory, 23*(1), 155–187.

Fetterman, D. M. (1996). Empowerment evaluation: An introduction to theory and practice. In D.M. Fetterman, S.J. Kaftarian, and A. Wandersman (Eds.), *Empowerment evaluation: Knowledge and tools for self-assessment and accountability* (pp. 3–46). Thousand Oaks, CA: Sage.

Fornell, C., & Larcker, D. F. (1981). Evaluating structural equation models with unobservable variables and measurement error. *Journal of Marketing Research, 18*(1), 39–50.

Fort, R. (2017). Reorganization challenges facing Korean baseball. In D. H. Kwak, Y. J. Ko, L. Kang, & M. Rosentraub (Eds.), *Sport in Korea: History, development, management* (pp. 190–206). London: Routledge.

Ghosh, K. (2015). Developing organizational creativity and innovation: Toward a model of self-leadership, employee creativity, creativity climate and workplace innovative orientation. *Management Research Review, 38*, 1126–1148.

Graen, G. (1976). Role-making processes within complex organizations. *Handbook of Industrial and Organizational Psychology, 1201*, 1245.

Graen, G., & Cashman, J. F. (1975). A role-making model of leadership in formal organizations: A developmental approach. In J. G. Hunt & L. L. Larson (Eds.), *Leadership frontiers*, (pp. 143–165). Kent, OH: Kent State University.

Graen, G., Dansereau, F., Minami, T., & Cashman, J. (1973). Leadership behaviors as cues to performance evaluation. *Academy of Management Journal, 16*(4), 611–623.

Graen, G., & Schiemann, W. (1978). Leader–member agreement: A vertical dyad linkage approach. *Journal of Applied Psychology, 63*(2), 206.

Graen, G. B., Orris, J. B., & Johnson, T. W. (1973). Role assimilation processes in a complex organization. *Journal of Vocational Behavior, 3*(4), 395–420.

Graen, G. B., & Scandura, T. A. (1987). Toward a psychology of dyadic organizing. *Research in Organizational Behavior, 9*, 175–208.

Graen, G. B., & Uhl-Bien, M. (1995). Relationship-based approach to leadership: Development of leader-member exchange (LMX) theory of leadership over 25 years: Applying a multi-level multi-domain perspective. *The Leadership Quarterly, 6*(2), 219–247.

Gutierrez, L., GlenMaye, L., & DeLois, K. (1995). The organizational context of empowerment practice: Implications for social work administration. *Social Work, 40*(2), 249–258.

Harris, K. J., Wheeler, A. R., & Kacmar, K. M. (2009). Leader–member exchange and empowerment: Direct and interactive effects on job satisfaction, turnover intentions, and performance. *The Leadership Quarterly, 20*(3), 371–382.

Hong, W., & Ahn, K. (2016). The relationship between empowerment and innovative behavior, and the moderating effect of psychological ownership in small business. *The Korean Society of Business Venturing, 11*(3), 145–155.

Hooper, D., Coughlan, J., & Mullen, M. (2008). Structural equation modelling: Guidelines for determining model fit. *The Electronic Journal of Business Research Methods, 6*(1), 53–60.

Houghton, J. D., & Jinkerson, D. L. (2007). Constructive thought strategies and job satisfaction: A preliminary examination. *Journal of Business and Psychology, 22*(1), 45–53.

Houghton, J. D., & Neck, C. P. (2002). The revised self-leadership questionnaire: Testing a hierarchical factor structure for self-leadership. *Journal of Managerial Psychology, 17*(8), 672–691.

Houghton, J. D., & Yoho, S. K. (2005). Toward a contingency model of leadership and psychological empowerment: When should self-leadership be encouraged? *Journal of Leadership & Organizational Studies, 11*(4), 65–83.

Jafri, M. H. (2010). Organizational commitment and employee's innovative behavior: A study in retail sector. *Journal of Management Research, 10*(1), 62.

Jennings, L. B., Parra-Medina, D. M., Hilfinger-Messias, D. K., & McLoughlin, K. (2006). Toward a critical social theory of youth empowerment. *Journal of Community Practice, 14*(1–2), 31–55.

Jeong, Y. (2017). Structural relationship among organizational culture, empowerment and job performance, and comparison of models – Focused on professional football corporate club and citizen club. Unpublished Ph.D. thesis, Kyonggi University, Suwon, South Korea.

Jeong, Y. (2018). The structural relationship between ethical climate, organizational effectiveness and innovative behavior of professional soccer front office. *The Korean Society of Sports Science, 27*(6), 649–661.

Jeong, Y., & Kim, Y. (2019). A strategy to strengthen the competitiveness of front office of professional football for promoting spectators – Focused on internal marketing. *Journal of the Korea Entertainment Industry Association, 13*(3), 169–180.

Jeong, Y., Kim, E., Kim, M., & Zhang, J. J. (2019). Exploring relationships among organizational culture, empowerment, and organizational citizenship behavior in the South Korean professional sport industry. *Sustainability, 11*(19), 5412.

Jeong, W., & Yun, I. (2016). The effects of self-leadership on innovative behavior – The moderating role of perceived procedural justice. *Korean Academy of Human Resource Management, 23*(5), 35–156.

Kanter, R. M. (1988). Three tiers for innovation research. *Communication Research, 15*(5), 509–523.

Kim, B. C. (2008). Professional baseball in Korea: Origins, causes, consequences and implications. *The International Journal of the History of Sport, 25*(3), 370–385.

Kim, B., & Kim, J. (2014). The relationship of transformational leadership and innovative behavior. *Korean Journal of Industrial and Organizational Psychology, 27*(1), 107–136.

Kim, K. S., & Kim, C. S. (2012). Relation of self-leadership and empowerment and organizational innovation action in private security guard. *Journal of the Korea Contents Association, 12*(11), 377–387.

Kim, T., Won, D., & Kwak, M. (2016). The relationships between leader-member exchange quality, empowerment, and job performance of the fitness center instructors. *Korea Institute of Sport Science, 27*(1), 88–104.

Kim, W. C., & Mauborgne, R. (2014). *Blue ocean strategy*. Boston, MA: Harvard Business School.

Kyoung, I., & Huh, J. (2018). The relationship among leader-member exchange (LMX), work engagement and innovation behavior on fitness centers. *The Korean Society of Sports Science, 27*(4), 427–439.

Lee, J. T. (2015). Long term trends in the Korean professional baseball. *Journal of the Korean Data and Information Science Society, 26*(1), 1–10.

Lee, K., Lee, M., & Kim, I. (2009). The effects of soccer leaders' self-leadership and empowerment on innovative behavior. *The Korean Society of Sports Science, 18*(3), 109–119.

Lee, M., & Koh, J. (2001). Is empowerment really a new concept? *International Journal of Human Resource Management, 12*(4), 684–695.

Lee, Y. H. (2006). The decline of attendance in the Korean Professional Baseball League: The major league effects. *Journal of Sports Economics, 7*(2), 187–200.

Lee, Y. H., & Fort, R. (2014). *The sports business in the Pacific Rim: Economics and policy*. New York: Springer.

Liden, R. C., & Maslyn, J. M. (1998). Multidimensionality of leader-member exchange: An empirical assessment through scale development. *Journal of Management, 24*(1), 43–72.

Locke, E. A., & Latham, G. P. (1990). *A theory of goal setting & task performance*. Englewood Cliffs, NJ: Prentice-Hall.

Luttrell, C., Quiroz, S., Scrutton, C., & Bird, K. (2009). *Understanding and operationalising empowerment*. London: Overseas Development Institute.

Manz, C. C. (1986). Self-leadership: Toward an expanded theory of self-influence processes in organizations. *Academy of Management Review, 11*(3), 585–600.

Manz, C. C. (1991). Leading employees to be self-managing and beyond: Toward the establishment of self-leadership in organizations. *Journal of Management Systems, 3*(3), 15–24.

Manz, C. C., & Sims Jr, H. P. (1987). Leading workers to lead themselves: The external leadership of self-managing work teams. *Administrative Science Quarterly, 32*(1), 106–129.

Manz, C. C., & Sims, H. P. (1980). Self-management as a substitute for leadership: A social learning theory perspective. *Academy of Management Review, 5*(3), 361–367.

Manz, C. C., & Sims, H. P. (2001). *The new superleadership: Leading others to lead themselves*. San Francisco, CA: Berrett-Koehler.

Menon, S. (2001). Employee empowerment: An integrative psychological approach. *Applied Psychology, 50*(1), 153–180.

Moon, Y., & Kang, N. (2010). The study of causal relationship model among LMX (leader-member exchange), empowerment and organizational commitment of workers in sports center. *Journal of Sport and Leisure Studies, 40*, 279–293.

Moon, Y., & Kang, N. (2010). The study of causal relationship model among LMX (leader-member exchange), empowerment and organizational commitment of workers in sports center. *Korean Society of Sport and Leisure Studies, 40*(1), 279–293.

Müller, T., & Niessen, C. (2018). Self-leadership and self-control strength in the work context. *Journal of Managerial Psychology, 33,* 74–92.

Mumford, M. D., & Gustafson, S. B. (1988). Creativity syndrome: Integration, application, and innovation. *Psychological Bulletin, 103*(1), 27.

Neck, C. P. (1996). Thought self-leadership: A self-regulatory approach towards overcoming resistance to organizational change. *The International Journal of Organizational Analysis, 4*(2), 202–216.

Neck, C. P., & Manz, C. C. (1996). Thought self-leadership: The impact of mental strategies training on employee cognition, behavior, and affect. *Journal of Organizational Behavior, 17,* 445–467.

Neck, C. P., & Manz, C. C. (2010). *Mastering self-leadership: Empowering yourself for personal excellence.* Upper Saddle River, NJ: Pearson Education.

Neck, C. P., & Milliman, J. F. (1994). Thought self-leadership: Finding spiritual fulfilment in organizational life. *Journal of Managerial Psychology, 9*(6), 9–16.

Neck, C. P., Neck, H. M., & Manz, C. C. (1997). Thought self-leadership: Mind management for entrepreneurs. *Journal of Developmental Entrepreneurship, 2*(1), 25–35.

Neck, C. P., Neck, H. M., Manz, C. C., & Godwin, J. (1999). "I think I can; I think I can": A self-leadership perspective toward enhancing entrepreneur thought patterns, self-efficacy, and performance. *Journal of Managerial Psychology, 14*(6), 477–501.

Neck, C. P., Smith, W. J., & Godwin, J. L. (1997). Thought self-leadership: A self-regulatory approach to diversity management. *Journal of Managerial Psychology, 12*(3), 190–203.

Neck, C. P., Stewart, G. L., & Manz, C. C. (1995). Thought self-leadership as a framework for enhancing the performance of performance appraisers. *The Journal of Applied Behavioral Science, 31*(3), 278–302.

Northouse, P. G. (2015). *Leadership: Theory and practice.* Thousand Oaks, CA: Sage.

Nunnally, J. C., & Bernstein, I. H. (1994). *Psychometric theory* (3rd ed.). New York: McGraw-Hill.

Oladipo, S. E. (2009). Psychological empowerment and development. *Edo Journal of Counselling, 2*(1), 118–126.

Pfeffer, J. (2010). Building sustainable organizations: The human factor. *Academy of Management Perspectives, 24*(1), 34–45.

Phillips, R. L., Duran, C. A., & Howell, R. D. (1993). An examination of the multidimensionality hypothesis of leader-member exchange, using both factor analytic and structural modeling techniques. *Proceedings of the southern management association* (161–163).

Pieterse, A. N., Van Knippenberg, D., Schippers, M., & Stam, D. (2010). Transformational and transactional leadership and innovative behavior: The moderating role of psychological empowerment. *Journal of Organizational Behavior, 31*(4), 609–623.

Preacher, K. J., & Hayes, A. F. (2008). Asymptotic and resampling strategies for assessing and comparing indirect effects in multiple mediator models. *Behavior Research Methods, 40*(3), 879–891.

Prussia, G. E., Anderson, J. S., & Manz, C. C. (1998). Self-leadership and performance outcomes: The mediating influence of self-efficacy. *Journal of Organizational Behavior, 19*(5), 523–538.

Rappaport, J. (1981). In praise of paradox: A social policy of empowerment over prevention. *American Journal of Community Psychology, 9*(1), 1–25.

Roberts, H. E., & Foti, R. J. (1998). Evaluating the interaction between self-leadership and work structure in predicting job satisfaction. *Journal of Business and Psychology, 12*(3), 257–267.

Saleebey, D. (1992). Biology's challenge to social work: Embodying the person-in-environment perspective. *Social Work*, *37*(2), 112–118.

Schermuly, C. C., Meyer, B., & Dämmer, L. (2013). Leader-member exchange and innovative behavior. *Journal of Personnel Psychology*, *12*, 132–143.

Scott, S. G., & Bruce, R. A. (1994). Determinants of innovative behavior: A path model of individual innovation in the workplace. *Academy of Management Journal*, *37*(3), 580–607.

Seo, H. (2018). The influence of self-leadership on innovative behavior of sports center instructors: Focused on the moderating effect resistance to organizational change. *The Korean Journal of Physical education*, *57*(5), 225–239.

Spreitzer, G. M. (1995). Psychological empowerment in the workplace: Dimensions, measurement, and validation. *Academy of Management Journal*, *38*(5), 1442–1465.

Stewart, G. L., & Barrick, M. R. (2000). Team structure and performance: Assessing the mediating role of intra-team process and the moderating role of task type. *Academy of Management Journal*, *43*(2), 135–148.

Tabachnick, B. G., & Fidell, L. S. (2007). *Experimental designs using ANOVA*. Belmont, CA: Duxbury.

Thomas, K. W., & Velthouse, B. A. (1990). Cognitive elements of empowerment: An "interpretive" model of intrinsic task motivation. *Academy of Management Review*, *15*(4), 666–681.

VanSandt, C. V., & Neck, C. P. (2003). Bridging ethics and self-leadership: Overcoming ethical discrepancies between employee and organizational standards. *Journal of Business Ethics*, *43*(4), 363–387.

Wallerstein, N. (2002). Empowerment to reduce health disparities. *Scandinavian Journal of Public Health*, *30*(59), 72–77.

Wayne, S. J., Shore, L. M., & Liden, R. C. (1997). Perceived organizational support and leader-member exchange: A social exchange perspective. *Academy of Management Journal*, *40*(1), 82–111.

Yang, D. S., Kim, H. Y., & Jang, S. Y. (2015). The effect of self-leadership on psychological empowerment and innovative behavior of taekwondo preliminary instructors. *Korean Journal of Sports Science*, *24*(2), 595–607.

Young, L. D. (2012). How to promote innovative behavior at work? The role of justice and support within organizations. *The Journal of Creative Behavior*, *46*(3), 220–243.

Yuan, F., & Woodman, R. W. (2010). Innovative behavior in the workplace: The role of performance and image outcome expectations. *Academy of Management Journal*, *53*(2), 323–342.

Zhang, Y. B., Lin, M. C., Nonaka, A., & Beom, K. (2005). Harmony, hierarchy and conservatism: A cross-cultural comparison of Confucian values in China, Korea, Japan, and Taiwan. *Communication Research Reports*, *22*(2), 107–115.

Zimmerman, M. A. (2000). Empowerment theory. In J. Rappaport & E. Seidman (Eds.), *Handbook of community psychology* (pp. 43–63). New York: Springer.

Chapter 7

Governing economic flows in European professional football clubs

Jan Šíma and Tomáš Ruda

Introduction

Football is a global phenomenon. According to the "Big Count" study published by FIFA (Fédération Internationale de Football Association, the main international football governing body), the number of players exceeded 250 million in 2006, which makes it the most popular sport in the whole world. Composed of 211 national football associations, the international football federation, FIFA now has six more members than the International Olympic Committee (FIFA, 2018). Not all members, however, are sovereign states.

This paper focuses solely on professional football clubs playing in top-tier league competitions. According to the FIFA's Report (2018), a total of 2,671 clubs participate in 204 top-tier competitions worldwide.

With the ever-growing commercialisation of professional football, not only league competitions but also national competitions have become a money-making business for more stakeholders. The income not only of players and clubs, but also of organisations involved in organising the competitions, increases each year (Deloitte, 2018). The structure of the income changes rapidly with time. Gone are the days when clubs resisted TV broadcasts of their league matches, as they were afraid of a decrease in proceeds from gate receipts. More than the attention of active fans as spectators in football stadiums, clubs now depend on the favour of passive fans who are willing, often in return for a fee, to follow their matches through the media, support their favourite club on social media, or buy club-related merchandise on the Internet. At the same time, these fans become potential customers of companies which sponsor the clubs.

The difference between the previous (traditional) and current structure of revenues generated by European professional sports clubs was described by Andreff and Staudohar (2000). The traditional model of a professional club is abbreviated as SSSL. The abbreviation stands for an income pattern typical for most of the 20th century (Spectators – Subsidies – Sponsors – Local). Gate receipts used to be the primary source of income. In addition to that, clubs in some countries were subsidised by local or national governments. Sponsorship increasingly gained importance in the second half of the 20th century, even though the contribution of

DOI: 10.4324/9781003213673-7

this income source had not exceeded gate receipts for a long time. Usually, only companies residing in the vicinity of the sponsored club became its sponsors.

The current financing structure of professional clubs is abbreviated by Andreff and Staudohar (2000) as MCMMG (Media – Corporations – Merchandising – Markets – Global). This model is typical for the majority of top European professional football clubs. As early as the 1990s, gate receipts were no longer the main source of income and, also, income from subsidies decreased significantly. Revenues from selling TV broadcasting rights have become the main source of finance for top professional football clubs and leagues. In the Premier League, the richest football league, these revenues have already accounted for the major share of income (Deloitte, 2018a).

Moreover, 2018 was a breakthrough year for professional football as the broadcasting rights were bought by the first technology corporation – retail giant Amazon (Kanter, 2018). According to Pedersen (2017), the main explanation for the increase in income from selling TV broadcasting rights is the ever-growing competition in this industry. In the past, there were only a few public-service stations, while now customers can choose from numerous, mostly private, TV channels. These channels derive their revenues mainly from advertising, the price of which is directly related to the audience share. Attracting huge attention from spectators, football is naturally a preferred sport. Another interesting aspect of the model devised by Andreff and Staudohar (2000) is the emergence of a new generation of entrepreneurs in the environment of professional football who seek to improve financial results of the clubs through ownership and control.

At present, the best-known examples of such relations are Sheikh Mansour bin Zayed Al Nahyan and Manchester City, Roman Abramovich and Chelsea, and Ahmad Al Sayed and Paris Saint Germain. It was this practice of rich entrepreneurs who can invest a lot of money that led the Union of European Football Associations (UEFA) to introduce the Financial Fair Play rule (Peeters & Szymanski, 2014). The purpose of this regulation is to bind clubs to spend only what they are able to generate (Preuss, Haugen & Schubert, 2014). Another synergy which occurs between sports and business is merchandising – sales of club shirts, clothing items, and other goods bearing the club's logo. Merchandising of club-related goods existed in the past, of course, but revenues in this domain have been gradually increasing with improved marketing practices, increasing globalisation, and the opportunity to buy on the Internet (Statista, 2019). Merchandising together with sponsorship, collectively referred to as "commercial revenue", account for 40% of all revenues of the 20 richest football clubs in Europe (Deloitte, 2019).

According to Andreff and Staudohar (2000), "markets" means the possibility to trade talented players in the market. Notably, clubs from lower grade competitions have become suppliers of talented players to football mega clubs, and these sales are a major source of their revenues. The UEFA Report (2019) suggests that, with only one exception, the Premier League clubs are net buyers, while clubs from the Dutch, Belgian, Czech, and Polish leagues are net sellers in the majority of cases. As a matter of fact, this is the most significant revenue for many of them.

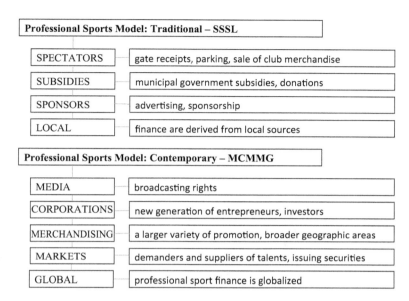

Figure 7.1 European model of professional sports finance by Andreff and Staudohar.
Source: Adapted from Andreff and Staudohar (2000).

Andreff and Studohar (2000) conclude that the model is based on four pillars: "Media-Corporations-Merchandising-Markets". They emphasize that the link between the nationality of the professional club and the television broadcaster, or the company that has an investment stake, is no longer important. This is the reason why this model is also referred to as MCMMG. The above information is summarized in Figure 7.1, where the authors list the most significant revenues of professional football clubs in both models defined.

Globalisation of football

The essential difference between the traditional professional sports model and the contemporary professional sports model is related to the globalisation of professional sports. Compared to other sports, football has advanced most in this respect. It has become the only truly global sport in the world. Not only is football played in almost every country, but it is the most popular sport worldwide. It is no wonder that football provides a perfect insight into various globalisation processes, i.e. the ever-increasing interconnection of people, products, and values all over the world. European professional football, especially, has been affected by globalisation. It is based in Europe where players from all continents play in the richest leagues (Mudde, 2017).

According to Beek, Ernest, and Verschueren (2018), the following are the most important globalisation trends in football: geographical globalisation, commercial globalisation, and digital globalisation. Geographical globalisation has been influenced mainly by the migration of professional football players in Europe after the Bosman affair. Since 1995, professional football players have been considered to be employees who should not be prohibited from moving to another club after the termination of their contract. Moreover, their home clubs are not eligible for any financial compensation. The verdict also removed the existing limitation on the number of foreigners in European leagues as, according to the court decision, this contradicts the principle of free movement of labour in the EU countries (Hamernik, 2007).

Commercial globalisation is related to the development of social and cultural relationships, which essentially influence the demand for, and offer of, work in European football. Wages of elite players and coaches have increased at a fast pace. The revenue mix of professional clubs has also changed significantly. Gate receipts have declined as a percentage of overall revenue, while the revenues from the sales of broadcasting rights have substantially increased (UEFA, 2019). The approach of sponsors and investors also changes with the ever-increasing commercialisation of football. Local organisations at one time, football clubs are becoming global brands which are more and more often supported by foreign investors. In England, the cradle of football, the majority of first and second league clubs are owned by foreigners (Cleland, 2017). Private investments also flow to other elite league competitions with the aim to acquire at least partial ownership. According to Ghemawat (2017), this is the most important condition which reduces the differences among countries and contributes significantly to commercial globalisation.

According to Beek, Ernest, and Verschueren (2018), digital globalisation started to gain importance with the birth of satellite television. Football became interesting for new sponsors who intended to present their brand to spectators watching television rather than to spectators on a stadium tribune. Marketing strategies have changed and the pressure on managers responsible for finding the right sponsors and orchestrating cooperation with many social entities has grown. This has intensified with the advancement of the Internet and social networks like Facebook, Twitter, and Instagram. These platforms have extended the reach of media and marketing communication, as customers need only to switch on their computer, laptop, or smartphone. They can watch football matches online on their devices and be in contact with other fans at the same time. Numerous other digital innovations are being developed, e.g. LED screens available to referees on the pitch where they can review their decisions with the help of the video assistant referee (VAR). Bringing digital globalisation to another level, FIFA's computer games and Pro Evolution Soccer have gradually become a self-contained phenomenon (e-sport) (Beek, Ernest & Verschueren, 2018).

The way fans discuss football determines its dynamics and predetermines social changes in the new media era. Digital communication induces a feeling of fellowship to communities due to which fans can share their experience during matches both in and out of the stadium. The power of social networks to appeal to millions of people is now changing the game mainly in marketing. In football, this form of influencing people is becoming more and more dominating and all-embracing. More number of professional football clubs invest in the creation of databases with the help of which they can better understand their fans and this makes it possible for them to discover new advertising opportunities (Beek, Ernest & Verschueren, 2018). According to Scelles and Andreff (2017), marketing is necessary to optimise club revenues and therefore requires support from specialists in its thinking and implementation. They add, however, that this reflection on engaging clubs in modernity must be done with respect for their past and lend value to their historical sports performances.

Goals of a professional football club

Goals of sports clubs can be assessed from several aspects. Quirk, Fort, and Fort (1997) described two basic goals of professional sports clubs – profit and reward. The authors explain *Profit* as the difference between revenues and expenses and, thus, as a purely economic indicator. As described above, professional football clubs can be considered to be businesses and their profit orientation is, therefore, natural. To say that profit maximisation is the only and crucial objective of each club would be misleading. It is obvious in the professional football environment, and in Europe in particular, that clubs and their owners are willing to spend considerable sums of money (often exceeding the revenues) on achieving the desired sports results – victory in the league, qualification for Cups or, possibly, being rescued in the league. This goal is described by the authors as *Reward*.

There are many individuals in the sports business who are very competitive and enjoy winning. Social recognition and profit may not be their priority. For these individuals, reward resulting from excellent sport achievement takes different forms, e.g. increasing fame, getting new business contacts, or achieving a better position for negotiating with banks and other institutions (Novotny, 2011). Caslavova (2009) classified goals of a sports club into three categories – sport goals, economic goals, and social goals – and formulated long-term, medium-term, and short-term goals for each of them. According to Sima (2019), the classification can be further specified in the professional football environment as follows:

Sport goals. These goals are mainly connected with a good position in the league or European cups. Logically, not all clubs share the same goal as they are aware of their potential with regard to their economic background and the quality of their roster. Some clubs declare their goal to win the league title or qualify for European competitions before the season starts, others are happy to "nestle" in the middle of the league table, and some make no secret of their struggle to remain in the competition. Sport goals can comprise other sport activities like support of talent in youth and junior competitions.

Economic goals. Each club sets economic goals mainly out of the necessity to ensure its financial resources. The club's management assumes the task to raise enough funds to cover the budget for one season and, also, to ensure the long-term sustainability of the club. The fact that spiralling costs, mainly staff expenditure, are perceived as an investment that will guarantee higher revenues in the future is a specificity of this environment. Therefore, partial goals can include investments in the roster and technical staff, marketing support, construction of sports facilities, reconstruction of player and spectator amenities etc.

Social goals. Although it may sound like a cliché considering the current form of professional football and its commercialisation, football is played for fans. In spite of this, it is repeatedly and often declared by clubs and both national and international associations. Football – both professional and non-professional – should bring people together, stimulate their positive emotions and satisfaction with being fans of their club, motivate them to support their club on a long-term basis, and to identify themselves with the club. Traditionally, fans demonstrate their passion for the club by their presence in the stadium, by purchasing the club's merchandise and, currently, also by their active support on the club's website. Social networks especially are the main means for clubs to communicate with their fans. The purpose of these activities is not to sell the club's services or merchandise, but to build awareness and image for the club. Establishing new trends of communication with fans or support to the existing ones is, thus, an example of a social goal. According to Sima (2019), the goals described above influence and support one another.

Achieving an excellent result in the given competition means to meet a sports goal that increases the club's revenues in the form of prize money received from the organiser and bring higher revenue from the sales of broadcasting rights. The income from selling players who achieved the success, typical for economically less advanced competitions, may also increase. Resources generated in this way can be used to hire new players and coaches whose task is to achieve the same or even better result. It has been proven that excellent sport performance and results boost fans' interest in the club (social goal). They help create a better atmosphere in the stadium contributing to sporting success ("the twelfth player"). Moreover, a higher number of supporters finds a direct expression in the sales of tickets, snacks, and club's merchandise. Club merchandise is sold in the stadium and official fan shops, but mainly over the Internet to fans all over the world. The crucial importance of the fans' interest in the team manifests itself in higher attractiveness of cooperation with the club for sponsors. The road to a larger inflow of fans, however, does not go through only meeting sports goals. Clubs spend considerable resources on attracting fans, and players are also selected according to their marketing value (Sima, 2019).

Model of economic flows in European football clubs

The suggested model is based on a review and analysis of reference literature, football regulations, and financial reporting of professional football clubs. Semi-structured interviews have been conducted with representatives of European

Economic flows in European football clubs 109

professional football clubs to collect necessary additional information on relationships among the club and other stakeholders. Neither the amount of pecuniary performance, nor appropriateness of the executed consideration have been dealt with. A description of specific links between professional football clubs and their partners, including national and international associations, sponsors, fans, and TV broadcasters, is the output of the review. There, mutual relationships among these partners were also investigated. Additionally, certain attention was paid to the relationships with investors and public institutions, and operations in the transfer market were described (Figure 7.2).

A football match, or a competition including more football matches, is the main product which is traded. On a national level, this comprises a league or a cup, while on an international level, clubs can take part in the UEFA Champions League or the UEFA European League. The prize money for participation in the European cups is paid by UEFA. It is an essential source of income for all participants. The proportion made up by these premiums differs in the budgets of the participating clubs. Real Madrid, the winner of the most desired cup for victories in the Champions League (CL) in 2016, 2017, and 2018, has become the most

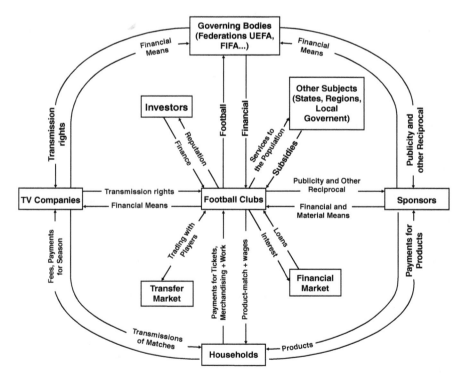

Figure 7.2 Model of economic flows in European professional football clubs.

successful club in the whole history of CL. If looked at from the perspective of proportion of the income for the team budget and compared with poorer leagues, the proportion of the budget that, for example, Slavia Prague will receive just for participation in the group will be much higher than the proportion that Real Madrid will get for winning the CL. As implied from the interviews with managers, this "paradox" may even apply to clubs which fail to qualify for the main CL competition and receive "solidarity payments" from UEFA. The purpose of these contributions is to maintain competitiveness of these clubs on the European scene. Clubs failing in the third qualifying round of the CL receive EUR 400,000 and this is an amount which, in certain extreme cases, can cover the whole budget of an economically weaker club.

Traditionally, the organisation of league competitions falls within the competence of national associations. Their role consists of the distribution of finance generated by collective selling of TV broadcasting rights, sales of advertising etc. to clubs. It has been a recent trend to exclude the top-tier competitions from the national union and allow the clubs in such top-tier competitions to decide about their sponsorship agreements and selling of broadcasting rights. Both of the interviewed managers agreed that this practice is significantly more favourable for the clubs, since the national associations are not always able to trade the rights in an efficient way. Moreover, the whole executive committee, including many members focused more on amateur football, was involved in the decision-making on important issues related to professional football.

National or international competitions are attractive for sponsors who become either direct partners of the club, or partners of the association. In the first case, sponsors usually pay for a type of advertising to approach spectators both in the stadium and in front of the television. Presentation of the sponsor's name or logo within the stadium premises or on shirts is a traditional form of cooperation. At present, contracts with sponsors also include "hospitality programmes" or bespoke activation of sponsorship. If the sponsor is a member of the organising association, advertisements are displayed during all matches and, usually, are given the best visibility. The current trends in sponsorship in European professional football include "naming rights", a form of advertising whereby a competition bears the name of its most important partner (e.g. LaLiga Santander in Spain, Fortuna Liga in the Czech Republic).

Football is played for people, for fans. This is the most usual proclamation of all clubs even though it might sound rather insincere, to say the least, as gate receipts are no longer the most significant source of finance. It should be borne in mind that a club's other revenues are also linked to fans and their support. At present, top football clubs generate huge revenues from selling the club's merchandise and this is also the reason why they frequently use new forms of communication with fans (e.g. social networks, mobile applications, etc.). Moreover, members of households in particular demand products of sponsoring companies and show their willingness to pay fees to TV companies in return for the possibility of watching their favourite team playing.

Attractive league competitions are now broadcast predominantly on private television channels. Spanish LaLiga Santander, an attractive product for many TV broadcasters all over the world, is no exception. Spanish top-tier league competition, which ranked the last among the top 5 best leagues (English Premier League, Spanish LaLiga, German Bundesliga, Italian Serie A, and French Ligue 1), used to trade the broadcasting rights for its matches individually and this resulted in huge differences in revenues from the sales of these rights among football clubs. Since the 2015/16 season, broadcasting rights have been sold collectively and the revenues have been distributed according to an agreed upon distribution formula. As in the other leagues listed above, most revenues are distributed evenly among all participants in the league. According to the manager of Real Madrid, the management of this Spanish club had expected lower revenues from the sales of TV broadcasting rights before the new policy was introduced. Eventually, their concerns proved to have been unfounded and in the 2016/17 season the Spanish mega club collected the same amount in revenues from the sales of TV broadcasting rights as in the 2014/15 season before the new system was introduced (in total, EUR 140 million). Even though collective selling of TV broadcasting rights is typical for other league competitions, there are many competitions in Europe where clubs trade the rights to broadcast their matches on their own.

The financial market gives clubs additional opportunities to access finance for their operation or new investments. Construction of a new stadium is an example of this. Thus, some room is given to investors and public institutions which can take part in the construction. Cooperation of the private and public sectors is typical for PPP (Public Private Partnership) projects, in the frame of which the stakeholders cooperate not only to jointly finance construction of a new stadium or any other facility, but also to operate and maintain it, or ensure services provided by the new facility. PPP projects were used to build stadiums for both Euro 2016 in France and the World Cup 2018 in Russia. Transfer of players is the last item on the list of considerable sources of income. As explained above, the transfer market is, in this respect, an opportunity mainly for economically weaker clubs.

Conclusion

The presented model is based on a review of reference and specialised literature, and on interviews with managers of professional football clubs. Having performed long-term analyses of top professional football clubs, auditing company Deloitte classifies their income into three categories – *matchday*, *broadcast*, and *commercial*. *Matchday* includes revenues generated on the day on which the match is played, i.e. gate receipts (including the share in the sales of season tickets), and sales of snacks and club merchandise sold on matchday in the stadium. *Broadcast* represents the share in the sales of TV broadcasting rights for the domestic competition and, also, European club competitions. *Commercial* includes mainly revenues from sponsorship and merchandising, including premiums for participation in the European cups. In the 2016/17 season, these commercial revenues accounted for, on average, the biggest part of income in all first league football clubs in Europe (UEFA, 2019).

Having a list of the main revenue items is essential to understand the different structure of total revenue generated by the followed clubs. Revenues from *commercial* prevail especially if revenues from participation in European club competitions are included. Net income from the player's purchase/sale balance is a separate category. For economically advanced clubs, this item is not significant, or it is almost never a positive number. Mostly, rich clubs spend more on buying players than what they get for selling them. It is different for clubs playing in average and smaller league competitions. This is also confirmed by the UEFA Report (2019) stating that the clubs in smaller leagues (outside the richest top 20) reported that their revenues from transfers were, on average, double compared to what they spent on purchase and that their net gains were equivalent to approximately 20% of their total revenue. This can be interpreted as evidence that the transfer market serves as an indirect tool of financial solidarity between the economically stronger and weaker clubs.

The managers confirmed the relations in the suggested model, as indicated above, especially that the amount and percentage of finance generated by means of these links differ. The link perceived by the managers of football clubs as essential is the relationship with spectators, sponsors, and the umbrella association, the organiser of the lucrative CL and European League. Any direct relation with TV broadcasting companies is not important any more as the practice of collective trading of the rights for both domestic and foreign competitions has become the prevailing trend of the recent years. Clubs, however, do not question the importance of the media. Rather than traditional media, they rely on the so-called new media as a means to communicate with their fans. For all the managers who were interviewed, sporting success is a prerequisite for successful marketing.

The ever-growing globalisation and also commercialisation of football was a widely discussed issue. Partners of top football clubs are no longer local companies residing in the vicinity of the sponsored club, they are described by Andreff and Staudohar (2000), but they are international corporations, often with their headquarters in another country. Nowadays relation between households and corporations is not understood as a connection with the club's fan who buys a matchday ticket or a season ticket. For mega clubs like Real Madrid, support from fans outside Spain and even outside Europe is important. The sales manager of Real Madrid said that most revenues from merchandising were from sales in Asia. Only 5% of the amount was collected in Spain and most often, from tourists. The popularity of a club (or attractiveness of the whole competition) is an essential factor for all the links described above. Clubs are aware of this and, therefore, the importance of marketing continues to grow. The banal and sometimes questionable slogan "Fan First" is still valid.

Acknowledgement

This work was supported by the scientific branch development program PRO-GRESS [Q19] at the Charles University in Prague.

References

Andreff, W., & Staudohar, P. D. (2000). The evolving European model of professional sports finance. *Journal of Sports Economics, 1*(3), 257–276.

Beek, R. M., Ernest, M., & Verschueren, J. (2018). Defining the rules of the changing game. In *Routledge handbook of football business and management*. Retrieved from https://www.routledgehandbooks.com/doi/10.4324/9781351262804-3

Caslavova, E. (2009). *Management a marketing sportu*. Prague, Czech Republic: Olympia.

Cleland, J. (2017). The English Premier League in a global context. In *The English Premier League* (pp. 70–83). Routledge. https://doi.org/10.4324/9781315636696-6

Elliott, R. (2017). *The English Premier League: A socio-cultural analysis*. London: Routledge, Taylor & Francis Group. https://doi.org/10.4324/9781315636696

Deloitte. (2018). *Roar power. Annual Review of Football. Finance 2018*. Retrieved from https://www2.deloitte.com/content/dam/Deloitte/uk/Documents/sports-business-group/deloitte-uk-sbg-annual-review-of-football-finance-2018.PDF

Deloitte. (2019). *Bullseye. Football Money League*. Retrieved from https://www2.deloitte.com/content/dam/Deloitte/uk/Documents/sports-business-group/deloitte-uk-deloitte-football-money-league-2019.pdf.

FIFA. (2007). *FIFA Big Count 2006. FIFA Communication Division*. Retrieved from https://resources.fifa.com/image/upload/big-count-summary-report-association-520044.pdf?cloudid=vrnjcgakvf7nds6sl5rx.

FIFA. (2018). *Global Club Football 2018 Report*. Retrieved from https://resources.fifa.com/image/upload/fifa-global-club-football-report-2018-web.pdf?cloudid=plstmtbjzbps7c2vkfir.

Ghemawat, P. (2017). *The laws of globalization and business applications*. Cambridge: Cambridge University Press. https://doi.org/10.1017/9781316678503

Gimet, C., & Montchaud, S. (2016). What drives European Football Clubs' stock returns and volatility? *International Journal of the Economics of Business, 23*(3), 351–390.

Hamernik, P. (2007). *Sportovní právo s mezinárodním prvkem*. Prague, Czech Republic: Auditorium.

Kanter, J. (2018). Amazon just made history by buying rights to show live Premier League games. *Business Insider*. Retrieved from https://www.businessinsider.in/amazon-just-made-history-by-buying-rights-to-show-live-premier-league-games/articleshow/64494249.cms.

Mudde, C. (2017). *Football and globalization: The EURO 2016 in numbers*. Huffpost. Retrieved from https://www.huffpost.com/entry/football-and-globalizatio_b_10424170.

Novotny, J. (2011). *Sport v ekonomice*. Prague, Czech Republic: Wolters Kluwer.

Pedersen, P. (Ed.). (2017). *Routledge handbook of sport communication*. London, UK: Routledge.

Peeters, T., & Szymanski, S. (2014). Financial fair play in European football. *Economic Policy, 29*(78), 343–390.

Preuss, H., Haugen, K., & Schubert, M. (2014). UEFA financial fair play: The curse of regulation. *European Journal of Sport Studies, 2*(1), 33–51.

Quirk, J., Fort, R. D., & Fort, R. (1997). *Pay dirt: The business of professional team sports.* Princeton, NJ: Princeton University.

Scelles, N., & Andreff, W. (2017). Economic model of a professional football club in France. In *Routledge handbook of football marketing* (pp. 60–72). Routledge. https://www.routledgehandbooks.com/doi/10.4324/9781315267203.ch2

Sima, J. (2019). *Ekonomika evropských profesionálních fotbalových klubů a soutěží.* Prague, Czech Republic: Ekopress.

Statista. (2019). *Total revenue generated from sports merchandising worldwide from 2006 to 2015.* Retrieved from https://www.statista.com/statistics/269797/worldwide-revenue-from-sports-merchandising/.

UEFA. (2019). The European Club Footballing Landscape. Club Licensing Benchmarking Report Financial Year 2017. Retrieved from https://www.uefa.com/MultmediaFiles/Download/OfficialDocument/uefaorg/Clublicensing/02/63/79/75/2637975_DOWNLOAD.pdf.

Chapter 8

Efficiency of financial investment in Formula One racing

A new era in motor sport

William Oster and Brandon Mastromartino

Introduction

To be a F1 driver, one must possess an elite level of stamina, physical strength, and agility, all of which are qualities that could be used to define an athlete (Potkanowicz & Mendel, 2013; Yeung, 2017). The stamina and strength of these drivers truly rival athletes of any sport in the world, mainly due to the extreme gravitational force equivalent, more commonly known as G-Force, that these drivers experience. A G-Force is the force acting on a body as a result of acceleration or gravity, meaning that a G-Force of 1G is the normal gravitational pull that we experience here on earth. F1 drivers today can experience around 5G when taking corners; putting that into perspective a high-end commercial road car may allow for a driver to feel 1.2–1.3G, and almost all of this force is put onto the head and neck of the driver (Saunders, 2017). The head of a driver, including the helmet, weighs approximately 15 lbs, and that multiplied by the G-Force means that the driver is relying on their neck strength to keep nearly 80 lbs upright while entering a turn at a high rate of speed (Auty, 2017).

If a non-trained driver was put behind the wheel of a F1 car, it would just be a matter of a few laps before they would be physically unable to hold their head up enough to actually see the road. However, F1 drivers do this for approximately two hours on a race day, experiencing high levels of G-Force up to 20 times a lap, and sometimes in brutal heat and weather conditions. Due to this, the focal part of a F1 driver's training includes exercises that are designed to strengthen and build stamina in their neck muscles (Rosalie & Malone, 2018). Additionally, these drivers must apply an extreme force when braking, as there is no assisted braking system like there is in a normal road car. This means that drivers need to apply up to 175 lbs of pressure to the brake pedal in order to slow properly (Auty, 2017).

F1 drivers are agile in the sense of their incredible reaction times. When braking at speeds of 200 mph, braking just a tenth of a second too late can be the difference between taking the apex of the corner versus crashing into the back of the car ahead, ending the driver's race. When attempting to overtake another vehicle or defend a position at these high speeds, failure to maintain focus and

DOI: 10.4324/9781003213673-8

reaction speed can also result in crashes. Additionally, these drivers must have great reaction times off the line, as each race begins with a starting light system, which is random every time. Reaction times also play a key role when shifting gears, as being too slow to shift can take time off of a lap, which is a big deal when tenths of a second can mean the difference in the results of a race (Jutley, 2003). Due to all of these factors, it seems clear that F1 drivers fit the mold of an athlete, and thus F1 should be considered a sport.

Overview and history of F1

Formula One is the highest class of single-seater auto racing that is sanctioned by the Fédération Internationale de l'Automobile (FIA) and is owned by the Formula One Group, which exercises the sport's commercial rights. The sport has grown exponentially over the decades, largely under the leadership of Bernie Ecclestone (Ciolfi & Stuart, 2013), and ultimately lead to Liberty Media purchasing Formula One Group for $4.6 billion in 2017. Formula One cars are the fastest road racing cars in the world, with an unmatched combination of engine power and downforce for turning corners, making this the absolute pinnacle of motor sport for millions of fans across the world (Mastromartino, 2020). The races are referred to as "Grands Prix" and take place either on specifically built circuits or on public roads throughout major cities, making for an incredible backdrop as these cars race around metropolitan areas at speeds reaching 210 mph and higher. There are traditionally 21 races in a year, each in a different country, with 11 out of 21 taking place in Europe.

The inaugural F1 season took place in 1950, a seven-race season that featured automobiles that are certainly quite different from what is seen today. Most of the cars in the early years were developed and raced by small scale private racing companies, however the sport quickly saw an influx of major manufacturers, such as Ferrari, enter the scene and that changed the sport forever. The evolution of this sport and just what the cars have become capable of is one of the more fascinating aspects of Formula One. There have been all sorts of engines used, from V6 to V12, with everything in between. There have been technological developments that have transferred from the track to the public sphere, with the lightweight materials used for these vehicles as well as different electronic technologies (Young, 2012). One of the most important changes over time to these vehicles comes from a safety standpoint (Lippi et al., 2007). Early iterations of F1 cars were severely lacking in this area as many of the sport's 26 driver deaths were in the first 30 years of racing. In fact, before the unfortunate death of Jules Bianchi in 2014 as a result of a collision with a safety vehicle off-track, the most recent F1 driver death came in 1994 with the legendary Ayrton Senna's passing. This was a true turning point in the sport, as drivers demanded additional steps and measures be taken to provide for a safer racing environment.

Team-based structure of F1

Over the 70 years of F1 there have been many different structures in terms of number of cars and teams. Essentially, there are ten "teams", which can be more formally referred to as manufacturers, and these teams each employ two drivers to race their two car slots throughout the season, leading to a 20-car racing field in each of the 21 races. Now, while two drivers for a team are referred to as "teammates", they are often each other's biggest rivals as they drive the same machines with the same quality parts, leading to direct comparisons to one another. Additionally, a team will often pick a lead driver who will receive the benefit of a better pit stop strategy, among other things, which can certainly lead to tension as egos clash. The reason why those teammates will be compared to each other a lot more closely than to other drivers in the field is a very important point to understand in this paper.

Unlike other forms of motor sport around the world, F1 teams are not regulated to manufacture cars in the same exact way that would result in an entire field of very similarly performing cars. Rather, teams are given a set of technical regulations by the FIA for the season with certain specifications for the car's chassis and engine, among other areas. At that point, it is completely up to the team to manufacture a car in the way they see fit and is compliant with those regulations. Additionally, up to this point in F1 history, there have not been any spending regulations for teams, meaning that teams with a better financial backing are often able to produce a faster and more reliable car (Mourão, 2017). They are able to do that by hiring higher quality technical directors and engineers, along with investing in higher quality materials that yield a better result on track. Teams with a lower financial capability often do not have as many engineers employed, and sometimes do not have the capability to actually produce their own parts inhouse, so they have to outsource the manufacturing of many of their parts. All of this is why teammates are compared so much throughout a season especially since all these cars are very different, with some teams focusing more on engine power than aerodynamics and vice versa, leaving no two teams with an exactly comparable car.

The Drivers' Championship and the Constructors' Championship are the two championships being sought after throughout an F1 season. Both of these championships are decided by points, and points are earned through on-track race results. The top-ten finishers of a Grand Prix being the only ones that are awarded these points, with the winner receiving 25, second place receiving 18, with 15, 12, 10, 8, 6, 4, 2, and 1 points for positions 3 through 10 for each and every competition. The Drivers' Championship is the competition for the best individual driver for a season, with the highest individual point earner claiming that trophy at the end of the year. The Constructors' Championship is a team-based competition, with the points that a team's drivers earn adding together to count for this competition. The team with the highest number of combined driver points wins this award, which is why it is important to have two very skilled drivers on a team.

The importance of winning in F1

The Constructors' Championship is of vital importance to these teams, as it directly correlates to the performance based tiered payout system that F1 disburses to teams at the end of a season (Judde et al., 2013). Currently, every team receives a fixed $35 million from F1, yet the difference in overall payouts once performance and popularity payouts are considered produces an approximate $150 million difference between the highest and lowest earning team, as shown in the chart below, with a column for the corresponding season's budget and standings for reference (Sportekz, 2020). The order of the payouts appears to be not that different from the 2019 standings (Table 8.1).

Note that this is payout from F1 and certainly not all the revenue that a team brings in, as they have many sponsors and other sources of revenue that help make them profitable. However, just as with the F1 disbursement, there is a correlation between winning and revenue generation capacity for a team through these other avenues. Sponsorships are the largest source of revenue for F1 (Cobbs et al., 2017), having received $30 billion from sponsors over the last 15 years (Sylt, 2019). These sponsors include team sponsorships, which include naming rights and decals on the most visible part of the cars, and made up 44.7% of F1's sponsorship revenue. There are also payments from team owners in exchange for branding, which represented 38.9% of F1's haul, followed by 12.6% from series partners such as Heineken and Rolex, that are featured in a specific way at every Grand Prix. Additionally, there are trackside advertisements from individual races that make up 3.8% of F1's sponsorship haul (Sylt, 2019). The team sponsorship, which makes up the highest percentage of sponsorship revenue, is the most relevant to this section, as it directly ties in with a team's performance.

While specific sponsorship deals are not made readily available to the public, it is logical that the better teams would attract sponsors that would be willing and able to pay more for naming rights and decals on the car. This is due to the fact that there are more eyeballs on these front running teams, along with a prestige

Table 8.1 Order of the Payouts from the 2019 Standings

Team Name	2019 Season Payout	2019 Season Budget	2019 Standings
Ferrari	$205 million	$463 million	2
Mercedes	$177 million	$484 million	1
McLaren	$152 million	$269 million	4
Red Bull Racing	$100 million	$445 million	3
Renault	$73 million	$272 million	5
Haas	$70 million	$173 million	9
Williams	$60 million	$132 million	10
Racing Point	$59 million	$188 million	7
Alfa Romeo	$56 million	$141 million	8
Toro Rosso	$52 million	$138 million	6

factor that goes with being associated with a top team in F1, or one that has a great history and reputation (Jensen & Cobbs, 2014). In 2019, F1 reached a total audience of 1.9 billion people, a truly astounding number that would be attractive to any sponsor (F1, 2020). The battles going on for the top positions in a Grand Prix dominate all the air time, with the back markers really only being shown on camera if there is a crash or if they are being lapped by the leaders. "Pay Drivers" have become a popular way for teams to bring in additional sponsorship revenue as well. This term refers to drivers who can bring to the table a great deal of personal sponsorships or other financial backing, in exchange for a driver's seat in F1. Examples of this in the recent past include Sergio Perez, who has significant financial backing from both the Mexican government as well as one of the richest men in the world, Carlos Slim (Mattocks, 2019). Another example of this would be Lance Stroll, whose billionaire father invested heavily in the meager Williams team in order for his son to obtain his first seat in F1. This type of sponsorship is one that usually comes with criticism, and may be one that is not seen as much in the future for reasons that will be discussed later in the paper.

There is also a prevalent type of partnership in F1 that does not include the transfer of money, but rather the transfer of technology. Technology is vital in F1, as in each car there are 1.3 kilometers of wiring and around 300 sensors that can give around 1,000 readings per second back to the engineers in the paddock (Sylt, 2019). Thus, an area for mutually beneficial partnerships has arose, with various technology based companies using F1 to test their equipment in a high pressure and demanding environment, that will serve to benefit their commercial products. In exchange, teams get the benefit of having their performance increased by working with some of the best companies in their respective fields. Examples of these partnerships include Williams and British Telecoms, McLaren and Dell Technologies, Mercedes and Petronas, and many more (Mattocks, 2019). This also acts as a way for these technology companies to have the prestige of working with an F1 team, something that can be very valuable when they are selling their industrial and commercial products. Thus it would make sense that they would prefer to be associated with a winning team, leading to the higher performing teams getting their pick when it comes to these partnerships.

Unlike most businesses, profit is not the benchmark for a team's success in F1. This is especially true for teams' whose owner is a company that sells a product, such as Mercedes, Ferrari, and Red Bull. These teams may struggle to break even from a pure accounting standpoint as a team, given how much more they spend compared to other teams, but they benefit in other areas significantly due to their success on track. One of these areas is the television exposure their logos get during the race, which is known as the Advertising Value Equivalent (AVE), which is a measure of how much the team's partners would have had to pay for a similar amount of on-screen exposure. According to Mercedes, its team made a $17.2 million net profit in 2017, while generating $3.4 billion in AVE, giving the prestigious brand quite the return on investment (ROI). This ROI is a very important concept as it pertains to teams and sponsorships. Sponsors are looking for a team that can do more with their investment level than others. Additionally, brands like Mercedes and Ferrari can use F1 as a radical testing ground to make significant technological advancements that will trickle down into their commercial vehicles. It also helps the prestige of these brands to have good results on track, as running at the back of the pack or breaking down often would reflect very poorly on their commercial vehicles.

Current landscape of F1

The current era of F1 is dominated by the three teams: Mercedes, Ferrari, and Red Bull Racing. These three teams have combined to win every single one of the last 139 races, a truly unbelievable feat that makes it tough to draw accurate comparisons with any other sport (Fair, 2020). There is also a substantial drop in team budgets after these three, something that will be looked at in-depth during the data analysis portion of the paper. Over the period of time from which data was drawn for the analysis part of this paper, from 2014 through to the 2019 season, Mercedes has won every single Constructors' Championship with either Ferrari or Red Bull Racing finishing in second place. Additionally, Mercedes has had one of their drivers win the Drivers' Championship in every single one of these years. Just knowing that information makes it is easy to understand why FIA may want to institute rule changes that would promote competitive balance, something that is not even remotely present in the current landscape of the sport. In 2019, the average budget per team was $271 million, but that number was skewed by these top three teams. As seen in the chart below, with all of the numbers in terms of millions, these teams have had substantial financial backing over that time frame (Table 8.2).

It makes sense that these three teams would have the highest budgets, as Mercedes and Ferrari are certainly two of the most successful luxury car brands in the entire world. For them, F1 serves as a way to increase their brand reputation, while having some of the world's best engineers develop technologies that could be used in some form in their commercial cars, and profit while doing so. Red Bull is a brand that is involved in many extreme sports, though they have probably seen the most success worldwide with their F1 venture, having won four consecutive Drivers' and Constructors' championships from 2010 through 2014. This was quite a feat for a team that is considered to be an outsider by many in the F1 community.

Table 8.2 Teams with Substantial Financial Backing over Time

Team Name	2019 Budget	2018 Budget	2017 Budget	2016 Budget	2015 Budget	2014 Budget	Average Budget
Mercedes	$484	$400	$390	$338	$509	$262	$397
Ferrari	$463	$410	$400	$421	$456	$358	$418
Red Bull	$445	$310	$273	$275	$510	$371	$364

Financial investment efficiency in F1   121

Table 8.3 Level of Midfield Group of Teams' Funding

Team Name	2019 Budget	2018 Budget	2017 Budget	2016 Budget	2015 Budget	2014 Budget	Average Budget
Renault	$272	$190	$187	$192	$152	$140	$189
McLaren	$269	$220	$231	$237	$507	$201	$277
Racing Point	$188	$120	$112	$114	$141	$65	$123
Haas	$173	$130	$125	$128	N/A	N/A	$139

Consider the midfield group of teams, known as the best of the rest, which in today's F1 include Renault, McLaren, Racing Point, and Haas. Their funding, while significant, is around half that of Mercedes, Ferrari, and Red Bull, as seen in the following chart, with the numbers in terms of $ millions (Table 8.3). Renault is a French automotive manufacturer that has a long history in F1, dating back to the 1970s. They have been the engine supplier to many other teams over the years and had great success as a team in 2005 and 2006, winning both the Drivers' and Constructors' Championships. They also have the advantage of being partially state-owned, by France, which helps to bring their funding to a level higher than many of their competitors. McLaren is arguably the second most storied name in F1 history, behind Ferrari, and has been in F1 since the 1960s. Over their time in F1, they have seen great success, winning eight Constructors' Championships with the last one being in 1998, and 12 Drivers' Championships with the last one being in 2008.

Racing Point and Haas are two of the newest teams in the paddock, but have solidified themselves as contenders in the midfield, and have a reputation of doing more than some of those with greater resources. Racing Point was known as Force India, from 2008 to 2018, having been forced into a sale at the end of 2018. Despite the sale, it appears as though most of the infrastructure remained the same, as the team has enjoyed strong performances over the years, finishing fourth in back to back years from 2016 to 2017. Haas F1 team is the lone American owned team, operated by Gene Haas. Haas is the newest team on the scene, with their first season in 2016. While 2019 was a struggle for them, finishing 9th in the Constructors' Championship, in 2018 they finished 5th and will look to get back to that form in the seasons to come. The team has adopted a very low-cost model of operating that has yielded a mixed response from fellow teams. The main issue some teams have with Haas, is that they do not really manufacture anything. They have chosen to form partnerships with other teams, especially Ferrari, buying so many parts from them that some say there is nothing unique or manufactured in-house by Haas. The flip side of this, is that it is very difficult for these smaller, privately owned teams to have any measure of success trying to develop and build parts in-house, so this may be their best option of surviving in F1 both financially as well as from an on-track results standpoint. Finally, the back of the pack includes the teams Alfa Romeo, Alpha Tauri, and Williams Racing. Their respective budgets are another step down from the previous midfield teams, as shown in the chart below, in terms of $ millions (Table 8.4).

Table 8.4 Financial Level of the Bottom Tier Teams

Team Name	2019 Budget	2018 Budget	2017 Budget	2016 Budget	2015 Budget	2014 Budget	Average Budget
Alfa Romeo	$141	$135	$119	$121	$112	$74	$117
Alpha Tauri	$138	$150	$125	$128	$149	$70	$127
Williams	$132	$150	$131	$134	$203	$131	$147

Alfa Romeo has a long and storied history in F1, sporadically operating as either a race team or parts supplier since the formation of F1 in 1950. They have changed their name and ownership several times over the years, but are still identified with the original team with the historic involvement in the sport. In fact, Alfa Romeo actually won the first two Drivers' Championships, before Constructors' Championships were an award. They have contributed to the success of teams that use their engines, including playing a role with Ferrari over the last decade, but unfortunately have not ever really found success as an independent team. The team was rebranded Alfa Romeo for the 2018 season, and hopes to find success as a constructor.

Alpha Tauri is a very interesting team, as they are actually also owned by Red Bull Racing. Alpha Tauri essentially acts as a junior team to Red Bull Racing, often times employing very young but promising drivers that have ended up making the jump to the senior team in the past. As seen in the charts, they receive a fraction of the funding as the senior team, oftentimes seeming to act as a testing ground for new engines or other developments. Red Bull has achieved great success through their driving academy, as some of the most talented drivers of the last 15 years have gone through their ranks, and Alpha Tauri certainly plays a role in that. It appears that Red Bull has been content with this team being a lower quality version of their senior team, with this junior team mostly finishing in the latter third of the Constructors' Championship, however in 2019 they did have a strong year as they finished 6th overall.

Williams Racing is currently the worst team on the grid, though this certainly has not always been the case. In fact, Williams is one of the most successful stories in F1, they have just been marred by inconsistency. Their history dates back to the late 1970s as a very small and independent setup which quickly grew to become a leading force in the sport, having won 9 Constructors' Championships, the last one in 1997. In fact, as recently as the 2014 and 2015 seasons they placed 3rd overall as a team, but have had quite the fall from grace, having scored just eight combined points over the 2018 and 2019 seasons. They have had a lot of trouble keeping sponsors and investors with their poor performance on-track, as well as turnover within their technical department. Williams has certainly bounced back from poor years in the past, and they hope to return to their desired form in the near future.

Incoming rule changes

Due to the wide disparity among the financial capabilities of teams, there are some monumental rule changes coming ahead of the 2021 season. Beginning that year, there will be a spending cap in place that is set at $175 million, a far cry from the nearly $300 million spent per year on average by teams (Gitlin, 2019). This cap does not include driver salaries, marketing costs, or operation costs associated with team travel to the 21 Grands Prix around the world. Thus, this financial restriction is really centered around the engineering and technical side of the sport, with the hope to prevent a team like Mercedes from having the resources to produce the best car for every track. Given the unprecedented success by the three teams with the largest budgets, the FIA believed the high correlation of more money with more points to be very true, and believed a financial restriction of this nature would be the best way to inject more unpredictability into the sport. Naturally, Mercedes, Ferrari, and Red Bull have resisted this change, but it seems to have been welcomed by most of the others in the sport. The thought is that now, there will be more parity in the sport, with anybody having a shot to win on race day and thus, an open competition for Drivers' and Constructors' Championships.

This best comparison for this would be the National Football League (NFL) salary cap. This salary cap allows a smaller market team, such as the Green Bay Packers, to compete for Super Bowls year in and year out with teams of better financial standing. This certainly does not mean that there is perfect parity across the NFL, as after 52 Super Bowls, 12 of the 32 NFL franchises have yet to win one, with 4 of those 12 never even making an appearance on the game's greatest stage. Simply restricting the money that the teams can spend does not mean that everybody now has the same chance of being successful, as there is a large human element at play, with important decisions to be made on how that money is spent. The structure of F1 has been akin to Major League Baseball in the United States, a league which has no salary cap and as a result the best teams are usually located in the biggest markets such as Los Angeles or New York, while teams in Kansas City or Oakland have to be innovative in order to find a way to compete. It is important to view this new landscape from an analytical approach to understand if and how these changes will impact competitive balance in F1.

Method

The budgets and point totals for each of the 10 teams in F1 dating back to the 2014 season is the primary data being analyzed in this study (see Table 8.5). The decision to only include data dating back to 2014 was made for a few reasons. First, the sport has changed immensely since then, especially with regard to car regulations and money that the teams spend. In order for the most comparable context and setting today, data before this time was not considered. Second, F1 is an ever-changing sport from a team and organization standpoint. Going too far back results in viewing teams that do not operate in the same manner as they do today.

Table 8.5 Data Used for the Analyses in Which All Dollar Amounts Are in Terms of $ Millions

Team Name	2019 Budget	2018 Budget	2017 Budget	2016 Budget	2015 Budget	2014 Budget	Average Budget	2019 Points	2018 Points	2017 Points	2016 Points	2015 Points	2014 Points	Average Points
Mercedes	$484	$400	$390	$338	$509	$262	$397	739	655	668	765	703	701	705.17
Ferrari	$463	$410	$400	$421	$456	$358	$418	504	571	522	398	428	216	439.83
Red Bull	$445	$310	$273	$275	$510	$371	$364	417	419	368	468	187	405	377.33
Renault	$272	$190	$187	$192	$152	$140	$189	91	122	57	8	78	10	61.00
McLaren	$269	$220	$231	$237	$507	$201	$277	145	62	30	76	27	181	86.83
Racing Point	$188	$120	$112	$114	$141	$65	$123	73	52	187	173	136	155	129.33
Haas	$173	$130	$125	$128	N/A	N/A	$139	28	93	47	29	N/A	N/A	49.25
Alfa Romeo	$141	$135	$119	$121	$112	$74	$117	57	48	5	2	36	0	24.67
Alpha Tauri	$138	$150	$125	$128	$149	$70	$127	85	33	53	63	67	30	55.17
Williams	$132	$150	$131	$134	$203	$131	$147	1	7	83	138	257	320	134.33

Going back far enough, most teams have had great success, and including that data could skew the results if those teams have not proven capable of operating at that level over the last decade. The sources for those budgets are not all the same, as neither F1 nor FIA discloses those records to the public, so they were gathered from secondary sources deemed to be reputable and accurate, such as Forbes and Bleacher Report. Several of these teams have had their name changed in the recent years, as indicated in the breakdown of the teams, but those teams still operate with the same relative budget and in the same facilities, so this data set has treated those teams as the same organizations. Additionally, Haas did not start racing until the 2016 season, so they will not have any data points for the 2015 or 2014 season, though they are the only team that will be left out in any capacity. Some of the numbers are listed in Euros and conversions to USD was conducted based on the exchange rate of that year.

The first aim of this study was to determine how much of a correlation there is between a team's budget and their points earned on-track. The idea that these two variables are highly connected may seem obvious to most people who follow the sport, but it is important to know and understand from a statistical standpoint just how much financial backing is responsible for a team's success. This was done by conducting a regression analysis in order to find the R-Squared, which is the statistical measure of variance for a dependent variable that is explained by the independent variable(s) in a regression. In this analysis, the dependent variable was the points earned by the teams, and the independent variable is the teams' budgets. It was designed this way because it is thought that a team's budget explains their race results, thus their points earned are dependent on how much they spend. Ideally, there would be multiple independent variables, however in this case it is quite difficult to obtain meaningful quantitative variables for each of the teams that would be applicable to this model.

The second aim of this study was to better understand the efficiency of the F1 teams, essentially taking a look at who is getting the most value for their spending. While Mercedes has amassed the most points annually during the time period this study examines, a lower performing team could be earning more points per million dollars spent, which would indicate they could be positioned to contend for a championship once the rule changes are implemented. Having the quality of efficiency is arguably going to be the most important thing for these teams moving forward into this new era of F1. With everybody on the same playing field from a financial standpoint, a team that can do the most within the new budget structure will certainly have more success than those which are inefficient. Upon discovering exactly how these teams rank against one another from an efficiency standpoint, there will be an interpretation of those results and a discussion as to which teams may rise or fall in the standings in the wake of these rule changes, as well as possible limitations to the study that are difficult to account for in a data analysis.

Results

Regression analyses revealed that the corresponding teams' budgets over time frame were significantly predictive of the average points earned from 2014 to 2019 (R^2 = .75; β = .71; SEE = 121.04; p < .001). A regression analysis was conducted for the 2019 season only, just for comparison purposes. The corresponding teams' budgets were also significantly predictive of the average points earned (R^2 = .88; β = .86; SEE = 96.61; p < .001), indicating stronger relationships. An analysis of each teams' efficiency was done by determining the points earned per 1 million dollars spent. To do this, the average points earned by a team from 2014 to 2019 were divided by the average budget of that team over the same time frame, giving a ratio for each team. Following that, just as with the regression, the same steps were applied to strictly the 2019 season for comparison as well as to possibly draw conclusions from the most recent data available (Tables 8.6 and 8.7).

Table 8.6 Analysis of Each Team's Efficiency in Terms of Budget and Average Points Earned (2014–2019)

Team Name	Points per Million Dollars (2014–2019)
Mercedes	1.78
Ferrari	1.05
Red Bull	1.04
Renault	0.32
McLaren	0.31
Racing Point	1.05
Haas	0.35
Alfa Romeo	0.21
Alpha Tauri	0.44
Williams	0.92

Table 8.7 Analysis of Each Team's Efficiency in Terms of Budget and Average Points Earned (2019)

Team Name	Points per Million Dollars (2019)
Mercedes	1.53
Ferrari	1.09
Red Bull	0.94
Renault	0.33
McLaren	0.54
Racing Point	0.39
Haas	0.16
Alfa Romeo	0.40
Alpha Tauri	0.62
Williams	0.01

Discussion

The results from this study lend some valuable information that could be used to predict the future standings in the new era of Formula One racing. The purpose of the regression analysis using the data from 2014 to 2019 was to determine how much of a team's points earned were explained by their respective budgets. This test was statistically significant and indicated that approximately 74.5% of the points earned by a team were explained by their budget. In the second regression analysis examining just the 2019 season, it resulted in a higher R-Squared of 0.875, meaning 87.5% of last season's results were explained by the independent variable (team budget). However, given that this was just the result of one season's worth of data, this will not factor in too much in the subsequent predictions.

These regression results show that the assumption that more money translates to more points is supported by data. From a quantitative standpoint, the coefficients table shows us that with every $1 million spent after $100 million spent, adds approximately 1.60 points to a team's season result. The ability for teams to have information like this is very important, as it can allow them to make accurate cost-benefit analyses to determine how much money they should spend to compete at a certain level. Of course, with the new financial regulations, this particular data point will be greatly changed, but it is important to look back and view the quantitative impact that a team's budget has had on their performance in order to adjust to the new rules accordingly.

With regard to efficiency, the higher the metric, the more efficient the team (see Tables 8.6 and 8.7). Another way to think about this is that the number represents a return on investment, with some of these teams performing at a higher level than where their corresponding financial backing is. Mercedes is by far, the leader on both charts, with Ferrari and Red Bull trailing at a distance, but competing neck to neck with each other. After those teams, in the 2014–2019 seasons, most teams are somewhere between .20 and .45, with Racing Point and Williams sticking out far above the pack, with 1.05 and .92 scores, respectively. It is very impressive that Williams would out-perform so many in this regard, given their historically poor performances. It is less surprising that Racing Point ranks well against other teams in this regard, given their aforementioned reputation for being able to do more than many of their competitors, especially with fewer resources. Additionally, for the 2019 season alone, apart from the "big three", Alpha Tauri and McLaren stick out as leaders in efficiency.

As the landscape of F1 is ever-changing, with ownership and technical directors seemingly in a constant state of flux, these predictions may only be applicable for the first season or two under the new rules, as teams will certainly adjust to these new budget restrictions after that. Additionally, it is assumed that the lowest funded teams will attempt to increase their budgets as much as they can now that everybody has a chance to compete. Given the information at hand, primarily consulting the 2014–2019 efficiency chart, Racing Point, Williams, and Alpha

Tauri should be the three teams most likely to make a big jump in performance in the upcoming seasons.

Given Racing Point's performance on a moderate budget over the years, including the 2019 budget which was very close to what they will have to operate on in 2021, it appears as though they are the most likely team from the midfield to break into the top three standings. The fact that they were right there competing with Red Bull and Ferrari from an efficiency standpoint is indicative of very good things for them in the future. While 2019 was a bit of a dip for them performance wise, that is certainly something that happens from time to time in the sport, as unexpected circumstances can arise. Given Williams' disastrous results in 2018 and 2019, it is tough to imagine them bouncing back and being in the fray for a championship anytime soon, but they have shown themselves capable of doing it in the past and on a more even playing field and hence, with their resourcefulness and efficiency, they may be able to rise again. Given their history and prestige as an organization, they can certainly acquire top talent in the technical department, and now they will not have to worry about being outbid by the top teams for that talent. Additionally, their lower manufacturing capabilities should be offset with so many teams being brought down closer to their financial status. It may not be a coincidence that both of these teams run on Mercedes power units, arguably the highest quality power unit on a yearly basis in F1 over the recent years, as that may turn out to be a key partnership for them moving forward.

Alpha Tauri is perhaps the most interesting team to keep an eye on in the following seasons. Now that the senior team, Red Bull Racing, will have their budget significantly cut, will some of that funding find its way to the junior team? If Alpha Tauri does indeed see their budget increase closer to the $175 million cap, there is a very good chance that they will find success, as they have been in very good form recently. They have always had the benefit of having young, star drivers at the wheel of their vehicles, something that does not appear to be changing anytime soon as the Red Bull Driving Academy is still one of the best in the world. With drivers of such high quality in a more even field, they could see their standing in the grid change significantly. However, there may be discussions at Red Bull if they want to see that happen, as they may not want their two teams battling at every Grand Prix and taking points from one another, making it much more difficult to win a championship. This could be a very difficult relationship to manage for Red Bull, as with a relatively even field those in charge of Alpha Tauri may no longer be content with being the test team for new power units and designs, and may voice their desire to compete at the same level as the senior team.

The other big unknown moving forward is what is going to happen to Mercedes, Ferrari, and Red Bull, in terms of their on-track results. From the results of this study, it is clear that they are very proficient at being top of the line F1 teams. However, their impending budget cuts have the potential to expose any weaknesses that have been covered up by their immense spending. Given their efficiency, as supported by the data, these three teams should certainly still expect to perform very well, provided that they can bring their operations to scale which will not be an easy task. It is unlikely that these teams will continue their uncontested reign of dominance, with likely an additional three or four teams spending just as much as these top three teams.

The impact that a quality driver has for a team will be of much more importance beginning in 2021 as driver salaries will not be counted toward the team's budget. Thus, teams that have been operating well above the future budget cap, such as Mercedes, Ferrari, Red Bull, Renault, and McLaren, would be wise to invest those funds that would have otherwise gone towards research and development, into acquiring and retaining the top drivers in the sport. The days of considering a driver's marketability or how many sponsors they may attract, may be over now that every team will feel like they have a chance at the championship any given year. This should ultimately be a positive change for the sport, as fewer undeserving drivers, from a pure driving ability and skill standpoint, should make the leap to F1 before they are actually ready to do so. This will hopefully only go to create more parity and uncertainty in the sport, making it more attractive and entertaining for fans.

This study comes with inherent limitations that should be considered by the reader. The biggest limitation of this study comes from the data itself, as the numbers are not budgets officially published by F1, thus there is a chance for some inaccurate data points. The numbers still do come from reputable sports journalism websites, and if they indeed are not 100% correct, they still provide a very good basis for the study. Also, it would have been ideal to include more independent variables in the regression analysis, but with a sport like F1 that is something really difficult to come by. Additionally, it is difficult to quantify exactly how much the top three teams will suffer from this budget cut, leading to some uncertainty in the predictions section. A lot of that is due to this rule change being unprecedented in the sport.

Overall, the results of this study provide some new insight into the efficiency of F1 team spending. For example, based on the opinions of some fans and media pundits, it seems as though many are expecting Renault and McLaren to start winning championships again, which is certainly understandable given their respective histories. However, the results of this study contradict that way of thinking. There is a great deal of uncertainty in the future of F1, and this can lend an understanding of what may come in the new era of the sport. It will be very interesting to see how these new financial restrictions actually impact the standings moving forward, and if the efficiency metrics from this study can be viewed as an accurate indicator.

References

Auty, B. (2017, October 3). Formula 1: Are F1 drivers considered athletes? Retrieved from https://bleacherreport.com/articles/30864-formula-1-are-f1-drivers-considered-athletes

Ciolfi, J. L., & Stuart S. (2013). Organizational succession in F1: An analysis of Bernie Ecclestone's roles as CEO of Formula One management. *International Journal of Motorsport Management*, 2(1), 1.

Cobbs, J., Tyler, B. D., Jensen, J. A., & Chan, K. (2017). Prioritizing sponsorship resources in Formula One racing: A longitudinal analysis. *Journal of Sport Management, 31*(1), 96–110.

F1. (2020, January 22). Formula 1 viewing figures 2019: F1 broadcast to 1.9 billion total audiences in 2019: Formula 1®. Retrieved from https://www.formula1.com/en/latest/article.f1-broadcast-to-1-9-billion-fans-in-2019.4IeYkWSoexxSIeJyuTrk22.html

Fair, A. (2020, April 4). Formula 1: The last time Mercedes, Ferrari or Red Bull Racing didn't win. Retrieved from https://beyondtheflag.com/2020/04/04/formula-1-last-time-mercedes-ferrari-red-bull-racing-didnt-win/

George, D. (2019, December 20). Amid Budget Cap for 2021, how much is the current budget of teams in 2019? Retrieved from https://www.essentiallysports.com/what-are-the-budgets-for-all-10-formula-one-teams-2019/

Gitlin, J. M. (2019, November 4). Formula 1 gets radical new rules for 2021, plus a budget cap. Retrieved from https://arstechnica.com/cars/2019/11/formula-1-gets-radical-new-rules-for-2021-plus-a-budget-cap/

Jensen, J. A., & Cobbs, J. B. (2014). Predicting return on investment in sport sponsorship: Modeling brand exposure, price, and ROI in Formula One automotive competition. *Journal of Advertising Research, 54*(4), 435–447.

Judde, C., Booth, R., & Brooks, R. (2013). Second place is first of the losers: An analysis of competitive balance in Formula One. *Journal of Sports Economics, 14*(4), 411–439.

Jutley, R. S. *Fit for Motor Sport: Improve Your Race Performance with Better Physical and Mental Training: With a Chapter on Motorsport Medical Emergency Procedures.* Somerset: Haynes Pub., 2003.

Lippi, G., Salvagno, G. L., Franchini, M., & Guidi, G. C. (2007). Changes in technical regulations and drivers' safety in top-class motor sports. *British Journal of Sports Medicine, 41*(12), 922–925.

Mastromartino, B. (2020). Motor sports. In J. Nauright & Zipp, S. (Eds.), *Routledge Handbook of Global Sports* (pp. 302–311). London, UK: Routledge.

Mattocks, H. (2019, April 21). Who benefits the most from F1 sponsorship: The team or the sponsor? Retrieved from https://drivetribe.com/p/who-benefits-the-most-from-f1sponsorship-QjpzASLyTl6D-sfxRsiSkw?iid=JF9FEMEoQo-fNmZZjcJloQ

Mourão, P. (2017). How to be a winning team in Formula One. In *The Economics of Motorsports* (pp. 165–201). London: Palgrave Macmillan.

Potkanowicz, E. S., & Mendel, R. W. (2013). The case for driver science in motorsport: A review and recommendations. *Sports Medicine, 43*(7), 565–574.

Rosalie, S. M., & Malone, J. M. (2018). Effect of a halo-type structure on neck muscle activation of an open-cockpit race car driver training under qualifying conditions. *Case Reports, 2018.*

Saunders, N. (2017, March 3). 2017 cars will take F1 drivers 'close to blackout point' – Pirelli. Retrieved from https://www.espn.com/f1/story/_/id/18811957/2017-cars-take-f1-drivers-close-blackout-point-pirelli

Sportekz. (2020, February 8). Formula 1 prize money 2020 winning bonus (revealed). Retrieved from https://www.sportekz.com/f1/formula-one-prize-money/

Sylt, C. (2019, April 26). Revealed: The \$285 million cost of winning the F1 championship. Retrieved from https://www.forbes.com/sites/csylt/2019/04/26/revealed-the-285-million-cost-of-winning-the-f1-championship/#e0236bd23d81

Sylt, C. (2019, May 19). Revealed: Sponsors fuel Formula One with $30 billion. Retrieved from https://www.forbes.com/sites/csylt/2019/05/19/revealed-sponsors-fuel-formula-one-with-30-billion/#2a5a19702416

Walthert, M. (2017, October 3). F1 team budgets: Which teams are getting the best value for their money in 2015? Retrieved from https://bleacherreport.com/articles/2550212-f1-team-budgets-which-teams-are-getting-the-best-value-for-their-money-in-2015

Yeung, J.-T. (2017, October 18). Scientific scribbles. Retrieved from https://blogs.unimelb.edu.au/sciencecommunication/2017/10/18/formula-1-is-not-a-sport/

Young, S. (2012). Formula One racing: Driver vs. technology. *Intersect: The Stanford Journal of Science, Technology, and Society, 5*, 1–11.

Chapter 9

Policy implications in rhythmic gymnastics judging

A case analysis

Rosa López de D'Amico and Mayerlith Canelón

Introduction

The sport judge or referee is an important component of the sport structure, their presence is essential in the sense that their absence could detract the competitive character (Guillen, 2003). In this research we work with elite athletes whose performance is expected to be properly evaluated by a qualified judge. But the judge does not value only the athlete per se, but the coaches' work, the organization's development and even the country's performance in a sport. So judges should be the guarantee of transparency and fair evaluation of the athlete's performance. The questions arise in terms of the inconsistencies and concerns that have been raised in relation to the subjective component of the judging and whether it is an aspect that is related with training or policies in place that regulate the sport. There are many cases in the world of sport, e.g. in some matches at the FIFA World Cup 2014, and in other sports (see Paiva, 2013) as well as in rhythmic gymnastics (Busbee, 2017). Several studies have looked at the judge's performance but mostly from different perspectives: competences for judges (Guardo, 2013); training (Betancort, 1999; López de D'Amico, 2001), instrument to assess judges' performance (Bobo, 2001), but not much analysis has been done towards the implications for the management of the sport.

The performance of sport referees or judges is a topic that has been discussed but little supported by literature. In rhythmic gymnastics it is a key element and this sport is characterized by its competitive art, beauty and plasticity in a composition; the audience might confuse a high technical performance, but the difference for the judges is the technical and normative character of the sport. Judging in rhythmic gymnastics, could also be considered a key factor for the advancement and development of this sport, because what is accepted as valid by the judges will become the tendency to be followed by many gymnasts. Even though the technical norms about performance are in the Code of Punctuation, the acceptance by the judges is for many coaches the validation of the work they develop. Besides that, there are many coaches that fulfil the double role of judges and coaches in this sport; it brings comments about tendencies of favouritism, preferences for particular teams and gymnasts of those judges who are also coaches.

DOI: 10.4324/9781003213673-9

In the judges' work there are many elements that are present, not just the technical elements of the code of points but feelings and values that interact when judging. Those are not just pressures; it depends on the judge's situation. When evaluating their own gymnasts, as it is facing their own work as coach, there is no surprise factor, for example, as one of the cases that can be experienced. To indicate if a judgement is positive or negative is a characteristic of axiology and considering subjectivity as a common factor in judging artistic sports besides the fact that judgements have relationship with the subject's will. So judging is more that the mere application of the Code of Points. The purpose of the study is to provide theoretical support to guide the formation of judges in rhythmic gymnastics, particularly in the axiological component as it is not included in the minimal standard requirements by the International Gymnastics Federation (FIG).

This research looks at whether the assessment of sport judgement is objective or not, correct or not, if they are right or wrong evaluations, to know why inconsistencies are visible and why the organizations in charge of the sport do not make the appropriate corrections. In consequence this denotes that professional ethics and morals have an effect on the subjective value and that it has no relationship with the evaluation system in sports, but on whom they evaluate and apply their judgment on, with particular criteria that are not subject to the sports norms; in short it is an element that has to do with values and respect. López and Arango (2002) indicate that values are created in the first years of the human being, slowly developed throughout life and they regulate the moral behaviour of the person. In consequence the formation of morals and ethics in relation to the sport judge and referee should be in place alongside the technical preparation itself. This research looks at understanding the performance of the rhythmic gymnastics judges, particularly making a reflection about the values that influence the judging process, including the responsibility of the sport organizations to guarantee fair play. The Kazan Action Plan contains three main policy areas and 20 specific ones. This research is framed in the third main area, 'protecting the integrity of sport', and particularly in the specific area III.3 i.e. foster good governance of sport organizations (MINEPS VI, 2017). Not to mention that it might also be connected with the wellbeing of the participants and protection of the participants' rights (III.1 and III.2), but for the purpose of this study it is used as a reference for the governance policy.

Review of literature

Among all the norms in sport, the well-known ones are those regulations that control the participation in the main scenario, i.e., competition. If a competition does not have regulation and judges, then the competitive character goes to a second place. Guillen (2003) indicates that the absence of the sport judge or referee represents the diminishment of the competitive character. All athletes who follow a full regimen of training and compete are expected to be evaluated by qualified people – judges – certified by the governing body of the discipline.

The theoretical framework is based on Roger Humanistic theory and Kohlberg's moral development theory. Kohlberg (1974) in the moral development theory presents three levels with two phases each; the purpose is the process that takes place in judgement so from there the moral judgements can be analyzed. Humans' moral development goes along the person's evolutionary trajectory throughout the years as well as the intellectual, cognitive, emotional and social. The intellectual evolution is strongly connected with the emotional component and the position taken in the social roles. Morality is conditioned by biological, psychological and social variables. The third level is the post conventional moral, approximately from 23 years old; the person fulfills society's perspective then is approved by all. However there is a clash with inalienable elements such as freedom; there might also arise internal confrontations between some moral and juridical norms. At this level the subject recognizes the universal norm and the actual social norms. This phase is difficult to access and it is considered to belong to philosophers. The post conventional morals based on judgement are not defined by social norms and are evident in adulthood; this idea supports this research. The universal ethical principles together with the job of the gymnastics judge should prevail in their performance.

Roger Humanist theory indicates that each person has a particular view of reality and this is precisely the focus of this theory, the private world that determines behaviour. Roger basically reviewed the semantic components such as ethics, moral and axiology. This is connected with this research as the subjective value of the sport judgement is not characteristic of the sport but of the person – in essence, for a judge in action, it is important to consider the personal characteristics of the judge. Roger refers to the 'experience sphere' as everything that happens to the individual (facts, perceptions, sensations) to which there is no consciousness at first but later there could be if concentrated in the experience. This theory was helpful in understanding the complexity of the judgement process, starting with the traditional composition of the judges, mostly coaches of the same gymnasts as judges. The personal sphere, as described in the theory, intervenes in the particular reality of each one at the moment of executing a dual function in the triad that is represented by the competition moment: it is visualized that the gymnast's performance is guided by a coach and valued by a judge.

Besides these theories and the review of the terms morality and ethics, Maslow's theory of basic needs was also studied. To be a judge of rhythmic gymnastics becomes a necessity because it is the easiest way to know in details the value of the technical elements and difficulties. In Maslow's theory, motivation is a hierarchy that is formed by five basic needs: physiological, security, belonging, esteem and self-realization, so people will have motives to satisfy any of the needs they feel is prominent in a given moment. A satisfied need generates the need to satisfy another of a higher need in the hierarchy. This is the area of Philosophy that studies the nature of values, between positive and negative, good and bad, as well as their influence. If values are analyzed from the moral point of view, then they are practical, and human beings behave self-consciously with attitudes that are relative to values. Piña (2004) indicates that values are intrinsic; they become instrumental through education and become extrinsic or social values. This means that it is possible to have a formation guided towards values.

According to Avelino (1994) the axiological behaviour of human beings exists since the origins of humanity, but the philosophical reflection about values is more recent. Humans beings are formed to grab, create and live in values; to capture the axiological dimension of the being and concrete values that already exist. Human beings live in a determined hierarchy of values; the human being is essentially axiological. Values exist even when the subject is not aware of them; they exist independent of the human being but human beings' actions are intentional. Every value has its anti-value, the presence of one or another depends on the human being's actions. For this research, the value definition chosen is from the axiological point of view, basically because through the rhythmic gymnastics judging a fair result is intended instead of an unfair one, however the appreciation could be a wrong assessment or the judge might do good work but it is not valued as such. The latter could impact on the judges' ethic considering that it is a job done in the sport field. That is why the study is centered in axiology and not in ethics or morality explicitly, even though there is relationship.

According to Bobo (2001), a system of performance indicators had to be created in order to improve the judging quality in rhythmic gymnastics; the model should respect evaluation principles such as: objectivity, validity, reliability, practical use and discrimination power. In the Olympics cycle 2005–2008 and 2009–2012 the forms used by the FIG rhythmic gymnastics technical committee for the evaluation system included some elements mentioned by Bobo. So the axiology of sport judging as an element that can influence the judgment in sport needs to be researched deeply as it can improve the general development of any sport discipline. López de D'Amico (2008) indicated that in New Zealand the national association of gymnastics has a norm that parents cannot participate as judges if their child is participating in the event. In the same sense judges who are affiliated as administrators of clubs, coaches or gymnasts, cannot be in the judges list until their period of membership is over. In a previous study, a similar situation is presented from Italy in which double roles are not allowed during the registration period (López de D'Amico, 2001).

It has to be analyzed how representative is the reality of each gymnastics judge to understand their behaviour in the judging which affects others (gymnasts, coaches, administrators and family). Due to the impact of the judging in the sporting life of a gymnast, the judge should have an element of understanding that s/he is a subject of action. When it comes to appreciation sport, also named competitive art, there is considered to be a qualitative and subjective qualification system. However, if the sport has a regulation that guides the competition then it is not subjective, because it assesses everything within the regulations and it cannot be considered qualitative as the result is in a number that is generated not by its beauty but the mastery of the sport technique. What could be subjective in the assessment process is the control of the performance by one person, wherein by human nature, subjectivity exists.

The consequences of mis-judgement are not just for the athletes, but coaches, sport organizations, states and even countries. A referee is judged daily by the sport viewers, for example in the FIFA World Cup 2014 in Brazil during the Uruguay vs. Italy match, the referee did not penalize the fault committed by the Uruguayan player Luis Suarez, who bit the Italian player Giorgio Chiellini during the game. This situation was recognized when FIFA indicated a fault against the Suarez, but what did it happen with the referee who did not use the regulation during the game? Another example of how the judge's appreciation affects sport results can be found in case of the Montreal Olympic Games at the welterweight boxing match, with the boxer José Gamarro from Venezuela. According to Paiva (2013) 'Gamarro was ripped of the gold medal' as two judges saw the Venezuelan win, two judges saw the European boxer win and the fifth judge indicated a tie but later voted for Bachfell. In this case Venezuela missed the chance of a gold medal that, through appreciation was given by a judge who at first evaluated it as a tie.

Since 1962 FIG recognized rhythmic gymnastics as a sport, and the first world championship took place in 1963. Thereafter, in 1984 it was included in the Olympic Games. In 1965, the first international judges course (Mendizabal, 2000) was celebrated and in 1970, the first Code of points was presented – this being the basic document for evaluation which is updated frequently. The formation of rhythmic gymnastics judges is administered by the Federation, following the FIG guidelines, and the periodicity is per Olympic cycle. It basically focuses on the study of the code of points and the technical regulation of the discipline. In 1970, rhythmic gymnastics was introduced in Venezuela and in 1984, the first national club championship was celebrated. It is governed by the Venezuelan Gymnastics Federation (FVG) and has been supported in various programs by the Ministry of Education as well as the Ministry of Sport since it started to be practised in the country. The training course for judges are abided by the rules of the FVG. At the moment the rhythmic gymnastics is the discipline that has more practitioners registered, but still it is not practised nationwide. In the Olympic cycle 2013–2016 just two courses were offered. Those who do not get approved might work as regional judges. In sport with subjective appreciation, the results of the competition depend on the assessment of the athlete's actions, it can be given by a person or a group in immediate results and others after the athlete's participation. For example, in Karate Do during combat, the judge gives constant judgement until the final verdict; it could be called an instant appreciation judgement. On the contrary, in gymnastics the judge assesses each movement from the beginning but it is a minute later, after the end of the full exercise, when the result is given.

In rhythmic gymnastics, by the judging characteristics, it is referred to as a subjective action or not fair. Some scandals have occurred for lack of confidence in the judging process, or even in the judging formation. In the news about the results of a competition, it was inferred that the particular judging scandal affected more than 60 persons (The New York Times, 2013). It also indicated the risk of the individual judgement and if this is a recurrent practice in the competitive field, then the power of the judges could be above athletic training and preparation. In 2015 the FIG suspended five judges after analyzing the results of the Esmirna World Championship 2014. The need for judges to be competent, independent and impartial was indicated, and that any judge not following these principles damages the image of gymnastics, not just in the face of the audience but also in opinion of athletes and coaches (El Universal, 2015).

This situation is not new, for example, before Sydney 2000, a research about the punctuations at the 1999 European championship conducted by FIG revealed generalized incompetence and conspiracy among judges. FIG prohibited eight judges from participating in the 2000 Olympic Games and six more were suspended for a year (ABC, 2004; Deporte Castilla-La Mancha, 2004). With the aforementioned facts, a question arises as to how a rhythmic gymnastics judge, a subject of poor confidence, could evaluate the work that is presented in a competition. In Venezuela during the National Sport Games 2013, the gymnasts themselves after the final award ceremony declared to the press their concern about the judges' appreciation, and two of them suggested that judges do influence results. So, the question is, whether this influence is positive or negative. Did they judge the technical quality or was the 'influence' present prior to the technical demonstration? The consequences of the judgement also affect the general development of the sport, particularly rhythmic gymnastics which is classified as competitive art, in which the performance of the winner becomes the model to follow; technically, this result becomes the target to follow by all those who want to get the best competitive result. Consequently, judges should respond in the competition to what is technically acceptable to guarantee quality in the sport.

Due to the constant questioning of the judging, the FIG developed its system to improve the evaluation system. It is called *Instant Replay and Control System* (IRCOS), with the implication that this tool had to be strategic and educative (FIG, 2004). In 2005 IRCOS began to be implemented and it provided, for the first time, the possibility to gymnasts and coaches, to impugn the difficulty grade of the judges. A camera and computer generate proof together, images that could verify decisions. The technical committee is benefited with the impact of IRCOS as they have a detailed analysis of the exercises after the competition. Consequently, judges can learn more about the evolution of the discipline, judges' behaviours, and, moreover, to reach a conclusion and rectify situations. As the IRCOS images are at the disposition of the federations, coaches, judges and audience, the analysis lead the action. This system is compulsory at intercontinental multisport events such as: Olympic Games, Junior Olympic Games, World Championships, FIG World Championship, African, Asia, Pan-American and University Games. IRCOS is the product of years of reflection by those who have administered FIG; it is sophisticated, but it has no influence on judging in the sport and the behaviour of its users.

Judges in rhythmic gymnastics have to receive their training from their national federations (NF), or FIG, for international judges. The requisites vary according to each NF, but the most fundamental one is to approve the training course for judges. The test has three components for testing: Practical Difficulty (35% approved), Practical Execution (40% approved) and Theory (75% approved) (FIG, 2013). According to the Code of Points 2013–2016, the body of the jury is formed by 12 persons (maximum) and 6 as a minimum, a reference judge for difficulty and a reference judge for execution, with each one presiding a specific panel. This should be respected in multisport competitions. The difficulty judges give the value of the technical elements presented by the gymnasts; the execution judges deduce the execution and composition as well as corporal faults and poor work with the apparatus. At the National Sport Games in Venezuela, the composition is six judges where two work with difficulty and four with execution, along with the reference judge.

In 2015, FIG approved that besides the Code of Points, there are three documents that are references in the work of the judges: (a) Regulations that rule the work of the Superior Judge and FIG competition supervisors, as well as the appellation jury and body of the competition control; (b) Regulation of the reference judges and (c) Regulation for the use of IRCOS. All this demonstrates the constant review that the FIG gives to the judges' evaluation process, and more responsible persons for the process (observers, evaluators and supervisors) have been included to make the judgement more objective. However, the courses are still oriented toward technical and practical components of the judging process in rhythmic gymnastics while there are other elements such as axiology in the judging process, which are not mentioned. In Venezuela, the reason to become a judge in rhythmic gymnastics is mostly personal motivation. It is ideal if the person has previous experience with the sport, but it is not a requisite.

Method

The main purpose of the study is to review the ethical and moral dimension in the formation of rhythmic gymnastics judges. It also looks at the axiological reality of the judgement together with the protagonists of the sport and what organization can do to guarantee fairness in the sport. Martínez (2006) used the term 'emerging paradigm' for the combination of qualitative and quantitative methods; he strongly promoted overcoming the naïve realism, suffocating reductionism and to go into the logic of comprehensive coherence. It is a paradigmatic approach that allows the researcher to approach the individual in their personal dimension and even feelings from the own experiences; in essence it is the quest for deeper comprehension.

The methodology was based on hermeneutic phenomenology as it values observation and interpretation; it looks at the way people experience their world, what is meaningful and how to understand it (Leal, 2005). It valued the meaning that each participant gives to his or her value system. The dynamic of this study looks at the sport judging process as an element of the sport phenomenon and the connotation it has; a dissatisfaction about the judging mistakes that are just expressed without consistent register. The judging decisions in sport are not measured just by the results in a competition, it goes beyond that moment itself and that is rarely appreciated by those who experience this reality. Semi-structured interviews were conducted with key informants: one international judge, one elite gymnast, one coach and one administrator, all of them working at an elite level. A questionnaire was applied to six national judges. In total five different instruments were designed and validated. Triangulation was applied to the collected data.

Results

The interviews conducted were analyzed in 28 long matrices which compared all the answers (Canelón, 2018). Some of the most common comments are presented in this section and the categories that emerged are summarized in the end and answer the purpose of the study. What is your opinion of a judge who evaluates their own gymnasts? Most of the judges indicated that there would be a tendency to favour the gymnasts and few indicated that they could do objective work – "unfortunately subjectivity prevails in most rhythmic gymnastics judges … but those who are objective and neutral in her judging work it should not create interference" (J.1). But it could also be the case that their gymnasts might not be fairly evaluated because the coach who is acting as a judge demands much more from the performance, "I feel a lot of pressure … it tends to be more demanding" (J.6).

The coach, gymnast and administrator believe that coaches should not evaluate their own gymnast. "I disagree, of course anyone could say you could also do it, but I don't think that is my role … it is like (silence) cheating, they let themselves be manipulated, well, not all of them, but many" (C.). The gymnast indicated that this possibility is 50%, but in any case this judge/coach will not let their gymnast down. The administrator even indicated two more elements – "sometime during a break they will approach us as delegates to ask for the grades… there is a tendency to make your own's win". There are cases in which a judge might evaluate a relative, and this is common. If there is objectivity, it should not create conflict, but again it could be either in favour or in detriment. "It should be neutral, but there have been cases in which problems have arisen in which accusation of bias or disgust for not a fair grade have taken place" (J.6).

The ethical component is expressed as the most important element judges should have,

> All those who have decided to participate as judge must respect the fundamental principles that as human beings should have …. In rhythmic gymnastics subjectivity rules, not just at national level but also international and it is obvious… judges who let their feeling evaluate their team or gymnast or just for other variables …unfortunately we have got used to live in a world in which not everybody keeps balance and objectivity.
>
> (C.)

Judges indicate that they rarely are evaluated in competition and even less, does a follow up of their work happen. The technical director of the competition should be responsible for the evaluation and the technical commission should review the results of the competition. This could support the follow up and feedback for the judges.

The grade represents the evaluation of all the preparation and performance of a gymnast, and is the result of the judges' appreciation. The gymnast indicated

> sometimes grades are unfair, you might feel that you did it great, but (silence) the judges' appreciation is different, sometimes I feel the grade could go further than the judge appreciation... the sport is unfair because it is much appreciation, from my international experience I have seen this in other places ... but it is the same at national level ... I consider judges' mentality should change.

Ferreira and Valdés (2003) indicated that the judge's task is always of appreciation with all the error that it implies. Appreciation is among other things, an aspects that generates many interests and this means there are different ways to perceive and it greatly pressures judges on different fronts.

The perceived unfairness in the sport has made the coach and the gymnast, on occasion, feel that they want to stop participating in this sport "In Toronto I was given an unfair grade ... I said stop, this is it, I don't continue, this sport is very, very, very (silence) ... unfair. I deserved to go to the finals" (G.). There is the possibility to appeal to a grade that is considered unfair. The coach requests the delegate to proceed. In the interview the administrator indicated that even though the procedure exists, there are elements that are not clear by the way they are applied in competitions in Venezuela. According to Ramírez (2014) a sport competition is an activity that has emphasizes results, but it also allows appreciating and controlling the good or bad development of the sport organizations, coaches, athletes (gymnasts), judges and referees, in an effective way.

The coach and administrator question the ethic of those judges who create rumours or comments about the judging, blame other judges because of grades, protect well-known athletes irrespective of their performance etc. In general, their request is that judges should judge what they see in the performance, not names, state or stereotype; they should be discreet about the comments they make in their meetings, unless it is something of general interest. The international judge indicated that theoretical and practical knowledge of the technical aspects of the sport is necessary but values are also of high relevance; the ethical aspects she reinforced are: respect, responsibility, objectivity when judging even one's own gymnasts as there is follow up of the grades and evaluation of the judge's performance at international level. This judge is in favour that during the Olympic cycle each person should register for one role only, in that way "coaches won't be officially judging".

In the interviews, it became evident that the universe of rhythmic gymnastics judges is small, there is a high level of technical specificity but through training it can be achieved. It is also a fact that judges in their courses do not receive an ethical component, it is centered on the technical regulations. Freitas and Guardo (2006) indicated a strategy to incorporate values in the sport judging based on two principles. The principle of values transmission indicates that along with all the formation of judges, general values such as: honesty, discipline, courage, responsibility, dignity, humility, persistence and exemplariness should be incorporated. This specific principle refers to respect of the rules, shamefulness, fighting spirit, fair play and passion for the sport movement; all of them characteristic of the intellectual practical activity. Two general categories emerged with subcategories in each: (a) Axiology of sport judging: subjectivity, objectivity, to be neutral, impartiality and favouritism. (b) Judges Formation: responsibility, knowledge of the code of points, technical profile of the gymnast, capacity, practical skill to evaluate, communication.

Discussion

Everything that is allowed or not is written in the sport regulations; FIG has made many attempts to achieve fairness in competitive results. However in rhythmic gymnastics it is a fact that most of the judges get there as a result of their coaching role. The reason is that their involvement contributes towards the gymnasts' preparation and then their presence becomes a normal situation in the judges' panels. The judges' formation is focused on the study of the code of points, technical regulations and to pass a test that will allow them to work for the respective Olympic cycle. At international competitions, judges receive the evaluation of their performance and they continue participating depending on the results. The duality of judge/coach roles in competitions is a recurrent phenomenon. Objectivity in judging is at the level of each judge's conscience, and interference of feelings and affinity with the gymnast should be avoided in the evaluation. Even though the regulations appreciate objectivity in the evaluation of the punctuation curve, the grade could also harm one's own gymnast as expressed by J.6 "I feel I am tougher with my own gymnasts"; this is another version of subjectivity in the judging.

Having as a reference the ethical values in consonance with the application of the norm, an objective judgment could be obtained, but it is necessary for a judge to exercise conscience as well as the equity principle in course of the exercise presented by the gymnast. The latter are not normative elements but they are a determinant of the sport results. As indicated by FIG (2017), to evaluate does not mean to know the rules but to apply them in a conscious way. The code of points provides the technical demands, it is precise, so it is necessary to acknowledge objectivity as an essential value, making the judges aware of using their conscience while applying the norms. Conscience is an important element of knowledge and practical guidance, it is related to the knowledge of attribute obtained through psychological contents (perceptions) supported by the acknowledgment of reality and nature (Abbagnano, 1993).

Impartiality over favoritism should prevail for the sake of rhythmic gymnastics. What makes this sport attractive is precisely its artistic composition, technical mastery and to go beyond the regulation limits by performance of extraordinary exercises. This is not just observed by the audience, judges are quiet aware of the countries, regions of the world where there is a tradition of excellence in the sport, and this also happens at all levels, even in clubs. Gymnasts deserve to be evaluated with equity and equality. Malem (2001) indicated that impartiality is related to the judge's mood while judging. This indicates that personal conditions influence the judgement, so the condition of being a coach will always have the judge interested in their gymnast's performance, as it is also a consequence of their coaching job. The affinity to gymnasts who participate in the competition is a circumstance that is associated with favoritism. Occasionally there have been comments that a gymnast or team won because the judges helped them, it seems to be a comment with no sense, however once we analyze the judges' panel, they mostly are the coaches of the competing gymnasts.

Judges' training and updating is a logical process that all organizations should practise, particularly the national federations that follow the standards of the FIG. But the standards of the follow up of the judges at national level, in this case, are not clear; the interviewees indicated that the evaluation model that is used at the international level is rarely applied nationally. The judging skill at the competitions is a reflection of judges having a long trajectory in the sport, but the updating and feedback should be the resource to make a standard in judging. Kohlberg's theory of moral development indicates that formation is the first step to achieve the intellectual development that allows maturity; in this research it means the reflexive and conscientious judging process.

The use of an evaluation and control form to keep the records of the judges' performance in competitions could support the technical committees' evaluation at the end of the year or even the Olympic cycle. For example, after a competition, a well-developed form could be used (Table 9.1).

Sport organizations should support impartiality and equality in competitions. It is team work that will allow rhythmic gymnastics to garner a good image. Judging supports the teaching of techniques and the artistic characterization, in consequence, a judge's performance is important at all competitive levels, so the axiological level should also be ideal. A gymnast after long hours of preparation wishes to be treated fairly and the grade is the only valid result; so, it should be objective. If it is not, then the gymnasts and coaches would gradually abandon the sport, which leads to the hypothetical question of what will the judges judge? The standard established by FIG should be followed. In places in which there are not many judges, constant efforts should be made to make updates and new courses introduced to gain more followers. It has to be remembered that the judges are not just evaluating a gymnast, but coaches, club, states, nations and even their evaluations establish the tendency to follow about elements and styles.

Rhythmic gymnastics judging   143

Table 9.1 Instrument for the Judge's Evaluation

Judge's Evaluation after the Competition		
Sample Indicators	*Yes*	*No*
Her or his gymnasts participated in the competition		
The punctuation given to her/his athletes is in the general media.		
The punctuation given in the competition by her/him mostly (90%) are in the media		
Did she/he communicate with any delegation (coaches, gymnasts or delegates)		
Arrival on time every day of the competition		

To be a judge is a profession of seriousness in sport, so the performance and general formation of the judge should be taken seriously. The active life of a gymnast might depend on the results in the competition, as well as the coaches' or administrators' performance in the job. Judging in rhythmic gymnastics tends to be referred to as a subjective action but it is not, the subjectivity is by the judge as a subject. It is also indicated that favoritism exists and great scandals have taken place when there is no confidence in the judging process, so it is about time to understand that good judging is a fundamental component for the quality and development of the sport. If individual criteria become a practice then it endangers the future of the sport, in this case rhythmic gymnastics. The power judges have when evaluating cannot be imposed to the technical and athletic preparation.

The sport organizations, clubs, associations and federations associated with rhythmic gymnastics could create strategies of inclusion, so people could start being trained and more judges be incorporated, in this way there will be fewer coaches judging their own gymnasts in competition. In this case it became evident that there are not enough courses and follows up to judges. Values of neutrality and impartiality can be achieved only when there are no particular conflicting interests in the judges' panels. The organizations in charge of the competitions must present the judges' evaluation once the competition is finished, besides the data on all the judges' performance.

Sport organizations should promote comprehensive models to train judges, in which besides the own sport technical regulations of the sport, elements related with personal development that influence rhythmic gymnastics judging could be incorporated, as well as a specific number of compulsory activities within a year. The values of quality that are applied in sport are related to all the stakeholders. Sport judging is fundamental at all levels of sport development – grassroots, elite, professional; the quality in judging will allow the solid advancement of the athlete and society. This is a task shared by judges and sport organizations, particularly federations and associations in charge of coaches' education. Venezuelan state institutions should be more involved in coaches' education; they should support

144 Rosa López de D'Amico and Mayerlith Canelón

it together with the federation as it is imperative in the country's constitution and the sport law to protect all sport systems and particularly, practitioners. This process should not be left to the responsibility of federations alone.

References

Abbagnano, N. (1993). *Diccionario de filosofía*. México: Fondo de Cultura Económica.

ABC. (2004). Aumentan las quejas en los Europeos de Kiev. [on-line paper] Available: https://www.abc.es/deportes/abci-aumentan-quejas-europeos-kiev-200406070300-9621907522030_noticia.htmlABC Madrid, España [Consulta: 2016, Mayo 2].

Avelino, J. (1994). *Educación, axiología y utopía*. Spain: Universidad de Oviedo.

Betancort, M. (1999). El árbitro de baloncesto. Principios y bases teóricas para su formación. *Lecturas: Educación Física y Deportes*, 17(4). Available: http://www.efdeportes.com/efd17/arbal.htm [Accessed: 2015, May 15].

Bobo, M. (2001). El juicio deportivo en gimnasia rítmica. Una propuesta de evaluación basada en indicadores de rendimiento. [Online thesis] Available: http://ruc.udc.es/dspace/handle/2183/1013 [Accessed: 2016, July 28].

Busbee, J. (2017). Low-rent scandal hits all levels of rhythmic gymnastic judging. Available: https://sports.yahoo.com/blogs/olympics-fourth-place-medal/low-rent-scandal-hits-levels-rhythmic-gymnastic-judging-215902482.html

Canelón, M. (2018). Axiología del juzgamiento deportivo: Un Complexus Teórico para la formación de jueces deportivos en la gimnasia rítmica. Unpublishedthesis. Universidad Pedagógica Experimental Libertador, Venezuela.

Deporte Castilla-La Mancha. (2004). Conspiración entre jueces en campeonato europeo de gimnasia 1999. Available at: http://deporteclm.com/

El Universal. (2015) La FIG castiga a 5 jueces de gimnasia rítmica. Caso. Available: http://104.239.237.37/articulo/deportes/mas-deportes/2015/09/4/la-fig-castiga-cinco-jueces-de-gimnasia-ritmica EFE Madrid, España [Consulta: 2016, Octubre 2].

Ferreira, M., & Valdés, H. (2003) *La personalidad de los árbitros y jueces. Psicología del arbitraje y el juicio deportivo*. Barcelona: INDE publicación.

Freitas, I., y Guardo, M. (2006). Hacia una teoría del arbitraje deportivo. *Lecturas: Educación Física y Deportes*, 68(10). [online journal] Available: http://www.efdeportes.com/efd94/arbit.htm [Consulta: 2015, May 20].

FIG. (2004). The IRCOS by FIG project. [online document] Available: http://www.fig-gymnastics.com [Accessed: 2017, April 20].

FIG. (2013). Specific judges' rules for rhythmic. [online document] Available: http://www.fig-gymnastics.com/ [Accessed: 2015, July 15].

FIG. (2015). Código de Puntuación 2013–2016 Gimnasia Rítmica. [online document] Disponible: http://www.fig-gymnastics.com/ [Accessed: 2015, February 15].

FIG. (2017). Reglamento general de jueces. [online document] Available: http://www.fig-gymnastics.com/ [Accessed: 2017, September 2].

Guardo, M. (2013). Competencias necesarias para los árbitros y jueces en el deporte. *Lecturas en Educación Física y Deporte*, 177(17). Available: http://www.efdeportes.com/efd177/competencias-necesarias-para-los-arbitros-del-deporte.htm [Accessed: 2015, May 20].

Guillen, F. (2003). *Psicología del Arbitraje y el Juicio Deportivo*. España: INDE Barcelona.

Kohlberg, R. (1974). La Teoría del Desarrollo Moral de L. Kohlberg. Rogers [Documento en Línea]. Disponible http://www.fcctp.usmp.edu.pe. [Accessed: 2014, July 05]

Leal, J. (2005). *La autonomía del sujeto investigador y metodología de la investigación.* Mérida-Venezuela: Litorama.

López de D'Amico, R. (2001). *Organisation and regulations in national sport bodies: A comparative study in artistic gymnastics.* Michigan: UMI.

López de D'Amico, R. (2008). Reglamentos de las organizaciones deportivas nacionales: un estudio comparativo. *Revista investigación y postgrado,* 24(2), 202–240.

López, M., & Arango, M. (2002). *Estimule sus Aptitudes, Virtudes y Fortalezas.* Colombia: Editorial Gamma.

Malem, J. (2001). ¿Pueden las malas personas ser buenos jueces? *Revistas - DOXA,* 24, 379–403. Available: rua.ua.es/dspace/bitstream/10045/10214/1/doxa24_14.pdf.

Martínez, M. (2006). *Ciencia y Arte en la Metodología Cualitativa.* México: Editorial Trillas.

Martínez, M. (2011). *Paradigmas emergentes y ciencias de la complejidad.* Caracas Venezuela: Universidad Simón Bolívar.

Maslow, A. (1943). Abraham Maslow. [on-line] Disponible: http://encina.pntic.mec.es/plop0023/psicólogos/psicólogos_maslow.pdf/ [Consulta: 2017, agosto 21].

Mendizabal, S. (2000). *Fundamentos de la gimnasia rítmica, mitos y realidades.* Madrid: Editorial Gymnos.

MINEPS VI. (2017). *KazanAction Plan.* Kazan: UNESCO.

Oropeza, N., Narváez G., & López de D'Amico, R. (2012). Jueces y Puntuación en Nado Sincronizado: caso Venezuela. In M. Cornejo, C. Matus & C. Vargas (Comps.), *Proceedings III Encuentro ALESDE Congreso Latinoamericano de estudios socioculturales del Deporte* (pp. 158). Concepción: Universidad de Concepción.

Paiva, C. (2013). *Venezuela en los juegos olímpicos.* Caracas: Author.

Piña, J. (2004) La responsabilidad moral individual [Online document]. Available: http://www.monografias.com/trabajos15/eticaaxiologia/etica-axiologia.shtml [Accessed: 2015, July 15]

Ramírez, J. (2014). *Thesaurus de la Actividad Fisicorporal y Deportiva.* Caracas: Cuentahílos.

The New York Times. (2013). Yahoo sports. Available: http://sports.yahoo.com/blogs/olympics-fourth-place-medal/low-rent-scandal-hits-levels-rhythmic-gymnastic-judging-215902482.html [Accessed: 2015, June 16].

Chapter 10

Restructuring CUBA and Chinese collegiate sports
Learning from the governing success of NCAA

Runtao Mao

Introduction

The Chinese University Basketball Association (CUBA) is the officially recognized five-person basketball league for Chinese college students, it is hosted by the Chinese University Sports Association and exclusively operated by Ali Sports. The league was conceived in 1996 and officially launched in 1998. Over the last two decades, the CUBA League has made significant progress in terms of scale and impact (Wang, 2019). Until 2019, more than 1,600 college teams participate in the CUBA League each year on the three levels, covering 32 provinces, cities and autonomous regions throughout China. CUBA is the top amateur league in Chinese sports industry in terms of scale, level of competition and talent incubation. It has constantly precipitated the atmosphere of Chinese college students' sports culture through the event. Today, CUBA has become the collegiate basketball "Hall of Fame" for more than 40 million college students. In addition, more than 1 billion audiences watch or follow CUBA games live via television and Internet each year.

On the other side of the Pacific, the most famous collegiate athletic league worldwide, the National Collegiate Athletic Association (NCAA) regulates and organizes nearly 1,300 North American institutions and conferences, where more than 480,000 college student-athletes compete annually in college sports. The NCAA Division I Men's Basketball Tournament, also known as March Madness, is definitely a signature college sports event. The tournament was created in 1939, and top basketball teams compete in a six-stage, single elimination tournament. The significance of March Madness goes far beyond basketball itself, it represents the highly developed collegiate athletic industry in the United States (US).

US sports media and commentators are talented at creating gimmicks for March Madness. For example, the games between Michigan and Ohio State are always a "War". According to Novak (2013), there is no better feeling in college sports than ruining a rival's perfect season, an opportunity the Ohio State Buckeyes took to heart when Michigan was the last remaining unbeaten team in the country in January. Moreover, for every single person who has watched or followed sports games, Duke versus University of North Carolina is on the shortlist

DOI: 10.4324/9781003213673-10

for the greatest rivalries in any sport, both because of the insanity of the two rabid fan bases and because of the extraordinary quality of play on court. Indeed, great rivals and hot topics can always encourage people to follow and get involved in college sports games. Another interesting phenomenon indicates how impactful March Madness is. The popularity of internet make fans more likely to watch games and discuss the results during working hours, rather than concentrate on their work, which causes many American companies' profits decrease dramatically every March. Moreover, most American fans prefer to watch the Final Four instead of National Basketball Association (NBA) games or other sport leagues games, so they stop for a day to avoid time conflict with NCAA Final Four.

The CUBA League is the top domestic collegiate basketball league in China. However, compared to the NCAA, it has far less influence on Chinese collegiate and professional sports than the NCAA does in the US. In light of these facts, this study demonstrates several limitations that restrict the further development of the CUBA basketball league. Moreover, this paper employs the NCAA as a parameter, and identifies some crucial factors driving the success of the NCAA while examining some issues the NCAA has confronted. More importantly, this paper provides recommendations for the CUBA League, covering the following aspects: (1) Organization Structure; (2) Game Culture and Game Design; (3) Team Management and; (4) Market Development. Furthermore, this study discusses the feasibility of establishing a Chinese collegiate athletic league with distinctive Chinese characteristics in the near future.

Review of literature

The earliest memory of NCAA basketball was the game between the University of Oregon and Ohio State University. This game was designed and organized by the National Association of Basketball Coaches (NABC) in 1939 (Cole, 1976), and this was the very beginning of the NCAA basketball tournament. The 1960s were called the "Golden Time" of NCAA basketball; UCLA was dominant and they captured their first national championship under the stewardship of John Wooden. Then, Bruins became unstoppable, Wooden led his team to sweep the NCAA basketball tournament, winning ten national titles over a 12-year stretch before the coach's retirement in 1975. As "UCLA Era" become one of the most influential phenomenon in sports history, a couple of television networks such as CBS, TBS and TNT announced to partially televise NCAA March Madness tournament on their television channels, since 1969.

26 March, 1979 was a big day in the history of March Madness and North American TV broadcasting. Indiana State's Larry Bird and Michigan State's Magic Johnson launched their rivalry in the 1979 championship game, and more than 35 million viewers watched Johnson's Michigan State Spartans defeat Bird and the Indiana State Sycamores, making it the most-watched NCAA championship game in history. More importantly, this game marked a new era in March

Madness broadcasting, with a couple of major broadcast rights deals coming after this game. Then, since 2011, all March Madness games are available for viewing nationwide and internationally. As television coverage has grown, so too has the tournament's popularity (Ausick, 2019).

Nowadays, other than college students and college basketball fans, numerous non-sports fans are crazy about following and predicting the outcomes of the March Madness games. Obviously, television and online media serve a significant role; mainstream media outlets such as ESPN, CBS Sports and Fox Sports host tournaments online where contestants can enter for free. Also, many sites cater to corporate marketing and public relations to get in on the excitement such as Big Tourney.com. According to US media reports, NCAA "March of Crazy 2018" was broadcast to more than 180 countries, with more than 97 million viewers (Friedman, 2018). The viewership increased by 28% compared with 2017, and the length of time watching live broadcast increased 14%, advertising revenue reached $1 billion, up 5.4% from 2017 and 391 advertisements for 142 brands were actually placed, a total of 6,761 (Wu, 2018).

Corresponding to the NCAA, the CUBA League is the most influential collegiate athletic league in China. It was conceptualized and introduced first in 1996, and the first game was held in 1998 in Beijing, China (Huo, 2011). Specifically, the development of CUBA went through three main stages. From 1998 to 2004, CUBA cooperated with the Henghua International Group, jointly introducing the Chinese version of March Madness "CUBA" to the public. At the beginning, CUBA consisted of 617 university teams from 26 provinces and autonomous regions including Hong Kong and Marco. The number of competitions exceeded 2,600, with 1.46 million live spectators, and the total number of audiences outnumbered 1.5 billion. Moreover, national television channel CCTV conducted live broadcast of 20 final stage games, and more than 100 central and local media conducted intensive coverage of the League. According to Zhuang (2013), the "CUBA phenomenon" brought fresh air to Chinese basketball at a time when it was in a historical trough. Numerous college students were inspired and started to practise basketball and other sports.

From 2004 to 2015, CUBA launched the Chinese University Basketball Super League (CUBS), allowing registered players, professional players to participate without affecting training and learning, and develop parallel to CUBA (Wang & Yao, 2015). In 2015, CUBS merged with CUBA, and they are collectively known as the Chinese University Basketball League. The CUBA committee divided the league into three levels: Recreational, Higher Vocational and Technical Colleges, and Elite.

The year 2018 is a defining one in the history of CUBA. On 6 August 2018, Ali Sports announced that they invested more than 1 billion yuan to take over CUBA's exclusive rights for the next seven seasons until September 2025 (Zhang, 2018). In 2018, Ali Sport successfully held the first joint competition between Peking University and Tsinghua University. At the same time, the CUBA Board of Governors and Ali Sports jointly made some big changes in the competition system: (1). Increased the number of teams in each division from 64 to 80, which increases the possibility of promotion, especially for these teams with poorer competitiveness; (2) expanded the traditional "Elite 24" to "Elite 32", and adopted a double knockout system; (3) changed men's "Final 8" teams from "stable location" to "host and guest" system, so that CUBA is able to better integrate into campus and deeply connect with students; (4) integrated "Recreational" and "Elite" group into the same system, recasting "Recreational" group as the third level compared to "Elite" group at the first level. Meanwhile, women's basketball league expanded from two-level to three-level. Eventually, the CUBA version of "Final Four" was held at the stadium of Beijing College of Physical Education. Peking University successfully defeated their traditional and most competitive opponent, Tsinghua University, winning their successive CUBA championship.

Organization structure

The main body of the NCAA is the Board of Governors consisting of legislative bodies that come from member schools. Each division has a separate Board of Directors, and they provide strategic direction and oversight for each division collegiate model, leadership and direction for each division and for the Association as a whole. According to Zhuo (2014), members of the Executive Committee come from public and private universities, and relevant sports associations. The NCAA legislative body comprises experts and scholars who work for management of higher education institutions, or physical education programmes. As an example, Mark Emmert, the current president of the NCAA, was previously the 30th president of the University of Washington (UW), his alma mater, taking office in June 2004, becoming the first alumnus in 48 years to lead UW (Griffin, 2004). All these experiences and backgrounds make running the team more professional and efficient. Besides, Management Council legislation goes on to the Board of Directors, consisting of school presidents, for final approval. The NCAA staff provide support, acting as guides, liaisons, researchers, and managing public and media relations. All members are elected as members of the Executive Committee in accordance with the relevant system of the NCAA (Yuan, 2008).

Compared to the NCAA, the Chinese University Sports Association (CUSA) and the Executive Committee Organization make up the main body of the CUBA. CUBA is also a non-profit organization, its staff and personnel consist of experts or scholars who come from a great variety of professional or academic groups, such as education, sports and media (Chen, 2007; Li, 2006; Li & Qiu, 2003). The main responsibilities of the CUSA and the Executive Committee Organization are to: (1) Carry out the relevant plans of the CUBA League; (2) Set up key principles and policies, formulate strategic plans, arrange and organize regular season games and tournaments; (3) Guide and coordinate various subordinate departments such as Department of Secretary, Competition and Media Center; (4) Event check and final approval. Developing for nearly a hundred years, the NCAA has developed a highly mature and complete management and operation system. It is important to note that the NCAA Board of Governors has independent leadership and a majority of decision-making powers, allowing them to make efficient decisions in a short time. Different from the NCAA, considering the actual situation in China, CUBA maintains closer relationship with government department, CUSA under the General Administration of Sport. CUSA is also responsible for supervising management and operation processes of the CUBA League (Wang, 2014).

Game design and culture

North America (US and Canada) is one of the biggest regions worldwide where the sports industry plays a key role for socioeconomic development and benefits society with job creation, brand recognition, promotion of volunteerism and development of better sports facilities (Dezsenyi, Patrucco & Wolfel, 2017). Different from professional sports leagues, the NCAA earned reputation as the only sports league in North America to provide "pure" sports to fans. Indeed, for students and fans, the significance of March Madness has surpassed basketball, it is a crucial part of their college life. In each sports season, from fall to the next spring, more than a thousand universities and colleges compete for victory, winning fame for their schools. Athletes, basketball fans, casual fans or non-fans watch games together and celebrate victories for their schools. Obviously, these memories are treasured ones for them.

Yan (2009) points out that when people do one thing over and over again, generation to generation, it becomes a part of their life, and culture. There are some factors that make the NCAA and March Madness so unique. First, athletes and competitions are the main body of March Madness. High level athletic performances make most games extremely intense with unpredictable results, and this is the essential reason that March Madness attracts millions of basketball fans. Moreover, it is worth mentioning that the single elimination format plays an important role in standardizing the sports competition, improving the quality of the competition and ensuring the competition runs smoothly and in order (Huo, 2011). According to former NCAA standout Kenny Anderson "To win it all you have to win six games, If you lose one game, it's over, and it's an especially large amount of pressure to continue to win" (Anderson, 2016). Different from professional leagues' playoff system, single elimination tournament makes every game a life-and-death battle, and players and coaches must do their best to win (Wu, 2018). Since all qualified teams are from top basketball programs in the nation, games between them are extremely exciting and fierce, drawing the fans' full attentions and involvement.

Furthermore, March Madness provides more than just a branch of competitive basketball games, it has also created a great culture. As NCAA men's and women's basketball adopt the host and guest system to regular season, teams and fans are able to have more direct interactions. Then, the athletic department utilizes these opportunities, creating a great variety of game-day events such as Family

Brunch, so fans can bring their family to watch games and enjoy quality family time. When most fans have a strong sense of identity with their alma mater team or local team, regardless of team performance, they always stay with their "home" teams, and become the "loyal fan base". As an example, Michael Jordan, the former "Hometown Hero" of UNC and the greatest basketball player of all time, flew to the scene to cheer for the UNC (Yan & Zhang, 2009).

Market development

Obviously, the NBA is one of the most successful commercial sports league in the world, having a great number of loyal fans in the US and overseas (Figler, 2009). Influenced by market effect of the NBA, the NCAA basketball league has a strong brand recognition and market influence. Firstly, the NCAA is able to independently pick their broadcasting channels and networks. Basically, they employ a professional team to evaluate and determine which channel or network is qualified for TV and online broadcasting, based on the cost, national influence and time (Trail & Yu, 2014). The "Golden" broadcasting condition ensures the exceptional popularity of March Madness nationwide.

At the same time, Mcfall (2014) suggests that the NCAA is an expert at utilizing the physical market, so most NCAA teams have a team-specific jersey, mascot and team fan base. Some famous NCAA basketball stars, such as Zion Williamson, draw even more market attention than NBA stars do. Finally, Treme, Burrus and Sherrick (2013) indicate that sponsorship is crucial for a sports league of any level. The NCAA emulates the sponsoring model of the NBA, carrying out team title and player endorsements. Related endorsement brands are world-renowned brands such as Nike, Adidas and Under Armour Both the sponsors and the NCAA could benefit from a consistent business alliance. On one hand, brands rely on the "Superstars Effect" to capture broader social attention, on the other hand, the NCAA can capitalize on its own social influence to continuously attract the sponsorship and titles of famous sports brands (Ye, 2014).

Limitations of the CUBA league

Wu (2010) points out that the CUBA League imitates the model of the NCAA basketball league, and makes many changes and adjustments in accordance with the actual situation in China. However, previous research on the limitation of the CUBA League indicates that shortage of talent supply (Li, Lai, Liu & Zhang, 2010) and unreasonable game arrangements (Wang, 2019) negatively influence the overall quality and attention of the league. According to Wu (2018), although the CUBA League officially set up a draft system for college players in 2015, professional basketball leagues did not entirely open their gates for college athletes. The draft system is naive and incomplete, and many professional teams abstain from picking players. In the case of those college players selected by a CUBA team, they spend most of their time sitting on the bench. This phenomenon can partly be attributed to college players' unsatisfactory skills and influence. In other words, professional teams do not give full credit to the competitive level of CUBA, simply opining that CUBA cannot serve the role as a talent pool for professional level leagues. In addition, most of college level games are organized and hosted in one city performing as tournament games. Ding (2015) suggests that CUBA tournament system leads to most student fans not having the opportunity to watch games and support their teams in person. This phenomenon further reduces the attention garnered by the tournament and hurts the home court atmosphere.

It is also important to realize that CUBA desperately needs to extend its social participation. Only a few of the matches in the final stage were broadcast on TV, while the other games were mainly broadcast on the Internet. Actually, this is a huge factor in making "March Madness" gathering a high degree of attention at the event. However, in China, considering profits and the rate of return, only a few live broadcasts and Internet platforms are willing to broadcast collegiate games. Insufficient broadcast channels limit CUBA in promoting public awareness and attention. In addition, CUBA has not developed inimitable event culture as March Madness has. Most players merely focus on training and games, while they look too busy to have extensive contact with fans. Therefore, insufficient interaction negatively affect the relationship between players and fans, and this hurts the formation of "home team identity".

Lastly, from the perspective of basketball games, it mainly consists of athletes and coaching staff. Management of athletes and coaches is significant for a successful basketball team (Treme et al., 2013). Wang (2019) compares and analyzes the daily class attendance and basketball training between athletes in the NCAA and CUBA. Results show that most NCAA member schools have strict requirements for student athletes' attendance on daily classes, and establish corresponding requirements for results in the final assessment. More importantly, schools set up a mature and efficient incentive mechanism for athletes. Student athlete's athletic performance is directly linked to the scholarship evaluation system, so that the athlete's own interests are closely correlated with training and competition. By contrast, CUBA member schools have not created a comprehensive athlete incentive system which results in some athletes with poor self-discipline, often absent from training. Over time, these athletes may be absent from team practice frequently and eventually quit the team. There is also a contradiction between academics and training. Daily training and games can be burdensome, as some athletes cannot handle both academic and athletic tasks. This system that separates athletic and academic success is not conducive to student athletes' employment in the future.

Meanwhile, Li, Lang and Yang (2006) demonstrates several factors related to coach recruitment and management in CUBA and compare them to the NCAA's system. They find that the NCAA basketball programs implement a complete recruitment system. Member schools prefer to hire coaches with rich coaching experience, background, advanced training theory and skills, rather than overemphasize their academic titles. They believe that their knowledge will help their team in cultivating first-class athletes. Also, most young coaches in the NCAA study sports-related majors and earn degrees while coaching sports teams. This bi-disciplinary talent guarantees that coaches adopt important skills to become excellent coaches. In contrast, most CUBA coaches are "part-time", and they may have a responsibility as a physical education (PE) teacher, since they are generally appointed by school administration (Qu, 1999). In recent years, a few universities have started to adopt a recruitment system to hire retired players or coaches from professional teams, and facts have proven that this method has a significant effect on improving a team's performance.

Li et al (2006) also suggest that coaches in the NCAA basketball teams usually consists of one head coach, three to four assistant coaches and a couple of voluntary assistants. Head coaches of some famous college are well-known nationally even worldwide, such as Coach K in Duke and Tom Izzo in Michigan State University. They have great coaching philosophy and experience, know how to manage their teams, and communicate with assistant coaches and players in efficient ways. Nevertheless, the CUBA head coaches generally take full responsibility of their team, make every decision by themselves and take care of every aspect of the team. As these head coaches are college PE teachers at the same time, they spend a lot time on PE courses. Considering most of them have no professional knowledge or experience in sports coaching, this dispersion could damage the quality of practice and team performance.

Issues of the NCAA

Traced back to 1920s, the NCAA was established on the basis of Big Ten and Southeastern Conferences (SEC). The NCAA initially runs as a "Declarant of Ideals", which allows colleges paying "scholarships" to their student athletes a way to recruit premier talent. However, the increase of recruitment battles between the Big Ten and SEC greatly threatened the Big Ten colleges' on-field dominance in college football (Edelman, 2002). Thus, the Big Ten Conference worked to transform the NCAA from a "declarant of ideals" into an association with direct authority to punish colleges that did not adhere to its vision of "amateurism." In 1948, the NCAA adopted a "Sanity Code" that empowered the association to ban any member school that compensated a student athlete with more than just the cost of tuition. In other words, if student athletes wanted something to eat or a place to sleep, they had to pay for it themselves or work for it.

Developing for nearly a century, the NCAA capitalizes on its television broadcast rights and commercializes most aspects of college sports, including the sale of rights to use student athletes' names and likenesses. The rapid growth of NCAA's popularity and the broadcasting and licensing arms of college sports transformed Division I college athletics into revenue-producing machine akin to a professional sports league. According to Edelman (2002), these revenues, in turn, are passed along in the form of higher salaries and other fringe benefits for NCAA officers, college presidents, athletic directors, and coaches. Nevertheless, NCAA rules continue to require conferences and member schools to strictly control the commercial rights to student-athlete identities, as well as to prevent member colleges from sharing licensing revenues with their student-athletes (Edelman, 2013). Thus, the fact is that compared to the NCAA executives, college presidents, athletic directors, and coaches have all become exceedingly wealthy, and most student-athletes remain poor. The NCAA's paradoxical goal of maximizing revenues in college sports while preventing Student-Athletes from participating in commercial ventures triggers numerous conflicts and legal issues between schools and Student-Athletes.

One of the most representative lawsuit was established by Ed O'Bannon, a former basketball player for UCLA who was a starter on the UCLA 1995 national championship team. He filed a lawsuit in 2009 against the NCAA and the Collegiate Licensing Company, alleging that the NCAA amateurism rules, insofar as they prevented student-athletes from being compensated for the use of their "Name, Image and Likeness", were an illegal restraint of trade under Section 1 of the Sherman Act. In addition to O'Bannon, 20 current or former student-athletes from either College Football of Division 1 men's basketball programs filed antitrust suits against NCAA for the rule prohibiting schools from offering football and basketball players a limited share of the revenues generated from the use of their names, images and likenesses. Moreover, Trey Johnson, a former Villanova defensive back who is playing in the Canadian Football League filed a class-action suit arguing that the organization and its member schools had violated minimum wage laws (Witz, 2019). According to the plaintiff, athletes' hours are tracked in the same way as those of students in a work-study program, and that if student ticket-takers, seating attendants and concession workers are being paid at least a minimum wage, so do the players performing on the field.

Baker (2019) notes that the NCAA designed its amateurism model since its establishment. This model does not restrict either the NCAA, its members or coaches from generating billions of dollars, but college athletes who actually play the games have compensation that is capped at the cost it takes to attend their college or university. It is obviously unfair and the NCAA critics have referred to the amateurism model as the "shame of college sports." In response to these issues, recently, the NCAA's Board of Governors released a statement – it had unanimously voted in favor of permitting college athletes to financially profit from the use of their names, images and likenesses, and the new NIL policy is set to go into effect in 2021 (Baker, 2019). Obviously, it will be a pioneering breakthrough for the NCAA, representing an apparent transformation for an NCAA model for amateur intercollegiate athletics that restricted college athletes from benefiting from any commercial value built from their reputation.

Besides, as a high-competitive athletic league, player safety is another big concern for the NCAA. In fact, it is the responsibility of each member institution to protect the health of and provide a safe environment for each participating student-athlete; the NCAA and member schools are supposed to guarantee a certain amount of Catastrophic Injury Insurance to ensure their athletes' safety and well-being. However, there is a case that shows something different. In 1972, former Texas Christian University football player Alvis Kent Waldrep signed a pre-enrollment form and a financial aid agreement documenting TCU's agreement to pay for his cost of attendance, and he also got the assurance from his head coach that if an injury occurred, TCU "would take care of them". Unfortunately, Waldrep's playing days were cut short by a horrific spinal cord injury in a 1974 game against the University of Alabama that left him paralyzed from the neck down (Rhodes, 2011). Waldrep tried to bring a worker's compensation lawsuit against TCU for his injury, but he failed since the District Court of Texas held that TCU intended Waldrep to participate as a student, not an employee when he was injured, and thus he was not entitled to workers' compensation. According to Armstrong (2012), no athlete is willing to play for an institution that cannot secure their safety, with the result that the NCAA would lose the trust of S-As and their parents in the long term.

Method

The information and relevant data of this study are sourced mainly from previous literature that focused on the comparison of the NCAA and CUBA leagues in terms of league management and operation, game arrangement, athlete and coaching staff management, and market development. The author also conducted interviews with players and coaches who are serving or have served in the NCAA basketball team via email or face to face conversations. Interviewees include Jordan Harris, current basketball player in the Georgia Bulldogs team; Mark Slonaker, former assistant coach in Georgia Bulldog men's basketball team and current Executive Director of Athletics Alumni Relations; Aifei Shao, former basketball player at Shanghai University of Sport, currently working for the Chinese national women basketball team. The author listened to their thoughts as a player or a coach in a college team, and compiled their opinions in the following section.

Findings and discussion

Management ideology

The NCAA realized the market-oriented management of the league through the form of corporate legal person. The Board focuses on strategic leadership, and it shifts more operational and legislative issues to the Council to study and resolve. The NCAA's Board of Directors authorized the five conferences and their 65 member institutions who find themselves in the forefront of public attention and criticism to expand their influence and to provide leadership on matters that directly address student-athlete well-being. More importantly, the NCAA emphasized S-A voice and vote, allowing efficient and scientific league management.

The NCAA delivers its identifiable Core Ideology to all its sub conferences, institutions and sports teams. According to the NCAA Committee (2004), they focus on historic values to ensure that the NCAA continues to advance in the right direction, and have an absolute obligation to make certain that intercollegiate athletics is successfully woven into the fabric of higher education. The Core Ideology consists of shared purpose, values and vision. They describe their purpose as to govern competition in a fair, safe, equitable and sportsmanlike manner, and to integrate collegiate athletics into higher education so that the educational experience of the student-athlete is paramount.

Furthermore, according to the NCAA values and belief, the collegiate model of athletics is one in which students participate as in an avocation, balancing their academic, social and athletic experiences. In other words, athletes are responsible for not only their athletic performance, but also excellence in academics, integrity and sportsmanship. Athletes also need to serve a supporting role in the higher education mission, in enhancing the sense of community and strengthening the identity of member institutions. Indeed, as celebrities and the face of schools, S-A's behaviors can significantly influence the reputation of schools and even the association; they are understood as a valued enhancement to a quality higher education experience. Student-athletes should achieve academic success and be better prepared to achieve their potential because they have participated in collegiate athletics. They should regard athletics endeavors as a valued part of their undergraduate education, and as a corollary, academic success among student-athletes enables the Association and its members to positively influence the perception of college sports.

Compared to the NCAA, the CUBA League mainly focus on basketball events, even though management noticed that ignorance of athletes' all-round development and value delivery will definitely hurt the attention and participation of younger generations. CUBA should utilize its educational value to cultivate young sports talent, and promote its popularity to influence more students participating in sports with healthy and positive attitudes. With the help of sports, college students are more likely to take challenges, and actively take action to build strength on-field and live up to their youth. It is important to let them feel the positive energy brought by basketball, and reshape the joy of sports.

Game design

Tournament design is an integral part of any sports league or event (Baumann, Matheson & Howe, 2010). Normally, the NCAA's regular season begins from November to the following year's spring, and it consists of home, guest games and intercollegiate invitational tournaments. NCAA Division I teams have to play about 30 games in the regular season. The March Madness tournament starts in mid-March, and champions from 32 Division I conferences and 36 teams which are awarded at-large berths qualify for the tournament. Sixty-eight teams are divided into four regions and organized into a single-elimination "bracket", which is predetermined. The first round consists of 64 teams playing in 32 games over the course of a week, followed by "Sweet Sixteen" and "Elite Eight". Then, the champions of the four divisions will make the "Final Four" that compete in a preselected location for the national championship. According to coach Slonaker, the single elimination format excites the nation because if you lose, your journey is done. So this concept leads to many dramatic upsets or near upsets in the first two rounds. There is no doubt that the game design significantly improves fans' interest and attention nationally. The fans, students and alumni of the schools that are in the tournament have a special interest in the tournament as they support their team.

CUBA adopts its format from the NCAA by introducing regular qualifiers, regional games and national tournament to the league. However, there is still a huge gap between a CUBA and NCAA match in terms of number and intensity. The good news for the CUBA League came in the summer before the 2018–2019 regular season, with Ali Sports winning the exclusive business operation right for the next seven seasons from 2018 to 2025, and announcing some crucial reforms of scale and arrangement of games. First, it divided competitions into five levels, starting from the Grassroots matches in 32 provinces, followed by the Regional competition, the top 32, Elite Eight and Final Four. More importantly, CUBA implemented an unprecedented home-guest competition system in Grassroots tournaments for more than 100 universities in the following Season 2018–2019.

Moreover, CUSA carefully picks more than 80 schools from 14 provinces and large cities to package and promote them for television and Internet viewers. The tournament increases regional spots from 16 teams to 20 from the second round qualifiers onwards. Then, 80 qualified teams gather in one city to fight for the national "Top 32". The national "Top 32" tournament employs the system of double defeat and elimination which eliminates losing teams and crowns the last team standing as the national champion.

Social participation

The NCAA is a non-profit organization, and amateurism is the most important character that differentiates it from professional sports leagues. Even so, the NCAA can still capture national attention and obtain considerable annual income, thus, the market development plan definitely makes a huge difference. Wang (2004) notes that broadcast revenue accounts for a large proportion of NCAA annual revenue. The NCAA closely cooperates with social media to obtain funds and social support. As an example, the NCAA and CBS signed an 11-year television broadcast contract in 2003 worth more than $6 billion. Meanwhile, CBS owns the rights to television, radio, Internet, satellite transmission, the rebroadcasting and distribution of home CDs. The NCAA's huge social influence made CBS package the television broadcasting rights as a huge asset that competed with other national broadcasters. For sports leagues, television and Internet broadcast rights are important resources, influencing social impact and sustainable development of the league.

Sponsorship is another big part on the NCAA's market development plan. Sponsor associations and member schools jointly organize a wide variety of game-day events. While helping sponsors promote their products, these events capture audiences' attention, allowing them to enjoy basketball games and relevant events with friends and family. Basketball fans can cheer for the team's great performance, while causal fans can also participate in the game through fans' interaction and other entertaining events. Such a strong alliance not only earns revenue for the team, but also improves the team's visibility and social influence.

Also, with the support of school officials and local communities, numerous NCAA member schools design team-specific nicknames, team colors, mascots and slogans, and these symbols represent the fame and spirit of schools. For instance, Duke Blue Devils, UNC Tar Heels and Kentucky Wildcats, all these recognizable names are introduced into basketball's "Hall of Fame" and become a part of the school identity. From the perspective of fans, these names can always remind them of the time they were in college, standing together when their team went through losses, celebrating victory with friends and family. In fact, fan' passion for their college athletic team reflects their affection for their school, which is passed down from generation to generation, resulting in the NCAA's unique game culture and enormous social participation and influence.

Using the NCAA as a parameter, the CUBA League is gradually moving to the right track. In the 2018–2019 season, more than 300 CUBA games were broadcast live on TV and network media, including the national television channel CCTV 5, and other influential media outlets like Five Star Sports Television, Guangzhou Radio and TV Channel. Ali Sports, as the exclusive operator of CUBA, increased investment in visual systems in the new season, when it announced that each player will have his own photo starting from the Grassroots events in the new season. In addition, CUBA launched a new trophy for the champion to build up its distinguished game culture. This trophy uses a wooden trophy base and a five-star surround trophy embedded with the CUBA tournament logo. The new slogan is "Conquer Disapproval", showing the world that the young Chinese generation is not afraid of challenge, fights for its identity and dreams even if it costs sweat and tears, and this is also the CUBA League's heroic declaration for victory.

The 2019 CUBA Tournament pioneered the new era of the CUBA League and Chinese collegiate sports. The Top 32 men's basketball teams gathered in Hangzhou, and the defending champions Peking University and Central South University sat in the North and South region respectively. At the opening ceremony, 32 teams appeared one by one on live video with gorgeous stage effects, enjoying NBA star-like cheers. The signatures of each team's representatives were assembled onto a giant honor platform, symbolizing the basketball "Hall of Fame for" Chinese college students. For CUBA, it is a huge step which extends basketball games to an all-round entertainment mode, making the CUBA not limited to a few students obsessed with basketball, and a part of Chinese entertaining industry. Ali Sports and Youku jointly created a show "Battle! Basketball", and the open ceremony gave it the first chance to move their live broadcast from the studio to the CUBA Top 32 tournament. Such a sports show that combines sports and entertainment has ignited more Zhejiang University students' enthusiasm for sports. Obviously, this event is the first large-scale combination of sports and entertainment in the history of CUBA, and is in resonance with Ali's entertainment ecology, which simultaneously opens up the sports and entertainment industries, allowing intercollegiate sports event to affect a wider range of people.

It may be predicted that, in the future, CUBA will continuously build up league culture, encouraging member schools to adopt the way of professional teams that design a fancy team-specific nickname, mascot, colors and jersey. This could be the next revolutionary step for CUBA to establish league culture and elevate league's social participation.

Team management

Sports attract a huge number of spectators, the most important reason being the level of intensity in competitions. Athletes and coaches are the main body of basketball teams, and they are also the decisive factor for the level of intensity of basketball matches. Basically, high-level basketball leagues are closely related to player and coaching staff management. Based on athletic performance, NCAA Division I schools provide athletes with tuition and fees, room and board, books and other expenses related to attendance at the school. Most Student-Athletes who receive athletics scholarships receive an amount covering a portion of these costs. In the season 2005–2006, the NCAA funded athlete scholarships and educational programs to the tune of $5.33 million, and used another $22.88 million assistantship grants to help Student-Athletes with their academic success. In fact, the availability of scholarships is crucial for most Student-Athletes, as it is related to their academic and future career. Therefore, generous scholarships could serve as an important incentive to enhance athletes' training and learning enthusiasm.

Moreover, it is notable that the NCAA and schools that compete in the league prioritize Student-Athletes' status as students, instead of athletes. Student-athletes need to constantly balance their academic and athletic commitments. The NCAA policies regarding time demands must ensure that student-athletes can successfully pursue both of these commitments while benefitting from the same educational opportunities available to the rest of the student body (Dirks, 2000). To enhance Student-Athletes' academic success, the NCAA sets targets and standards for academic achievement of student-athletes that meaningfully measure their academic progress toward a degree in a program or major offered to the student body. Also, member schools' function is to provide Student-Athletes with the best possible information regarding their careers inside and outside of athletics, and help them translate their skills, mindsets and athletic experiences from athletes to prospective employers.

Another important part of team management is the quality of training. In the NCAA, coaches and athletic directors jointly make strict training plans on a daily basis, regulating the training content, intensity and time. According to

University of Georgia men's basketball player Jordan Harris, the 2019 off-season training camp consisted of strength and conditioning that takes up a big part, followed by basketball fundamentals and a small piece of tactical practice. The head coach Tom Crean set up goals for individuals and the whole team, and he also cooperated with assistant coaches and voluntary assistants to monitor practice, guide young players with basic skills like shooting form, defense footwork and passing. It is impressive that the coaching staff clearly understand their respective jobs, so their cooperation turns out not only concise but efficient, making the practice run in an orderly and smooth way. To improve the training quality, a lot of huge athletic programs hire technical personnel to assist coaches with the daily training. Li (2006) found that athletic departments equip these technical personnel with advanced computers and other analysis equipment to help coaches breakdown and analyze athletes' motions such as shooting, dribbling, thereby allowing athletes to visually see the quality of their motions and make modifications.

Running in a different system, CUBA and its member schools manage athletic teams in another way. Most of the CUBA athletes are basketball majors coming from normal high schools. As normal students, they are required to participate in the national college entrance examination, and universities will pick athletes based on the grade in general subject and sports test. After entering the school team, Student-Athletes confront burdensome work from training and competitions, and regularly Student-Athletes choose to sacrifice the time they are supposed to spend on classes to participate in team practice. However, other than athletic performance, academic achievement should also be proposed and emphasized by schools and athletic teams. For CUBA member schools, it is necessary to share the primary goal that provides the best possible education for their student-athletes, while recognizing they have different roles to play in achieving that goal. To make Student-Athletes realize that participation in college sports has an important and substantial educational value, schools should develop effective measurement that evaluates Student-Athletes' academic progress, ensuring that this educational value is received by athletes and promoted among member schools and in the media.

Coaches makes a huge difference in shaping young players' mindset and character, in and outside of basketball. As mentioned above, coaches who serve in CUBA teams are directly appointed by school administrations, and most of them are part-time coaches who are required to coach athletic teams and teach PE classes. Hence, they cannot pay full attention to team training, and this negatively affects the quality of training. To promote training efficiency and effectiveness, schools should establish criteria that evaluates coaches' performance, clarifies their responsibilities, and is linked to the workload, titles and rewards. In addition, schools should upgrade coaching staff quantitatively and qualitatively, hiring experienced basketball experts such as former professional players to guide team practice, clarifying each coach's responsibility, and equipping coaches with modern educational techniques such as with a digital computer or projector.

Feasibility of the Chinese collegiate athletic league

The idea of the intercollegiate sports originated from the US in 1852, when crews from Harvard and Yale universities met in a challenge race in the sport of rowing (Whitmer, 2015). Later on, with the emergence of other sports such as football and basketball, many of these similar concepts and standards were adopted on 28 December 1905 when 62 higher-education institutions became charter members of the Intercollegiate Athletic Association of the United States (IAAUS), which marks the official initiation of the NCAA. The first NCAA national championship was conducted in 1921, with the National Collegiate Track and Field Championships. Developing for nearly 150 years, the NCAA integrates more than 30 men's and women's sport programs, and in 2014, it set a record high of a $989 million in net revenue, among the highest of all large sports organizations.

Over the last two decades, CUBA has become the third impactful sports league in China and its rapid growth reflects the significant progress in Chinese collegiate sports. In addition to CUBA, CUFA (Chinese University Football Association) and CUAFL (Chinese University American Football League) are also popular in China. However, for a long time, these leagues' viewership and market development were far worse than the professional leagues, with viewer groups limited to college athletes and sports fans. In 2018, Ali Sports obtained exclusive rights to operate CUBA for the next seven seasons until September 2025. At the same time, Ali Sports continues to deepen cooperation with other collegiate sports leagues including the CUFA and the CUAFL, managing and operating three major collegiate leagues in parallel (Zhang, 2018).

There is no doubt that this powerful alliance is a milestone for the development of Chinese collegiate sports, as Ali Sports is able to utilize the influence of CUBA to unite other sports leagues together, creating a comprehensive collegiate sports league. In fact, basketball and football (soccer) are the most popular sports among the young generation Chinese, with the highest participation in Chinese colleges and universities. According to statistics, more than half of Chinese college students participate in basketball, while football is close to 40%. Besides, millions of Chinese college students participate in physical exercise or pay attention to sports news and events, the "occasional" crowd is the largest. Most Chinese college students are casual sports fans who have the potential to transform into the "loyal fan base". When driven by the surrounding sports atmosphere, this group of students is very likely to become sports fans. Therefore, integrating different collegiate sports leagues into a comprehensive league, the CUSA can establish a more influential sports brand and extend its social awareness and participation, motivating more "casual sports fans" to support their schools and participate in sports.

It is notable that unlike the US or European countries, China does not have a century-old professional sports club or a century-old team, but China has numerous century-old universities, and most of them have at least 50 years of sports tradition. This sports tradition is able to generate a unique identity and honor to the college culture. To inspire more people and inherit this unique alumni culture generation by generation, Chinese college students and Student-Athletes need a sports league that specifically belongs to them. Moreover, to encourage more young people from various age and gender groups to get involved in sports, the Collegiate Athletic League is not supposed to be limited to merely one or two sports, more sports that are popular among Chinese youth should be formulated and combined into the league, such as Badminton, Tennis, Aerobics and so on. Also, founders can introduce some sports with Chinese characteristics to the league, such as Chinese martial arts and dragon boat race.

It takes a decade to foster trees, but a century to foster people. It requires confidence and patience to create the Chinese college sports Intellectual Property and cultivate college sports culture. For people who intend to develop Chinese sports, it is necessary to continuously promote Chinese sports from the bottom up. The group of college students from 18 to 25 years old are supposed be the most active sports crowd. A comprehensive college sports league is able to optimize resources from different aspects, providing a platform for all these students who are passionate and intend to participate in sports. It may be predicted that the future of Chinese sports industry is rooted in the soil of college sports, and the Chinese Collegiate Athletic League is undoubtedly a good starting point to cultivate the seed.

Conclusion

The NCAA is well-known as the most successful intercollegiate association in the world, and the March Madness basketball tournament earns its name by its incomparable popularity and influence in North America. There are some factors behind its success: the single elimination format excites the nation, if you lose, you are eliminated; amazing social participation gathering fans, students and alumni of the school together to support their team; enduring game culture makes every single game draws fans' full attention, and so on. This paper collects information from previous studies and research, and analyzed the NCAA and March Madness, and this analysis provides some valuable recommendations for the CUBA League.

More importantly, this paper offers an exciting possibility that in the future, China will be able to establish its own collegiate athletic association on the basis of the CUBA League. The vision of the Chinese Collegiate Athletic Association is to strengthen the educational function of sports to reform the traditional education model in the context of exam-oriented education, attracting more students to get involved in sports and become the core of Chinese sports. Furthermore, it will open a new vein that transforms numerous talented college athletes into players of professional leagues, and ultimately the national teams.

References

Anderson, K. (2016, March 22). In March Madness, anything can happen [Blog post]. Retrieved from http://kennyanderson.sportsblog.com/posts/14575807/in-march-madness-anything-can-happen.html

Armstrong, D. A. (2012), Emerging issues in collegiate athletics, current issues and potential future developments. Retrieved from https://www.stetson.edu/law/conferences/highered/archive/media/Emerging%20Issues%20PPT.pdf

Baker, T. (2019). 5 issues to keep an eye on with the NCAA's new NIL policy. Retrieved from https://www.forbes.com/sites/thomasbaker/2019/11/01/examining-the-ncaas-evolving-nil-policy-keep-an-eye-on-the-following-issues/#4a1af5087591

Bell, R., & Fernandez, C. (2017), The impact of cross-cultural communication on collective efficacy in NCAA basketball teams. *International Journal of Cross Cultural Management* 17(2), 175–195.

Chmielecki, M. (2012), Teaching intercultural communication in Polish higher education management programmes – A critical look. *Journal of Intercultural Management* 4(4), 79–89.

Cole, L. (1976, September), The NCAA: Mass culture as big business , *Change* 8(8), 42-46. (July 28, 2021), Retrieved from http://www.jstor.org/stable/40176893

Daniel, D., Fiorella, P., & Kim, W. (2017), Sports industry research North America: USA & Canada. Retrieved from https://open.bu.edu/

Dirks, T. (2000), Trustin leadership and team performance: Evidence from NCAA basketball. *Journal of Applied Psychology* 85(6): 1004–1012.

Edelman, M. (2002), Reevaluating amateurism standards in men's college basketball. *University of Michigan Journal of Law Reform* 35, 861.

Edelman, M. (2013), A short treatise on amateurism and antitrust law: Why the NCAA's no-pay rules violate Section 1 of the Sherman Act. *Case Western Reserve Law Review* 64, 61.

Friedman, W. (2018), March Madness grows 5% in National TV Ad dollars, ratings down.

Griffin, T. (2004, June). "The Homecoming". The University of Washington Alumni Magazine. Retrieved June 13, 2014.

Huo, Z. (2011), Thinking of CBA competition system reform and development. *Journal of Xi'an Institute of Physical Education* 28(6):680–682.

Kuaizhe, L. (2019), The CUBA 32 competition officially opened, 32 schools gathered in Zhejiang University to compete for the elite eight. Retrieved from http://www.lanxiongsports.com/posts/view/id/15629.html

Li, X., Liu, Y., Lai, X., & Zhang, Z. (2010), A study of the talent transfer chain of American college athletic basketball. *Journal of Beijing Sport University* 33(05):126–128.

Madlock, P. E. (2008), The link between leadership style, communicator competence, and employee satisfaction. *Journal of Business Communication* 45(1): 61–78.

National Collegiate Athletic Association. (2020, April 15), Retrieved from https://en.wikipedia.org/wiki/National_Collegiate_Athletic_Association

Novak, T. (2013), Ranking the 25 best rivalries in college basketball. Retrieved from https://bleacherreport.com/articles/1719358-ranking-the-25-best-rivalries-in-college-basketball#slide25

Pifer, N. David et al. The advantage of Experience: Analyzing the effects of player experience on the performances of March Madness Teams. *Journal of Sports Analytics* 5(2): 137–152.

Powell, B. (2012). How these 11 college teams got their nicknames. Retrieved from https://awfulannouncing.co/2012-articles/how-these-11-college-teams-got-their-nicknames.html

Rhodes, L. (2019), It's not as easy as it looks: Why the NCAA refuses to pay college athletes what they rightfully deserve. Retrieved from https://ubaltlawreview.com/2019/03/08/its-not-as-easy-as-it-looks-why-the-ncaa-refuses-to-pay-college-athletes-what-they-rightfully-deserve/

Schroeder, P. J. (2010, March), Changing team culture: The perspectives of ten successful head coaches. *Journal of Sport Behavior* 33(1), 63 (Academic Research Library).

Stockdale, M. S., & Crosby, F. J. (2004), *The psychology and management of workplace diversity*. Malden, MA: Blackwell Publishing.

Vallée, C. N., & Bloom, G. A. (2005). Building a successful university program: Key and common elements of expert coaches. *Journal of Applied Sport Psychology* 17, 179–196. doi:10.1080/10413200591010021

Vallée, C. N., & Bloom, G. A. (2016), Four keys to building a championship culture. *International Sport Coaching Journal*, 3, 170–177.

Wang, H. T. (2019), The comparative study of the operation modes of CUBA and NCAA basketball league. The Graduate School of Hunan Normal University.

Wang, J, & Yao, Y. (2015), College basketball league brews major reforms, merger of CUBA and CUBA. Retrieved from http://sports.sina.com.cn/cba/2015-08-10/doc-ifxftkpv6978679.shtml

Wang, N. (2014), A comparative study of the CUBA and the NCAA basketball tournament system development models. The Graduate School of Henan Normal University.

Wei, Y. (2018), Ali sports announces CUBA competition system: Team expansion, host and guest system, increases the number of on-site packaging activities. Retrieved from http://www.lanxiongsports.com/posts/view/id/13377.html

Whitmer, M. (2015, June 6). Harvard and Yale crews celebrate the 150th Boat Race. Boston Globe. Retrieved from https://www.bostonglobe.com/sports/2015/06/06/harvard-and-yale-crews-celebrate-boat-race/uFRfgEVkENrWKXAUDoQVPK/story.html

Witz, B. (2019). N.C.A.A. is sued for not paying athletes as employees. Retrieved from https://www.nytimes.com/2019/11/06/sports/ncaa-lawsuit.html

Wu, Q. (2018), The revelation of NCAA March Madness to China University Basketball Association. Sports Department of Xiamen Institute of Technology. *Journal of Jilin Sport University*. doi:10.13720/j.cnki.22-1286.2018.06.007

Yan, Z., & Zhang, Z. (2009), Research on the organization of NCAA National basketball tournament. *Chinese School Sports*, 2009(S2), 48–50.

Zhang, A. (2018), The 21st CUBA opens the Battle Burton, the new home- away system starts from the basic level competition. Retrieved from: https://baike.baidu.com/reference/4506884/ff4cqktWojjtpL5gSjESMelJxVo74EUVv5b5UENeFJQ5cli8ADEW1kvC7KkJiMrKwnmOoLhi0NvkOQUZRpyJEz1yPBnqfG-Sd-Bv6zr2OOlEIH7dzFuPvQ

Zhang, A. (2018), Ali sports gains CUBA operation rights, Zhang Dazhong: Let the campus become the main body of sports. Retrieved from: http://www.xinhuanet.com/sports/2018-08/06/c_1123231474.htm

Zhuang, W. (2013), *Comparative analysis between Basketball League and Chinese College Basketball League from the perspective of social concern*. Jinan: Shandong University.

Zuo, Y. (2014), The present situation of college students in China and the United States basketball league. The Graduate School of Henan Normal University

Chapter 11

Impact of athletic talents on team structure

Marquee players in Major League Soccer

Andrew Macuga and Euisoo Kim

Introduction

Soccer is the most global sport in the world. Fans everywhere support the game from the stands or their couches. Major League Soccer (MLS) is an ever-expanding league; the presence of great players such as David Beckham and Kaka assists in developing popularity of the league abroad and domestically. Having world-class players in MLS is a critical factor for its success as the league is not seen as one of top leagues in the world. Within the United States, MLS also competes with other professional sports such as the National Football League (NFL), the National Basketball Association (NBA), and Major League Baseball (MLB). Competition to secure fans among diverse professional sports is tough; generating popularity through association with major names is one of the oft employed means for sport teams.

As fandom picks up, many teams that are struggling with results and with generating support of fans for the team are willing to take every step to keep up with the rest of the league and make headlines. Signing the biggest names in soccer gains huge attention. But, does it actually show results on the pitch and in the stands? These marquee players make the most salary in the league; however, many of the superstars who are playing for MLS are at the end of their careers and cannot really help make a huge impact on team performance. There are a couple stars, who are able to bring results on both the pitch and in the stands, but a majority of these marquee players turn out as to be busts and a waste of money.

The purpose of this study is to examine the impact of some of the biggest names in MLS on the pitch and in the stands. It is our expectation that influence of star players in MLS does not meet the expectation of teams in terms of performance on the pitch as well as financial benefits.

History of MLS

MLS is the professional top tier men's soccer league in the United States. MLS is sanctioned by the United States Soccer Federation, which is a 501 nonprofit organization that manages the official governance of soccer in the United States.

DOI: 10.4324/9781003213673-11

MLS was founded in 1993 with the first season taking place in 1996. In the 1996 MLS season, there were ten original teams. Today, MLS is made up of 26 teams, 23 in the United States and 3 in Canada. By 2022, there are expected to be 30 teams with future franchisees lined up in cities in the United States. MLS is a single entity, instead of operating as an association of independently owned teams like in most professional sports leagues in the United States (Brown et al., 2016). MLS acts as a single entity in "attempt to avoid antitrust litigation, they tried to centralize and control their respective sports by having the league own all teams, hold all player and coaching contracts and pay those salaries, and maintain sponsorship deals and broadcasting rights" (Kaiser, 2004, p. 1). MLS struggled financially, early on. MLS "was reported to have lost an estimated $250 million in its first five years and more than $300 million overall" (Eligon, 2005). Then, in 2004, MLS turned a corner and started generating profits with new television and jersey deals negotiated from the single entity structure (Eligon, 2005). The policy concerning player acquisition in MLS was created here. According to MLS Players Association, the average salary of an MLS player is $373,094 (MLSPA, 2020c). In 2015, the average salary of a Liga MX (Mexico's league) player was roughly $415,000 (ESPN, 2015). This huge gap in player salaries is due to rules such as the salary cap in the MLS, which hinders the recruitment of talent among MLS teams to a certain degree. The current MLS salary cap is $3.845 million per team. MLS has two transfer windows that allow team to acquire players. Via the MLS website, the primary transfer window of 2019 was from 13 February to 7 May and the Secondary Transfer Window was opened on 9 July until 7 August. There have always been two transfer windows usually in Winter/Spring and Summer. These are the only times teams can acquire players, according to MLS Policy. It is important to understand the player acquisition rules in the league to fully comprehend what these teams are sacrificing by signing marquee players. These marquee players are meant to be the biggest stars on the pitch.

Designated player rule

When thinking about MLS, the first world-class star player most people think about is David Beckham of L.A. Galaxy. He was considered the first major name in the MLS and ignited the huge growth of the league from a worldwide perspective. The Designated Player (DP) Rule contributed to the transfer of the star player into MLS. Currently, the DP rule "allows clubs to acquire up to three players whose total compensation and acquisition costs exceed the maximum budget charge, with the club bearing financial responsibility for the amount of compensation above each player's budget charge" (MLS, 2017a). In 2007, this rule was made to encourage clubs to sign higher quality stars and increase league popularity on a global and local perspective.

In 2007, $400,000 of a DP's salary counted against the salary cap while the remaining portion of the contract becomes the responsibility of that team's ownership group (MLS, 2006). Teams, at the time, were allowed to trade these DP slots by holding a maximum of 2. If the team chooses to have a second DP, then $350,000 of the second DP's salary counts against the salary cap while the remaining portion of the contract becomes the responsibility of that team's ownership group. In 2009, Don Garber, commissioner of MLS, met with a Board of Governors to review the Designated Player Policy.

In 2010, the Designated Player Policy changed. For each DP, $335,000 of salary is charged to the salary cap and paid by the league, $167,500 for DPs joining during the MLS Summer transfer window, with any remaining salary being paid by the team's owner (Marcus, 2010). They made the adjustment that every club in MLS was allowed 2 DPs and the slots could not be traded, like in the previous seasons.

In 2012, the rule was adjusted again. MLS added a 3rd DP slot and kept the no trade rule. Additional price adjustments were also made. If a club signs a player who is 24 years old or older, the maximum budget charge will be $504,370, unless the player joins during the Secondary Transfer Window, in which case his budget charge will be $252,188 (MLS, 2012). MLS added the Young DP to encourage clubs to sign younger developing talent because the league was looked at as being a retirement league, in terms of the age of the stars that they were bringing in. The Young Designated Player (YDP) rule is that if the player is between 21 and 23 years old during the League Year, they will have a budget charge of $200,000, while a YDP age 20 or younger will have a budget charge of $150,000. If any YDP age 23 or younger joins his club after the opening of the Secondary Transfer Window, his charge will be $150,000. These YDPs still count as one of the 3 DPs allowed to clubs.

These DPs have created a problem in MLS, although their purpose was to bring better talent. The Designated Player Rule has created a large income inequality within MLS with top DPs earning as much as 180 times more than a player earning the league minimum (MLSPA, 2020a). According to Reese (2014), 29% of the MLS's wage spending went to just 6 DPs. This disparity upsets players who are working as hard as the DPs and are just as important to the team (Reese, 2014). The disparity is also a cause of the salary cap. Referring to these findings, it is assumed that the DP rule is outdated and does not fit with today's MLS environments.

Despite problems stated above, the Designated Player Policy has impacted MLS to a certain degree. It allows high quality talent to be paid by clubs. This high-quality talent leads to more exciting and enjoyable matches, which leads to increased fan interest. The Designated Player Policy has given life to an outdated structure of not paying players in MLS. It allows MLS to gain competitiveness and attract high profile talent. MLS is always evolving and changing the policy to make it more viable for the future. The Designated Player Policy was the first step MLS took toward exponential growth.

General allocation money

MLS is always looking for different ways that they can give teams opportunity to attract better and more popular talent to the league. One of these ways is the General Allocation Money (GAM). GAM is money that a club can use in addition to its salary cap (Brennan, 2018). MLS provides allotments of GAM to each team annually, which can be used to pay off a portion of a players' salary. However, a club cannot use GAM to reduce more than 50% of a player's salary cap hit. If a club chooses not to use it for salary, then the amount can be used to help pay for the transfer fees of a player.

Every club receives a different amount of GAM at the beginning of each season. To begin with, there is a base amount. In 2016, the allotment of GAM to each club was $150,000 (Stejskal, 2017). In 2019, the allotment was increased to $200,000 in GAM (Baer, 2017). After the base, there have been several cases where clubs would receive additional allotments of GAM. All of the following information is drawn from the Major League Collective Bargaining Agreement effective between February 2015 and January 2020 (MLSPA, 2020b). A club in MLS will receive $200,000 if they do not make the post season. If a club is an expansion club, meaning it is their first year in MLS, the club will receive $1.1 million in GAM. Whenever there is a soccer club expansion within MLS, all clubs, excluding the expansion club, will receive $100,000 in GAM. If a club qualifies for the region Concacaf Champions League, then the club will receive $140,000. If a club transfers or loans a player outside of Major Soccer, then the club could receive up to $750,000 in GAM. If a club does not have a 3rd DP, then the club will receive up to $200,000. When a club loses players who become free agents, the club receives $50,000 per lost player of GAM at the beginning of each year. Finally, when there is an Expansion Draft, clubs that draft players will receive $50,000 per recruited player in GAM while those clubs that choose not to use their draft picks do not receive any. GAM can be traded between clubs. Sometimes clubs trade GAM for players if they choose not to use it on their current salaries. This money is to be used by the end of the season and does not roll over to the following season. So, there is a number of ways that clubs may receive GAM.

This policy of GAM is to lighten up the load that the salary cap takes every year. MLS wants to offer competitive salaries with other leagues. The more the clubs can pay players, the more quality and popular talent the league can attract. This money is crucial for some clubs especially as some clubs do not have owners who are willing to invest in it. These clubs must rely on GAM to pay players' and transfer fees. The policy of GAM is one of three ways clubs can acquire talent in MLS.

Target allocation money

Introduced in 2015, Target Allocation Money (TAM) Policy is another way that MLS provides teams opportunities to improve the quality of the team roster by giving additional financial flexibility. In other words, TAM is "funds provided by the league strategically to add or retain players that will make an impact on the field immediately" (MLS, 2017b). TAM is intended to help afford talent that is almost as good as the club's DPs. In order to use TAM, the player has to make more than the league threshold maximum ($480,625 in 2017); every penny after that threshold is paid by TAM. When TAM was announced in 2017, it started with giving each team $100,000 per year for the next five years. Eventually MLS "raised the amount of TAM given to each team to $800,000 per year in 2016, $1.2 million per year for the 2017 season and $1.2 million per year plus an additional $2.8 in optional, discretionary TAM for 2018 and 2019" (MLS, 2017b).

TAM gives the roster even more talent. This can help free up DP spots on a roster. TAM is intended for clubs to be able to pay players more and attract higher talent from MLS's competitors. However, TAM is not allowed to be used in combination with GAM (Brennan, 2018). TAM Policy has been used smartly and efficiently by some clubs. For example, L.A. Galaxy used TAM to pay Zlatan Ibrahimović. L.A. Galaxy had a maximum of three DPs in the roster already, then offered Zlatan $1.5 million by using TAM (Stejskal, 2018). Similarly, FC Cincinnati used TAM to acquire Leonardo Bertone in 2018, although the amount of TAM was undisclosed (Brennan, 2018).

How do these rules compare around the world?

The salary cap is a widely used and understood policy in the professional sports world in the US. NFL has a hard salary cap, meaning no team is allowed to exceed the cap limit (Brown et al., 2016); there is no DP, TAM, or GAM. This is probably due in part because NFL does not have any real competing leagues as MLS does. MLB and NBA employ a soft salary cap, which places a limit on how much money each team can spend on all of their players while allowing teams to go over that limit by requiring teams to pay a luxury tax (Brown et al., 2016). For instance, there are five MLB teams that paid luxury tax in 2020 (Spotrac, 2020). In the case of MLS, although salary cap is considered a hard cap, policies like DP, TAM, or GAM make it a blurry line.

When it comes to soccer, the idea of a salary cap is not commonly used in other professional soccer leagues. Leagues in Europe, such as the Premier League and Bundesliga, do not limit the salary of players, as long as teams in Europe follow the Union of European Football Associations (UEFA) Financial Fair Play. UEFA Financial Fair Play states that a club can spend up to $5 million more than what it makes per three years; if any team violates these rules, then teams will usually be suspended for a transfer period (UEFA, 2015). Considering these differences, MLS is not capable of competing with these renowned leagues. In most cases, professional athletes are going after money; MLS is not capable of attracting world talent with its current pay system. As stated above, players in Liga MX make more than the average MLS Player. The average Premier League player makes roughly over $65,000 per week (BBC Sport, 2017). That is almost what some of the lower tier players make in MLS per year. Some of these Premier League players make over $190,000 per week, for instance, Raheem Sterling. Thus, it is almost impossible for MLS to compete with these leagues with the current salary cap system. These salary restriction policies that are implemented in the MLS make it more difficult to compete with leagues abroad.

Review of literature

MLS has always been looking for different ways to provide teams the opportunity to attract better and more popular talent to the league. MLS created the DP in 2007 and expanded it to three players in 2012. MLS created GAM to help spending within the league. They also announced TAM to bring additional higher-level talent to the league. All these different policies are intended to help clubs acquire talented players and secure a high level of quality and competitiveness of MLS. However, these policies are unique to the league compared to other leagues across the globe. Ultimately, it is begs a question whether these policies are actually working. Are they giving competitive advantages, but also keeping the league fair? Does the increased spending lead to an increase in spectators? The next section will examine a couple of previous studies on the topic. These studies are mainly on DP because of the lack of information on GAM and TAM due to the policies' recent introduction. Most DPs are considered the marquee talent that will be analyzed later.

The first study that was looked at was 'Beyond Beckham: The Designated Player Rule in MLS' which was conducted by Warren and Ross (2011). They examined the actual "David Beckham Effect" and the effect of other DPs to the attendance to MLS Matches. The salary of David Beckham was $6.5 million, whereas the entire salary cap for a club in 2008 was $2.1 million. This one player was making as much as three clubs could spend on talent. Other DPs of the time were still making as much as an entire team. The median MLS salary at the time was $53,000. Back in 2008, the main source of revenue for teams in MLS was gate revenue; therefore, getting people in the stadium was the first priority. In their regression analyses of the 15 MLS clubs, Warren and Ross (2011) factored in DPs, attendance, location, weather conditions, and match day promotions. The results showed that the presence of David Beckham in MLS matches was significant: his presence yielded about 12,698 more spectators per match that season. However, excluding David Beckham, DPs were not significant predictors of match attendance. On average, DPs brought 90 more spectators per match, while even a negative influence of DPs on attendance was found. Although DPs' contribution to team performance was not considered, DPs did not bring positive numbers in financial statements (Warren and Ross, 2011). Considering additional attendance and the average ticket price in 2008 which was $22.47, Beckham contributed to collect more than $9 million in ticket sales during the season; however, all other DPs added about $194,140 more in ticket sales to the MLS while teams spent more than $8 million on DPs' payroll (Warren and Ross, 2011). Although other important revenue sources DPs could bring such as sponsorship, luxury box, television revenue, and marketing correlation revenue were not considered, additional revenue incurred by DPs in ticket sales was too trivial compared to their salary. This study suggested that the DP rule would not end up working well for MLS. Ultimately, however, the DP rule turned out to be the source of what made the league as popular as it is today.

The second study that was examined to look at the effects of DPs was 'The Effect of Marquee Players on Sports Demand: The Case of U.S. Major League Soccer' which was conducted by Jewell (2017). Unlike Warren and Ross (2011) who examined a single season, Jewell considered a six-year period from 2007 to 2012. Furthermore, he had not examined the impact of all DPs in the league but only world-famous players such as Henry in his study. The study suggested that Designated Player Policy contributed to the increase of attendance in a league level as they attract more fans both for home and away matches; since the business model of MLS is a single entity model, overall increase of attendance due to marquee players is meaningful (Jewell, 2017). However, large market teams appeared to benefit more from the DP policy than smaller market teams (Coates et al., 2016). Another finding of his research is that DPs attract more spectators to the stadiums; however, impacts were the greatest in their first year of appearance while their power to attract fans to the stadium diminished over time. Overall, "when one considers the longer term impact of marquee players on the league, specifically in terms of league viability and franchise values, the 'Beckham Rule' may turn out to be extremely financially beneficial for MLS" (Jewell, 2017, p. 249). Considering business development stage of MLS, having marquee players in the late 2000s was crucial for growth as they provide positive impact both on and off the pitch.

Definition and background of marquee player in this study

A marquee is a structure that is commonly placed over an entrance with head liners of a concert or advertising a big event. In this study, players who attract all of the cameras and are worshipped by fans are the names on the marquee and the following four players who have played for MLS will be considered as marquee: Zlatan Ibrahimović, Kaka, David Villa, and Wayne Rooney. MLS heavily utilizes these names every chance they get for branding and marketing tools.

"Dare to Zlatan" is a phrase that truly encompasses Zlatan Ibrahimović. He is probably one of the most well-known players in the soccer universe. He is also probably the least loyal player and has the biggest personality. Hailing from Sweden and first seen by the world at Ajax, in the Netherlands, Zlatan went on to play for European giants such as Juventus, Barcelona, Paris Saint Germain, Manchester United, Inter Milan, and A.C. Milan. He is known for his audacious goals and his outspoken personality. He has won countless trophies and awards all over Europe, which is considered the highest level of soccer, winning over 31 trophies. Then in spring of 2018, Zlatan joined L.A. Galaxy with $1.5 million in salary, which increased to $7.2 million in 2019 (Simpson, 2019). Zlatan is one of the most recognizable names in soccer and one of the most decorated players ever. He has over 6.4 million Twitter followers, which is double the total of MLS's follower count. He also has 43 million Instagram followers, which is over 40 times more followers on Instagram than MLS. He was huge for MLS with his capacity to gain attention from around the globe.

Known for winning the Ballon d'Or, the world's most prestigious soccer accolade, is Kaka. He played for European giants A.C. Milan and Real Madrid. The Brazilian player is one of the most creative midfielders of all time. Orlando City targeted and signed him when he was 34. Kaka was making at the time, a record breaking base salary of $6 million and a guaranteed compensation of $7.2 million per season with Orlando City (Carlisle, 2014). He has over 29 million followers on Twitter and over 17 million followers on Instagram.

With long, creative passes from Messi, David Villa would strike goals into the back of the net on the big stages. The Spanish striker is one of the most prolific strikers of his generation. David Villa is known for winning many titles in Europe and even the World Cup. He has a niche in finding the back of the net. In 2015, New York City FC (NYCFC) were looking to find their goal scorer in the inaugural season. Villa was making a hefty $5.6 million during his last season with NYCFC in 2018 (Boniface, 2018). Villa has over 9 million followers on Twitter and over 6 million on Instagram.

The iconic bicycle-kick in the Manchester Derby that led to a win is a memory that most soccer fans in the world would have. Wayne Rooney is an English soccer legend, having started his career at Everton, he made his way over to Manchester United and became a club legend. His jersey is worn in almost every household in Manchester. He is the record goal scorer for England and Manchester United, two of the most historic soccer organizations in the world. In July 2018, he decided to take his career with D.C. United, signing at annual base salary of $2.7 million with additional $5 million in the form of image rights and commercial incentives (Reed, 2019). This was huge for a struggling club looking to become relevant again. Nobody would have guessed that Rooney would end up playing soccer in the United States. Rooney has over 17 million followers on Twitter and over 15 million followers on Instagram.

Method

Data collection and analyses

Data was collected through the MLS Player Database and MLS match archives. All match statistics for each of the four marquee players as well as team performance during their stay at MLS were collected. Items collected were minutes played, starting status for each match (e.g. starter, substitution, not played), number of goals and assists, match results, and attendance of each match. Furthermore, the team's performance during the year prior to each marquee player's arrival was also collected to compare overall attendance differences before and after these super stars' arrival.

After the statistics of players and teams were collected, means of each item were calculated to analyze effectiveness of these players on the pitch and in the stands. In the case of on pitch performance of each player, play time, goals, assists, and team records were analyzed. The means of these statistics and team

Marquee players in MLS   173

performance were compared with team performance at matches without these marquee players during the same season. This study considers team winning percentage and points gained per match (e.g. 3 points for a win, 1 point for a draw, and 0 point for a loss) as an indicator of effectiveness of marquee players: these two factors are critical in evaluating team performance.

In order to evaluate the impact of marquee players in the stands at home, comparison between the average stadium attendance at home of the previous year of the player's arrival and the average attendance while the player was with the team were analyzed. In the cases of Kaka and David Villa, they joined an expansion franchisee, meaning attendance of the previous season of home matches is not available. Instead, the average attendance of home matches during their stay was compared to the attendance of home matches of the following season after they left to estimate the impact on their home attendance. The assumption is that if there is a significant decrease in average home attendance in the following season of marquee player's departure, it is highly likely that the loss of marquee player would attribute to the decrease. Furthermore, comparison of away team's stadium attendance between the season average attendance and having the marquee player on the pitch as an opponent were also evaluated to see if these players attracted more fans of opponent team's home matches. Since additional spectators to a stadium means additional revenue for MLS, their impacts were calculated as a form of ticket price and concession spent at a stadium. In order to do so, ticket price was set at $46.22, which was the average price in 2018 (Lukas, 2018). In case of concession spent per spectator, $47.31 was used; according to the report by Oracle (2016), $47.31 was spent by the average fan in the US across all major sports leagues.

Result

On the pitch impact

To analyze an impact on the pitch, winning percent and points per match were compared. Comparing winning percent when marquee players are on and off the pitch can show the positive impact these players bring to the team. Points per match is even more critical in that every match carries a lot of weight. In soccer, draws (ties) are possible and these points can make a huge difference in the end of season standings.

Zlatan Ibrahimović. In 2 seasons with L.A. Galaxy, Zlatan played in 56 matches, including the 53 he started. Zlatan was a striker and his role was to put the ball in the back of the net. He scored 52 goals in his 56 matches and also had 17 assists. In Zlatan's 56 matches, he won 24, drew 11, and loss 21. His winning percent when starting is 43%, which is quite strong. Points gained per match when being a starting were 1.49 points. Zlatan on the pitch made a large difference compared to the matches that he did not play in for ten matches. When Zlatan did not play, the team had a winning percent of 40% and points gained per match was

1.3. Although not much difference was found in the winning percent, the points gained per match when he played makes a huge difference. For example, hypothetically, during 2018 season, having him on the pitch for his missed five matches would give L.A. Galaxy a point more, making their final standing from 6 to 5: its final points were 48 with goal difference of 2 while points for Real Salt Lake, which finished its season as 5, was 49 with goal difference of −3. Playoff spots run tight in MLS. The marginal point difference shows his impact. He averages almost a goal a match and has proven to be a game changer for L.A. Galaxy. He also led the team to the MLS post season in 2019 with his 30-goal campaign. Zlatan, from a marquee player impact on the pitch perspective, has proven his worth. L.A. Galaxy were definitely not the best team in the league, but the team was better when Zlatan was playing (Table A.1).

Kaka. Orlando City was an expansion franchise, so the team had to start its roster from scratch. Kaka played 3 seasons with Orlando City. Kaka's position was a center attacking midfielder. His role was to make the key passes in the match. Considering this role, his stats for goals and assists will not be outstanding. The impact of midfielder is difficult to evaluate with individual stats, but match results would be a good indicator. Kaka played in 75 matches, starting 69 of them. Kaka's record in matches that he played in was 22 wins, 22 draws, and 31 losses. When he started, winning percent of the team was 28.9%, which is not outstanding. Points gained per match were 1.14 points. During his 3 seasons and 75 matches, Kaka accounted for 24 goals and 22 assists, which is less than expected. When Kaka did not play, Orlando City went on to win 9, draw 9, and lose 9. Winning percent of Orlando City without Kaka was 33%, while points gained per match were 1.33. Orlando City did better in the matches without Kaka on the pitch. Kaka also never led the team to a post season appearance. Kaka, from his results on the pitch, does not appear to worth investment of the team put on him. Orlando City has never been a good team, but buying Kaka appears to be even more hurtful to their success on the pitch (Table A.2).

David Villa. David Villa played 4 seasons with NYCFC. NYCFC was an expansion franchise, so the team also had to start its roster from scratch. David Villa was a striker. In his 4 seasons at NYCFC, Villa played in 117 matches, starting 109 of them. With him on the pitch, the team resulted in 47 wins, 31 draws, and 39 losses. The team's record indicates that winning percent of the team was 40% and gained 1.467 points per match when he was a starting member. In his 117 matches, Villa scored 77 goals and had 26 assists, which is pretty productive. However, without Villa on the pitch, NYC FC won 10, drew 2, and loss 7, recorded winning percent of 52% and points gained per match of 1.68. Although he was a productive striker, these results show that NYCFC played better without David Villa. During 4 seasons of his playing with the NYCFC, the team made to a post season three times and appeared in a conference championship in 2018 (Table A.3).

Wayne Rooney. Rooney played a season and a half with D.C. United as a striker, who played in 48 matches with starting 45 matches. While he was on the pitch, the results of the team were 23 wins, 13 draws, and 12 losses. Winning percent of him as a starting was 48% and points gained per match was 1.64, which are outstanding figures. Although the winning percent was little bit below 50%, points gained per match when he was on the pitch was the highest among 4 marquee players analyzed in this study. Furthermore, in his 48 matches, he scored 23 goals and racked up 15 assists. On the contrary, when Rooney did not play D.C. United went on to win 2, draw 2, and lose 2. The winning percent was 33% and points gained per match were 1.33 points, which display positive influence of having Rooney on the pitch for sure. Rooney made an instant impact when he joined D.C. United in the middle of 2018 season, carrying the team from almost last place to just barely missing the playoffs (Table A.4).

Beyond the pitch impact

These marquee players are some of the most well-known players in the world. Part of signing these marquee players is not just for the results that they can bring on the pitch, but also for putting spectators in the stands. Getting fans in the seats is a huge piece to MLS team's revenue; it is found that venue generated income represents 69% of MLS team revenues (Olshansky, 2013). To calculate additional revenue these players generated to the MLS, ticket price was set at $46.22, which was the average price as of 2018 (Lukas, 2018). Furthermore, according to the report by Oracle (2016), the average fan in the U.S. across all major sports leagues spent $47.31 in concessions. This study employed this figure to calculate revenue generated by additional fans spending during their staying at a stadium.

Zlatan Ibrahimović. When his attendance effect is examined, noticeable differences were found in L.A. Galaxy's home attendance. Over his two seasons at L.A. Galaxy, an average of 1,578 more fans attended home matches compare to the previous season. Over 34 matches (17 home matches per season), the L.A. Galaxy had 53,652 more fans at the stadium. For L.A. Galaxy, Zlatan had brought $2,479,795 as a form of gate revenue and $2,538,276 as concession sales; he helped L.A. Galaxy generate additional revenue of about $5 million over the two years.

Zlatan had a significant impact when it comes to attendance at away matches. Over his two seasons in MLS, he added almost 200,000 more spectators, compared to the away teams' average attendance figure during his appearance. In sum, it is estimated that he had brought 252,164 more fans to the stands during his period at MLS, which is equivalent to an additional $11,655,020 in ticket revenue as well as $11,929,878 in concession spending to MLS. Over the two years, L.A. Galaxy paid him $14.4 million dollars. From a league stand point, he was almost worth the value in just gate revenue. Gate revenue and concession sales combined, an additional revenue of $23,584,898 was generated for MLS from Zlatan being in L.A. Galaxy.

Kaka. He was part of an expansion franchise so no information was available on attendance before him; therefore, as stated previously, average home attendance in 2018 was compared. Orlando City opened up their franchise playing in the Citrus Bowl through the 2015 and 2016 seasons due to their stadium being under construction. The attendance capacity at the Citrus Bowl for MLS matches capped out at around 33,000 fans for most matches and rarely up to 60,000 fans for one or two special matches a season. When Orlando City moved to their new stadium, Exploria Stadium, their new capacity was 25,500. This change in available fans in the stadium skews Kaka's numbers when taking the mean and makes it less accurate. Instead, for Kaka, the ratio of the percentage of the capacity that the average season attendance of home matches to the 33,000 capacity of home matches and same for Exploria Stadium, but with 25,500, will be used to see his impact in the stands when he left Orlando City. In 2015, Orlando City filled up 99.61% of the Citrus Bowl capacity. In 2016, they filled 94.92%. In 2017 at Exploria Stadium, they filled 98.14% of the 25,500 capacity on average. On average, Kaka filled 97.55% of stadium capacity for home matches. The number that will be used to see his impact once he leaves is 24,875 fans. Kaka added 1,009 more fans per home match throughout his career. This is equivalent to 17,153 more fans per season and $1,604,320 more in revenue per season. Over his career, he added over 51,459 more fans to home matches and $4,812,960 in estimated total gate revenue and concession spending, together. He also added 52,532 more away fans to 51 away matches over his three seasons, which is $2,428,029 in ticket revenue and $2,705,569 in concession sales to MLS. His impact in the stands does not reflect well on the salary that he was paid over his time in MLS.

David Villa. As Villa joined NYCFC as an extension franchise as well, his home attendance figure was compared to the year after he left the team. Over his four seasons at NYCFC, an average of 25,516 spectators attended for home matches, whereas an average of 21,107 fans attended for 17 home matches during 2019 season, the year Villa left the franchise. Therefore, it is estimated that he had brought 74,953 more spectators every year; and during his career at NYCFC, he added about 299,812 more spectators, which is equivalent to gate revenue of $13,857,310 and concession revenue of $14,184,106. In other words, Villa contributed to almost $28 million additional revenue that was generated at the stadium while he played for NYCFC. In case of away matches, he also attracted 143,655 more away fans to matches over his four seasons and his 68 away matches. This is equivalent to additional gate revenue of $6,639,734 and $6,769,792 from concession sales, a total of $13,436,525 to MLS. Considering Villa's paycheck of $5.6 million per season, his contribution to the NYCFC and MLS was far beyond his salary.

Wayne Rooney. Rooney did not have any effect when it comes to home attendance: his arrival kept the home attendance about even. Similarly, he had a smaller role in bringing in more league gate revenue for away matches as well. He had brought 22,387 more away fans to matches during his 23 away matches over one and half seasons with D.C. United. Overall, it is estimated that his contribution to the MLS in terms of additional revenue is about $2,093,856, which was not enough to cover his paycheck of $2.7 million per year (Table A.5).

Conclusion

From an on the pitch impact perspective, the findings of this study are controversial; while Zlatan and Rooney made a significant positive impact to the team performance in terms of winning percent and points gained each match, team performance was better when Villa and Kaka were not playing for their team. However, considering their paychecks, which are usually more than the salary cap of the entire team, it is questionable whether the investment is worth the enhanced performance. In spite of their big names, most of these players are at the end of their career, inferring that they do not have the same spark that they used to have. When it comes to off the pitch or bringing additional spectators to the MLS, most of them had positive impacts for both home and away matches, except Rooney. However, it can be claimed that their contribution to generate additional revenue at the gate as well as concession sales for both home and away matches seem not large enough to justify their paycheck.

In spite of the above findings, it should not be concluded that these marquee players are not worth investing in. In this study, when on the pitch impact of these marquee players was evaluated, the performance level of opponent teams was not considered. It may be the case that these players did not play for a specific match because it would not be too difficult to win the match without marquee players on the pitch. There are other occasions when the losses had nothing to do with the performance of these super stars. For instance, Kaka played for Orlando City, which has been a struggling franchise on the results side. As soccer is a team sport played by 11 players, it is extremely difficult for one exceptional player to bring victory every time.

Furthermore, although this study investigated their impact on and off the pitch, there are several other factors that should be considered. For instance, this study fails to consider the marketing and brand advertisement money involved with these players. Due to the high attention these players draw, it is often a means to gain global recognition when they score, which affects brand awareness of the club associated with the players. Moreover, it is also true that these renowned international players attract overseas media, audiences, and potential corporate sponsors (Zhang et al., 2018), whose impacts are not easy to calculate in monetary value.

In spite of these unaccounted factors in this study, it is not worth investing significant amount to sign a marquee player, when considering only on and off the pitch impact this study has estimated. They typically do not produce on the pitch performance like managers think they would nor do they necessarily draw in fans the way the owners think they would. It is very few times that we see the 'Beckham effect' or the 'Zlatan effect'. Moreover, having these players in a team is not a sustainable strategy to enhance team performance or to attract fans to a stadium from a long-term perspective. The common finding across these four players is that home team attendance after these players' exit dropped significantly. These players had attracted temporal fans rather than 'true' fans to the team. One of the main motivations to sign these players is to secure more fans for the team, who usually leave with the exit of marquee players. Considering these factors, the direction of new strategy in MLS, MLS 3.0, which extensively searches for young and potential talent seems to be on the right track from a long-term perspective, as the impact of signing big names lasts for a short while and diminishes once they leave the team.

References

Baer, B. (2017, December 8). MLS announces increase in Targeted Allocation Money for 2018 and 2019. *Major League Soccer.* https://www.mlssoccer.com

BBC Sport. (2017, November 28). Premier League average weekly wage passes £50,000, says new study. *BBC.* https://www.bbc.com/

Boniface, D. (2018, May 10). New York City FC player salaries 2018. *The Denver Post.* https://www.denverpost.com/

Brennan, P. (2018, December 18). How the money works: Understanding Major League Soccer's financial rules. *The Enquirer.* https://www.cincinnati.com/

Brown, M. T., Rascher, D. A., Nagel, M. S., and EMcEvoy, C. D. (2016). *Financial management in the sport industry* (2nd ed.). Taylor & Francis.

Carlisle, J. (2014, September 29). Kaka tops Clint Dempsey as the highest-paid player in MLS. *ESPN.* https://www.espn.com/

Coates, D., Frick, B., and Jewell, T. (2016). Superstar salaries and soccer success: The impact of designated players in Major League Soccer. *Journal of Sports Economics, 17*(7), 716–735.

Eligon, J. (2005, November 11). For M.L.S., the sport's future is in the eye of the beholder. *The New York Times.* http://www.nytimes.com

ESPN. (2015, January 7). MLS confident new CBA will be done in time for March 6 season start. *ESPN.* https://www.mlssoccer.com

Jewell, R. T. (2017). The effect of marquee players on sports demand: The case of US Major League Soccer. *Journal of Sports Economics, 18*(3), 239–252.

Kaiser, L. L. (2004). The flight from single-entity structured sport leagues. *DePaul Journal of Sports Law, 2*(1), 1–27.

Lukas, M. (2018, September 17). NFL vs MLS: Revenue, salaries, viewership and ratings. *WSN.* https://www.wsn.com

Marcus, J. (2010, April 2). M.L.S. expands designated player rule. *The New York Times.* https://www.nytimes.com/

MLS. (2006, April 1). MLS implements designated player rule and other competition initiatives. *Major League Soccer.* https://www.mlssoccer.com

MLS. (2012, Febraury 16). MLS roster rules. *Major League Soccer.* https://www.mlssoccer.com

MLS. (2017a, January 1). MLS designated players. *Major League Soccer.* https://www.mlssoccer.com

MLS. (2017b, February 2). Targeted Allocation Money. *Major League Soccer.* https://www.mlssoccer.com/glossary/targeted-allocation-money

MLS. (2020). Stats. *Major League Soccer.* https://www.mlssoccer.com/stats/players

MLSPA. (2020a). *2014 salary report.* M. L. S. P. Association. http://s3.amazonaws.com/mlspa/September-15-2014-Salary-Information-Alphabetical.pdf?mtime=20180416202413

MLSPA. (2020b). *2015–2019 CBA in English*. M. L. S. P. Association. https://s3.amazonaws.com/mlspa/Collective-Bargaining-Agreement-February-1-2015.pdf?mtime=20180213190926

MLSPA. (2020c). *2019 salary report*. M. L. S. P. Association. http://s3.amazonaws.com/mlspa/Salary-List-Fall-Release-FINAL-Salary-List-Fall-Release-MLS.pdf?mtime=20190927175823

Olshansky, A. (2013, April 30). Greed is good: Why MLS must feed the monster. *The Shin Guardian*. https://www.mlssoccer.com

Oracle. (2016). The fan experience changing the game with food and beverage technology. O. F. a. beverage. www.oracle.com/fanexperience

Reed, A. (2019, August 6). Wayne Rooney is leaving his $2.7 million a year salary in the US to play soccer in England's second tier. *CNBC*. https://www.cnbc.com/

Reese, B. (2014, January 30). A look at income inequality in MLS. *Empire of Soccer*. http://www.empireofsoccer.com/

Simpson, C. (2019, June 13). MLS salaries released: Zlatan Ibrahimovic sets record with $7.2M 2019 wage. *Bleacher Report*. https://bleacherreport.com/

Spotrac. (2020). *MLB team luxury tax tracker*. https://www.spotrac.com/mlb/tax/

Stejskal, S. (2017, February 2). General allocation money. *Major League Soccer*. https://www.mlssoccer.com

Stejskal, S. (2018, March 27). Stejskal: The inside story of how the LA Galaxy landed Zlatan Ibrahimovic. *Major League Soccer*. https://www.mlssoccer.com

UEFA. (2015, June 30). Financial fair play: All you need to know. https://www.uefa.com/

Warren, C. J., and Ross, S. D. (2011). Beyond Beckham: The designated player rule in Major League Soccer. *International Journal of Sport Management*, *12*(2), 208–220.

Zhang, J. J., Kim, E., Mastromartino, B., Qian, T. Y., and Nauright, J. (2018). The sport industry in growing economies: Critical issues and challenges. *International Journal of Sports Marketing and Sponsorship*, *19*(2), 110–126

Appendix 11.1

Player statistics and attendance (MLS, 2020)

Table A.1 Performance Statistics of Zlatan Ibrahimović (from 2018 to 2019 Season)

Regular Season

Date	Match	Result	Appearance	MINS	G	A	Attendance
3/24/18	LA @ VAN	T 0-0	Unused Sub	0	0	0	22,120
3/31/18	LAFC @ LA	W 3-4	Subbed on	19	2	0	27,068
4/8/18	SKC @ LA	L 2-0	Subbed on	28	0	0	25,846
4/14/18	LA @ CHI	W 1-0	Started	80	1	0	21,915
4/21/18	ATL @ LA	L 2-0	Started	90	0	0	25,846
4/28/18	RBNY @ LA	L 3-2	Started	90	0	2	26,704
5/5/18	LA @ HOU	L 2-3	Started	90	0	1	22,320
5/12/18	LA @ DAL	L 2-3	Started	90	0	0	18,355
5/21/18	LA @ MTL	W 1-0	Started	41	0	0	20,801
5/25/18	SJ @ LA	W 0-1	Unused Sub	0	0	0	23,118
5/30/18	DAL @ LA	L 3-2	Started	90	2	0	18,003
6/2/18	LA @ POR	T 1-1	Subbed on	18	0	0	21,144
6/9/18	RSL @ LA	W 0-3	Started	86	2	0	25,462
6/30/18	LA @ SJ	T 3-3	Started	90	2	0	50,743
7/4/18	DC @ LA	T 2-2	Started	90	1	0	25,462
7/7/18	CLB @ LA	W 0-4	Started	71	1	0	21,211
7/14/18	LA @ NE	W 3-2	Unused Sub	0	0	0	36,573
7/21/18	LA @ PHI	W 3-1	Started	90	1	1	19,013
7/26/18	LA @ LAFC	T 2-2	Started	90	0	1	22,716
7/29/18	ORL @ LA	W 3-4	Started	90	3	1	24,941
8/4/18	LA @ COL	L 1-2	Unused Sub	0	0	0	17,837
8/11/18	MIN @ LA	T 2-2	Started	90	0	1	24,891
8/14/18	COL @ LA	T 2-2	Started	90	0	0	16,231
8/18/18	LA @ SEA	L 0-5	Unused Sub	0	0	0	44,213
8/24/18	LAFC @ LA	T 1-1	Started	90	1	0	27,068
9/1/18	LA @ RSL	L 2-6	Started	90	0	1	21,363
9/15/18	LA @ TOR	L 3-5	Started	90	1	0	30,799
9/23/18	SEA @ LA	W 0-3	Started	90	1	1	25,503
9/29/18	VAN @ LA	W 0-3	Started	90	2	0	25,659
10/6/18	LA @ SKC	T 1-1	Started	90	1	0	20,092
10/21/18	LA @ MIN	W 3-1	Started	90	1	1	52,242
10/28/18	HOU @ LA	L 3-2	Started	90	0	0	27,068
3/2/19	CHI @ LA	W 1-2	Started	90	1	0	25,866
3/9/19	LA @ DAL	L 0-2	Unused Sub	0	0	0	17,220
3/16/19	MIN @ LA	W 2-3	Unused Sub	0	0	0	21,177
3/31/19	POR @ LA	W 1-2	Started	90	2	0	23,820

Marquee players in MLS 181

Date	Match	Result	Appearance	MINS	G	A	Attendance
4/5/19	LA @ VAN	W 2-0	Started	90	1	1	22,120
4/13/19	PHI @ LA	W 0-2	Started	90	2	0	24,053
4/19/19	HOU @ LA	W 1-2	Started	90	1	0	21,503
4/24/19	LA @ MIN	T 0-0	Started	90	0	0	19,779
4/28/19	RSL @ LA	W 1-2	Started	90	1	0	20,615
5/4/19	LA @ RBNY	L 2-3	Started	90	1	1	20,128
5/8/19	LA @ CLB	L 1-3	Started	90	0	0	13,207
5/11/19	NYC @ LA	L 2-0	Started	90	0	0	22,806
5/19/19	COL @ LA	L 1-0	Unused Sub	0	0	0	19,015
5/24/19	LA @ ORL	W 1-0	Unused Sub	0	0	0	24,712
5/29/19	LA @ SKC	W 2-0	Started	90	1	1	19,979
6/2/19	NE @ LA	L 2-1	Started	90	1	0	20,828
6/22/19	LA @ CIN	W 2-0	Started	90	0	0	32,250
6/29/19	LA @ SJ	L 0-3	Started	90	0	0	50,850
7/4/19	TOR @ LA	W 0-2	Started	90	2	0	25,482
7/12/19	SJ @ LA	L 3-1	Started	90	0	0	22,508
7/19/19	LAFC @ LA	W 2-3	Started	90	3	0	27,088
7/27/19	LA @ POR	L 0-4	Started	90	0	0	25,218
8/3/19	LA @ ATL	L 0-3	Unused Sub	0	0	0	72,548
8/11/19	LA @ DC	L 1-2	Started	90	0	0	20,006
8/14/19	DAL @ LA	W 0-2	Started	90	2	0	19,653
8/17/19	SEA @ LA	T 2-2	Started	90	2	0	26,213
8/25/19	LA @ LAFC	T 3-3	Started	90	2	0	22,757
9/1/19	LA @ SEA	L 3-4	Started	90	1	1	46,673
9/11/19	LA @ COL	L 1-2	Started	90	0	0	10,945
9/15/19	SKC @ LA	W 2-7	Started	90	3	0	22,465
9/21/19	MTL @ LA	W 1-2	Started	90	1	1	25,482
9/25/19	LA @ RSL	W 2-1	Started	90	1	1	20,838
9/29/19	VAN @ LA	L 4-3	Started	90	1	1	25,903
10/6/19	LA @ HOU	L 2-4	Started	90	1	0	21,777

Post Season

Date	Match	Result	Appearance	MINS	G	A
10/24/19	LA @ LAFC	L 3-5	Started	90	1	1
10/20/19	LA @ MIN	W 2-1	Started	90	0	0

Career Statistics – Regular Season

Year	Club	GP	MINS	G	A
2019	LA Galaxy	29	2,610	30	7
2018	LA Galaxy	27	2,143	22	10
Career totals		56	4,753	52	17

Career Statistics – Post Season

Year	Club	GP	MINS	G	A
2019	LA Galaxy	2	180	1	1

Note: MINS = Minutes played, G = Goal, A = Assist, GP = Game Played.

182 Andrew Macuga and Euisoo Kim

Table A.2 Performance Statistics of Kaka (from 2015 to 2017 Season)

Regular Season

Date	Match	Result	Appearance	MINS	G	A	Attendance
3/8/15	NYC @ ORL	T 1-1	Started	90	1	0	62,150
3/13/15	ORL @ HOU	W 1-0	Started	82	0	0	22,407
3/21/15	VAN @ ORL	L 1-0	Started	90	0	0	31,072
3/28/15	ORL @ MTL	T 2-2	Started	90	1	1	25,245
4/3/15	DC @ ORL	L 1-0	Started	90	0	0	32,822
4/12/15	ORL @ POR	W 2-0	Started	90	1	0	21,144
4/18/15	ORL @ CLB	L 0-3	Started	90	0	0	15,655
4/26/15	TOR @ ORL	L 2-0	Started	90	0	0	30,908
5/8/15	NE @ ORL	T 2-2	Started	90	0	0	27,243
5/13/15	ORL @ DC	L 1-2	Started	90	0	0	12,532
5/17/15	LA @ ORL	W 0-4	Started	90	1	1	40,122
5/24/15	ORL @ SJ	T 1-1	Started	90	1	0	36,224
5/30/15	CLB @ ORL	T 2-2	Started	90	1	0	31,430
6/6/15	ORL @ CHI	W 3-2	Started	89	0	0	20,124
6/14/15	DC @ ORL	W 0-1	Started	89	1	0	30,054
6/20/15	ORL @ MTL	L 0-2	Started	90	0	0	17,820
6/24/15	COL @ ORL	W 0-2	Started	90	1	0	23,372
7/4/15	ORL @ RSL	T 1-1	Started	44	1	0	20,956
7/11/15	DAL @ ORL	L 2-0	Unused Sub	0	0	0	30,513
7/18/15	RBNY @ ORL	L 2-0	Started	90	0	0	33,518
7/26/15	ORL @ NYC	L 3-5	Started	90	0	1	32,041
8/1/15	CLB @ ORL	W 2-5	Started	90	0	1	26,586
8/5/15	ORL @ TOR	L 1-4	Unused Sub	0	0	0	26,648
8/8/15	PHI @ ORL	T 0-0	Started	90	0	0	28,495
8/16/15	ORL @ SEA	L 0-4	Started	70	0	0	40,453
8/22/15	ORL @ TOR	L 0-5	Started	85	0	0	26,397
8/29/15	CHI @ ORL	T 1-1	Started	90	0	0	28,921
9/5/15	ORL @ NE	L 0-3	Unused Sub	0	0	0	18,854
9/13/15	SKC @ ORL	W 1-3	Unused Sub	0	0	0	22,241
9/19/15	ORL @ CHI	W 1-0	Unused Sub	0	0	0	20,280
9/25/15	ORL @ RBNY	W 5-2	Started	90	0	3	20,695
10/3/15	MTL @ ORL	W 1-2	Started	90	0	0	35,421
10/16/15	NYC @ ORL	W 1-2	Unused Sub	0	0	0	43,179
10/25/15	ORL @ PHI	L 0-1	Started	90	0	0	17,309
3/6/16	RSL @ ORL	T 2-2	Unused Sub	0	0	0	60,147
3/11/16	CHI @ ORL	T 1-1	Unused Sub	0	0	0	29,041
3/18/16	ORL @ NYC	W 1-0	Unused Sub	0	0	0	24,597
4/3/16	POR @ ORL	W 1-4	Started	80	1	2	31,114
4/8/16	ORL @ PHI	L 1-2	Started	90	0	0	15,011
4/17/16	NE @ ORL	T 2-2	Started	90	1	0	36,048
4/24/16	ORL @ RBNY	L 2-3	Unused Sub	0	0	0	18,238
4/30/16	ORL @ NE	T 2-2	Unused Sub	0	0	0	25,203
5/6/16	RBNY @ ORL	T 1-1	Started	90	0	0	31,264
5/15/16	ORL @ SKC	L 1-2	Started	90	0	0	19,080
5/21/16	MTL @ ORL	W 1-2	Started	90	0	2	34,081
5/25/16	PHI @ ORL	T 2-2	Started	90	0	1	24,109
5/29/16	ORL @ NYC	T 2-2	Unused Sub	0	0	0	15,039
6/18/16	SJ @ ORL	T 2-2	Unused Sub	0	0	0	37,194

Date	Match	Result	Role	Min			Att
6/25/16	TOR @ ORL	W 2-3	Started	90	1	0	27,818
7/4/16	ORL @ DAL	L 0-4	Started	45	0	0	16,195
7/8/16	HOU @ ORL	T 0-0	Unused Sub	0	0	0	28,104
7/13/16	ORL @ RBNY	L 0-2	Unused Sub	0	0	0	19,121
7/16/16	ORL @ VAN	T 2-2	Unused Sub	0	0	0	22,120
7/23/16	ORL @ CLB	T 2-2	Subbed on	30	0	0	20,034
7/31/16	NE @ ORL	W 1-3	Started	84	0	1	27,768
8/7/16	SEA @ ORL	L 3-1	Started	90	0	1	28,247
8/14/16	ORL @ CHI	T 2-2	Started	90	1	1	18,148
8/20/16	ORL @ COL	T 0-0	Started	90	0	0	16,813
8/24/16	TOR @ ORL	L 2-1	Started	90	0	0	23,802
8/28/16	NYC @ ORL	W 1-2	Started	74	2	0	27,482
9/7/16	ORL @ MTL	W 4-1	Started	65	2	0	17,389
9/11/16	ORL @ LA	L 2-4	Started	73	0	0	27,167
9/17/16	CLB @ ORL	L 4-1	Started	90	0	0	30,218
9/24/16	ORL @ DC	L 1-4	Started	64	0	0	25,842
9/28/16	ORL @ TOR	T 0-0	Started	90	0	0	23,805
10/2/16	MTL @ ORL	L 1-0	Started	90	0	0	26,041
10/16/16	ORL @ PHI	W 2-0	Started	90	0	0	18,007
10/23/16	DC @ ORL	W 2-4	Started	90	1	2	30,022
3/5/17	NYC @ ORL	W 0-1	Started	11	0	0	25,527
3/18/17	PHI @ ORL	W 1-2	Unused Sub	0	0	0	25,527
4/1/17	ORL @ CLB	L 0-2	Unused Sub	0	0	0	12,226
4/9/17	RBNY @ ORL	W 0-1	Unused Sub	0	0	0	25,527
4/15/17	LA @ ORL	W 1-2	Unused Sub	0	0	0	25,527
4/23/17	ORL @ NYC	W 2-1	Unused Sub	0	0	0	22,470
4/29/17	COL @ ORL	W 0-2	Subbed on	30	1	0	25,527
5/3/17	ORL @ TOR	L 1-2	Started	65	1	0	25,200
5/6/17	ORL @ HOU	L 0-4	Subbed on	32	0	0	19,292
5/13/17	SKC @ ORL	T 2-2	Started	90	1	0	25,527
5/17/17	ORL @ SJ	T 1-1	Subbed on	27	0	1	18,000
5/21/17	NYC @ ORL	L 3-0	Started	60	0	0	25,527
5/27/17	ORL @ MIN	L 0-1	Unused Sub	0	0	0	18,896
5/31/17	DC @ ORL	W 0-2	Unused Sub	0	0	0	24,112
6/4/17	CHI @ ORL	T 0-0	Subbed on	31	0	0	24,469
6/17/17	MTL @ ORL	T 3-3	Started	90	0	1	25,527
6/21/17	ORL @ SEA	T 1-1	Started	90	0	1	42,333
6/24/17	ORL @ CHI	L 0-4	Started	64	0	0	20,000
6/30/17	ORL @ RSL	W 1-0	Started	72	0	0	19,218
7/5/17	TOR @ ORL	L 3-1	Started	90	0	1	25,029
7/21/17	ATL @ ORL	L 1-0	Started	90	0	0	25,527
7/29/17	ORL @ ATL	T 1-1	Started	90	1	0	45,006
8/5/17	ORL @ MTL	L 1-2	Started	90	0	0	20,801
8/12/17	ORL @ RBNY	L 1-3	Started	89	0	1	25,219
8/19/17	CLB @ ORL	T 1-1	Unused Sub	0	0	0	25,527
8/26/17	VAN @ ORL	L 2-1	Started	90	0	0	24,406
9/2/17	ORL @ NE	L 0-4	Started	90	0	0	17,865
9/9/17	ORL @ DC	W 2-1	Subbed on	13	0	0	18,028
9/16/17	ORL @ ATL	T 3-3	Unused Sub	0	0	0	70,425
9/24/17	ORL @ POR	L 0-3	Unused Sub	0	0	0	21,144
9/27/17	NE @ ORL	W 1-6	Started	80	2	0	23,018
9/30/17	DAL @ ORL	T 0-0	Started	90	0	0	24,007
10/15/17	CLB @ ORL	L 1-0	Started	90	0	0	25,166
10/22/17	ORL @ PHI	L 1-6	Unused Sub	0	0	0	18,595

Career Statistics – Regular Season

Year	Club	GP	MINS	G	A
2017	Orlando City SC	23	1,564	6	5
2016	Orlando City SC	24	1,955	9	10
2015	Orlando City SC	28	2,439	9	7
Career totals	–	75	5,958	24	22

Note: MINS = Minutes played, G = Goal, A = Assist, GP = Game Played.

Table A.3 Performance Statistics of David Villa (from 2015 to 2018 Season)

Regular Season

Date	Match	Result	Appearance	MINS	G	A	Attendance
3/8/15	NYC @ ORL	T 1-1	Started	90	0	0	62,510
3/15/15	NE @ NYC	W 0-2	Started	90	1	1	43,507
3/21/15	NYC @ COL	T 0-0	Started	90	0	0	17,692
3/28/15	SKC @ NYC	L 1-0	Unused Sub	0	0	0	27,454
4/11/15	NYC @ PHI	L 1-2	Started	90	1	0	18,603
4/16/15	PHI @ NYC	T 1-1	Started	45	0	0	20,461
4/19/15	POR @ NYC	L 1-0	Unused Sub	0	0	0	21,891
4/24/15	NYC @ CHI	L 0-1	Unused Sub	0	0	0	19,124
5/3/15	SEA @ NYC	L 3-1	Subbed on	36	0	0	25,384
5/10/15	NYC @ RBNY	L 1-2	Started	68	0	0	25,217
5/15/15	CHI @ NYC	T 2-2	Started	90	0	1	23,315
5/23/15	NYC @ RSL	L 0-2	Started	90	0	0	20,801
5/30/15	HOU @ NYC	T 1-1	Started	90	1	0	26,211
6/6/15	NYC @ PHI	W 2-1	Started	90	0	0	18,517
6/13/15	MTL @ NYC	W 1-3	Started	90	1	1	24,042
6/20/15	NYC @ TOR	W 2-0	Started	90	2	0	30,029
6/28/15	RBNY @ NYC	L 3-1	Started	90	0	0	48,047
7/4/15	NYC @ MTL	W 2-1	Started	90	2	0	18,112
7/12/15	TOR @ NYC	T 4-4	Started	90	2	0	27,533
7/18/15	NYC @ NE	L 0-1	Started	90	0	0	28,811
7/26/15	ORL @ NYC	W 3-5	Started	90	2	1	32,041
8/1/15	MTL @ NYC	L 3-2	Started	90	1	1	27,645
8/9/15	NYC @ RBNY	L 0-2	Started	90	0	0	25,219
8/13/15	DC @ NYC	W 1-3	Started	90	1	1	28,262
8/19/15	NYC @ CLB	T 2-2	Started	90	0	1	15,514
8/23/15	NYC @ LA	L 1-5	Started	90	1	0	27,000
8/29/15	CLB @ NYC	L 2-1	Started	90	0	0	30,018
9/12/15	NYC @ DAL	L 1-2	Started	45	0	0	16,937
9/16/15	TOR @ NYC	W 0-2	Unused Sub	0	0	0	25,075
9/19/15	SJ @ NYC	W 2-3	Started	70	1	1	28,231
9/26/15	NYC @ VAN	W 2-1	Started	90	1	0	21,000
10/2/15	NYC @ DC	L 1-2	Started	90	0	0	21,517
10/16/15	NYC @ ORL	L 1-2	Started	90	0	0	43,179
10/25/15	NE @ NYC	L 3-1	Started	90	1	0	34,150
3/6/16	NYC @ CHI	W 4-3	Started	90	0	0	17,768
3/13/16	TOR @ NYC	T 2-2	Started	90	2	0	30,321
3/18/16	ORL @ NYC	L 1-0	Started	90	0	0	24,597
3/26/16	NE @ NYC	T 1-1	Started	90	0	0	23,425

4/10/16	CHI @ NYC	T 0-0	Started	90	0	0	22,930
4/16/16	NYC @ CLB	L 2-3	Started	90	2	0	16,715
4/23/16	NYC @ PHI	L 0-2	Started	90	0	0	18,681
4/27/16	MTL @ NYC	T 1-1	Started	90	0	0	23,352
4/30/16	VAN @ NYC	W 2-3	Started	90	2	0	25,438
5/8/16	NYC @ DC	W 2-0	Started	90	1	0	14,504
5/15/16	NYC @ POR	W 2-1	Started	90	1	0	21,144
5/18/16	NYC @ TOR	T 1-1	Subbed on	16	0	0	30,262
5/21/16	RBNY @ NYC	L 7-0	Started	90	0	0	37,858
5/29/16	ORL @ NYC	T 2-2	Started	90	1	0	25,039
6/2/16	RSL @ NYC	L 3-2	Started	90	1	1	22,736
6/18/16	PHI @ NYC	W 2-3	Started	90	1	0	27,456
6/25/16	NYC @ SEA	W 2-0	Started	90	0	0	47,537
7/3/16	RBNY @ NYC	W 0-2	Started	90	1	0	33,613
7/6/16	NYC @ NE	W 1-0	Started	90	0	0	18,187
7/10/16	NYC @ SKC	L 1-3	Started	90	0	0	19,881
7/17/16	NYC @ MTL	W 3-1	Started	90	1	0	20,801
7/24/16	NYC @ RBNY	L 1-4	Started	90	0	0	25,218
7/30/16	COL @ NYC	W 1-5	Unused Sub	0	0	0	25,711
8/5/16	NYC @ SJ	T 0-0	Started	90	0	0	18,000
8/13/16	NYC @ CLB	T 3-3	Started	90	2	0	18,189
8/20/16	LA @ NYC	W 0-1	Started	90	1	0	35,509
8/28/16	NYC @ ORL	L 1-2	Started	90	0	0	27,482
9/1/16	DC @ NYC	W 2-3	Started	90	1	1	23,768
9/10/16	NYC @ NE	L 1-3	Started	63	0	0	23,325
9/17/16	DAL @ NYC	T 2-2	Started	90	0	0	25,204
9/23/16	CHI @ NYC	W 1-4	Started	90	2	1	25,011
9/30/16	NYC @ HOU	W 2-0	Started	90	2	0	19,616
10/16/16	NYC @ DC	L 1-3	Started	90	1	0	30,943
10/23/16	CLB @ NYC	W 1-4	Started	90	1	1	30,374
3/5/17	NYC @ ORL	L 0-1	Started	90	0	0	25,527
3/12/17	DC @ NYC	W 0-4	Started	78	2	1	24,259
3/18/17	MTL @ NYC	T 1-1	Started	90	0	0	18,515
4/1/17	SJ @ NYC	W 1-2	Started	89	0	2	20,066
4/8/17	NYC @ DC	L 1-2	Started	90	1	0	18,855
4/14/17	NYC @ PHI	W 2-0	Started	90	1	0	16,553
4/23/17	ORL @ NYC	L 2-1	Started	90	1	0	22,470
4/29/17	NYC @ CLB	W 3-2	Unused Sub	0	0	0	17,336
5/7/17	ATL @ NYC	W 1-3	Started	89	1	1	25,605
5/14/17	NYC @ DAL	T 1-1	Started	90	0	0	14,665
5/17/17	NYC @ RSL	L 1-2	Subbed on	36	0	0	16,434
5/21/17	NYC @ ORL	W 3-0	Started	86	2	0	25,527
5/28/17	NYC @ ATL	L 1-3	Started	90	0	0	44,901
5/31/17	NE @ NYC	T 2-2	Started	90	0	2	20,193
6/3/17	PHI @ NYC	W 1-2	Started	90	0	0	24,290
6/17/17	SEA @ NYC	W 1-2	Started	89	2	0	25,073
6/24/17	NYC @ RBNY	W 2-0	Started	83	0	0	25,219
6/29/17	MIN @ NYC	W 1-3	Started	90	1	0	21,572
7/5/17	NYC @ VAN	L 2-3	Started	90	1	0	22,120
7/19/17	TOR @ NYC	T 2-2	Started	90	1	1	22,011
7/22/17	CHI @ NYC	W 1-2	Started	89	1	0	26,025
7/30/17	NYC @ TOR	L 0-4	Started	77	0	0	29,203
8/6/17	RBNY @ NYC	W 2-3	Started	89	3	0	33,679
8/12/17	NYC @ LA	W 2-0	Started	90	1	0	25,667
8/20/17	NE @ NYC	W 1-2	Started	90	1	1	22,415
8/25/17	NYC @ RBNY	T 1-1	Started	90	0	1	25,219

(Continued)

Date	Match	Result	Appearance	MINS	G	A	Attendance
9/6/17	SKC @ NYC	W 0-1	Unused Sub	0	0	0	19,353
9/9/17	POR @ NYC	L 1-0	Unused Sub	0	0	0	23,651
9/16/17	NYC @ COL	T 1-1	Subbed on	18	0	0	14,336
9/23/17	HOU @ NYC	T 1-1	Started	84	0	0	10,165
9/27/17	NYC @ MTL	W 1-0	Subbed on	29	0	0	16,005
9/30/17	NYC @ CHI	T 1-1	Started	90	1	0	20,195
10/15/17	NYC @ NE	L 1-2	Started	90	0	0	33,767
10/22/17	CLB @ NYC	T 2-2	Started	90	2	0	20,113
3/4/18	NYC @ SKC	W 2-0	Started	85	0	1	20,831
3/11/18	LA @ NYC	W 1-2	Started	86	1	0	26,221
3/17/18	ORL @ NYC	W 0-2	Unused Sub	0	0	0	18,584
3/24/18	NYC @ NE	T 2-2	Unused Sub	0	0	0	12,376
3/31/18	NYC @ SJ	W 2-1	Unused Sub	0	0	0	18,000
4/11/18	RSL @ NYC	W 0-4	Subbed on	31	0	0	18,603
4/15/18	NYC @ ATL	T 2-2	Subbed on	55	1	1	45,001
4/22/18	NYC @ POR	L 0-3	Started	90	0	0	21,144
4/29/18	DAL @ NYC	W 1-3	Started	87	2	0	22,115
5/5/18	NYC @ RBNY	L 0-4	Started	66	0	0	25,219
5/13/18	NYC @ LAFC	T 2-2	Started	87	1	0	22,000
5/19/18	COL @ NYC	W 0-4	Started	90	2	1	21,494
5/25/18	NYC @ HOU	L 1-3	Started	90	1	0	18,123
6/2/18	ORL @ NYC	W 0-3	Subbed on	25	0	0	22,103
6/9/18	ATL @ NYC	T 1-1	Started	90	0	1	25,628
6/24/18	TOR @ NYC	W 1-2	Started	28	0	0	23,930
6/30/18	NYC @ CHI	L 2-3	Unused Sub	0	0	0	15,204
7/8/18	RBNY @ NYC	W 0-1	Unused Sub	0	0	0	30,027
7/11/18	MTL @ NYC	W 0-3	Unused Sub	0	0	0	18,706
7/14/18	CLB @ NYC	W 0-2	Unused Sub	0	0	0	21,085
7/26/18	NYC @ ORL	W 2-0	Unused Sub	0	0	0	23,790
7/29/18	NYC @ SEA	L 1-3	Unused Sub	0	0	0	39,528
8/4/18	VAN @ NYC	T 2-2	Unused Sub	0	0	0	20,802
8/12/18	NYC @ TOR	W 3-2	Started	71	1	0	27,935
8/18/18	NYC @ PHI	L 0-2	Started	56	1	0	17,594
8/22/18	RBNY @ NYC	T 1-1	Started	87	1	0	30,139
9/1/18	NYC @ CLB	L 1-2	Started	90	0	0	11,991
9/5/18	NE @ NYC	L 1-0	Started	90	0	0	18,884
9/8/18	DC @ NYC	T 1-1	Started	90	1	0	2,829
9/22/18	NYC @ MTL	T 1-1	Started	90	0	0	20,801
9/26/18	CHI @ NYC	W 0-2	Started	90	1	1	21,582
9/29/18	NYC @ MIN	L 1-2	Unused Sub	0	0	0	21,926
10/21/18	NYC @ DC	L 1-3	Started	90	1	0	20,249
10/28/18	PHI @ NYC	W 1-3	Started	90	1	0	26,441

Post Season

Date	Match	Result	Appearance	MINS	G	A
11/11/18	NYC @ ATL	L 1-3	Started	90	0	0
11/4/18	ATL @ NYC	L 1-0	Started	90	0	0
10/31/18	PHI @ NYC	W 1-3	Started	84	1	0
11/5/17	CLB @ NYC	W 0-2	Started	90	1	0
10/31/17	NYC @ CLB	L 1-4	Started	90	1	0
11/6/16	TOR @ NYC	L 5-0	Started	90	0	0
10/30/16	NYC @ TOR	L 0-2	Started	78	0	0

Marquee players in MLS   187

Career Statistics – Regular Season

Year	Club	GP	MINS	G	A
2018	New York City FC	23	1,754	14	5
2017	New York City FC	31	2,556	22	9
2016	New York City FC	33	2,869	23	4
2015	New York City FC	30	2,514	18	8
Career totals		117	9,693	77	26

Career Statistics –Post Season

Year	Club	GP	MINS	G	A
2018	New York City FC	3	264	1	0
2017	New York City FC	2	180	2	0
2016	New York City FC	2	168	0	0
Career Totals		7	612	3	0

Note: MINS = Minutes played, G = Goal, A = Assist, GP = Game Played.

Table A.4 Performance Statistics of Wayne Rooney (from 2018 to 2019 Season)

Regular Season

Date	Match	Result	Appearance	MINS	G	A	Attendance
7/14/18	VAN @ DC	W 1-3	Subbed on	32	0	1	20,504
7/21/18	DC @ ATL	L 1-3	Started	66	0	0	45,087
7/25/18	RBNY @ DC	L 1-0	Subbed on	33	0	0	15,655
7/28/18	COL @ DC	W 1-2	Started	90	1	0	18,931
8/4/18	DC @ MTL	T 1-1	Started	90	0	0	19,152
8/12/18	ORL @ DC	W 2-3	Started	90	0	2	17,020
8/15/18	POR @ DC	W 1-4	Started	86	2	0	18,219
8/19/18	NE @ DC	W 0-2	Started	90	0	0	20,198
8/26/18	DC @ RBNY	L 0-1	Started	79	0	0	22,324
8/29/18	PHI @ DC	L 2-0	Started	90	0	0	17,692
9/2/18	ATL @ DC	W 1-3	Started	85	1	2	20,557
9/8/18	DC @ NYC	T 1-1	Started	90	0	1	28,239
9/12/18	MIN @ DC	W 1-2	Started	90	0	0	16,114
9/16/18	RBNY @ DC	T 3-3	Started	90	1	0	18,331
9/29/18	MTL @ DC	W 0-5	Started	90	2	1	20,573
10/7/18	CHI @ DC	W 1-2	Started	90	2	0	20,064
10/13/18	DAL @ DC	W 0-1	Started	90	0	0	19,610
10/17/18	TOR @ DC	W 0-1	Started	90	1	0	18,562
10/21/18	NYC @ DC	W 1-3	Started	90	2	0	20,249
10/28/18	DC @ CHI	T 0-0	Started	90	0	0	19,459
3/3/19	ATL @ DC	W 0-2	Started	90	0	1	16,942
3/10/19	DC @ NYC	T 0-0	Started	90	0	0	24,361
3/16/19	RSL @ DC	W 0-5	Started	90	3	1	17,190
3/31/19	DC @ ORL	W 2-1	Started	90	1	1	22,481
4/6/19	LAFC @ DC	L 4-0	Started	52	0	0	20,600

(Continued)

Date	Match	Result	Appearance	MINS	G	A	Attendance
4/9/19	MTL @ DC	T 0-0	Unused Sub	0	0	0	18,116
4/13/19	DC @ COL	W 3-2	Started	90	0	0	15,094
4/21/19	NYC @ DC	L 2-0	Started	90	0	0	18,004
4/24/19	DC @ CLB	W 1-0	Started	89	1	0	10,169
4/28/19	DC @ MIN	L 0-1	Started	90	0	0	19,620
5/4/19	CLB @ DC	W 1-3	Started	90	1	0	16,687
5/12/19	SKC @ DC	W 0-1	Started	90	0	1	12,521
5/15/19	DC @ TOR	T 0-0	Subbed on	42	0	0	26,116
5/18/19	DC @ HOU	L 1-2	Started	90	1	0	15,811
5/25/19	DC @ NE	T 1-1	Started	90	1	0	20,131
5/29/19	CHI @ DC	T 3-3	Started	90	0	1	14,201
6/1/19	SJ @ DC	T 1-1	Started	90	0	0	18,002
6/26/19	ORL @ DC	W 0-1	Started	90	1	0	17,398
6/29/19	TOR @ DC	T 1-1	Started	90	1	0	18,854
7/4/19	DC @ DAL	L 0-2	Started	90	0	0	19,096
7/12/19	NE @ DC	T 2-2	Started	90	0	1	18,903
7/18/19	DC @ CIN	W 4-1	Started	83	1	1	28,774
7/21/19	DC @ ATL	L 0-2	Unused Sub	0	0	0	44,405
7/27/19	DC @ CHI	T 0-0	Started	89	0	0	18,232
8/4/19	PHI @ DC	L 5-1	Started	90	0	0	18,697
8/11/19	LA @ DC	W 1-2	Unused Sub	0	0	0	20,006
8/17/19	DC @ VAN	L 0-1	Started	74	0	0	22,120
8/21/19	RBNY @ DC	L 2-1	Started	24	0	0	18,302
8/24/19	DC @ PHI	L 1-3	Unused Sub	0	0	0	18,781
8/31/19	DC @ MTL	W 3-0	Unused Sub	0	0	0	18,285
9/15/19	DC @ POR	W 1-0	Started	79	0	0	25,218
9/22/19	SEA @ DC	W 0-2	Started	77	0	1	18,489
9/29/19	DC @ RBNY	T 0-0	Started	89	0	0	20,118
10/6/19	CIN @ DC	T 0-0	Unused Sub	0	0	0	18,732

Post Season

Date	Match	Result	Appearance	MINS	G	A
10/19/19	DC @ TOR	L 1-5	Started	105	0	1
11/1/18	CLB @ DC	T 2(3)-(2)2	Started	120	0	0

Career Statistics – Regular Season

Year	Club	GP	MINS	G	A
2019	D.C. United	28	2,318	11	8
2018	D.C. United	20	1,641	12	7
Career totals		48	3,959	23	15

Career Statistics – Post Season

Year	Club	GP	MINS	G	A
2019	D.C. United	1	105	0	1

Note: MINS = Minutes played, G = Goal, A = Assist, GP = Game Played.

Marquee players in MLS 189

Table A.5 Average Home Attendance vs. Attendance on the Day Marquee Player Visited

2015	Team	Avg	Zlatan	Kaka	Villa	Rooney
1	Seattle Sounders	44,247		40,453		
2	Orlando City SC	32,847			52,845	
3	NYC FC	29,016		32,041		
4	Toronto FC	23,451		26,523	30,029	
5	LA Galaxy	23,392			27,000	
6	Portland Timbers	21,142		21,144		
7	San Jose Earthquakes	20,979		36,224		
8	Houston Dynamo	20,658		22,407		
9	Vancouver Whitecaps	20,507			21,000	
10	Real Salt Lake	20,160		20,956	20,801	
11	Sporting KC	19,687				
12	New York Red Bulls	19,657		20,695	25,218	
13	NE Revolution	19,627		18,854	28,811	
14	Montreal Impact	17,703		21,533	18,112	
15	Philadelphia Union	17,451		17,309	17,665	
16	Columbus Crew	16,513		15,655	16,603	
17	DC United	16,244		12,532	21,517	
18	FC Dallas	15,981			16,937	
19	Chicago Fire	16,003		20,202	19,214	
20	Colorado Rapids	15,657				
	Overall Average	21,546		23,323	24,288	

2016	Team	Avg	Zlatan	Kaka	Villa	Rooney
1	Seattle Sounders	42,636			47,537	
2	Orlando City SC	31,324			27,482	
3	NYC FC	27,196		19,818		
4	Toronto FC	26,583		23,805	30,262	
5	LA Galaxy	25,147		27,167		
6	Vancouver Whitecaps	22,330		22,120		
7	Portland Timbers	21,144			21,144	
8	Montreal Impact	20,669		17,389	20,801	
9	New York Red Bulls	20,620		18,680	25,218	
10	NE Revolution	20,185		25,203	20,756	
11	San Jose Earthquakes	19,930			18,000	
12	Real Salt Lake	19,759				
13	Sporting KC	19,597		19,080	19,881	
14	Houston Dynamo	19,021			19,616	
15	Philadelphia Union	17,519		16,509	16,681	
16	Columbus Crew	17,125		20,034	17,452	
17	DC United	17,081		25,842	22,499	
18	Colorado Rapids	16,278		16,813		
19	Chicago Fire	15,602		18,148	17,768	
20	FC Dallas	14,094		16,195		
	Overall Average	21,692		20,485	23,221	

2017	Team	Avg	Zlatan	Kaka	Villa	Rooney
1	Atlanta United FC	48,200		57,716	44,901	
2	Seattle Sounders	43,666		42,333		
3	Toronto FC	27,647		25,200	29,203	

(Continued)

2017	Team	Avg	Zlatan	Kaka	Villa	Rooney
4	Orlando City SC	25,028			25,527	
5	NYC FC	22,643		22,470		
6	LA Galaxy	22,246			25,667	
7	Vancouver Whitecaps	21,416			22,120	
8	New York Red Bulls	21,175		25,219	25,219	
9	Portland Timbers	21,144		21,144		
10	Minnesota United	20,538		18,896		
11	Montreal Impact	20,046		20,801	16,005	
12	San Jose Earthquakes	19,875		18,000		
13	Sporting KC	19,537				
14	NE Revolution	19,367		17,865	26,311	
15	Real Salt Lake	18,781		19,218	16,434	
16	DC United	17,904				
17	Houston Dynamo	17,500		19,292		
18	Chicago Fire	17,383		20,000	20,195	
19	Philadelphia Union	16,812		18,595	16,533	
20	Columbus Crew	15,439		12,226	17,336	
21	Colorado Rapids	15,322			14,336	
22	FC Dallas	15,122		18,028	14,665	
	Overall Average	22,106		24,768	22,461	

2018	Team	Avg	Zlatan	Kaka	Villa	Rooney
1	Atlanta United FC	53,002			45,001	45,087
2	Seattle Sounders	40,641	44,213		39,528	
3	Toronto FC	26,628	30,799		27,935	
4	LA Galaxy	24,444				
5	Minnesota United	23,902	52,242		21,926	
6	Orlando City SC	23,866			23,790	
7	NYC FC	23,211				28,239
8	LAFC	22,042	22,716		22,000	
9	Vancouver Whitecaps	21,946	22,120			
10	Portland Timbers	21,144	21,144		21,144	
11	Sporting KC	19,950	20,092		20,831	
12	San Jose Earthquakes	19,032	50,743		18,000	
13	Real Salt Lake	18,605	21,363			
14	New York Red Bulls	18,601			25,219	22,324
15	Montreal Impact	18,569	20,801		20,801	19,152
16	NE Revolution	18,347	36,573		12,376	
17	D.C. United	17,635			20,249	
18	Houston Dynamo	16,906	22,320		18,123	
19	Philadelphia Union	16,518	19,013		17,594	
20	FC Dallas	15,512	18,355			
21	Colorado Rapids	15,333				
22	Chicago Fire	14,806	21,915		15,204	19,459
23	Columbus Crew	12,447	17,837		11,991	
	Overall Average	21,873	27,640		23,107	26,852

2019	Team	Avg	Zlatan	Kaka	Villa	Rooney
1	Atlanta United FC	52,510	72,548			44,405
2	Seattle Sounders	40,247	46,673			
3	FC Cincinnati	27,336	32,250			28,774
4	Portland Timbers	25,218	25,218			25,218
5	Toronto FC	25,048				26,116
6	LA Galaxy	23,205				
7	Orlando City SC	22,761	24,712			22,481
8	LAFC	22,251	22,757			
9	NYC FC	21,107				24,361
10	Minnesota United	19,723	19,779			19,620
11	Vancouver Whitecaps	19,514	22,120			22,120
12	San Jose Earthquakes	18,781	50,850			
13	Sporting KC	18,601	19,979			
14	Real Salt Lake	18,121	20,838			
15	D.C. United	17,744	20,006			
16	New York Red Bulls	17,281	20,128			20,118
17	Philadelphia Union	17,111				18,781
18	NE Revolution	16,737				20,131
19	Montreal Impact	16,171				18,285
20	Houston Dynamo	15,674	21,777			15,811
21	Columbus Crew	14,856	13,207			10,169
22	FC Dallas	14,842	17,220			19,096
23	Colorado Rapids	14,284	10,945			15,094
24	Chicago Fire	12,324				18,232
	Overall Average	21,310	28,129			22,366

Note: Avg = Average Home Attendance during the season; Zlatan = Attendance on the day Zlatan visited the away game; Kaka = Attendance on the day Kaka visited the away game; Villa = Attendance on the day Villa visited the away game; Rooney = Attendance on the day Rooney visited the away game.

Chapter 12

Endorsing public diplomacy through international sport events

Impact of sport fan engagement

Kevin K. Byon, Sung-Un Yang, Wooyoung (William) Jang, and Taeyoung Kim

Introduction

For effective public diplomacy outcomes for which authentic people-to-people interactions are critical, as opposed to traditional government-sponsored diplomatic activities, countries have been using international sport events in light of *cultural diplomacy* as a core linchpin for public diplomacy (Grix & Lee, 2013; Melissen, 2005). The recent case of the 2018 Winter Olympics in Pyeongchang, South Korea, is a great example of how international sport events can be utilized as a public platform to nurture genuine spectator interactions, such as the inclusion of North Korean guests and the South-North unifying team. Beyond the economic impacts associated with the 2018 Winter Olympics (Lee, 2018), its social impact was unprecedented. It initiated political breakthroughs between South Korea and North Korea (Garofalo, 2018).

As shown in the previous example, by intertwining an international sport event and cultural diplomacy, the current research aims to fill the void in the existing literature on the impacts of international sport events, the majority of which is limited to the assessment of economic impacts (e.g. Hiller, 1998; Hiller & Wanner, 2015; Huang, Mao, Kim & Zhang, 2014; Roche, 1994; Zhang, Byon, Huang & Xu, 2020). For instance, the hosting city residents can foster positive attitudes and behaviors to support the hosting city. Hilgers, Maenning, and Porsche (2010) suggested that one of the most important social effects of the 2006 World Cup was the 'feel-good' effect among the residents in security, transportation, and ecology. Beyond the domestic public, international sport events can demonstrate attractive attributes of the event-hosting city and country to the foreign publics. As a result, a favorable reputation of the event-hosting country can be enhanced, leading to the country's competitive advantages over other countries.

In addition, scholars have found that the concept of engagement is a central concept to promote supportive behavioral intentions, commitment, and loyalty behaviors (Kang, 2014; Lim, Hwang, Kim & Biocca, 2015). Thus, focusing on the concept of engagement developed in public diplomacy, public relations, and sport management, the current study aimed to examine the event attendees engagement in the sporting event. Specifically, the present study examined how

DOI: 10.4324/9781003213673-12

the international sport event of interest influenced sport fan engagement, which affected the event attendees' perception of the event-hosting city and country.

Review of literature

The ATP World Tour in Shanghai, which is the current study context, is one of China's three largest international sport events, with the Formula One Grand Prix and Shanghai International Marathon (Huang et al., 2014). The ATP World Tour is part of the global men's professional tennis circuit, administrated by the Association of Tennis Professionals (ATP). The tour began in 1990 and is now comprised of the ATP World Tour Masters 1000, ATP World Tour 500 series, ATP World Tour 250 series, and ATP World Tour Finals. At the end of the season, the top eight players qualify for the final event and compete for the season's last title. Although the Grand Slams are not ATP events, ranking points are awarded. As the world's biggest tennis event, the ATP World Tour provides an opportunity to introduce "the world's most exciting venues" to sports fans worldwide (ATP, n.d.). According to the ATP, the ATP World Tour holds 62 tournaments in 31 countries.

The Shanghai ATP Masters 1000 is held annually in early October, for a week, at the Qizhong Forest Sports City Arena in the Minhang District of Shanghai, China ("Shanghai Masters," n.d.). Shanghai has been selected as one of the nine locations to hold the Masters 1000 tournaments since 2009 and was awarded the ATP World Tour Masters 1000 Tournament of the Year between 2009 and 2012 as voted by the ATP players ("ATP World Tour Masters 1000 Shanghai," n.d.). Huang et al. (2014) assessed the economic impact of the above three major events in China using an input-output model. They reported that the ATP was estimated to generate "340.89 million Yuan of output, 131.20 million Yuan of income, 34.19 million Yuan of indirect tax" and "create 2,627 full-time equivalent jobs" (p. 29).

While the common approach to studying the impact of international sport events has been the analysis of economic and tourism outcomes (Hiller, 1998; Hiller & Wanner, 2015; Huang et al., 2014; Roche, 1994; Zhang et al., 2020), the current study focused on the event attendees' perceptions of sport fan engagement in the event, and how it influenced their perceptions of the event-hosting city and country from a public diplomacy perspective. To this end, we examined the literature regarding destination image and reputation management.

Destination image of the event-hosting city

Destination image is defined as individuals' subjective perceptions of a particular destination, which incorporates cognitive and affective dimensions (Baloglu & McCleary, 1999; Byon & Zhang, 2010; Koo, Byon & Baker, 2014; Woodside & Lysonski, 1989; Zhang, Byon, Williams & Huang, 2019). A destination image's cognitive dimension refers to the beliefs, knowledge, and perceptions that an individual holds about a destination (Byon & Zhang, 2010). Scholars in tourism studies (Aksu, Caber & Albayrak, 2009; Alcaniz, Sanchez & Blas, 2009; Hui & Wan, 2003) have identified various attributes that could influence tourists to form cognitive images: social, cultural, and environmental attractions (e.g. sightseeing, shopping, and leisure amenities, nightlife), convenience (e.g. accommodation, transportation, facilities), and safety (e.g. risk, friendly atmosphere, political stability). The affective dimension of destination image refers to individuals' feelings about a destination (Baloglu & Brinberg, 1997; Byon & Zhang, 2010). Arousing, exciting, pleasant, and relaxing are the typical types of feelings that have been identified as representing the affective image component (Baloglu & McCleary, 1999).

Destination image has been widely studied in sport and tourism research as one of the focal factors that may affect tourists' travel-related intentions and behaviors (Byon & Zhang, 2010). Scholars (e.g. Chalip, Green & Hill, 2003; Gibson, Qi & Zhang, 2008; Kaplanidou, 2009; Kim, Han, Holland & Byon, 2009; Xing & Chalip, 2006; Zhang et al., 2020) have particularly paid attention to the impact of hosting international sport events on destination image and sport tourists' behavioral intentions. They argued that hosting a major sport event could also be an effective tool for enhancing a city's image, not only among sport tourists, but also among general tourists (i.e. non-sport tourists). In other words, well-organized sport events can increase the awareness and image of host cities.

Several researchers have found that destination image is positively associated with actual and potential tourists' attitude (Aksu et al., 2009; Alcaniz et al., 2009; Baloglu & McCleary, 1999; Byon & Zhang, 2010; Hui & Wan, 2003). For example, destination image was found to be a critical predictor of people's attitudes toward a destination (Jalilvand, Samiei, Dini & Manzari, 2012). Besides influencing their attitudes toward the destination, destination image also positively impacts tourists' future travel intentions (Hui & Wan, 2003; Kim et al., 2009). As one of the components of tourism behavioral intentions, a visit or revisit intention has been the most commonly investigated outcome of destination image (Byon & Zhang, 2010; Chalip et al., 2003; Chen & Chen, 2010; Gibson et al., 2008; Jalilvand et al., 2012; Kaplanidou & Vogt, 2007). According to previous studies, a more favorable destination image is expected to cause a stronger intention to revisit a destination in the future (see Byon & Zhang, 2010; Chalip et al., 2003; Koo et al., 2014).

Engagement in international sport events

Sport fan engagement is a specific type of engagement in which a sport fan invests both decisions and resources to support a particular sport or sport team (Stander & De Beer, 2016; Yoshida, Gordon, Nakazawa & Biscaia, 2014). Yoshida et al. (2014) categorized sport fan engagement into three types: management cooperation, prosocial behavior, and performance tolerance. *Management cooperation* refers to the intentions of sport fans to make cooperative efforts to the management of preferred sport teams. *Prosocial behavior* describes the intention to enhance interactions with fellow sport fans either directly by attending games together at the stadium or indirectly through social/digital channels. *Performance tolerance* is defined as the intention to keep supporting specific sport teams regardless of those teams' performances. Among these three types, prosocial behavior has relevance to the current research from the public diplomacy perspective since the dimension emphasizes the processes and outcomes of the interactions among stakeholders (Taylor & Kent, 2014). After reviewing multiple perspectives on the engagement concept in the existing literature, Taylor and Kent (2014) defined engagement as "part of the dialogue and, through engagement, organizations, and public can make decisions that create social capital" (p. 384).

Recently, scholars have studied the concept of engagement as a central variable of positive public behaviors (e.g. Kang, 2014; Taylor & Kent, 2014). Among them, Kang (2014) defined public engagement as "a psychologically motivated affective state that brings voluntary extra-role behaviors and is characterized by affective commitment, positive affectivity, and empowerment that an individual [member of] public experiences in interactions with an organization over time" (p. 402). Since the current study examines a specific context of engagement (i.e. sport fan engagement) in which individuals attend a sport event directly as members of the community of fans, the dimension of *communal* engagement (Lim et al., 2015) is also relevant. Lim et al. (2015) used the concept of communal engagement to study how users of social TV engaged in international sport events to "feel a sense of community while communicating with other fans" (p. 159). Both studies by Kang (2014) and Lim et al. (2015) found that engagement is a central concept facilitating supportive behavioral intentions, commitment, and loyalty behaviors. Therefore, the following research hypothesis is proposed for the current study to test:

H_1. Greater fan engagement in the ATP World Tour will be significantly associated with a more favorable destination image of Shanghai, which will increase supportive behavioral intentions toward both the event-hosting city and the event-hosting country.

Soft power and country reputation enhanced by international sport events

As an effective means of high profile, dialogic engagement with domestic and international stakeholders, organizations and countries may utilize international sport events to showcase essential authentic values and drive competitive advantages in the global marketplace (Anholt, 2007a, 2007b). From a critical and cultural approach, L'Etang (2006) suggested that mega sports events can be pertinent to the role of *cultural intermediary*, since such sport events can become "circuits of culture" (p. 388) where "meaning is created, modified, and reinvented during processes of symbolization, representation, consumption, and identity formation within particular cultural contexts" (p. 388). International sport events are often conceived as economic initiatives (Hiller, 2000). Still, they can also enhance people-to-people interaction, which can serve as a good means for public diplomacy (Grix & Lee, 2013). For example, Grix and Houlihan (2014) mentioned that substantial governmental efforts exist to project and boost soft power through such events, such as Germany's staging of the 2006 FIFA World Cup and the UK's hosting of the 2012 London Olympic Games.

Differentiating from the traditional (coercive) power of nations, Nye (2008) coined a new framework of power called *soft power*, which he defined as "the ability to affect others to obtain the outcomes one [a state] wants through attraction rather than coercion or payment. A country's soft power rests on its resources of culture, values, and policies" (p. 94). Applying Nye's soft power concept to international sport events, Grix and Houlihan (2014) identified strong links between international sport events and soft power in two ways. First, an international sport event is "a collective event, which is culturally understood and socially played out through the lens of shared and celebrated universal values" (Grix & Houlihan, 2014, p. 12), unlike unilateral values, which stem from a state's own political or economic initiatives. Second, international sport events are critical cultural sources of a state's soft power (e.g. the World Cup and Olympic Games), which, in turn, become "a perfect platform to showcase the hosting nation [and its] culture and image" (Grix & Houlihan, 2014, p. 12).

Now that the close link between international (mega-) sport events and soft power has been discussed, we will delve into outcomes of such sport events in terms of the event-hosting country's reputation. The pivotal premise of the soft power concept is a state's ability to garner and enhance favorable perceptions of a country, which in turn encourage supportive behaviors for the state in various ways (Nye, 2008), including supportive behaviors toward the state's policies (Golan & Yang, 2014), purchasing products/services that originate from the state (Kang & Yang, 2010), and travel to the state (Anholt, 2002; Yang, Shin, Lee & Wrigley, 2008). Speaking of such favorable perceptions of a state, Passow, Fehlmann, and Grahlow (2005) claimed the relevance of country reputation as follows: "reputation management is, by no means, restricted to companies and other organizational entities. Nations today are increasingly concerned with their reputations relative to other nations and turn to actively measuring and managing that reputation" (p. 309). Country reputation refers to collective representations that individual members of the domestic/foreign publics hold of a state based on experiences, including information received about the state and other direct/indirect personal experiences (Passow et al., 2005; Yang et al., 2008).

In past research, scholars have studied country reputation in terms of strategic public diplomacy (Kruckeberg & Vujnovic, 2005), effective nation-building (Taylor & Kent, 2006), and national branding (Anholt, 2002; Yang et al., 2008), suggesting that favorable country reputation often drives positive perceptions of the country and, in turn, supportive behaviors toward the country by the members of the foreign publics. Based on the previous literature on reputation management and engagement, the following hypothesis is proposed:

H_2. Greater fan engagement in the ATP World Tour will be significantly associated with a more favorable reputation of China, which will increase supportive intentions toward the hosting country.

For the current study, we also explored possible links between the destination image of the event-hosting city and the country's reputation of the event-hosting country. Despite the absence of previous research, we posit that China's country reputation would be positively affected by the destination image since the image of multiple dimensions of an entity becomes the basis of the overall reputation (Fombrun & Shanley, 1990). As such, we posited the following research question:

RQ$_1$. To what extent did the event-hosting city's travel destination image positively influence the country's reputation of the event-hosting country and supportive intentions toward the country?

Additionally, in terms of the positive spillover effect of international sport events, we explored the possible impact of supportive intentions about the event-hosting city on the event-hosting country's supportive intentions. Therefore, we proposed the following research question:

RQ$_2$. How strongly did supportive intentions about the event-hosting city influence supportive intentions toward the event-hosting country?

Method

Sample and data collection procedure

Data were collected at the Qizhong Forest Sports City Arena in Shanghai, China, from 8 October to 16 October, 2016. The arena has 25 courts, including three main courts (i.e. center court, grandstand court 2, and court 3). The arena is located in southwest of Shanghai and is in its eighth year of hosting the Shanghai Rolex Masters. Efforts were made to approach all in attendance. For the survey, *systematic random sampling* was used. This sampling included distributing surveys to every tenth person entering each of the 25 courts and those individuals in line at concession stands. Second, the respondents were approached by research assistants and asked to complete the survey. If the individual declined to participate, the interviewer was instructed to intercept the next person passing by until the interviewer identified an individual who agreed to participate in the survey. After the individual agreed, the purpose of the study was explained in detail by the interviewer. Finally, the respondents filled out the questionnaires on-site and returned them when completed. The response rate was 94%. A gift branded with the Shanghai ATP symbol was given in exchange for participation in the study.

A total of 986 responses were collected and used for the analyses. The sample was 52.9% male. In terms of marital status, 55.3% were single, and 36.1% were married. The median income was between $40,000 and $59,000 (USD). For education level, around 60% possessed either college or advanced degrees (e.g. master's or doctoral degrees). The survey respondents include 354 Shanghai residents (n = 354, 35.9%), 322 non-residents (n = 322, 32.7%), and 310 foreigners (31.4%).

Measurement

We measured travel distance toward the international sport event destination and controlled for the travel distance in the data analysis. Given the size of Shanghai (i.e. 2,448 square miles) according to World Population Review (2017), travel distance (i.e. "How many miles did you travel to attend the ATP event?") was measured on a five-point interval scale: 1 (> 50 miles), 2 (> 100 miles), 3 (> 200 miles), 4 (> 500 miles), and 5 (500 miles or longer). The mean of travel distance was 1.96 with SD of .82. Out of the 986 respondents who answered the question, the mode was less than 50 miles (n = 501, 52.3%), followed by 500 miles or longer (n = 214, 22.3%).

A seven-point Likert scale (e.g., 1 = "Strongly Disagree" to 7 = "Strongly Agree") was used to measure the perceptions that the ATP attendees held of the travel *destination image* of Shanghai. These seven items were used to measure perceived value and affective value, modified from the scale of destination image (Byon & Zhang, 2010). The overall reliability of the seven items was α =.91. The following items measured the dimension of perceived value (M = 5.10, SD = 1.25, α =.86): (1) Shanghai's accommodations were reasonably priced, (2) Shanghai is an inexpensive place to visit, and (3) Shanghai offers good value for my travel money. The *affective* dimension was measured by the following items (M = 5.66, SD = 1.04, α =.92): (1) Shanghai is a pleasing travel destination, (2) Shanghai is an enjoyable travel destination, (3) Shanghai is an exciting travel destination, and (4) Shanghai is a novel travel destination.

To measure the *country reputation* of China, we modified a scale of country reputation (Passow et al., 2005). On a seven-point Likert scale (e.g., 1 = "Strongly Disagree" to 7 = "Strongly Agree"), 13 items were used to assess China's country reputation as held by the ATP attendees. This assessment was broken into five dimensions: physical appeal, financial appeal, leadership appeal, cultural appeal, and social appeal. The overall reliability of the 13 items was α =.94. Among the 13 items, the following two items measured the dimension of *physical* appeal (M = 5.82, SD = 1.08, α =.75): (1) China is a beautiful place and (2) China has a good infrastructure of roads, housing, services, health care, and communications. The dimension of *financial* appeal was measured by the following three items (M = 5.60, SD = 1.08, α =.85): (1) China is an inviting place to do business, (2) China has a well-developed industrial sector, and (3) China is a safe place in which to invest. The following two items measured the dimension of *leadership* appeal (M = 5.56, SD = 1.19, α =.84): (1) China communicates an appealing vision of the country, and (2) China is well-managed. The dimension of *cultural* appeal was measured by the following three items (M = 5.90, SD =.97, α =.77): (1) China is socially and culturally diverse, (2) China has a rich historical past, and (3) China offers enjoyable entertainment activities. The following three items measured the dimension of *social* appeal (M = 5.58, SD = 1.23, α =.88): (1) China supports good causes, (2) China is a responsible member of the global community, and (3) China supports responsible environmental policies.

To measure *sport fan engagement* in international sport events, we adapted a scale measuring public engagement involving two dimensions of *positive affects* and *affective commitment* (Kang, 2014). For the dimension of *communal engagement*, we modified the measurement items of prosocial behavior from Yoshida et al.'s (2014) scale of sport fan engagement. The dimension of *positive affects* was measured by the following items ($M = 5.84$, $SD = 1.12$, $\alpha =.88$): (1) When I think about this sporting event, I feel enthusiastic and (2) When I think about this sporting event, I feel interested. The dimension of *affective commitment* was measured by the following items ($M = 5.44$, $SD = 1.14$, $\alpha =.77$): (1) I was emotionally attached to this sporting event, and (2) I was emotionally connected to this sporting event. Finally, the dimension of *communal engagement* was measured by the following items ($M = 5.44$, $SD = 1.14$, $\alpha =.77$): (1) I felt a sense of community during this sporting event, and (2) I liked to interact with other fans during this sporting event.

Modifying the scale of behavioral intentions from Byon, Zhang, and Connaughton (2010), on a seven-point Likert scale (e.g. 1 = "Strongly Disagree" to 9 = "Strongly Agree"), our study measured *supportive intentions toward the event-hosting city* using two measurement items. It computed a mean index ($M = 5.63$, $SD = 1.49$, $\alpha =.82$): (1) I am likely to recommend the city (Shanghai) to those individuals who want advice on places to travel and (2) I am likely to revisit (/keep residing in for the residents) this city (Shanghai) in the future.

On a seven-point Likert scale (e.g., 1 = "Strongly Disagree" to 7 = "Strongly Agree"), we measured *supportive behavioral intentions toward the event-hosting country* using eight items that assess the two aspects of *country* and *country products*. The following items measured the dimension of behavioral intentions for the event-hosting country ($M = 5.69$, $SD = 1.05$, $\alpha =.90$): (1) I would love to visit China, (2) I think other people want to visit China, (3) I would be satisfied visiting China, and (4) I would recommend visiting China.

The following items measured the dimension of behavioral intentions for the country products ($M = 5.22$, $SD = 1.27$, $\alpha =.93$): (1) I would love to purchase Chinese products, (2) I think that other people like Chinese products, (3) I would be satisfied with owning a Chinese product, and (4) I would recommend China's products to others.

Measurement model

First, to test the validity of the overall measurement model, a confirmatory factor analysis (CFA) was conducted: $\chi^2(76, N = 986) = 719.43$ $p <.001$, SRMR $=.036$, RMSEA $=.093$ (90% CI:.087, .099), and CFI $=.945$. The data-model fit indexes demonstrated that the proposed measurement model could be retained as a valid model (Holbert & Stephenson, 2002; Hu & Bentler, 1999). The lowest standardized factor loading found was .699 on the second indicator (i.e. perceived value) for destination image, indicating a strong degree of content and construct validity with average variance extracted (AVE) larger than .50 and CR larger than

.80 for all latent variables in the proposed measurement model (see Appendix 12.1).

As the proposed measurement model had a good data-model fit, we proceeded to analyze the overall validity of the proposed structural equation model (SEM) to test the research hypotheses and questions. The proposed SEM also had sound data-model fits: $\chi^2(78, N = 986) = 732.85$, $p <.001$, SRMR =.037, RMSEA =.092 (90% CI:.086, .098), and CFI =.944. In testing the research hypotheses and questions, we controlled for travel distance (See Table 12.1). Except for the variable of travel distance, all of the other constructs used in the structural model were latent variables with multiple measurement indicators.

Table 12.1 Results of Testing Hypotheses and Research Questions ($N = 986$)

H/RQ	IV		DV	b	SE	β (p)
	Travel distance[a]	→	Engagement in the ATP event	−.10	.05	−.07*
	Travel distance	→	Destination images of the city	−.03	.02	−.06 *(ns)*
	Travel distance	→	Country reputation	−.02	.02	−.04 *(ns)*
	Travel distance	→	Supportive intentions toward the city	−.06	.01	−.12***
	Travel distance	→	Supportive intentions toward the country	.05	.01	.10***
H1	Engagement in the ATP event	→	Destination images of the hosting city	.42	.04	.41***
	Destination images of the hosting city	→	Supportive intentions toward the city	.50	.03	.54***
	Engagement in the ATP event	→	Supportive intentions toward the city	.51	.03	.53***
H2	Engagement in the ATP event	→	Country reputation	.38	.04	.33***
	Country reputation	→	Supportive intentions toward the country	.55	.02	.71***
RQ1	Destination images of the hosting city	→	Country reputation	.54	.04	.49***
	Destination images of the hosting city	→	Supportive intentions toward the country	.05	.02	.06*
RQ2	Supportive intentions toward the city	→	Supportive intentions toward the country	.29	.03	.31***

Note. [a]Travel distance (i.e. "How many miles did you travel to attend the ATP event?") = 1 (> 50 miles), 2 (> 100 miles), 3 (> 200 miles), 4 (> 500 miles), and 5 (500 miles or longer).

$\chi^2(78, n = 986) = 732.85$, $p <.001$, Standardized RMR = .037, RMSEA = .092 (90% CI: .086, .098), and CFI = .944.
***p < .001. **p < .01. *p < .05.

Results

H_1 dealt with the effects of fan engagement on the destination image of Shanghai as the event-hosting city and the attendees' supportive intentions toward Shanghai. The results supported this hypothesis (see Table 12.1). With travel distance being controlled for, engagement in the ATP significantly led to an increase in the favorable destination image of Shanghai (b =.42, SE =.04, β =.41, p <.001) and resulted in stronger supportive intentions toward Shanghai (b =.51, SE =.03, β =.53, p <.001). In addition, the results indicated that, for the ATP attendees, the more favorable the destination image of Shanghai, the greater their intentions to support the city (b =.50, SE =.03, β =.54, p <.001). For the control variable, travel distance was found to be negatively associated with sport fan engagement in the ATP (b = −.10, SE =.05, β = −.07, p <.05) and was not found to be significantly associated with the destination image of Shanghai as the hosting city of the ATP (b = −.03, SE =.02, β = −.06, ns).

H_2 concerns the effects of the ATP at the country level. The results supported this hypothesis. Greater engagement in the ATP significantly resulted in a favorable reputation for China (b =.38, SE =.04, β =.33, p <.001), while a strong, positive effect existed related to country reputation and the ATP attendees' intentions to support the country (b =.55, SE =.02, β =.71, p <.001). We did not find a significant impact of travel distance on country reputation (b = −.02, SE =.02, β = −.04, ns).

We also examined the link between the destination image of Shanghai and the country reputation of China. First, the results revealed that the destination image of Shanghai significantly led to a favorable reputation for China as held by the ATP attendees (b =.54, SE =.04, β =.49, p <.001) as well as stronger intentions to support the country (b =.05, SE =.02, β =.06, p <.05). Related to the possible influence of the control variable, we found that shorter travel distance for the ATP attendees was significantly associated with greater intentions to support Shanghai as the event-hosting city (b = −.06, SE =.01, β = −.12, p <.001), whereas the effect on supportive intentions toward China as the event-hosting country was greater among those individuals who had longer travel distances for the ATP (b =.05, SE =.01, β =.10, p <.001). The second research question dealt with a possible positive spillover effect of an international sport event from the event-hosting city to the country level. We found that, among the ATP attendees, supportive intentions toward Shanghai significantly resulted in supportive intentions toward China as the event-hosting country (b =.29, SE =.03, β =.31, p <.001) (Figure 12.1)

Discussion

This study aimed to examine the effects of an international sport event, the ATP in Shanghai, from a cultural public diplomacy perspective. Before this study, existing research on international sport events had mostly focused on the economic/tourism outcomes (Hiller, 1998; Hiller & Wanner, 2015; Huang et al., 2014; Roche, 1994; Zhang et al., 2020). Emphasizing sports as a key vehicle for cultural public

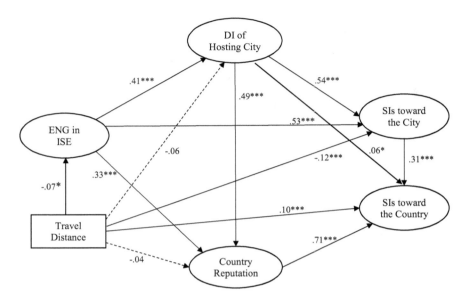

Figure 12.1 The Results of the Proposed Model.

diplomacy, the current study delimited its scope to examine the event attendees perceptions and behavioral intentions. Also, focusing on the concept of engagement in public diplomacy/public relations and sport management, the current study examined the event attendees engagement in the sporting event rather than their general perceptions. We posited two research hypotheses and two research questions. First, at the level of the event-hosting city, we found strong effects of engagement in the ATP regarding the positive travel destination image of Shanghai and the event attendees strong intentions to support the city. Second, at the level of the event-hosting country, we found that engagement in the ATP significantly led to an increase in a favorable reputation for China as the event-hosting country and strong intentions of supportive behaviors toward China.

Additionally, we examined the link between Shanghai's destination image and the country reputation of China to explore a possible positive spillover effect of an international sport event beyond the level of the event-hosting city. The results demonstrated a strong and positive association between the destination image of the hosting city and the reputation of the hosting country and a strong link between supportive intentions toward the city and country. Such relations were strong and positive, whereas the effect size was medium, suggesting that the effects of an international sport event at both levels (i.e. the event-hosting city and the event-hosting country) are strongly intertwined but distinctive. Those event attendees with shorter travel distances had a greater association with the destination image of the event-hosting city. In contrast, those with greater travel distances, including foreign travelers, had a greater association with the country's reputation.

Implications

This study's results have profound implications for the theory and practice of public diplomacy and management of place images and country reputation. First, this study extends the engagement literature by investigating the role of a specific type of engagement, sport fan engagement, in an international sport event context, which remains a relatively undiscovered area in public diplomacy research. We empirically demonstrated both direct and indirect linkages among engagement, destination image of a hosting city, and hosting country reputation by analyzing the data collected from an international sport event attendees. This finding is significant in that getting residents and travelers to be engaged with an international sport event plays a crucial role in positively determining the event attendees evaluations of the hosting city and the country's reputation. This empirical finding suggests that event organizers should create an engaging atmosphere around an international sport event so that the event attendees can form a strong sense of community, which will further help the event attendees develop not only a cognitive reaction but also affective and behavioral reactions (i.e. supportive behavior) toward the hosting city and country (Yoshida et al., 2014).

The current study also suggests that the impact of hosting an international sport event is not confined to the event-hosting city but also occurs at the country level. The findings provide strong empirical evidence for the positive spillover effect of an international sport event from the hosting city to the country, confirming that a strong link exists between the travel destination image of the event-hosting city and the overall reputation of the country. The results illustrate that a host country's reputation is significantly affected by event attendees perceptions of the host city's destination image, which leads to stronger intentions to support the country. In addition to the link between the destination image of the host city and the country reputation, this study demonstrates another spillover effect in perceptions across different levels. In other words, the event attendees' supportive intentions toward the host city increased their supportive intentions toward the host country. In this study, we empirically demonstrated Nye's (2008) *soft power* in an international sport event, which serves as a stimulus affecting attendees to positively form an image toward a hosting city and country and develop supporting behavior of hosting an international event.

Finally, the results of this study have implications from a cultural public diplomacy perspective. As stated earlier, we examined the impact of hosting an international sport event by measuring the event attendees' engagement through a survey to determine how their attendance would affect their perceptions and attitudes toward the host city and country. The survey results revealed that the event attendees with greater travel distances, including foreign travelers, showed stronger intentions to support the event-hosting country than those attendees with shorter travel distances. These results indicate that differentiated effects exist in international sport events engagement by travel distance.

Limitations and suggestions for future studies

The current study has several limitations. First, although we made a concerted effort to collect representative data from the sporting event attendees at the Shanghai ATP Masters 1000, the data used in the data analyses was cross-sectional. Therefore, the relationships examined in the hypothesized model is only assumed to be correlational, not causal. Therefore, caution is required when interpreting the results of this study. Second, other factors may influence the event attendees' perceptions and attitudes about the host city and country in addition to the engagement in an international sport event. Such factors include, but are not limited to, physical surroundings (Jang, Byon & Yim, 2020; Jang, Kim & Byon, 2020), frequency of attendance (Zhang, Pease, Hui & Michaud, 1995), identification of a sport (Trail, Robinson, Gillentine & Dick, 2003), and residency type (Stylidis, Shani & Belhassen, 2017).

Third, while we controlled for travel distance, which may have affected individuals' evaluation of image and reputation of the travel destination, the findings of this study require further examination with longitudinal data to see whether travel distance has a prolonged impact on sport spectators' attitudinal formation (i.e. cognitive, affective, and conative). Fourth, behavioral intentions rather than actual behaviors were measured, while intentions are not always flawless predictors of behavior. However, it is widely believed that behavioral intentions can be a close proxy for a given actual behavior (Ajzen, 1991), so it would be interesting if future scholars measure both supportive intentions and supporting behaviors to the extent to which supportive intentions actually would be translated into supporting behaviors. Such a finding would provide strong empirical evidence to prove the positive soft power stemming from an international sports event (Nye, 2008).

In conclusion, future studies should go beyond the above limitations to assess public diplomacy and communication management's specific roles during international sport events and their effects on destination image and country reputation. More research is also needed to examine the relationship between individuals' engagement in different contexts and their perceptions and attitudes about host destinations.

References

Ajzen, I. (1991). The theory of planned behavior. *Organizational Behavior and Human Decision Processes, 50,* 179–211.

Aksu, A. A., Caber, M., & Albayrak, T. (2009). Measurement of the destination evaluation supporting factors and their effects on behavioral intention of visitors: Antalya region of Turkey. *Tourism Analysis, 14,* 115–125.

Alcaniz, E. B., Sanchez, I. S., & Blas, S. S. (2009). The functional-psychological continuum in the cognitive image of a destination: A confirmatory analysis. *Tourism Management, 30*, 715–723.

Anholt, S. (2002). Nation-branding. *Journal of Brand Management, 9*, 229–239.

Anholt, S. (2007a). The role of culture in branding places. *Place Branding and Public Diplomacy, 3*, 268–331.

Anholt, S. (2007b). What is competitive identity? In *Competitive identity* (pp. 1–23). London: Palgrave Macmillan.

Baloglu, S., & Brinberg, D. (1997). Affective images of tourism destinations. *Journal of Travel Research, 35*, 11–15.

Baloglu, S., & McCleary, K. W. (1999). A model of destination image formation. *Annals of Tourism Research, 26*, 868–897.

Byon, K. K., & Zhang, J. J. (2010). Development of a scale measuring destination image. *Marketing Intelligence & Planning, 28*, 508–532.

Byon, K. K., Zhang, J. J., & Connaughton, D. P. (2010). Dimensions of general market demand associated with professional team sports: Development of a scale. *Sport Management Review, 13*, 142–157.

Chalip, L., Green, B. C., & Hill, B. (2003). Effects of sport event media on destination image and intention to visit. *Journal of Sport Management, 17*, 214–234.

Chen, C. F., & Chen, F. S. (2010). Experience quality, perceived value, satisfaction and behavioral intentions for heritage tourists. *Tourism Management, 31*, 29–35.

Fombrun, C. J., & Shanley, M. (1990). What's in a name? Reputation building and corporate strategy. *The Academy of Management Journal, 33*, 233–258.

Garofalo, P. (2018, February 8). The diplomacy Olympics. *U.S. News*. Retrieved from https://www.usnews.com/opinion/articles/2018-02-08/the-pyeongchang-olympics-might-be-worth-it-due-to-north-korea-diplomacy

Gibson, H. J., Qi, C. X., & Zhang, J. J. (2008). Destination image and intent to visit China and the 2008 Beijing Olympic Games. *Journal of Sport Management, 22*, 427–450.

Golan, G., & Yang, S. U. (2014). Introduction: Public diplomacy from public relations perspectives. In G. Golan, S. U., Yang, & D. F. Kinsey (Eds.), *International public relations and public diplomacy* (pp. 1–12). New York: Peter Lang Publishing.

Grix, J., & Houlihan, B. (2014). Sports mega-events as part of a nation's soft power strategy: The cases of Germany (2006) and the UK (2012). *The British Journal of Politics and International Relations, 16*, 572–596.

Grix, J., & Lee, D. (2013). Soft power, sports mega-events and emerging states: The lure of the politics of attraction. *Global Society, 27*, 521–536.

Hilgers, D., Maennig, W., & Porsche, M. (2010). The feel-good effect at mega sport events: Public and private management problems informed by the experiences of the FIFA World Cup. *International Journal of Business Research, 10*, 15–29.

Hiller, H. H. (1998). Assessing the impact of mega-events: A linkage model. *Current Issues in Tourism, 1*, 47–57.

Hiller, H. H. (2000). Mega-events, urban boosterism and growth strategies: An analysis of the objectives and legitimations of the Cape Town 2004 Olympic Bid. *International Journal of Urban and Regional Research, 24*, 449–458.

Hiller, H. H., & Wanner, R. A. (2015). The psycho-social impact of the Olympics as urban festival: A leisure perspective. *Leisure Studies, 34*, 672–688.

Holbert, R. L., & Stephenson, M. T. (2002). Structural equation modeling in the communication sciences, 1995–2000. *Human Communication Research, 28*, 531–551.

Hu, L., & Bentler, P. M. (1999). Cutoff criteria for fit indexes in covariance structure analysis: Conventional criteria versus new alternatives. *Structural Equation Modeling: A Multidisciplinary Journal, 6*(1), 1–55.

Huang, H., Mao, L. L., Kim, S. K., & Zhang, J. J. (2014). Assessing the economic impact of three major sport events in China: The perspective of attendees. *Tourism Economics, 20,* 1277–1296.

Hui, T. K., & Wan, T. W. D. (2003). Singapore's image as a tourist destination. *International Journal of Tourism Research, 5,* 305–313.

Jalilvand, M. R., Samiei, N., Dini, B., & Manzari, P. Y. (2012). Examining the structural relationships of electronic word of mouth, destination image, tourist attitude toward destination and travel intention: An integrated approach. *Journal of Destination Marketing & Management, 1,* 134–143.

Jang, W. W., Byon, K. K., & Yim, B. H. (2020). Sportscape, emotion, and behavioral intention: A case of four professional major league sport events. *European Sport Management Quarterly, 20,* 321–343.

Jang, W. W., Kim, K. A., & Byon, K. K. (2020). Social atmospherics, affective response, and behavioral intention associated with esports events. *Frontiers in Psychology, 11,* 1–11.

Kang, M. (2014). Understanding public engagement: Conceptualizing and measuring its influence on supportive behavioral intentions. *Journal of Public Relations Research, 26,* 399–416.

Kang, M., & Yang, S. U. (2010). Comparing effects of country reputation and the overall corporate reputations of a country on international consumers' product attitudes and purchase intentions. *Corporate Reputation Review, 13,* 52–62.

Kaplanidou, K. (2009). Relationships among behavioral intentions, cognitive event and destination images among different geographic regions of Olympic Games spectators. *Journal of Sport & Tourism, 14,* 249–272.

Kaplanidou, K. & Vogt, C. (2007). The interrelationship between sport event and destination image and sport tourists' behaviors. *Journal of Sport & Tourism, 12,* 183–206.

Kim, S. H., Han, H. S., Holland, S., & Byon, K. K. (2009). Structural relationships among involvement, destination brand equity, satisfaction, and destination visit intentions. The case of Japanese outbound travelers. *Journal of Vacation Marketing, 15,* 349–365.

Koo, S. K., Byon, K. K., & Baker, T. A. (2014). Integrating event image, satisfaction, and behavioral intention: Small-scale marathon event. *Sport Marketing Quarterly, 23,* 127–137.

Kruckeberg, D., & Vujnovic, M. (2005). Public relations, not propaganda, for US public diplomacy in a post-911 world: Challenges and opportunities. *Journal of Communication Management, 9,* 296–304.

Lee, Y. N. (2018, February 15). For the sake of the games, South Korea needs to show hosting an Olympics can be economically viable. *CNBC.* Retrieved from https://www.cnbc.com/2018/02/15/south-koreas-pyeongchang-winter-olympics-costs-benefits-of-hosting.html

L'Etang, J. (2006). Public relations and sport in promotional culture. *Public Relations Review, 32,* 386–394.

Lim, J., Hwang, Y., Kim, S., & Biocca, F. A. (2015). How social media engagement leads to sports channel loyalty: Mediating roles of social presence and channel commitment. *Computers in Human Behavior, 46,* 158–167.

Melissen, J. (2005). *Wielding soft power: The new public diplomacy* (pp. 1–29). Netherlands: Netherlands Institute of International Relations, Clingendael.

Nye, J. S. (2008). Public diplomacy and soft power. *The ANNALS of the American Academy of Political and Social Science, 616*, 94–109.

Passow, T., Fehlmann, R., & Grahlow, H. (2005). Country reputation - From measurement to management: The case of Liechtenstein. *Corporate Reputation Review, 7*, 309–326.

Roche, M. (1994). Mega-events and urban policy. *Annals of Tourism Research, 21*(1), 1–19.

Stander, F. W., & De Beer, L. T. (2016). Engagement as a source of positive consumer behaviour: A study amongst South African football fans. *South African Journal for Research in Sport, Physical Education and Recreation, 38*, 187–200.

Stylidis, D., Shani, A., & Belhassen, Y. (2017). Testing an integrated destination image model across residents and tourists. *Tourism Management, 58*, 184–195.

Taylor, M., & Kent, M. L. (2006). Beyond excellence: Extending the generic approach to international public relations: The case of Bosnia. *Public Relations Review, 33*, 10–20.

Taylor, M., & Kent, M. L. (2014). Dialogic engagement: Clarifying foundational concepts. *Journal of Public Relations Research, 26*, 384–398.

Trail, G. T., Robinson, M., Gillentine, A., & Dick, R. (2003). Motives and points of attachment: Fans versus spectators in intercollegiate athletics. *Sport Marketing Quarterly, 12*, 217–227.

Woodside, A. G., & Lysonski, S. (1989). A general model of traveler destination choice. *Journal of Travel Research, 17*, 8–14.

World Population Review. (2017). *Shanghai population 2017.* Retrieved from http://worldpopulationreview.com/world-cities/shanghai-population/

Xing, X., & Chalip, L. (2006). Effects of hosting a sport event on destination brand: A test of co-branding and match-up models. *Sport Management Review, 9*, 49–78.

Yang, S. U., Shin, H., Lee, J. H., & Wrigley, B. (2008). Measuring country reputation in multi-dimensions: Predictors, effects, and communication channels. *Journal of Public Relations Research, 20*, 421–440.

Yoshida, M., Gordon, B., Nakazawa, M., & Biscaia, R. (2014). Conceptualization and measurement of fan engagement: Empirical evidence from a professional sport context. *Journal of Sport Management, 28*, 399–417.

Zhang, J. C., Byon, K. K., Huang, H. R., & Xu, K. (2020). Event impact on residents' satisfaction and behavioral intention of the mega sporting event: Pre-post study. *International Journal of Sports Marketing and Sponsorship, 21*, 487–511.

Zhang, J. C., Byon, K. K., Williams, A. S., & Huang, H. (2019). Differential effects of event and destination image on sport tourists' attachment and loyalty to destination. *Asia Pacific Journal of Tourism Research, 24*, 1169–1185.

Zhang, J. J., Pease, D. G., Hui, S. C., & Michaud, T. J. (1995). Variables affecting the spectator decision to attend NBA games. *Sport Marketing Quarterly, 4*, 29–40.

Appendix 12.1

Measurement instruments

1 **Engagement in International Sport Events** (α =.88, CR =.822, AVE =.607)
   Positive Affects (M = 5.84, SD = 1.12, α =.88, r =.79)
   - When I think about this sporting event, I feel enthusiastic.
   - When I think about this sporting event, I feel interested.
   Communal Engagement (M = 5.44, SD = 1.14, α =.77, r =.63)
   - I felt a sense of community during this sporting event.
   - I liked to interact with other fans during this sporting event.
   Affective Commitment (M = 5.73, SD = 1.18, α =.85, r =.74)
   - I was emotionally attached to this sporting event.
   - I was emotionally connected to this sporting event.

2 **Reputation of the Event-Hosting Country** (α =.94, CR =.924, AVE =.708)
   Physical Appeal (M = 5.82, SD = 1.08, α =.75, r =.60)
   - China is a beautiful place.
   - China has a good infrastructure of roads, housing, services, health care, and communications.
   Financial Appeal (M = 5.60, SD = 1.08, α =.85)
   - China is an inviting place to do business.
   - China has a well-developed industrial sector.
   - China is a safe place in which to invest.
   Leadership Appeal (M = 5.56, SD = 1.19, α =.84, r =.72)
   - China communicates an appealing vision of the country.
   - China is well-managed.
   Cultural Appeal (M = 5.90, SD =.97, α =.77)
   - China is socially and culturally diverse.
   - China has a rich historical past.
   - China offers enjoyable entertainment activities.
   Social Appeal (M = 5.58, SD = 1.23, α =.88)
   - China supports good causes.
   - China is a responsible member of the global community.
   - China supports responsible environmental policies.

3 **Destination Image of the Event-Hosting City** (α =.91, CR =.811, AVE =.684)
   Economic Value (M = 5.10, SD = 1.25, α =.86)

- Shanghai's accommodations are reasonably priced.
- Shanghai is an inexpensive place to visit.
- Shanghai offers good value for my travel money.
  Affective Value (M = 5.66, SD = 1.04, α =.92)
- Shanghai is a pleasing travel destination.
- Shanghai is an enjoyable travel destination.
- Shanghai is an exciting travel destination.
- Shanghai is a novel travel destination.

4 **Supportive Behavioral Intentions toward the Event-Hosting City** (M = 5.63, SD = 1.49, α =.82, r =.70, CR =.872, AVE =.774)
- I am likely to recommend the city (Shanghai) to those individuals who want advice on places to travel.
- I am likely to revisit (/*keep residing in) this city (Shanghai) in the future.
- or the resident.

5 **Supportive Behavioral Intentions toward the Event-Hosting Country** (α =.93, CR =.916, AVE =.845)
  Country (M = 5.69, SD = 1.05, α =.90)
- I would love to visit China.
- I think other people want to visit China.
- I would be satisfied visiting China.
- I would recommend visiting China.
  Country Products (M = 5.22, SD = 1.27, α =.93)
- I would love to purchase Chinese products.
- I think other people like Chinese products.
- I would be satisfied with owning a Chinese product.
- I would recommend China's products to others.

Chapter 13

Transcending ball and ballin'
Connecting the Jordan Brand and college football fans

C. Keith Harrison, Kathy Babiak, Jacob Tingle, Jessie Dickens, Whitney Griffin, and Scott Bukstein

Introduction

Michael Jordan played 15 seasons in the National Basketball Association (NBA) between 1984 and 2003 and is considered by many to be the greatest basketball player of all time. Not surprisingly, he is the subject of much discussion and lore in today's popular culture. The Jordan Brand, first introduced in 1984, is famously characterized by the Jumpman logo: a silhouette of Michael Jordan that conjures images of Jordan flying through the air to dunk a basketball and is one of the most widely recognizable logos of athletes in the world (Rovell, 2006). The Jumpman logo has appeared on Jordan Brand products since 1988 and the brand has been wildly popular, valued at over $10 billion and generating more than $3.1 billion in revenue in the 2019 fiscal year. It has thus become one of Nike's largest business units. There has been much scholarly attention given to Nike and its strategy, business model, and innovation (Ramaswamy, 2008), its social responsibility (DeTienne & Lewis, 2005), and its branding and marketing (Coleman, 2013). However, much less attention has been given to Nike's individual business units. Given the Jordan Brand's substantial role and distinct position within the Nike business structure, the Jordan Brand business model merits focus due to its effective influence over the Nike brand, as well as its consumers, sport fans, and other influencers.

The role of Michael Jordan and his associated endorsement, brand, and marketing efforts with Nike has been examined in a broader analysis of Michael Jordan as a celebrity endorser (Mathur et al., 1997). This study highlighted the wealth effects (e.g., the increased values of Jordan's client firms) associated with a celebrity figure and specifically an iconic athlete, utilizing an event study methodology to collect data. At the time of their study, it was estimated that Michael Jordan's return to the NBA after his (first) retirement would be financially impactful for Jordan Brand and other associated brands. In 1997, Mathur et al indicated that "Jordan's expected return has increased the stock values of related firms by $1.016 billion. This illustrates the potential value of celebrity endorsements" (p. 67). However, there remain gaps in the understanding of the consumer experience, emotion, intentions, and behaviors related to brands that are so tightly linked to a company.

DOI: 10.4324/9781003213673-13

The Jordan Brand & college football fans 211

There is a myriad of evidence that discrete emotions play a pivotal role in product marketing, brand loyalty, and consumer purchasing behavior. Heavily documented is the role that emotions such as fear (Tannenbaum et al., 2015), attachment (Akgun et al., 2013), companionship, and love (Rossiter & Bellman, 1999) play in consumer responses across a variety of branding contexts. But what about awe? Awe is a powerful emotion characterized by vastness and the need for humans to adjust their cognitive framework to accommodate it. Keltner and Haidt (2003) explored the conceptual aspects and dimensions of awe, disaggregated its differences from other positive emotions, and noted the lack of consideration given to awe as an emotion. Consistent with this discussion is a lack of empirical investigation of the depth and breadth of the effects of awe in the branding and consumer behavior setting.

In 2016, the University of Michigan's athletic department announced a partnership with Jordan Brand wherein Air Jordan provided the equipment for the university's football team. Similar partnerships were subsequently announced between Jordan Brand and the University of North Carolina, the University of Oklahoma, and the University of Florida, along with the basketball programs at four other institutions. In addition to athletic uniforms at these universities that display the Jumpman logo, fans may also purchase merchandise such as jerseys, hats, t-shirts, and other items that display the logo. The partnerships between these large, tradition-laden football programs and the value created by the Jordan Brand invites several new lines of inquiry:

1   Does the experience of watching Michael Jordan's superior skills on the court carry over into consumer perceptions of the brand bearing his likeness?
2   Does the partnership between these athletic departments and the Jordan Brand evoke attachment and feelings that are documented as being associated with awe?
3   To what extent do the perceived quality, admiration, and tradition of the Jordan Brand influence behaviors of fans associated with athletic departments that chose to engage in the sponsorship?

The current study investigates the role that awe plays in sports branding by examining how the Jordan Brand's use of the likeness of an iconic athlete such as Michael Jordan, whose style of play elicited emotions of awe, impacts consumer responses.

Review of literature

Branding and the theory of awe

Scholarly research into the conceptual foundations surrounding the emotion of awe is relatively new within the context of the social sciences, but the breadth of knowledge is rapidly expanding. As stated above, Keltner and Haidt (2003), initially framed the construct defining two central elements to conceptualizing awe: *vastness* and *accommodation*. Weber (1978) detailed the importance of a charismatic person in changing attitudes and behaviors. This concept is central to corporate branding and/or athlete and celebrity endorsements where one charismatic individual can deeply influence customers and their behaviors. Keltner and Haidt (2003) further synthesized how "certain collective emotions have transformative powers; they change people's attitudes and inspire them to follow something larger than themselves" (p. 300). Successfully branding charismatic people, then, can have observable outcomes.

While awe is typically viewed as a relatively spiritual emotion without many concrete applications, recent research has shown that it has more positive, tangible associations that are unique relative to other positive emotions (Gottlieb et al., 2018). Some of these associations include wonder, admiration, respect, and reverence; additionally, it can drive outcomes such as intentions to generosity, helping behaviors, and have positive effects on self-image (Rudd et al., 2012). Thus, experiencing awe can produce changes in actions or behavior amongst those that experience it. When considering how awe relates to firms and companies, the concept is deeply connected with a feeling of admiration for the brand. Aaker et al. (2012) note that when consumers seek to express their intense feelings of admiration about the firm, there can be a spillover into feelings associated with awe. It is documented that awe can be present in settings such as sporting events (Ohlin, 2019) and that engaging in an awe-inducing conditions can cause the individual experiencing it to feel small relative to the world around them and feel more connected to the culture in which the experience was contextualized (Shiota et al., 2007). Michael Jordan's exceptional ability on the basketball court has precipitated many a fan to experience these feelings, and the growth of his legacy may continue to elicit levels of awe that can create spillovers into his brand; feelings which may ultimately be leveraged into enhancing consumer perceptions and influencing behaviors (Rudd et al., 2012).

While a gap exists in previous work surrounding the role that awe plays in branding, branding and consumer behavior have been examined from a variety of other angles. There is a general consensus that branding has become integral to product success – a critical element in today's market conditions (Chovanová et al., 2015). A company's brand provides products with identity and personality and often serves as a signal to consumers of product quality, market segmentation, and company values. A brand allows companies to build a relationship with consumers; this helps dictate consumer behavior. Sport literature also provides important insights into branding patterns and the people behind them. Sport organizations at both the professional and collegiate level often build their brands through corporate sponsorships that convey characteristics of the organizations' values, which then impacts consumer perceptions. Mason (2005) found that sport sponsorships can impact consumers' attitudes and can help build emotional attachments that favorably alter consumer behavior, particularly if there is a strong fit between the organization and the corporate sponsor, and if the consumer is a highly involved fan. A key distinction that separates the Jordan Brand from many other modern-day brands lies in the connection with Michael Jordan's name and likeness. Carlson and Donovan (2013) determined that consumers view athletes, such as Michael Jordan, as *human brands*. Thomson (2006) concluded that attachment to a human brand leads to higher levels of satisfaction, trust, and commitment associated with the brand – and an overall richer experience for consumers. In this context, factors such as prestige and distinctiveness led to higher levels of emotional attachment between the consumer and the brand, which in turn, resulted in higher levels of viewership of the athlete and more purchases of the athlete's brand merchandise. This is key for the Jordan Brand, as Michael Jordan is generally viewed as one of the most prestigious human brands in sports history (Crowley, 1999).

While the concept of awe has been studied in spiritual, artistic, and sociological contexts, the literature exploring the relationship between awe and consumer behavior is sparse. Examining the relationship between consumer behavior, branding, and awe through the lens of a sports brand is a logical progression to better understand the effects elicited by the performance of "once in a generation" athletes, such as Michael Jordan. Previous scholars build on the idea that as an emotion, awe can be elicited as a result of watching peak performances in sport and has become associated with athletes who have demonstrated these peak performances (Chidester, 2012; Ravizza, 1977). Given his remarkable performance while playing, it is intuitive that Michael Jordan would emerge as a natural figure to study awe. There is, however, a quality of wonderment inherently unique about Jordan (i.e. the Jordan Brand), for he is still perceived as one of the most prestigious athletes and human brands in sport history, despite not playing in nearly two decades (Crowley, 1999). Jordan seems to have transcended Weber's (1978) assertion that "charismatic authority is naturally unstable" and that one "gains and retains [power] solely by proving his powers in practice" (p. 1114). As such, exploring the Jordan Brand phenomenon is even more important, as it appears that through reputation and image alone, Jordan continues to inspire awe. Furthermore, the awe-inspiring nature of the Jordan Brand is evidenced by the extent to which youth and adults relate to and consume the Jordan Brand across the world. Whether it be parents taking their children out of school to stand in queue for the latest Jordan Brand sneaker release, or *sneaker heads* with their shoe collection including the original packaging preserved like a museum artifact, or those who get tattoos of the Jumpman logo – there appears to be some aspect of awe associated with the brand (Connolly, 2016; Jackson, 2016).

Fans and audiences of Michael Jordan and the Jordan Brand

Although Michael Jordan's playing career ended in 2003, he remains extremely popular in modern culture. He is revered as a symbol of greatness by former and current basketball players, other athletes/celebrities, and basketball fans both casual and devoted, alike. The on-court success of Jordan is undeniable – six NBA championships, five NBA Most Valuable Player Awards, ten NBA scoring titles, two Olympic gold medals, and much more. He is a two-time inductee into the Naismith Memorial Basketball Hall of Fame, and in 2016 was awarded the Presidential Medal of Freedom, the highest honor awarded to civilians of the United States. ESPN named Jordan the top North American athlete of the 20th century, ahead of famed athletes such as Babe Ruth, Muhammad Ali, and Wayne Gretzky (ESPN, n.d.). Perhaps the most remarkable feature of his career relative to those of legendary athletes, both in basketball and in other sports, has been his ability to leverage the emotional response from fans garnered by his on-court play into legacy effects and financial success in his business ventures off the court. Jordan is the wealthiest former professional athlete in the world (Gaines et al., 2020) and in 2013, ten years after his retirement from the NBA, was earning an estimated $30 million more than the highest paid active NBA player, stemming mostly from the Jordan Brand and various other endorsements (Lubin, 2014).

In the years since Jordan's retirement, a multitude of statements by former and current professional basketball players, media members, and other figures in popular culture have shed light on Jordan's long-lasting impact both on and off the court. In 2019, a poll of 117 current NBA players showed that 73% of players view Michael Jordan as the best basketball player of all time (Amick, 2019). His online NBA legends profile remarks that "he was an accessible [through the Air Jordan brand] star who managed to maintain an air of mystique" (NBA.com, n.d., para. 5). Current NBA star LeBron James remarked that the first time he met Jordan "it was like meeting God for the first time" (Olivieri, 2020). Likewise, NFL quarterback Tom Brady stated that he "was in awe of Michael Jordan and [is] still in awe of what he was and what meant (...) there's an art and a beauty to the way he played the game" (Conway, 2017). Current NBA player Chris Paul notes that the Jordan Brand is a large reason why Michael Jordan's legacy still inspires players in the modern NBA, aided by Nike's storytelling prowess, with many shoes associated with iconic moments from Jordan's career (Harris, 2018).

The Jordan Brand also has facilitated Michael Jordan's transcendence from a basketball player to a popular culture figure. Grammy Award-winning hip-hop artist DJ Khaled has stated "for me, he is the definition of greatness. His influence is generational. A brand you can trust forever, timeless. It represents winning and being the best period" (Harris, 2018). While the above quotations are anecdotal, they are illustrative of how Jordan's aura is perceived on and off the basketball court and the feelings of awe that are conjured by his performance and likeness. In a 2019 survey of over 1,000 basketball fans conducted by Business Insider, Michael Jordan was overwhelmingly supported (66% of participants) as the greatest basketball player of all time, with his overall influence in elevating the NBA's global profile and popularity cited as a major contributing factor (Davis et al., 2019). The results were consistent across fans who categorized themselves as only casual fans and those who identified themselves as loyal NBA supporters. They were also consistent across age groups with over 60% of the 18–29 age group recognizing Jordan's elite prowess. This is further illustrative of the long-lasting effects of Jordan's image, as many of the fans in this age group were born after the peak of Jordan's career in the mid-1990s, and thus never personally witnessed it. Providing an explanation for this phenomenon, former United States President Barack Obama notes that "Michael Jordan helped create a different way people saw athletics as part of the entertainment business (…) [he] changed the culture. He became an extraordinary ambassador, not just for basketball, but for the United States" (Manrique, 2020).

From a more academic perspective, Harrison et al (2010) further investigated the connection between the awe-like emotions that fans experience while watching Michael Jordan on the court to the emotional responses they experience when coming into contact with the Jordan brand and the Jumpman logo. This was accomplished by collecting responses from 89 college students using the photo elicitation technique to qualitatively analyze consumer perspectives related to the logo. With Jordan's on-court play serving as key facilitator of the strength of the emotional responses, the results demonstrated that Jordan's brand is capable of eliciting awe-like emotions. Examples of participant responses to the Jumpman logo included, "Michael Jordan, greatness"; "greatness and style"; "people want to 'be like Mike' on and off the court"; and "Michael Jordan – One of the greatest to ever play the game [of basketball]; It is a logo that represents a brand name – Jordan." Major themes of the findings stemming from the responses to the logo and the Jordan Brand included (a) *Be Like Mike*, (b) *The Branding Representation of Michael Jordan the athlete*, (c) and *Greatness, Style and Winning*. This further establishes a key link between Jordan's athletic performance and the brand bearing his likeness, and confirms that his image is capable of eliciting strong emotional responses from consumers engaging with his brand.

Given the strong emotional responses elicited by the Jordan Brand and Jumpman logo, particularly with younger audiences across all regions of the country, the partnerships between the Jordan Brand and the athletics departments at major universities, i.e. Big 10, Southeastern Conference (SEC), Big XII, and Atlantic Coast Conference (ACC), all seem intuitive. In 2015, when the University of Michigan officially announced the partnership with the Jordan Brand, interim athletic director Jim Hackett remarked, "this partnership is about more than Michigan athletics; at the core, it is about our University community and it is about two great names reuniting for an opportunity that speaks to more than uniforms and apparel" (University of Michigan, 2015). Michigan's basketball coach John Beilein concurred, stating that "the traditions and reputations of both brands make this relationship one of the best in college athletics" (University of Michigan, 2015). Similar characterizations were provided at other partnering institutions, with University of Florida athletic director Scott Stricklin noting that, "The Florida Gators and Jordan Brand are two of the more iconic brands in athletics and we are looking forward to our partnership that will be enjoyed by the student-athletes of our football and basketball programs and our fans," and Florida football coach Dan Mullen saying, "I know our players and staff will be pumped up" (Hutchins, 2017). It seems that the Jordan Brand elicits emotional responses from even the highest levels of athletic leadership in higher education.

The last dance phenomenon

In 2020, ESPN and Netflix released *The Last Dance*, a documentary centered on capturing the progression and impact of Michael Jordan's career. The series covers Jordan's playing career from high school through the end of his final season with the Chicago Bulls in 1998, airing footage from a film crew that followed the Bulls during the 1997–1998 season. It also features interviews and analysis from key figures, including Jordan himself, former teammates, coaches, media members who covered Chicago while Jordan was a member of the team, NBA players that Jordan played against, and other non-athlete public figures who offered their perspectives. Premiering during the 2020 COVID-19 global pandemic as live sports were indefinitely paused, the docuseries averaged 5.648 million viewers across the ten aired episodes, making it the most watched ESPN documentary ever released and top program viewed on television since live sports had been paused (Young, 2020). Since the premier, viewership has continued to increase with the first two episodes garnering an average audience of over 13 million viewers as of May 2020 (NBA, 2020).

The content and subsequent analysis of the docuseries has precipitated contemporary conversation surrounding Jordan's legacy, particularly with younger viewers. The series received overwhelmingly positive reviews with a 95% approval rating from audiences and a 96% approval rating from critics (Rotten Tomatoes, 2020). Critics remark that *The Last Dance* serves as an "education and spiritual reunion" with Jordan's Bulls and that viewers will be in "awe of [Jordan's] superpowers." Analysis of the docuseries yields that the content will change the way viewers think of Michael Jordan and his legacy (NBA Insiders, 2020). In a survey of ESPN NBA analysts, the docuseries is said to confirm that Jordan is the greatest and most charismatic player in history, appears invincible (Zach Lowe), and inspires awe for his life and basketball career (Brian Windhorst). The docuseries has changed the way that younger NBA players (born in the late 1990s to early 2000s) and current college players perceive the career and image of Jordan, even for those who have grown up watching video of him playing (Youngmisuk, 2020). Finally, college-going fans who watched the docuseries characterized their view of Jordan as being that of a dominating athlete and a global icon (Taub, 2020).

Method: collecting data in real time

The Last Dance phenomenon coupled with the enduring aura and legacy of Jordan and his brand necessitate further study surrounding the emotional responses from consumers who engage with products bearing his likeness. The newly minted partnerships between the Jordan Brand and athletic programs of elite universities serves as an optimal vehicle to conduct this study because (a) consumer responses are capturable as the transition to Jordan Brand products is being implemented and (b) resulting changes in behavior can be analyzed. Attendees of football games at the partner institutions serve as a primary population from which to sample for two reasons. First, these four football programs, each from a different major conference, were exclusively chosen to have their equipment and associated merchandise branded with the Jumpman logo. While there are other universities with basketball uniforms that contain the Jumpman logo, the inclusion of the logo on the football uniforms of these institutions received considerable promotion. Second, the surveying of fans at football games allows for the analysis of whether the Jordan Brand and the Jumpman logo elicit emotional responses strong enough to transcend the game of basketball. As discussed previously, even casual basketball fans revere Michael Jordan and his image. By examining football game attendees who have no outward affinity to the game of basketball, a richer analysis can be conducted. Additionally, in 2019 the University of Michigan led the nation in average football attendance at 111,459 attendees per game (NCAA, 2020). The University of North Carolina averaged 50,500, the University of Florida averaged 84,684, and the University of Oklahoma averaged 83,256. The two stated factors coupled with the large attendance at games from each partner institution provide a diverse population from which to sample.

To study the impacts of the partnership, the survey construction process was designed to gain a holistic view of the respondents' feelings and emotions toward the Jordan Brand, their university, and the partnership between the two. Survey questions were constructed so that subsequent analysis of the data allowed for the determination of key characteristics that serve as predictors of favorable consumer behavior (and feelings of emotional attachment and awe) in relation to the Jordan Brand. By measuring the level of affinity survey participants feel towards Jordan Brand, the potential gains from a partnership with a brand that elicits strong emotional responses such as the Jordan Brand does, can be examined. More specifically, the survey was designed to collect data on four dimensions: (a) the demographic background of the survey participants; (b) their level of connection to the University and Jordan Brand; (c) their emotional feelings and perceptions toward the Jordan Brand and its partnership with the university's athletic department; and (d) the likelihood that the Jordan Brand partnership would influence their future actions. Survey participants' emotions towards the Jordan Brand were captured using a 5-point Likert scale, in which a response of 1 generally indicated a strongly negative response while a response of 5 generally indicated a strongly positive/affirmative response.

Demographic data collected included information on participants' age, gender, race, and socioeconomic status. Data corresponding to the participants' relationships and prior interactions with the university and Jordan Brand were collected using objective, discrete choice questions. Information collected included the connection to the university (e.g. student, alumni, faculty), their typical level of home game attendance, season ticket holder status, level of awareness of the new partnership between the university and Jordan Brand, whether they had previously purchased their university's Jordan Brand merchandise, and the amount they previously spent on Jordan Brand merchandise.

Successfully quantifying the emotional attachment to Jordan Brand is a crucial feature of the survey design and data collection process. Given the anecdotal evidence of awe-like emotional responses to Michael Jordan the athlete and the connections between his athletic performance and his human brand, data were collected on a variety of variables that serve as proxies for awe, based on its definition and theoretical dimensions. A Likert scale allows for quantification of the strength of participants' feelings toward the Jordan Brand, as well as their beliefs as to how the partnership with it influences outside perspectives. With the theoretical sentiments surrounding awe in mind, the survey asked participants whether they perceived the Jordan Brand as representing quality, embodying tradition, and displaying excellence. Participants were also asked whether they believed the partnership with Jordan Brand would bring more attention to the athletic programs and create a more positive perception from those not affiliated with the university. As additional measures of emotional attachment and proxies for awe, participants were asked whether they felt Jordan Brand was a good fit for the university, whether it brought value to the university, and how they personally felt when wearing Jordan Brand apparel. In addition to measuring affinity to Jordan Brand partnership, these questions allowed for analysis of participants' perceptions of how others perceived the Jordan Brand partnership, and hence the collectiveness of the emotional response, a key theoretical construct of awe.

While understanding the emotional response to the branding partnership is an important first step, it was also important to understand how these emotional connections translated to impact in consumer behavior and other actions. Thus, participants were asked whether they intended to purchase their university's Jordan Brand apparel in the future or purchase additional apparel in the future if they had already done so. To understand whether the emotional response to the new branding would translate to non-purchasing behaviors, individuals were asked whether they were more likely to donate to the university and the university's athletic department as a result of the partnership with Jordan Brand, whether they were more likely to attend football games in the future as a result of the partnership, and whether the partnership encouraged them to purchase non-university Jordan Brand apparel. Finally, individuals were asked whether they were willing to pay more for their university's apparel because it has the Jordan Brand logo.

Data collection was completed in two phases. As the partnerships were first established at the University of Michigan and the University of North Carolina, the first phase of data collection occurred at these two institutions. Subsequent data collection occurred at both the University of Florida and University of Oklahoma. Data collection occurred in the tailgate areas around each stadium beginning four to five hours before the start time of the game taking place on the day of collection. The survey itself was distributed in paper form and participants were asked to answer each question with the response that best characterized their reaction to the stated question.

Findings

For the first phase of data collection, survey results were compiled and analyzed for over 1,000 participants. Results can be summarized into three main findings: (a) changes in perceived beliefs of outsiders as influences on consumer outcomes, (b) cultural relevance and historical significance as determinants of consumer behavior, and (c) the desire to be engaged in a broad, and collective movement. Before analyzing behavioral impacts that the partnership had on consumers, it is important to first understand their emotional responses along the dimensions mentioned above. Overall, participants agreed that the partnership with Jordan Brand created a more positive perception (Mean = 4.07) and brought more attention (Mean = 4.31) to the football program. They agreed that the Jordan Brand represents quality (Mean = 4.39), value (Mean = 4.36), excellence (Mean = 4.32), tradition (Mean = 3.96), and they experienced a positive personal response when wearing their university's Jordan Brand apparel (Mean = 3.77).

The mean response values for these questions indicate that the partnership was successful in eliciting awe-like emotions from fans and developing a level of emotional attachment to the merchandise. These response items provide insight not only into participants' personal feelings towards Jordan Brand and the partnership, but also insight into how they believed others perceive the partnership and the impact that these perceptions will have, highlighting the collective nature of their perception. Additionally, most survey participants indicated a high level of awareness regarding the introduction of the partnership between Jordan Brand and the university (Mean = 4.17), indicating that the launch of the new merchandise was sufficiently promoted. Just over half of participants (Mean = 0.51) indicated that they had purchased some of their university's Jordan Brand apparel and had spent on average about $100 on such merchandise.

The impact that emotional responses had on an individual's intention to purchase the university's Jordan Brand merchandise in the future was analyzed using a logistic regression. The results show that younger people, those with higher incomes, as well as those who are more engaged with the university's athletics (proxied by game attendance) are more likely to purchase the university's Jordan Brand merchandise on average. Additionally, individuals who are more aware of the partnership are more likely to purchase merchandise. Furthermore, the extent of previous purchases (proxied by amount spent) also positively influences likelihood of future purchases, indicating satisfaction with the product and brand loyalty. Finally, individuals who felt that the Jordan Brand invoked awe-like emotions, who perceived the partnership with Jordan Brand positively, and individuals who personally elicit a positive response to wearing Jordan Brand merchandise are all more likely to purchase merchandise in the future.

It is also of interest whether the feelings elicited by the branding can have broader effects that are more impactful for the university. The analysis provides insight into participants' propensity to donate, both to the university itself and to the university's athletic department. Individuals who previously spent more on the university's Jordan Brand merchandise are more likely to donate to both the university and the university's athletic department. Interestingly, more casual, younger fans who do not attend every game and thus, likely have not donated as much in the past as participants who attend every game, seem to be more influenced by the partnership to donate. This suggests that the partnership can help universities solidify their young alumni bases that could pay dividends as these individuals age and obtain the financial ability to donate larger sums. Variables that capture the historical significance of the Jordan Brand and that capture how outsiders perceive the university and its athletics program, as a result of the partnership with Jordan Brand, tend to be positive and significant. Taken together, this suggests that the ability of Jordan Brand to influence behavior outside of strict purchasing behavior hinges on the emotional vastness conjured by the historical significance of the brand, and the larger scale change in perception that the partnership has on the collective view of the university (accommodation).

Finally, the analysis investigates whether individuals are willing to pay more for the merchandise simply because it displays the Jumpman logo. Younger individuals, who have spent larger amounts of money on the university's Jordan Brand merchandise in the past, are more likely to spend more on future purchases simply because it has the Jordan Brand logo. Additionally, more casual fans of the university's athletic program that have strong emotional attachment to the Jordan Brand are also willing to pay more, suggesting that the partnership of the two entities together influences behavior. Factors relating to how individuals believe outsiders perceive the partnership (whether they believe it is a good fit, represents tradition etc.) also have a positive impact on willingness to pay. This suggests that the Jordan Brand logo raises the significance of the university's merchandise and places it within a cultural and historical context to a level sufficient to raise the individual's willingness to pay for the apparel.

Discussion

While the initial survey analysis serves as a first step at understanding the connections between Michael Jordan's athletic performance, the emotional responses to his brand and the power of the University-Jordan Brand partnership, there are still a variety of avenues of future research to be undertaken. Future scholarship should examine the next wave of schools partnering with athlete sport brands; specifically, to investigate what impact the history, traditions, and geographical locations of these institutions have on their fans' consumptions patterns. Different universities have varying compositions of students, alumni, and visitors, and future research will allow for a richer set of findings relative to those in the initial phase of results. Fans and their purchasing decisions are nuanced.

Thus, future studies should continue to tease out the major factor(s) for the support of the merger between these reputable institutions and the exceedingly popular global brand by Michael Jordan at Nike. Perhaps future research could investigate any differences in perception related to the Jordan Brand partnership that exist between game attendees and non-game attendees.

These findings suggest and support the expansion of partnerships between the Jordan Brand and athletic departments of Division I universities due to the mutual benefits experienced by each entity. For the Jordan Brand, a partnership is valuable as it allows them access to a segment of the market that it may not have had access to before. Consumers who are simply interested in buying the university's apparel appear inclined to purchase merchandise that is also Jordan Brand apparel, which they would not have been inclined to do so beforehand. The finding that previous purchasers are more likely to purchase again, bodes well for the Jordan Brand as it indicates that it can retain and expand its customer base. For a university, the partnership with Jordan Brand is advantageous because of its transcendent nature: the affiliation with a brand like Jordan causes those with a relationship to the university to believe that outsiders have a raised perception of the university brand, which positively influences the behaviors of those with a connection to the university. This ripple effect is illustrated by the finding that consumers are willing to pay more for apparel simply because it is affiliated with the Jordan Brand and by the fact that these individuals are more likely to donate to the university and its athletic programs.

The findings of this study can be used by both entities to better understand the types of consumers who are likely to elicit a response to a partnership between the university and Jordan Brand. This allows these entities to diversify branding strategies to best meet the needs of each customer base, i.e. students, alumni, and visitors, which will continue to increase brand awareness and loyalty. By continuing to strategically connect consumers to the university, the Jordan Brand, or both, the partnership will be able to enhance the cognitive identification that consumers associate with the brands, which will ultimately impact their behavior.

References

Aaker, J. L., Garbinsky, E. N., & Vohs, K. D. (2012). Cultivating admiration in brands: Warmth, competence, and landing in the "golden quadrant." *Journal of Consumer Psychology, 22*(2), 191–194.

Akgun, A., Kocoglu, I., & Imamoglu, S. (2013). An emerging consumer experience: Emotional branding. *Procedia – Social and Behavioral Sciences, 99*(6), 503–508.

Amick, S. (2019, April 09). The 2019 NBA Player Poll: MVP? The GOAT? Most overrated? Retrieved June 13, 2020, from https://theathletic.com/909752/2019/04/08/the-2019-nba-player-poll-mvp-the-goat-most-overrated-players-weigh-in-on-the-best-and-worst-in-the-game/

Carlson, B. D., & Donovan, D. T. (2013). Human brands in sport: Athlete brand personality and identification. *Journal of Sport Management, 27*, 193–206.

222 C. Keith Harrison et al.

Chidester, P. (2012). "Open-Mouth Awe": ESPN's streetball and the "Transcendant Simultaneity" of the media sublime. *Mass Communication and Society, 15*(1), 98–114.

Chovanová, H. H., Korshunov, A. I., & Babčanová, D. (2015). Impact of brand on consumer behavior. *Procedia Economics and Finance, 34*, 615–621.

Coleman, C. (2013). Classic campaigns- "It's gotta be the shoes": Nike, Mike and Mars and the "Sneaker killings". *Advertising and Society, 14*(2), 1–2.

Connolly, M. (2016, May 19). *Whether LeBron has a $1B deal or not, Michael Jordan is still the king of Nike.* Forbes. https://www.forbes.com/sites/mattconnolly/2016/05/19/despite-lebron-james-1-billion-deal-michael-jordan-still-king-nike/#3b2cb54d9cd0

Conway, T. (2017, September 29). *Tom Brady says he was in awe of Michael Jordan, talks retirement with ESPN.* Bleacher Report. Retrieved June 16, 2020, from https://bleacherreport.com/articles/2709711?fb_comment_id=1525476130817636_1526629164035666

Crowley, M. (1999). *Muhammad Ali was a rebel. Michael Jordan is a brand name.* Nieman Reports. https://niemanreports.org/articles/muhammad-ali-was-a-rebel-michael-jordan-is-a-brand-name/

Davis, S., Hickey, W., & Yuan, Y. (2019, March 18). *Most Americans think Michael Jordan is the 'GOAT' over LeBron James, and it's not even close.* Business Insider. Retrieved June 18, 2020, from https://www.businessinsider.com/jordan-lebron-goat-debate-americans-jordan-2019-3

DeTienne, K., & Lewis, L. (2005). The pragmatic and ethical barriers to corporate social responsibility disclosure: The Nike case. *Journal of Business Ethics, 60*(4), 359–376.

ESPN. (n.d.). *Top N. American athletes of the century.* ESPN. https://www.espn.com/sportscentury/athletes.html

Gaines, C., Borden, T., & Askinasi, R. (2020, June 07). How Michael Jordan makes and spends his $2.1 billion fortune. Retrieved May 30, 2020, from https://www.businessinsider.com/how-michael-jordan-spends-his-money-2015-3

Gottlieb, S., Keltner, D., & Lombrozo, T. (2018). Awe as a scientific emotion. *Cognitive Science, 42*(6), 2081–2094.

Harris, J. (2018, January 02). *MJ's influence as strong as ever in today's NBA.* Sports Illustrated. Retrieved June 16, 2020, from https://www.si.com/nba/2018/01/02/michael-jordan-sneaker-culture-influence-nba-chris-paul-nas

Harrison, C. K., Sutton, W., Lawrence, S. M., Buksten, S., Connolly, M., Dickens, J., & McArdle, D. (2010). The Jumpman logo and lovemarks theory. Paper presented at the Diversity and Social Issues in Sport Jordan Brand Symposium, Orlando, Florida.

Hutchins, A. (2017, December 06). *Florida announces switch to Jordan Brand for football, basketball.* SB Nation. Retrieved June 22, 2020, from https://www.alligatorarmy.com/2017/12/6/16742638/florida-gators-jordan-brand-uniforms-football-basketball-nike

Jackson, S. (2016). *Impact of Jordan Brand reaches far beyond basketball.* ESPN. http://www.espn.com/nba/story/_/id/14760324/cultural-impact-jordan-sneakers-goes-far-basketball

Keltner, D., & Haidt, J. (2003). Approaching awe, a moral, spiritual, and aesthetic emotion. *Cognition and Emotion, 17*(2), 297–314.

Lubin, G. (2014, June 05). *Michael Jordan is a billionaire thanks to soaring NBA team values.* Business Insider. Retrieved June 7, 2020, from https://www.businessinsider.com/michael-jordan-is-a-billionaire-2014-6

Manrique, B. (2020, May 18). *Barack Obama explains how Michael Jordan "changed the culture."* Clutch Points. https://clutchpoints.com/last-dance-news-barack-obama-explains-michael-jordan-changed-the-culture/

Mason, K. (2005). How corporate sport sponsorship impacts consumer behavior. *The Journal of American Academy of Business, Cambridge, 7*(1), 32–35.

Mathur, L. K., Mathur, I., & Rangan, N. (1997). The wealth effects associated with a celebrity endorser: The Michael Jordan phenomenon. *Journal of Advertising Research, 37*(3), 67–73.

NBA.com. (n.d.). *Legends profile: Michael Jordan.* https://www.nba.com/history/legends/profiles/michael-jordan

NBA.com. (2020, May 04). 'The Last Dance' continues to set ratings records for ESPN. Retrieved June 23, 2020, from https://www.nba.com/article/2020/05/04/last-dance-ratings-continue-impressive-run-official-release

NBA Insiders. (2020, May 17). *How 'The Last Dance' changed the way we think about Michael Jordan.* ESPN. https://www.espn.com/nba/story/_/id/29180240/how-last-dance-changed-way-think-michael-jordan

NCAA Football Attendance. (2020, April 09). Retrieved June 27, 2020, from http://www.ncaa.org/championships/statistics/ncaa-football-attendance

Ohlin, B. (2019, July 04). *What is awe? A definition and 3 ways to live an 'Awesome' life.* Positive Psychology. https://positivepsychology.com/what-is-awe-definition/

Olivieri, A. (2020, April 26). *GOATs on GOATs: LeBron and MJ in their own words through the years.* ESPN. https://www.espn.com/nba/story/_/page/allstarweekend25788027/the-comparison-lebron-james-michael-jordan-their-own-words

Ramaswamy, V. (2008). Co-creating value through customers' experiences: The Nike case. *Strategy and Leadership, 36*(5), 9–14.

Ravizza, K. (1977). Peak experiences in sport. *Journal of Humanistic Psychology, 17*(4), 35–40.

Rossiter, J., & Bellman, S. (1999). A proposed model for explaining and measuring web ad effectiveness. *Journal of Current Issues & Research in Advertising, 21*(1), 13–31.

Rotten Tomatoes.com. (2020). *The last dance: Season 1.* https://www.rottentomatoes.com/tv/the_last_dance/s01

Rovell, D. (2006). *First in thirst: How Gatorade turned the science of sweat into cultural phenomenon.* New York: Amacom.

Rudd, M., Vohs, K. D., & Aaker, J. (2012). Awe expands people's perception of time, alters decision making, and enhances well-being. *Psychological Science, 23*(10), 1130–1136.

Shiota, M. N., Keltner, D., & Mossman, A. (2007). The nature of awe: Elicitors, appraisals, and effects on self-concept. *Cognition and Emotion, 21*(5), 944–963.

Tannenbaum, M., Hepler, J., Zimmerman, R., Saul, L., Jacobs, S., Wilson, K., & Albarracin, D. (2015). Appealing to fear: A meta-analysis of fear appeal effectiveness and theories. *Psychological Bulletin, 141*(6), 1178–1204.

Taub, B. (2020, May 09). *The last dance: Younger fans react to Michael Jordan, whom they never saw play; Better than LeBron?* Sports Broadcast Journal. https://www.sportsbroadcastjournal.com/the-last-dance-young-fans-react-to-michael-jordan/

Thomson, M. (2006). Human brands: Investigating antecedents to consumers' strong attachments to celebrities. *Journal of Marketing, 70*(3), 104–119.

University of Michigan Athletics. (2015, July 6). Reunited: Michigan and NIKE announce partnership. Retrieved June 22, 2020, from https://mgoblue.com/news/2015/7/6/Reunited_Michigan_and_NIKE_Announce_Partnership.aspx

Weber, M. (1978). *Economy and society: An outline of interpretive sociology.* In G. Roth and C. Wittich (Eds.), (Based on 4th German edition). Berkeley, CA: University of California.

Young, R. (2020, May 21). *Viewership numbers from "The Last Dance" prove Michael Jordan documentary was a smash hit.* Yahoo. https://sports.yahoo.com/michael-jordan-the-last-dance-documentary-numbers-viewership-figures-espn-chicago-bulls-224004795.html

Youngmisuk, O. (2020, May 15). How modern NBA players grew up on Michael Jordan way after he retired. ESPN. https://www.espn.com/nba/story/_/id/29163950/how-modern-nba-players-grew-michael-jordan-way-retired

Chapter 14

Structuring sustainable sport events and achieving desirable impact on urban development

Cristiana Buscarini, Fabio Cerroni, and Sara Franzini Gabrielli

Introduction

Events bring people together and the industry supplies a high percentage of a country's Gross Domestic Product (GDP) (Celuch, 2018). Personnel involved in event creation and management have a strong and important position in that they can create unforgettable and sustainable memories (Moital et al., 2019). Event personnel not only provide the opportunity for participation and enjoyment but also train and inform all stakeholders. Events can make a difference and create change. Every day, event professionals see the value of people coming together to collaborate. It is time to build a new event vision and mission to define how people will come together. The future is uncertain, but events must both inspire and contribute to reaching sustainable goals in everyday life, organizations, governments' strategies, and all stakeholders' actions (Cavagnaro et al., 2016).

Sport can be used to spread sustainable values all over the world. It has great capacity to determine the correct sustainability principles that should be put into practice (Dudfield & Dingwall-Smith, 2015). A lot of sustainable principles are innate and already included in Olympic values, as outlined at the beginning of the last century by Baron Pierre de Coubertin, the father of modern Olympics. The Olympic Movement has embraced sustainable initiatives since 1994 when the environment was included as a third pillar of the Olympic Movement (Ross & Leopkey, 2017). The IOC (International Olympic Committee) has also paid a lot of attention to the legacy of sporting events and sport in general: within bid presentations, event organizers must specify the social, environmental, and economic benefits that the event will bring into the host country, city, and community. This is because the IOC's analysis phase places enormous importance on legacy management and sustainable strategies that the Organising Committees present and express within the bid.

All Olympic Games have demonstrated the importance of hosting big events for urban development of the city, especially in the development of transportation networks to be more comprehensive, efficient, and in helping to drive better social behaviours.

DOI: 10.4324/9781003213673-14

To deliver an event sustainably, the standard ISO20121 was developed, outlined by the International Organization for Standardization (ISO). This standard specifies the requirements for an event sustainability management system for any type of event or event-related activity and provides guidelines on how to comply with them. The aim of ISO20121 is to minimize the impacts of an event on the community and environment in which it takes place (Buscarini & Franzini, 2017). It also allows the organizing committee to align the event with the Sustainable Development Goals (SDGs), set out in the UN 2030 Agenda published by the United Nations in 2015, which outlines a new plan for global development with the ambition to 'transform our world by 2030'.

The 17 SDGs, with their 169 targets and 241 indicators, have replaced the Millennium Development Goals (MDGs) in providing the key reference point for global development efforts. The SDGs represent a common goal – for all countries and individuals – setting fundamental targets for future development, such as: reduce and remove poverty and hunger, fight against climate change, build more inclusive and sustainable cities etc. The 2030 Agenda requires governments to coordinate, consult, and work across policy areas in an unprecedented way. This calls for strategic use of budget, procurement, and regulatory tools and the design and implementation of innovative, forward-looking policies and programs. All these issues are part of a 'governance' agenda, which not only is a goal but also, more importantly, an essential enabler for the achievement of all other goals (comprehensive approach) (UN, 2015).

During the last few years, after SDGs gained increasing relevance within the sports sector, professionals started trying to develop easy guidelines and actions to enable organizers to attain SDGs within the sports sector. Some goals are ingrained in the sports world, but others require more work and a collaborative approach between sports professionals to create the basis to reach sustainable goals in sports activities, events, and strategies. With this paper, we would like to provide to the organizers of sporting events that use the Global Reporting Initiative reporting framework, a tool that allows them to link the GRI reporting with the targets of the SDGs, to better identify how the event contributes to sustainable development. For our exploratory study, we chose to examine the Gold Coast 2018 (or the XXI Commonwealth Games) because it was an event organized following ISO20121 (Bakos et al., 2020).

In its sustainability reports drafted following the GRI guidelines, it refers to the willingness to pursue the SDGs. In this chapter, our effort was to link the disclosure of the GRI with the targets of SDG 11, through the information provided in the sustainability reports on the impacts of the event on urban development. The UN document 'The contribution of Sports to the achievement of the sustainable development goals' (UN SDG Fund, 2018) and the Commonwealth document 'Sport for Development and Peace and the 2030 Agenda for Sustainable Development' (Dudfield & Dingwall-Smith, 2015) show how sport and sporting events can contribute to reaching the targets of the SDG 11, having an impact mainly on targets 11.3, 11.7, and 11.a. Besides, after analyzing the sustainability reports of the event mentioned above, we noticed that there are also other targets of this goal that sport can affect, i.e. 11.2, 11.4, and 11.6.

Sustainability in the sports sector

The first document in the history of the sports sector that has embodied the values of sustainability is the *Annuaire du Comité International Olympique* that outlined the fundamental principles of Olympism: this was first published in 1908 and was based on some rules written by Baron Pierre de Coubertin around 1898 (IOC). Throughout the following years, this document had taken various names up to the current name, 'Olympic Charter' adopted in 1978 (Figure 14.1). The Olympic Charter is the

> codification of the fundamental principles of Olympism, and the rules and bye-laws adopted by the International Olympic Committee. It governs the organisation, actions, and functioning of the Olympic Movement and establishes the conditions for the celebration of the Olympic Games. Among other things, it establishes the relations between the International Federations, National Olympic Committees, and the Olympic Movement.
>
> (IOC)

In 1978, UNESCO's International Charter of Physical Education and Sport was adopted (updated in 2015). The document, with its 12 articles, represents a universal reference for ethical and quality standards for physical education, physical activity, and sport. In 1992, during the Earth Summit, held in Rio de Janeiro, UNCED (United Nations Conference on Environment and Development) Agenda 21 was drafted, an action plan for the sustainable development of the planet. Few weeks later, at the conclusion of the XXV Olympics Games in Barcelona, various institutions of the sports world endorsed the Earth Pledge, committing to make the Earth a safe place (IOC, 2012). In the same year, the European Sports Charter was issued by the Council of Europe in Rodi (Greece). The document contains the "Sport and Sustainable Development principles" aimed at improving and ensuring people's physical, social, and mental well-being from one generation to the next, requiring that sporting activities including those in urban, open country, and water areas, must be adjusted to the planet's limited resources and be carried out following the principles of sustainable development (Council of Europe, 1992). The last document issued in 1992 was the 'Geneva Charter of the Rights of the Child in Sports' which claimed the right of children to benefit from a healthy environment during sports activities, including a commitment to fair play, and the fight against doping.

During the IOC centenary congress, environmental protection was included as the third pillar of Olympism, alongside sport and culture (Ross & Leopkey, 2017). In 1995, the IOC established the Commission for Sport and the Environment to outline principles to ensure that sport and its manifestations would no longer be

Figure 14.1 Historical Stages of Sport Sustainability.

damaging the environment. The birth of this commission followed the beginning of a collaboration between the IOC and the UNEP (United Nations Environment Programme), in 1994 – to spread awareness on the importance of sustainable development in the world of sport (IOC, 2012). Due to this collaboration, the Olympic Movement Agenda 21 was approved in 1999, a document inspired by the UNCED's agenda, which aims to encourage the Olympic Movement to play an active role in the sustainable development of our planet (IOC, 1999).

For sporting events, a milestone was posed at the end of 2002, when the International Olympic Committee organized an international congress on the 'Legacy of the Olympic Games from 1984 to 2000', to define all the potential strengths and drawbacks in the planning and management of long-term legacies (Leopkey & Parent, 2012). After this congress, in 2003, the generation of positive legacy was formally included in the Olympic Agenda (IOC, 2014). Since 2003, all bidding cities are expected to include a legacy plan in their bidding papers, outlining the use of sports facilities for post-events, and long-term plans for the Games regions (Azzali, 2017; Chappelet, 2008). In 2007, one of the European Commission's contributions to the world of sport was published, 'White Paper on Sport' and it states,

> the practice of sport, sports facilities, and sports events all have a significant impact on the environment. It is important to promote environmentally sound management, fit to address inter alia green procurement, greenhouse gas emissions, energy efficiency, waste disposal, and the treatment of soil and water. European sports organisations and sport event organisers should adopt environmental objectives to make their activities environmentally sustainable.
>
> (European Commission, 2007)

In 2012 the ISO20121:2012 was released which specifies requirements for an event sustainability management system. This standard was first applied to the 2012 London Olympics and provides guidance and best practices to help event organizers improve event-related activity and sustainability. The IOC adopted the Olympic Agenda 2020 in 2014, a roadmap for the future of the Olympic Movement. The document is made up of 40 recommendations for the safety of the Olympic Games is aimed at strengthening the practice of sport all over the world. We would like to highlight two recommendations, 4 and 5, which request that organizers implement sustainability in all the aspects of the Olympic Games and within the Olympic Movement's daily operations (IOC, 2014).

In 2015, the 2030 Agenda for Sustainable Development was introduced, which comprises the 17 SDGs, and recognizes sport as an important enabler of sustainable development. In fact, at point 37, it declares that

> sport is also an important enabler of sustainable development. We recognize the growing contribution of sport to the realization of development and peace in its promotion of tolerance and respect and the contributions it makes to the empowerment of women and young people, individuals and communities as well as to health, education and social inclusion objectives.
>
> (UN, 2015)

The importance of sport in achieving SDGs was also highlighted in the Kazan Action Plan, a call for action aimed at aligning the efforts of governments to make sports contribute effectively to reach the Sustainable Development Goals (Dudley et al., 2018; UNESCO, 2017).

The urban SDG: SDG 11

SDG 11, referred to by some as the 'urban SDG', represents one of the clearest examples of an evolving global development agenda – from one focusing on specific development issues to a more systemic approach which aims to address underlying factors that contribute to many human development challenges. SDG 11 covers an array of urban infrastructure targets. For many of these, sport will be of limited relevance. It is important to consider the interplay between SDG 11 and the other SDGs, recognizing that population density can mean that development challenges are intensified in urban areas. The role that sport and physical activity can play in target 11.7 is to consider that "by 2030, [to] provide universal access to safe, inclusive and accessible, green and public spaces, in particular for women and children, older persons and persons with disabilities." SDG 11, therefore, represents recognition of the need to adopt a systematic approach that addresses infrastructure implications of population-level changes, to realize the full scope of the 2030 Agenda for Sustainable Development.

It is clear that SDG 11 and its specific targets have relevance to sport and significant implications for its contribution to other goals. SDG target 11.7 identifies the importance of designing and maintaining all spaces, including those suitable for sport and active recreation, in a way that provides safe and inclusive access for all in society. Planning and management of such spaces must be participatory, integrated, and sustainable. SDG target 11.3, therefore, indicates both the importance and potential contribution of adopting such approaches within sport. The importance of ensuring adequate provision of space for sport and recreation is recognized in urban planning and design recommendations. The technical description of the indicators for Target 11.7 on access to green and public spaces cites the UN-Habitat guideline that a minimum of 15% of an urban area should be given over to 'green space', including athletic and recreational space (Dudfield & Dingwall-Smith, 2015; Lindsey & Chapman, 2017).

Background and review of literature

Sustainable development has become more and more incorporated into mega-event hosting objectives (Hall, 2012). Increasingly, cities are involved in the bidding and hosting mega-events. These events are considered vehicles for the economic growth of cities for many reasons. For instance, they can reinforce or establish a city's national or global status, they can be an impetus to construct new buildings and parks, they can draw visitors and tourists, and, lastly, they can legitimize a rapid infrastructure development program. It has become essential to adopt strategies to enhance gains from each stage and to plan and execute effective, sustainable, and long-lasting legacies (Azzali, 2019).

In the last 20 years, the issue of legacy has gained increasing attention both from academics and event organizers (Leopkey & Parent, 2012), and various definitions have been developed (Matheson, 2010). One of the most popular defines legacy as "all planned and unplanned, positive and negative, intangible and tangible structures created by and for a sports event that remain for a longer time than the event itself" (Preuss, 2007). The legacy may be tangible, such as constructing a new stadium or a new highway, or it can be intangible, such as fostering a sense of community or cultivating a professional information volunteer corps (Phillips & Bouchier, 2014). About the benefits of sporting events, they include such aspects as new or upgraded stadium facilities, tracks and pools, enhanced visibility on the world stage, and civic and national pride, among others. Also, a legacy can be negative – as in opportunity costs, the displacement of low-income housing as neighborhoods are 'rejuvenated', massive public debt, and sports facilities that are mothballed after the event. But there are questions in how one measures legacy, especially the intangibles, and exactly how long after an event one needs to wait before measuring any sustainable benefit. When all is said and done, policymakers must then decide whether the benefits were worth the overall costs (Phillips & Bouchier, 2014).

The majority of scholarly works focused on aspects related to legacy such as the environmental impacts of events (Chappelet, 2008; Collins et al., 2009; Ross & Leopkey, 2017), others on social (Raco, 2004; Smith, 2009; Waitt, 2003), and economic outcomes (Allmers & Maennig, 2009; Clark & Kearns, 2015; Gratton et al., 2006; Pham et al., 2019; Preuss, 2005). Instead, Zhang and Zhao (2009) focused on the impacts on the image of hosting cities, while others studies focused on the impacts on urban development (Liao & Pitts, 2006; Pillay & Bass, 2008; Pillay, Tomlinson & Bass, 2009). Essex and Chalkley (2015) explored how to utilize sporting events for urban regeneration and renewal purposes. Cleland et al. (2020) focused on opportunities for sports participation and increased levels of physical activity. Moreover, in recent years, driven by the IOC, hosting cities have started to integrate sustainability principles into their legacy strategies (Smith, 2009).

The sustainable organization of an event should therefore involve its stakeholders in identifying, understanding, and responding to the main sustainability themes, and communicating the performance achieved through reporting tools (Accountability, 2018). A strategic value of reporting could also be recognized, because it can help the organization to set goals, measure performance and manage change, combining long-term profitability with respect for people and care for the natural environment (GRI, 2013). After the adoption of the 2030 Agenda by the UN, it was recognized that the key role of sport in achieving SDG 11, with its ten targets lies in the hope to make cities and human settlements inclusive, safe, resilient, and sustainable by 2030 (UN, 2015).

A variety of international organizations, governing bodies, and research institutions, such as the Commonwealth and United Nations, have studied the implications of the implementation of the SDGs for sport-related policy. The Commonwealth has developed an analysis of the contribution that sport-based approaches can make to the 2030 Agenda (The Commonwealth, 2018). These documents recognize the role of sport in the achievement of three of the ten targets of SDG 11: 11.3, 11.7, and 11.a (Dudfield & Dingwall-Smith, 2015). Moreover, the Commonwealth Secretariat specifies that the contribution and catalyst role that major sporting events can bring to progress is a high-profile example of a place-based approach to maximizing the potential of sport. The experience of the organization of the XX Commonwealth Games (held in Glasgow, Scotland) has contributed to broader citywide efforts to promote economic development, improved physical activity levels, cultural activities, urban regeneration, and enhanced civic pride (Dudfield & Dingwall-Smith, 2015).

The Commonwealth Games is an international multi-sport event involving athletes from the Commonwealth of Nations. The event was first held in Hamilton, Canada in 1930, and since then it takes place every four years (the editions of 1942 and 1946 were cancelled because of World War II). The next Commonwealth Games edition (XXII) are to be held in Birmingham from 27 July to 7 August 2022. The Games are overseen by the Commonwealth Games Federation (CGF), which also controls the sporting program and selects the host cities. Over 5,000 athletes compete at the Commonwealth Games in more than 15 different sports and more than 250 events. Apart from many Olympic sports, the Games also include some sports which are played predominantly in Commonwealth countries, but which are not part of the Olympic program, such as lawn bowls, netball, cricket, and squash.

During the 20th and 21st centuries, the evolution of the Games' movement has resulted in several changes to the Commonwealth Games. Some of these adjustments include the creation of the Commonwealth Winter Games for snow and ice sports, the Commonwealth Paraplegic Games for Commonwealth athletes with a disability, and the Commonwealth Youth Games for Commonwealth athletes aged 14–18. There are currently 54 members of the Commonwealth of Nations, 71 teams currently participate in the Commonwealth Games, as several dependent territories compete under their flags. The most recent Commonwealth Games were held in Gold Coast from 4 to 15 April 2018. This edition has been organized with a strong commitment to diversity, inclusion, gender equity, and sustainability. Nearly 7,000 athletes from 71 countries of the world competed for 11 days in 18 different sports and 26 different disciplines. The Games are estimated to have created a gross state product (GSP) of approximately $2.5 billion to Queensland net costs incurred (Pham et al., 2019; Powell, 2019).

Given the commitment to deliver an event aligned with the sustainability principles, the Games were organized following the international framework ISO20121, achieving a second party conformity to ISO in 2015, which was reconfirmed in 2017. To report transparently on the economic, social, and environmental effects of the event, the GOLDOC has been preparing his Sustainability Reports using the GRI G4 version since 2014, including using the Event Organizers sector supplement of the GRI guidelines. Through stakeholder engagement nine key sustainability priority areas were identified for Gold Coast 2018: food and beverage, transport, accessibility, economy and community, carbon, inclusivity and diversity, sustainable procurement, environmental impact, and waste. These priority areas were organized in three main sustainability themes, and for each one of them, the SDGs impacted were identified. The Gold Coast 2018 Games can be considered a best practice to take into consideration in organizing sustainable events. Indeed, its vision "to show leadership in sustainability by delivering GC2018 to international standards of best practices, leaving positive economic, environmental, social, and community legacies" is being realized.

Method

Given the exploratory nature of our study, we opted for a qualitative method, analyzing the sustainability reports of Gold Coast 2018 which followed ISO20121 for sustainable event organization and the GRI guidelines for reporting. We have designed a specific process to link the disclosures of the GRI with the targets of the SDGs and to analyze the sustainability performance of the Games, allowing an integration in the sustainability reporting performed with the GRI guidelines. So, we analyzed the sustainability reports of Gold Coast 2018 to verify whether what was reported by the organizing committee was aligned with one of the 17 objectives of the SDGs. In this study, we have chosen the SDG 11 targets as an example.

The sustainability report of the Games was prepared following both the GRI-G4 guidelines and the GRI sector supplement for Event Organizers (GRI, 2013, 2014). So, the starting point of our analysis was the construction of an Excel matrix, built for this specific sporting event, which aims to correlate the indicators of the GRI with the targets of the SDG 11 (Table 14.1). This matrix was built starting from the Content Index, a table that, following the requirements of the GRI guidelines, was provided at the end of the sustainability reports, and then a column containing the targets of the SDG 11 was added. In this phase, a careful analysis of the requirements of the indicators was supported by the GRI linkage document named *SDG Compass Annex: Linking the SDGs and GRI Standards* (GRI, 2017). Hence, the matrix that has been constructed enabled us to highlight how reporting with the GRI can be useful also to report in terms of SDGs. This is detailed below in Table 14.1.

Results and discussion

Analyzing the Gold Coast 2018 sustainability reports we noticed how the organizing committee gave a strong contribution to reach some of the SDG 11's targets. Below, we report some of the most important and significant actions that have been put in place both before and post the event. Target 1 states that by 2030, there ought to be provision access to safe, affordable, accessible and sustainable transport systems for all, improvement of road safety, notably by expanding public transport, with special attention to the needs of those in vulnerable situations, women, children, persons with disabilities, and older persons. A well-managed transport system is crucial to the success of major sporting events. In the planning phase, it is necessary to take into account all the aspects that make it possible to

234 Cristiana Buscarini et al.

Table 14.1 GRI Content Index Integrated with SDGs: An Example of How SDG 11 Had Been achieved By GOLDOC

G4 Disclosure	GRI Standard	Disclosure Number	Disclosure Title	Gold Coast 2018 Sustainability Reports		SDG 11's Targets
				Pre-Event (2014–2015)	Post Event	
G4-EO2	Event organizers sector disclosures	EO2	Modes of transport taken by attendees as a percentage of total transportation, and initiatives to encourage the use of sustainable transport options	pp. 34–36, 43–45	pp. 89–95	Target 2
G4-EO3	Event organizers sector disclosures	EO3	Significant environmental and socio-economic impacts of transporting attendees to and from the event, and initiatives taken to address the impacts	pp. 34–36, 43–45	pp. 89–95	Target 2
G4-EO5	Event organizers sector disclosures	EO5	Type and impacts of initiatives to create a socially inclusive event	pp. 34–36, 50–52	pp. 96–128	Target 3
G4-EO6	Event organizers sector disclosures	EO6	Type and impacts of initiatives to create an accessible environment	pp. 34–36, 50–52	pp. 96–128	Target 3
G4-EO11	Event organizers sector disclosures	EO11	Number, type, and impact of sustainability initiatives designed to raise awareness, share knowledge, and impact behaviour change, and results achieved	pp. 34–36, 53–56	pp. 8, 12–13, 134	Target 4

G4-EO12	Event organizers sector disclosures	EO12	Nature and extent of knowledge transfer of best practice, and lessons learned	pp. 34–36, 53–56	pp. 8, 12–13, 134	Target 4
G4-EO13	Event organizers sector disclosures	EO13	Number, type, and impact of physical and technological legacies	pp. 34–36, 53–56	pp. 8, 12–13, 134	Target 2 Target 7
G4-EN3	GRI 302	302-1	Energy consumption within the organization	pp. 34–35, 38–39		Target 6
G4-EN15	GRI 305	305-1	Direct (Scope 1) GHG emissions		pp. 55–68	Target 6
G4-EN16	GRI 305	305-2	Energy indirect (Scope 2) GHG emissions	pp. 34–35, 38–39	pp. 55–68	Target 6
G4-EN17	GRI 305	305-3	Other indirect (Scope 3) GHG emissions		pp. 55–68	Target 6
G4-EN18	GRI 305	305-4	GHG emissions intensity			Target 6
G4-EN19	GRI 305	305-5	Reduction of GHG emissions		pp. 55–68	Target 6
G4-EN20	GRI 305	305-6	Emissions of ozone-depleting substances (ODS)			Target 6
G4-EN21	GRI 305	305-7	Nitrogen oxides (NOX), sulphur oxides (SOX), and other significant air emissions			Target 6
G4-EN23	GRI 306	306-2	Waste by type and disposal method	pp. 34–36, 40–42	pp. 70–88	Target 6
G4-EN24	GRI 306	306-3	Significant spills			Target 6
G4-EN25	GRI 306	306-4	Transport of hazardous waste			Target 6

ensure access to the games' locations and venues, to anyone regardless of physical ability, as well as to avoid a situation where a high level of people's participation during the competition period can cause the public transport system to go haywire. Events can also provide a good opportunity to educate about more sustainable forms of movement, which positively affect people's health and cut down environmental impacts.

Regarding the GC2018, a Transport Strategic Plan was developed with the efforts of all the stakeholders' groups, to provide a positive public transport experience to encourage better long-term outcomes. To reach this scope, extensive community engagement and consultation were performed and a transport target was set. This target provided that 80% of games' spectators should have attended GC2018 via public and active transport. Moreover, to manage the emissions related to transport, the organizing committee collaborated with the Queensland Department of Transport and Main Roads (TMR) and the City of Queensland, to plan and deliver an integrated transport service. To reduce the use of private vehicles to attend the competition and to encourage active forms of transport, GC2018 provided several opportunities. For example, free public transport was included in the ticket price on event days, hoping this new travel practice would continue after GC2018 as well. During the event, there was an unprecedented peak in average daily passenger journeys, with three times as many daily train and tram trips and four times as many bus trips with over 130,000 bus shuttles from park and ride locations. Moreover, an 8.5 km walking and cycling route (namely Borobi Fan Trail) was designed to encourage sustainable mobility. It was useful to link some of the venues to other key areas of the event and allows volunteers, spectators, and the workforce to embrace more active forms of travel.

To help people with accessible requirements, all of GC2018's park and ride sites, and accessible car parks were designed to be located as close as possible to the entrance and bus area. Bus monitors were also placed at different locations to look out for spectators with accessible requirements. There were dedicated accessible boarding points as well. All the vehicles, necessary for the operations of the games, were required to comply with safety, accessibility, comfort, reliability, fuel efficiency, noise, and emissions specifications. Hand controls in two fleet vehicles were also installed to enable people with accessibility needs to self-drive. The transport of GC2018 was designed to comply with sustainability requirements. Efforts have been made to ensuring access for all to the transport system and in promoting active forms of travel that the event organizers hope will last over time. After the event, a modified bus was donated to Southport Special School, and residents of Gold Coast were able to benefit from about $300 million in road infrastructure improvements. Development and town planning experts Urbis have identified 342 infrastructure projects across the Gold Coast and Tweed regions linked to GC2018, worth a total of $13.2 billion. Finally, GC2018 further enhanced Queensland's global reputation as a world-class event host, with a tourism legacy already underway.

Target 3 aims to, by 2030, enhance inclusive and sustainable urbanization and capacity for participatory, integrated and sustainable human settlement planning and management in all countries. GC2018 immediately committed itself to be accessible and inclusive, enabling all interested parties to participate without fear of discrimination regardless of age, gender, or ability; to be free from barriers, physical or otherwise; to be kept well informed through appropriate communications and media channels. GC2018 provides also an important opportunity to recognize the indigenous culture and respect traditional land custodians through the development of the GC2018 Reconciliation Action Plan (RAP), intending to outline objectives across areas such as employment, procurement, cuisine, language, and cultural awareness. The GC2018 RAP has been the first of its kind delivered by a major event in Australia and the first in Commonwealth Games history. During GC2018 observations were made on activities to support the GOLDOC Sustainability and Legacy Team by monitoring human and child rights related performance, to observe GC2018 in action with a focus on safety, athlete, worker, and spectator welfare, to identify potential human and child rights gaps and to engage stakeholders on a bilateral basis, and attend meetings with bearing on human and child rights including around the RAP and indigenous issues. These observations formed the basis of future work to further strengthen the approach by future organizing committees to human rights and child rights issues.

Other activities aimed at improving the accessibility and inclusivity of the Game were put in place: so as to improve the Village's accessibility pool, hoists were installed in every residential pool; a multi-faith centre, accessible 24 hours a day, was established within the Village residential zone, and provided formal religious services, individual prayer, meditation, individual counselling, and/or pastoral care, to provide spiritual support, encouragement and, confidential advice; a range of initiatives were implemented to encourage lesbian, gay, bisexual, transgender, intersexual, and queer (LGBTIQ) inclusion at GC2018; and GOLDOC's website has been designed with the aim of meeting Level AA of the Web Content Accessibility Guidelines Version 2.0. Finally, to ensure that public places were shared by all people during GC2018, GOLDOC assisted the Queensland Government in developing a protocol for working with people experiencing homelessness in public places during GC2018 to ensure that people experiencing homelessness were respected.

Target 4 is to strengthen efforts to protect and safeguard the world's cultural and natural heritage. The legacies left by GC2018 are incredibly important and defined the success of the event. The development of the legacy strategy, Embracing Our Games Legacy (Strategy), has been led by the State government in conjunction with the City of Gold Coast. So as to leave a strong legacy and to engage and form all stakeholders, educational activities have been organized and suppliers have been educated about sustainable procurement practices. GOLDOC and its GC2018 delivery partners developed the GC2018 Sustainable Goods and Services Guidelines as an initial educational piece to communicate to potential suppliers the importance of sustainability for GC2018 and to provide information about ways to contribute to the goal of delivering a sustainable event.

To avoid environmental damage and over-usage, wherever possible, preexisting venues were used for the events, with modifications or upgrades where required. Regarding the construction of the Commonwealth Games Village (CGV) which housed around 6,500 athletes and technical officials, including para-sport athletes, the development was part of a public-private partnership between the State and a private developer and incorporated design principles that aimed to achieve energy and water efficiency initiatives as well as a reduction in natural resource consumption. GOLDOC was working towards a 4 Star Green Star Interiors rating for its headquarters fit-out. Aside from the core work required to achieve the Green Star rating, they were also working towards several innovation points for the tenancy. GC2018 was always designed to be more than just a sporting spectacle: inspiring children to be fit and active, increasing public transport usage, encouraging recycling, showcasing the Gold Coast's natural beauty, or reducing plastic pollutants; these Games were a shift in the right direction.

Target 6 is that by 2030, reduce the adverse per capita environmental impact of cities, including by paying special attention to air quality and municipal and other waste management. GOLDOC put a lot of emphasis on carbon, waste management, energy, and water. This was also reported on all sustainability reports. Carbon and other greenhouse gas emissions have been identified as arguably the greatest environmental challenge of our time. So GOLDOC developed a carbon management strategy that supported its environmental and social legacy objectives. The strategy has also been designed to help to identify and wherever possible, deliver economic benefits through reduced energy expenditure. The strategy encouraged stakeholders to take steps to minimize their carbon impact. It is anticipated that the outcomes of carbon mitigation activities can serve as a benchmarking and capacity building tool for future events in the City. Organizers intended to develop a methodology to accurately estimate GOLDOC's organizational energy use and emissions impacts and begun development of its Workplace Travel Plan (WTP), aimed at reducing emissions from staff travel to and from work, as well as day-to-day business-related travel. Organizers also developed an Energy Management Policy for venues. Related to transport emissions, the following have been analyzed: Waste transport emissions, Games family bus fleet emissions, Workforce and spectator transportation, Workforce and spectators – Light Rail, Workforce and spectators – Rail (Queensland Rail), Games Family fleet vehicle emissions, Logistics fleet emissions. Rather, related to travel emissions, the following have been analyzed: flight emissions for the 'Games Family', both international and domestic.

Another focus was put on paper usage and several GOLDOC FAs worked to significantly reduce it with paper use for creative services, publication paper use, and Sport publications paper use. With a united commitment to demonstrating leadership in sustainability, TAFE Queensland and GOLDOC have saved over 1.8 million pieces of paper by providing volunteer training online instead of printed workbooks for the orientation and role-specific training components. The printed results distribution model moved towards a 'digital first', 'print second' model. In keeping with its sustainability targets and RAP commitments, GOLDOC sourced half of the carbon offsets from a project with Great Barrier Reef protection co-benefits and the other half from an Indigenous early dry season savannah burning project in Queensland's Cape York.

Huge work was done on waste management system planning and management. GOLDOC's waste management systems and practices were designed around a Waste Recovery Hierarchy that begins with waste avoidance/prevention and reduction followed by reuse, recycling, recovery, and lastly disposal to landfill. As an organization, this means that their staff was educated about waste management practices and steps that they can take to avoid or reduce the amount of waste they create. It also means that GOLDOC worked with suppliers, venues, and contractors to ensure they can support positive waste outcomes for GC2018. Furthermore, waste management has included setting up appropriate governance structures to manage and monitor actions around waste management. All existing venues that hosted GC2018 events had waste management practices already in place which provide an ideal opportunity to establish historical baselines for waste indicators. The newly built venues also provided an opportunity to establish sustainable waste practices from the beginning. The available infrastructure for waste processing in Queensland was largely limited to the recycling of co-mingled waste such as PET bottles, glass, paper and cardboard, and landfill.

Regarding look and signage, mega-events have the potential to generate significant waste. The GOLDOC Look and Signage team were committed to best practice from the start and designed the GC2018 look and signage Kit of Parts (KOP) with a range of sustainability considerations at the forefront. Readily renewable, low carbon, and recyclable materials like bamboo, ply, corn lute, and sandbags were used as a basis for design instead of traditional materials like concrete and metal. These lightweight materials also allowed faster, safer installation across GC2018. Signage was also designed to be installed on existing structures where possible to reduce production impacts, logistic overhead, and cost. Recycled materials and end-of-life disposal were also key tender considerations for GOLDOC when awarding the GC2018 look and signage production and installation contract. As a result of careful planning and innovative design, GOLDOC managed to avoid and reduce its look and signage waste impact significantly. The Sustainability team performed waste audits across venues during GC2018 in order to report the total operational waste across all competition venues and the Village. The organizers did this to better inform event waste management legacy learnings and to monitor on-venue compliance with GOLDOC's Materials and Packaging Policy. With the support of a team of 7 Griffith University interns, the Sustainability team audited 56 samples across 11 streams and 5 venues, plus the Village. Notably banned items like plastic straws and balloons were not present in any waste streams within the venue.

Target 7 is to provide, by 2030, universal access to safe, inclusive and accessible, green and public spaces, in particular for women and children, older persons, and persons with disabilities. Events bring a variety of legacy opportunities to a city or region. They may be physical and tangible legacies, such as new infrastructure or equipment, or intangible, such as education and behavioural change. Events also connect people from different social or interest groups who may not have had the opportunity to interact before. This cross-pollination of ideas and knowledge transfer can lead to innovative ideas and influence long term behavioural, social, cultural, institutional, and technological change. The impacts on the reputation of a city or region may also drive significant and long-lasting benefits.

GC2018 provided a perfect opportunity for people on the Gold Coast and in the event, cities to use public and active transport, access to green spaces, and sports areas. Moreover, thanks to a great stakeholder engagement in a lot of organizational areas, organizers created a really inclusive and co-created environment. There were many ways to participate in the GC2018 experience. This means enabling all interested parties to participate without fear of discrimination regardless of age, gender, or ability; to be free from barriers, physical or otherwise; to be kept well informed through appropriate communication and media channels. Another core commitment given by the Games partners was to deliver an accessible and inclusive GC2018. This means not only respecting the multi-cultural nature of this event, but also eliminating any physical or other barriers to a safe and dignified GC2018 experience. Several initiatives were put into action to support this commitment. For example, to improve the Village's accessibility pool hoists were installed in every residential pool. Rather than assuming that para-athletes needed to use them or wanted to use them, the teams at the resident centres would say: "Just to let you know, we're going to take the cover off the pool hoists now."

Future research

This process finalized to link the GRI disclosures with the SDGs targets, proposed through the example of Gold Coast, and enabled us to verify that, by adding information about the SDGs targets to the GRI Content Index, a more comprehensive view of the event's sustainability performance could be provided. Therefore, this study aimed to bring out how adoption of GRI guidelines allows event organizers to report what has been achieved also in terms of SDGs targets. We have made this link by analyzing and taking into consideration as an example, SDG 11. Nevertheless, it would be useful to do the same analysis with all the 17 SDGs. However, from the study of SDG 11, it has emerged that not all targets were affected by Gold Coast 2018. Therefore, this leads us to consider that for each SDG, everyone should inquire which SDG targets are relevant to the event industry with future research. So, it can be interesting to find and create a new area of research, aimed at finding and building a new reporting tool for event organizers. This can be done through an international network between universities, researchers, and professionals from both the sustainability and events worlds. Our final intent is to stress the importance of considering the SDGs with their targets in all productive activities to foster a more strategic approach to sustainability and improve organizations' accountability. This last goal can be reached through a reporting process that should be integrated with SDG targets that will be understood with future research.

References

Accountability (2018), "AA1000 Accountability Principles Standards", Accountability. Available from: https://www.accountability.org/standards/aa1000-accountability-principles

Allmers, S., & Maennig, W. (2009), "Economic impacts of the FIFA soccer world cups in France 1998, Germany 2006, and outlook for South Africa 2010", *Eastern Economic Journal*, 35(4), 500–519.

Azzali, S. (2017), "Queen Elizabeth Olympic Park: An assessment of the 2012 London Games Legacies", *City, Territory and Architecture*, 4(1), 1–12.

Azzali, S. (2019), "Mega sporting events and their impact on the built environment: Lessons learned from the past", *Journal of the Faculty of Architecture*, 16(2), 25–37.

Bakos, A. R. (2020), *"The institutionalisation of sustainability in event management: A case study of the diffusion of ISO 20121 at the Gold Coast 2018 Commonwealth Games"*, Bond University.

Buscarini, C., & Franzini, S. (2017), "Iso 20121 and Theory-U: A new way to manage sporting events", in I. Valantinė, B. G. Pitts, & J. J. Zhang (Eds.), *Global issues and new ideas in sport management* (pp. 5–6). Kaunas: Lithunia Sport University.

Cavagnaro, E., Postma, A. & de Brito, M. P. (2016), *"The sustainability agenda and events"*, in N. Ferdinand & P. J. Kitchin (Eds.), *Events Management: An International Approach* (288–316). London: Sage.

Celuch, K. (2018), "Impact of the events sector on the economy case study of Poland", *Ekonomiczne Problemy Turystyki*, 44(4), 69–81.

Chappelet, J.-L. (2008), "Olympic environmental concerns as a legacy of the winter games", *The International Journal of the History of Sport*, 25(14), 1884–1902.

Clark, J., & Kearns, A. (2015), "Going for gold: A prospective assessment of the economic impacts of the Commonwealth Games 2014 on the East End of Glasgow", *Environment and Planning C: Government and Policy*, 34(8), 1474–1500.

Collins, A., Jones, C., & Munday, M. (2009), "Assessing the environmental impacts of mega sporting events: Two options?", *Tourism Management*, 30, 828–837.

Council of Europe (1992), "The European Sports Charter", 7th Conference of European Ministers responsible for Sport, Rodi, Greece.

Dudfield, O., & Dingwall-Smith, M. (2015), "Sport for development and peace and the 2030 agenda for sustainable development", Commonwealth Secretariat, London, UK.

Dudley, D., Beighle, A., Schaefer, L., Cairney, J., & Vasily, M. A. (2018), "A review of the evidence and practices supporting the UNESCO Kazan Action Plan for Quality Physical Education", In AIESEP World Congress 2018 (p. 137), University of Edinburgh, United Kingdom.

European Commission (2007), "White paper on sport", Commission of the European Communities, Brussels.

Essex, S., & Chalkley, B. (2015), "Mega-events as a strategy for urban regeneration", University of Plymouth, UK.

Global Reporting Initiative (2013), "G4 sustainability reporting guidelines: Reporting principles and standard disclosures", *Global Reporting Initiative*, Amsterdam, The Netherlands.

Global Reporting Initiative (2014), "Event organizers sector supplement", *Global Reporting Initiative*, Amsterdam, The Netherlands.

Global Reporting Initiative (2016), "GRI sustainability reporting standards 2016", *Global Reporting Initiative*, Amsterdam, The Netherlands.

Global Reporting Initiative (2017), "SDG Compass Annex: Linking the SDGs and GRI standards", *Global Reporting Initiative*, Amsterdam, The Netherlands.

GOLDOC (2015), "Sustainability report 2014–15", *Gold Coast 2018 Commonwealth Games Corporation.*

GOLDOC (2016), "Sustainability report 2015–16", *Gold Coast 2018 Commonwealth Games Corporation.*

GOLDOC (2017), "Pre-games sustainability report", *Gold Coast 2018 Commonwealth Games Corporation.*

GOLDOC (2018), "Post-games sustainability report", *Gold Coast 2018 Commonwealth Games Corporation.*

Gratton, C., Shilbi, S., & Coleman, R. (2006), "The economic impact of major sports events: A review of ten events in the UK", *Sociological Review*, 54, 41–58.

Hall, C. M. (2012). "Sustainable mega-events: Beyond the myth of balanced approaches to mega-event sustainability", *Event Management*, 16(2), 119–131.

International Olympic Committee (1999), "Olympic movement's agenda 21: Sport for sustainable development", *International Olympic Committee.*

International Olympic Committee (2012), "Sustainability through sport: Implementing the Olympic movement's agenda 21," *International Olympic Committee.*

International Olympic Committee (2014), "Olympic Agenda 2020: 20+20 recommendations", *International Olympic Committee.*

Leopkey, B., & Parent, M. M. (2012), "The (Neo) institutionalization of legacy and its sustainable governance within the Olympic Movement", *European Sport Management Quarterly*, 12(5), 437–455.

Liao, H., & Pitts, A. (2006), "A brief historical review of Olympic urbanization", *International Journal of the History Of Sport*, 23(7), 1232–1252.

Lindsey, I., & Chapman, T. (2017), *Enhancing the contribution of sport to the sustainable development goals.* London: Commonwealth Secretariat.

Matheson, C. M. (2010), "Legacy planning, regeneration and events: The Glasgow 2014 commonwealth games", *Local Economy*, 25(1), 10–23.

Moital, M. (2019), "The impacts of sports events at tourist destination level". *Motricidade*, 15, 1–5.

Pham, T., Becken, S., & Powell, M. (2019), "Modelling the economic impacts of a large event: The case of the Gold Coast 2018 Commonwealth Games", *Queensland Review*, 26(1), 110–127.

Phillips, C., & Bouchier, N. (2014), "Building and re-building a city through sport: Hamilton, Ontario and the British Empire and Commonwealth Games, 1930–2003", *Sport in History*, 34(3), 390–410.

Pillay, U., & Bass, O. (2008), "Mega-events as a response to poverty reduction: The 2010 FIFA World Cup and its urban development implications", *Urban Forum*, 19, 329–346.

Pillay, U., Tomlinson, R., & Bass, O. (2009), *Development and dreams: The urban legacy of the 2010 Football World Cup.* Cape Town: HSRC.

Powell, M. (2019), "Commentary: Gold coast 2018- The innovative and inclusive Games", *Queensland Review*, 26(1), 156–165.

Preuss, H. (2005), "The Economic Impact of Visitors at Major Multi-Sport Events", *European Sport Management Quarterly*, 5(3), 281–301.

Preuss, H. (2007), "The conceptualisation and measurement of mega sport event legacies", *Journal of Sport and Tourism*, 12(3–4), 207–228.

Raco, M. (2004), "Whose Gold Rush? The social legacy of a London Olympics", in A. Vigor, M. Mean, & C. Tims (Eds.), *After the Gold Rush: A sustainable Olympics for London* (33–49). London: IPPR/Demos.

Ross, W. J., & Leopkey, B. (2017), "The adoption and evolution of environmental practices in the Olympic Games", *Managing Sport and Leisure*, 22(1), 1–18.

SDG Fund Secretariat (2018), *"The contribution of sports to the achievement of the Sustainable Development Goals: a toolkit for action"*, SDG Fund Secretariat. Available from: https://www.sdgfund.org/un-presents-new-toolkit-action-how-sports-can-contribute-achieve-sdgs.

Smith, A. (2009), "Spreading the positive effects of major events to peripheral areas", *Journal of Policy Research in Tourism, Leisure and Events*, 1(3), 231–246.

The Commonwealth (2018), "Measuring the contribution of sport to the sustainable development goals", Discussion Paper for the UN Expert Group Meeting on 'Strengthening the Global Framework for Leveraging Sport for Development and Peace', June 2018.

UNESCO (2015), "International Charter of Physical Education and Sport", United Nations Educational, Scientific and Cultural Organization. Available from: https://unesdoc.unesco.org/ark:/48223/pf0000235409

UNESCO (2017), "Kazan Action Plan", United Nations Educational, Scientific and Cultural Organization. Available from: https://unesdoc.unesco.org/ark:/48223/pf0000252725

United Nations (2018), "The contribution of sports to the achievement of the sustainable development goals", *SDG Fund*.

United Nations General Assembly (2015), "Transforming our World: The 2030 Agenda for Sustainable Development", United Nations: New York, NY, USA.

Waitt, G. (2003), "Social impacts of the Sydney Olympics", *Annals of Tourism Research*, 30(1), 194–215.

Zhang, L., & Zhao, S. X. (2009), "City branding and the Olympic effect: A case study of Beijing", *Cities (London, England)*, 26(5), 245–254.

Chapter 15

New directions for professional preparation

A competency-based model for training sport management personnel

Jana Nová

Introduction

The aim of this paper to propose a managerial competence model for sport managers that could be utilized in the design of sport management programs/ curriculum. Therefore, this paper includes a review of the considerable body of literature relating to professional competence for sport managers and managerial competence models as well as outcome and competency-based education. Empirical work was conducted during the NASME project in 2017–2019 New Age of Sport Management (NASME) ERASMUS+. The project was launched to improve the synchronicity between obtained skills through sport management education and demand in the labour market in nine European countries: Denmark, Finland, Czech Republic, Norway, Germany, France, Spain, Greece, and Lithuania. This was a follow-up to a previous AEHESIS (Aligning a European Higher Education Structure in Sport Sciences) study done in 2004 where only six countries participated (AEHESIS, 2006).

An online survey was implemented to gain the insights of experienced professionals from four sports sectors (sports clubs, sport managers in a city or municipality – public sector; sports association and federations; and private enterprises) in nine European countries on the competencies that are and will be important for sport managers in the future. Face to face interviews conducted with 78 interviewees supported the results from quantitative data in terms of the various aspects of the professional competence of sport managers (NASME, Concluding Report, 2019). A critical review of the managerial competency literature in sport management indicates that the managerial competency models are used just partially. This leaves a gap in managerial competency literature in sport management. The results from the NASME project provide an opportunity for testing the appropriateness of the most recent managerial competency models from general management in the sport management context. This would enable capturing systematically the core and generic competencies that should form the occupational and educational standards for sport managers.

The competency-based approach towards setting the competence profiles of sport managers would form the basic predispositions for implementation of the

DOI: 10.4324/9781003213673-15

competency-based approach to the curriculum design and education in sport management. Thus, this paper addresses the gap in the literature by proposing the utilization of a holistic-domain model of managerial competency for a competency-based approach in designing sport management curricula. First, the paper examines the concept and historical development of managerial competencies in sport management. Second, the paper provides evidence on the absence of existing managerial competency models in sport management by reviewing competency models located in the literature. Third, evidence on the international endeavours in the realm of sport management occupation standardization is provided. Fourth, drawing on the review, on conceptual and empirical grounds, the paper tests (based on the results from NASME project) the hypothesis in terms of the possibility to effectively utilize the existing managerial competency models for defining the competence models that would serve as a point of departure for sport management curriculum design and thus could enrich current accreditation standards. Finally, theoretical, practical, and research implications for sport management educators, researchers, professionals, and accreditation bodies are provided.

Review of literature

The competency-based approach toward designing sport management curricula is based on the premise that the design of sport management as a profession would reflect the occupational as well as educational standards and vice versa. Therefore, in this part of the paper, we will present the approaches towards the definition of the competencies of sport managers and occupational as well as educational standards, the managerial competence models, and the concept of competency-based and outcomes-based education.

Competencies for sport managers

The first study on competency-based approaches to sport management by Jamieson (1987) reviewed the development of interest in and concern for training and education of sport specialists. Not only does he emphasize functional aspects of all sport involvement such as organization, administration, finance, budgeting, marketing, staffing, coordination, planning, and evaluation but he also suggests identifying the competences or composite skills in sport management in practice and then to relate them to the training and education. The results were the competency statements for entry, middle, and top management. Since then, this hierarchical approach towards the identification of competencies for sport managers has not been replicated and it is unclear to what extent the results of this study have influenced sport management curricula or The Commission on Sport Management Accreditation (COSMA, 2016) accreditation standards.

Lambrecht (1987) identified the competencies needed to manage athletic clubs and determined the differences that exist in required competencies regarding the organizational size of the club. "Communication with clientele" was the top-rated competency regardless of the type of club. Cuskelly and Auld (1991) reviewed the perceived importance of selected job responsibilities of sport and recreation managers in an Australian context and provided with up to date results from studies on competence profiles from different sport settings and for different managerial posts (Brassie, 1989; Hardy, 1987; Hatfield et al., 1987; Jamieson, 1987; Lambrecht, 1987; Parkhouse, 1987; Parks & Quain, 1986). They concluded that the occupational competencies perceived as being most important to sport and recreation managers are management skills (e.g. marketing, personnel, financial); communication skills, particularly interpersonal; program development and administration; and public relations. Besides, their study revealed that public relations, financial management, program planning and management, and interpersonal communications were perceived as the most important competencies for sport and recreation managers.

Parkhouse (1987) and Brassie (1989) contributed to the debate significantly by promoting the inclusion of foundation courses in business administration and communications/journalism into curricula in sport management. Kelley et al. (1994) presented undergraduate and graduate sport management curricular models to facilitate the implementation of the National Association for Sport and Physical Education (NASPE)/the North American Society for Sport Management (NASSM) guidelines within five sport management concentrations with similar objectives but different settings (Sport for Leisure/Recreation; Sport and Athletics; Sport Merchandising; Hostelries/Travel; and Recreation Agencies). For each degree level, curricular models provide a professional core, focused specialization requirements, and defined culminating experiences. These models were projections derived from a synthesis of research results based on responses from employers in the sport management field, sport management academicians, and undergraduate and graduate students majoring in sport management. Practitioners noted six areas in which all sport managers need to be knowledgeable: communication, facility management, fiscal management, marketing/sales, program/event management, and personnel management/supervision (Kelley et al., 1994).

The undergraduate and graduate sport management models suggest the need for interdisciplinary programs across sport studies, leisure/recreation, and business/management. Ross et al (1999) examined the status of professional preparation programs in sport management at selected academic institutions in the United States. The study indicated that sport management curricula varied widely from one institution to another. It also showed variations in philosophy and primary emphasis of the programs when it comes to topics such as professional sport marketing, management, and marketing services for professionals, organization and coordination of recreational sports programming, and sport programming in recreational settings. They also stressed that sport management curricula must keep pace with and address the changes in society and the sport management field such as globalization, international sports events, and international sports broadcasting. Li et al (2002) stated that the trend in the globalization of sports has provoked sport management educators around the world to contemplate if sport management curriculum should be internationalized to become part of this globalization trend (p. 180). Chalip (2006) made it clear that sport management as an academic discipline is a young discipline and he argues that there are very important contributions sport management brings to the scholarly debate about the intersection of sport and business nationally and at the global level, regardless of where it may be housed in the university. He concluded that what sport management scholars contribute to the discipline is much more important than the argument about where sport management programs are housed.

While there is no clear consensus for the 'best' home for sport management programs, Parkhouse (1987) stated that regardless of the program's location, sport management requires the cooperation of several disciplines, especially business administration and physical education (p. 109). Jones et al (2008) concluded that the historical evolution of sport management programs in the United States moved from the physical education model to a more business-oriented curriculum. As they emphasized, since 1966, sport management programs in America have witnessed significant growth and increasing popularity due to enormous student interest and sport management outside the United States continues to grow as well. The content areas prescribed in the NASPE–NASSM standards provide students with a common body of knowledge around core content areas to prepare them for careers in sport management. As they stated the study programs also include behavioural dimensions in sport, management, and organizational skills in sports, ethics in sport management, marketing in sport, communication in sport, finance in sport, economics in sport, legal aspects of sport, governance in sport, and field experience in sport management. Notwithstanding they were also convinced that looking towards the future, it is important for sport management programs to gain a better understanding of skill sets and competencies needed to meet the demands of the global sport management workplace.

Differences that exist regarding the perception of importance concerning sport management competencies among sport management practitioners and students have been further explored by Mathner and Martin (2012). Sport practitioners ranked leadership, management skills, personality, and communication as the most important competencies and viewed technology as more important than marketing skills, which students had put more emphasis on. Yiamouyiannis et al (2013) discuss the COSMA accreditation process valid in 2010 and its eight principles and they concluded that when it comes to principle 3 – curriculum – the faculty applies various models to syllabi to enhance the measurement of student learning outcomes. Two models are mentioned – Dick and Carey's (2010) instructional design model and Wiggins and McTighe's (2005) backward instructional design. The latter involves fleshing out the exact skills students will be able to perform through the successful completion of various assessment techniques. Through this model, faculty develop syllabi from the perspective of understanding specific performance skills that can be demonstrated by the students. The backward design approach involves looking at the tangible skills that students need to achieve at various points of instruction within a course for the student to complete a larger assignment or project.

Zaharia et al (2016) stated that the growth of sport management programs housed in (or with formal curriculum-based ties to) a school of business indicates more academic institutions are reconsidering sport management as a business-oriented field. Considering this growth, sport management has the potential to shift to a more business-oriented discipline (Danylchuk & Boucher, 2003; Jones et al., 2008; Schwarz, 2010). The limitation of this study is that the research was developed within the US context and might not apply to other countries and it was recommended to test these findings in more countries and regions where sport business programs have experienced growth such as Australia, Canada, the United Kingdom, and continental Europe. Unfortunately, when it comes to the curriculum design or competence profile of a sport manager, they are not discussed in the study and preference is given to the issues such as administration, housing, accreditation, faculty performance indicators, and research requirements, as well as salaries for faculty and alumni of such sport management programs.

In 2017, Miragaia and Soares analyzed the literature on Higher Education in Sport Management published in leading international journals from 1979 to 2014 – curriculum and knowledge, and accreditation process and quality were among eight research themes. The former theme is introduced in general by guidelines prescribed by the NASPE and NASSM standards (NASPE–NASSM, 1993). They prescribed three components of a sport management curriculum: (a) the foundational areas of study, which comprise full courses in business management, marketing, economics, accounting, finance, and computer science; (b) the application areas (e.g. sports sociology, sports law, sports economics, sports marketing, and sports administration); and (c) field experiences, including practicums and internships (Brassie, 1989).Contributions from different authors are presented in this study as well but none of them offers a comprehensive view regarding the competence profile for sport managers as a basis for educational standards.

Based on the critical review of the literature that deals with the sport management study content and discusses the variety of competencies for sport management profession, we can state that what is missing in the literature is a clear explanation regarding, to what extent and how the results from the abundance of the abovementioned studies have been implemented into sport management curricula or any kind of occupational, educational, or accreditational standards in sport management.

Curriculum model development

Currently, there are two main sources when designing the content of sport management studies – the body of the knowledge in sport management and accreditation standards. Examination of the development of the body of knowledge in sport management could show how the science of sport management is developing in terms of the solidity of the study area (Kuhn, 1962) and can indicate the competence clusters for sport managers as well. Trying to find out what can currently be considered as a body of knowledge in sport management, we have conducted the content analysis of available studies concerning this problem (Ciomaga, 2013; Kim, 2012; Parkhouse et al., 1982; Pitts & Danylchuk, 2007; Pitts & Pedersen, 2005; Soucie & Doherty, 1996). The clusters of theoretical topics that were developing in the period from 1950 to 2010 are the leadership and administrative arrangement of sport management to sport marketing (motivation and behaviour of sport consumers), the organizational change, and organizational culture. Assessing the whole range of theoretical topics that have been identified in all studies, we could state that the body of knowledge generated so far in sport management is organized in clusters around marketing and organizational theory.

The COSMA accreditation (COSMA, 2016) standards and The Quality Assurance Agency for Higher Education (QAA) UK Subject Benchmark Statements for Events, Hospitality, Leisure, Sport, and Tourism (EHLST, 2016) are currently leading accreditation concepts for sport management curricula design internationally. Both of them are linked to the body of knowledge in sport management. COSMA defines the Common Professional Component (CPC) topical areas that should be adequately covered within the content of undergraduate sport management degree programs. QAA Subject Benchmark Statements not only defines the topical areas but also define the generic skills and behaviours and they form generic learning outcomes that are applicable to all bachelor's degrees with honours in the EHLST.

In the European Union (EU) we can observe the attempt to establish the Common European Reference for sports managers as a standard that would help to recognize the profession of sport management and sport management education across the EU. In sport management up to 2017, there were two milestones that are linked to the endeavour to define the profession, related competencies, and subsequently design of the sport management curricula. The first one was the project Sport Management Occupations in Europe involving seven countries within the Programme SOCRATES (Directorate General XXII) initiated by the European Network of Sport Sciences in Higher Education and the European Observatoire for Sport Employment (EOSE). They established the Permanent Management Committee and requested a report from the Sport Management Committee on the profession of sports management in Europe. The report issued in June 1997 outlines the work carried out in response to this request. The work aimed to build a Common European Reference for sports managers. This report took into consideration different jobs within the field of sport management and tried to describe the tasks, skills, and knowledge corresponding to them. Taking into consideration the sport environment (context), they elaborated on the Classification of Sport Management Occupations which contained five categories (manager in a training institute, manager of a facility, manager of a national sport organization, manager of a sport club, and manager of a sport service organization). Each category can be disaggregated in various 'levels' and specializations that represent the degree of complexity or standardization of the structure where managers are working.

To analyze the jobs of sport managers in a so-called Job Matrix, they used the concepts of task, skill, and knowledge. They have considered three categories of skills of a given job – conceptual, human, and technical, that were related to the managerial tasks. Their understanding of knowledge was that it is a theoretical and practical background that the manager must refer to achieve his or her objectives. The contribution of this study to the development of occupational standards was significant as they reflected the 'reality' of the job of sport managers. Unfortunately, the results from this project have not been either developed or researched further at all. As a second milestone in the endeavour to define the profession, related competencies and subsequently design of the sport management curricula is considered the Aligning a European Higher Educational Structure in Sport Science (AEHESIS) project. The project was funded by the SOCRATES Programme of the European Commission as a four-year project (2003–2007) and was coordinated by the Institute of European Sport Development & Leisure Studies at the German Sport University Cologne on behalf of the European Network of Sport Science, Education and Employment (ENSSEE).

The AEHESIS project identified four standard occupations for sport management: Local Sport Manager or director in a city or municipality; Sport club Manager or Director; Manager or Director in a National Sport Federation; Manager in a Fitness Club. Within the project, the research in six EU countries revealed Core Competencies of all four standard occupations: Will to succeed (motivation); Leadership; Capacity for planning and organizing; Marketing (commercialization); Capacity to adapt to new situations (internationalization); Creativity (demand, commercialization); Production (commercialization) Teamwork; Oral communication; Computing skills; and Interest in following the developments in the field (life-long learning). In terms of curricula development, the project suggested the methodological concept – the Six-Step-Model, reflecting the key principles of the Bologna declaration (1999) and the Tuning methodology (2000). Based on research findings the project strongly promoted four sector- specific Curriculum Models, to be used as reference models, but they have not been implemented widely as has been shown by the NASME project results (New Age of Sport Management, Concluding Report, 2019).

Similar to NASME in Europe, the European Association of Sport Management (EASM) was initiated in 1993 but after more than 25 years of its existence, EU accreditation standards similar to COSMA do not exist and considering the EASM strategic plan up to 2022 (EASM Strategic priorities 2018–2022, 2018) there is no intention to follow either the US or the UK approach to the standardization of sport management study programs accreditation across Europe. Many processes in the higher education area in Europe are led by Bologna declaration (1999) and subsequent actions bearing in mind the highest priorities – employability, and quality of the education using the European Credit Transfer and Accumulation System (ECTS, 2015) which is since 1989 used as a tool of the European Higher

Education Area for making studies and courses more transparent by internationally recognizing the variety of national education contexts.

The processes of study program design in higher education are also indirectly influenced by various EU policies. One of them is National and European Qualification Frameworks (2019) which should help in defining the skills in sport sector on the basis of the social dialogue mechanism and sectorial skills alliances. These are driven by the different schemes and movements so as to define the skills in the sport sector, such as the EU Sector skills alliances movement aimed at tackling skill gaps concerning one or more occupational profiles in a specific sector. For example, The Active Leisure Alliance (ALA) was established in 2012 as part of the European Skills Competencies Qualifications and Occupations (ESCO). Its referencing work combined the active leisure, fitness, and outdoor sectors of the active leisure sector. The EU also promotes the dialogue between the social partners in the sectors at the European level (Commission decision of 20 May 1998 – 98/500/EC) and as a result, the Sectoral Social Dialogue Committee for Professional Football exists since 2017 but it focuses mainly on Human Resources Management issue in professional sport, not on the relevance of education in sport.

Although at the EU level in the sport sector, few activities and alliances have been established, so far, the alliances in sport management have not been established. But it is worth mentioning that a new movement within the Chartered Institute of Management focuses on sport. The CIMSPA Professional Standards Matrix (2018) outlines occupations and job roles within the sport and physical activity sector, by defining what knowledge and skills an individual must understand and demonstrate in order to undertake a particular role. The Chartered Institute for the Management of Sport and Physical Activity (CIMSPA) in 2018 launched the CIMSPA Higher Education Partnership Pilot scheme. The two-year pilot will finalize the endorsement and recognition process for UK sport and physical activity-related degree programs. CIMPSA standards will be piloted by ten universities in the UK. A lot of activities in and for education in sport and sport management are conducted by the EOSE, an international organization working towards the development of the sport and active leisure sector, with expertise in building bridges between the worlds of education and employment, and ensuring the development of a competent workforce with the right skills.

The managerial competence models

A competence model, in a managerial context, describes the performance criteria or the description of the characteristics of a competence performance against which manager performance is measured, reviewed, and evaluated. It identifies and describes the knowledge, skills, and behaviours needed to perform a role effectively in an organization to achieve the organization's goals (Asumeng, 2014). The concept of managerial competence is rooted in the work of White (1959) who was the first to use the term 'competence' precisely to describe personality characteristics, in particular, scholastic intelligence/cognitive intelligence associated with high motivation and superior performance at work. McClelland (1973) argued that the definition of competency should relate to work behaviours and supported the proposition that behaviours were more likely to have stronger and better predictive validity for managerial performance and effectiveness. Based on the competence definition, a variety of the managerial competence models have been developed since then. They differ in terms of the variability of importance they assign to the different competencies or their cluster.

An overview of the various managerial competence models is offered by Asumeng (2014), and Cheetham and Chivers (1996). They not only critically assess the existing models but also suggest their own models. Moreover, they offer the definitions and clarifications of the terms such as core, generic, meta-competencies, and occupational standards that are in our view crucial for accurate understanding, and to design competence models for sport managers. The perceived importance of the need to differentiate between the functional and personal competence led to not only the existence of the functional competency models but also to the development of behavioural/personal competence models. In the functional model, competence criteria and occupational standards of competence are grounded in the reality of managerial work. It has been a UK tradition and has influenced the development of similar frameworks in some countries in the Commonwealth and the EU (Le Deist et al., 2005).

The model of management competence offered by Boyatzis (1982) contrasted with the UK approach, as many American researchers, especially within the management area, who have focused heavily on behaviours stated that personal competence may be a better predictor of capability than functional competence. Boyatzis (1982) defined competence as performance capability that distinguishes high performing managers from low performing managers, and empirically identified a list of managerial competencies including personality traits, cognitive skills, and interpersonal/social skills. Cheetham and Chivers (1996) describe a model of professional competence which attempts to bring together a number of apparently disparate views of competence, including the "outcomes" approach. The model incorporates both functional and behavioural competence as well as meta-competence and ethics. As they warn, the approach, when the competencies are derived by functional analysis, tends to ignore the personal behaviours which underpin them. Consequently, this aspect of competence has tended to be largely disregarded in training and development programs linked to the standards.

The job competence model, which is often closely associated with UK occupational standards, and the reflective practitioner approach are other competence models explained in detail by Cheetham and Chivers (1996). In the latter, competence is seen as having three basic components – tasks; task management; and the role/job environment. The ability to reflect is considered to be a primary competence of any professional. A new professional competence model suggested by Cheetham and Chivers (1996) is based on the meta-competencies such as communication, self-development, creativity, analysis, and problem solving, which are generic and overarching, i.e. common to all occupations by their nature. They are

Competency-based training: sport managers   253

also fundamental and transferable between different situations and tasks. At the core of the model, there are four key components of professional competence – functional competence; personal or behavioural competence; knowledge/ cognitive competence; and values/ethical competence. The meaning of each of these competencies is defined as well. Four key components of professional competence contain core skills known as constituents.

Asumeng (2014) described the historical development of generic Managerial Competence models and extended the overview by two more competency models. The first one is the domain model of managerial competencies developed by Hogan and Warrenfeltz (2003) that posited that all managerial competencies can be categorized into four main skills: intrapersonal skills; interpersonal skills; leadership skills, and technical/ business skills. The second one is a model suggested by Le Deist et al (2005) that argues for the usefulness of a holistic typology in understanding the combination of knowledge, skills, and social competencies that are necessary for particular occupations and accordingly proposed a multi-dimensional and holistic model of competencies. Building on the Domain Model, Asumeng (2014) defined the key elements in the proposed Holistic Domain Model of Managerial Competencies that comprise six key domains: intrapersonal skills, interpersonal skills, leadership skills, technical/business skills, career skills, and mentoring skills. In addition to the taxonomy of competencies, protocols for measuring and assessing the sample competencies are provided.

Competency-based vs. outcomes-based education

As previously explained, the definitions of the managerial competencies and their incorporation into the managerial competence models should be wisely translated into sport management curricula. Therefore, opinions about the concept of competency-based and outcomes-based education are of crucial importance. Mulder et al (2009) evaluated whether the new (comprehensive) concept of competence and the competency-based education approach are being used in, and perceived as being fruitful for, academic education. The opinions of the respondents from academia on the usefulness of the competency-based education approach were quite positive in so far as there is wide agreement on the necessity to align university curricula to the needs of society and of the labour market. But many hurdles were identified for implementing a competency-based approach in university curricula. The importance of the translation of the competence-oriented education philosophy to the curriculum which should start by the composition of the competence profiles was also highlighted. A way to get to a competence profile is to start with job roles and to define outputs and consequently competencies for those roles. Competencies can be formulated at a general level, but also at a very specific level. While formulating competencies in university education, over-generalization and over-specialization should both be avoided.

Malan (2000) discusses the similarities between the outcomes-based education (OBE) and competency-based education (CBE). The former was favoured internationally to promote educational renewal and has been implemented in countries such as Canada, the United States, and New Zealand whereas competency-based education were introduced in the United States towards the end of the 1960s in reaction to concerns that students are not taught the skills they require in life after school. For OBE, Bloom's (1956) taxonomy, particularly in the cognitive domain, remains invaluable. Competency-based education is based on six critical components (Van der Horst & McDonald 1997) and the explicit learning outcomes for the required skills and concomitant proficiency (standards for assessment) are stressed heavily. All six components are prominent in the outcomes-based education approach as well. Thus, Malan (2000) advocates not only competency-based education but also outcomes-based education approach. An example of how to conceptualize and advance approaches to competency-based learning is offered by Rivenbark and Jacobson (2014) who present lessons learned from the experience of the Master of Public Administration (MPA) program at the University of North Carolina at Chapel Hill (UNC) in its response to the new accreditation standards. A systematic competency-based learning system was adopted and implemented in support of its mission statement of preparing public service leaders. In the process, the most crucial was to identify 40 competencies critical to achieving the program's mission and to group them into eight major competency areas that reflect the universal competencies contained in the accreditation standards. Based on these, the new curriculum has been crafted.

The competence models for sport managers

Few systematic studies exist on competence models for sport managers taken from general management literature. In North America, the COSMA accreditation that replaced former Sport Management Program Review Council is in place although criticized and not accepted entirely especially by sport management programs housed in business schools (Zaharia et al., 2016). In Europe, the process of accreditation is still exclusively in the hands of the respective national bodies. But considering the EU principle of free labour market and movement, there are a lot of initiatives and projects supported that could lead to unified qualification and occupational standards. It is assumed that these will be a vital source for the EU educational standards. But the issue of competence models of sport managers has not been sufficiently discussed and researched yet. The issue of occupational competencies (competence models) of sport managers has been addressed comprehensively neither by academia nor by practice. This prevents linking the market needs and educational and accreditation standards which may cause the lower employability of sport management graduates. Thus, the proposition of a preliminary competency model for sport managers based on the real data from nine European countries (NASME Project) fills an important gap in managerial competency literature for sport management. It provides a conceptual framework for a comprehensive and holistic generic managerial competency model building which has implications for theory, practice, and empirical research.

Method

Based on the data from NASME project the suitability of a general managerial competency model to determine the competency model for the profession of sports manager will be tested. The NASME data were collected with an overall sample of 557 respondents from nine EU countries. A web-based questionnaire was applied to experts in the sport management labour market from four sectors (sport clubs – 30%; sport federations – 22%; public sector – 29%; private sector – 19%). The objective of the quantitative data collection was to examine the performance of competencies of current sport managers as well as the importance of the same competencies when it comes to the future performance of the sport manager profession.

The standardized questionnaire was translated into the languages of the respective project partner countries. Respondents were asked to rate their performance concerning 72 selected competencies on a scale ranging from 1 to 5 (1 = weak, 5 = excellent) and then they were asked to evaluate the future importance of these 72 competencies in the field of sport management on a scale ranging from of 1 to 5 (1 = not at all important, 5 = very important). The data was processed through SPSS, Excel, and/or Webropol. For this paper, the data was additionally analyzed descriptively as current and future competency mean average scores (see Appendix 15.1). Core competencies are highlighted, implying those competencies with mean averages of 4.0 and above for both current and future competencies. The special competencies represent those competencies which may have room for development in the future. They indicate competencies with a difference of at least 0.5 between future and current competencies. On the base of the results from the NASME data and to develop the competence model for sport managers that would reflect the future competencies portfolio of sport managers, the following hypotheses were examined:

H_1: Whether the practitioners from the sport would assign the highest importance to the meta-competencies as defined by the model of professional competence model suggested by Cheetham and Chivers (1996)?

H_2: Whether the future competences assigned by practitioners from sport can be allocated within the model of professional competence model suggested by Cheetham and Chivers (1996)?

H_3: To what extent the competence profiles of sport managers are currently operationalized in the COSMA accreditation manual and the UK Subject Benchmark Statements for Events, Hospitality, Leisure, Sport, and Tourism?

The reason why the model of professional competence model suggested by Cheetham and Chivers (1996) has been chosen as a reference model for testing the hypothesis was explained by the authors themselves:

> One fundamental difference between the provisional model and certain other models (including that implicit within UK occupational standards) is

that the former affords equal prominence to each of the core components. These are all explicit within the model. At the same time, it allows for the possibility that different professions will require a different mix of the core components.(pp. 26–27).

Thus, the chosen competency model offers a solution to the dilemma in sport management education when it comes to the generalist vs. specialist education debate. In other words, the potential differences between and within professions can be resolved by flexible utilization of the 'occupational competence mix' model where the relative importance of each of the core components to different occupations is indicated by the size of the segments.

Results

The first hypothesis has only partially been confirmed. In assessing the validity of H_1, the results from NASME project (Appendix 15.1) namely future mean average of the relevant competencies have been used. Due to the fact that the NASME competencies do not copy in their words those entirely used in the competence model suggested by Cheetham and Chivers (1996), we assessed the meta-competencies either as a stand-alone competency or as a group of competencies which fall under the respective meta-competencies. Meta competencies – communication, self-development, creativity, analysis, and problem solving have been rated as a future competency by sport professionals on a scale ranging from of 1 to 5 (1 = not at all important, 5 = very important) and they all belong to the group of Core Competencies with mean averages of 4.0 and above. But only communication (namely oral) and problem solving skills belong to the group of top 10 future competencies that achieved the highest score among all 72 competencies.

The group of competencies related to the meta-competency Communication achieved a high rate in all sub-components of communication: Oral communication (mean average 4.41); Written communication (mean average 4.28); Communication skills and management (mean average 4.35); Ability to communicate with experts in other fields (mean average 4.23). Thus, this group of competencies belong to the top 15 future competencies for sport managers. Self-development meta-competency was in the NASME survey represented by two single competencies – Capacity to learn (mean average 4.34), and Interest in following the development of the sport management field (mean average 4.03). Creativity meta-competency was also represented by two competencies – Capacity to generate new ideas /Creativity (mean average 4.28), and the Ability to create new products or services (mean average 4.14). Problem solving skills as a stand-alone meta competence achieved the mean average 4.40 as well as analyzing skills with mean average 4.07.

The second hypothesis has been confirmed as far as the future competencies assigned by practitioners from sport can be allocated within the model of professional competence model suggested by Cheetham and Chivers (1996).

We were able to allocate all surveyed future competencies, thanks to the fact that the mean average for all respondents and all 72 competencies was 4.10 (n = 516). This average indicates the high importance of all surveyed competencies for the future performance of sport managers in all sectors. It means we could place all competencies surveyed by the NASME project (except Psychomotor competence) within the model as it is shown in Figure 15.1, which represents the suggested Competence model for sport managers based on the managerial competence model suggested by Cheetham and Chivers (1996) using the results from NASME project.

The question is to what extent digital competence affects the acquisition of other competencies. As a result, we suggest classifying digital competence as a new meta-competence in the proposed model. Digitalization is touching all functional areas of managerial work and without possessing digital competence, current managers cannot possess other competencies that have been identified in the NASME project by practitioners as important for the future such as data management skills, business intelligence in sport, customer relationship management, and ability to use big data.

The proposed competency model uses the results of research within the project on what competencies are necessary for the profession of sports manager in the next ten years and reflects the views of experts from practice in which competencies are to be developed.

To confirm or reject H3 we have conducted a profound analysis of the COSMA accreditation manual (2016) and the QAA UK Subject Benchmark Statements for Events, Hospitality, Leisure, Sport and Tourism (SBS EHLST, 2016), which led us to the decision that we will further deal with just the COSMA manual as far as the QAA UK SBS is relevant for a broad range of Sports programs and not exclusively Sport management programs, and the specific topic areas for sport management programs are not selected. Although the QAA UK SBS is in comparison to the COSMA manual enriched by the list of generic skills and behaviours shared by graduates of all EHLST, their purpose is to form generic learning outcomes using the Bloom taxonomy. Therefore, it is very difficult to find the link between those generic skills and competencies assessed in the NASME project.

COSMA is a leader in outcomes-based assessment and accreditation, in which excellence in sport management education is evaluated based on the assessment of educational outcomes, rather than on prescriptive input standards (COSMA accreditation manual, 2016, p. 1) Excellence in sport management education at the undergraduate level requires coverage of the key content areas of sport management – the Common Professional Component (CPC). The CPC topic areas should be adequately covered within the content of undergraduate sport management programs (COSMA accreditation manual, 2016, p. 15). Each topic area is described in terms of content in detail indicating the potential learning outcomes. Although the Outcomes Assessment Plan is required as a part of the accreditation documentation and the template for its development is provided,

258 Jana Nová

Meta – competencies (Cheetham & Chivers, 1996)	Corresponding competencies from NASME Project
Communication	(Oral communication; Written communication; Communication skills and management; Ability to communicate with experts in other fields)
Self-development	(Capacity to learn; Interest in following the development of the sport management field).
Creativity	(Capacity to generate new ideas - Creativity; Ability to create new products or services)
Analysis	(Analyzing skills)
Problem solving	(Problem solving skills)
Digital competence (newly identified meta competence as a result of NASME project)	*New meta – competence due to digitalization trend* (Use of social media in sport; Digital marketing; Use of virtual media/ platforms in work)

Core components

Competencies defined by (Cheetham & Chivers, 1996)	Corresponding competencies from NASME Project
Knowledge/ cognitive competence	**Corresponding competences from NASME Project**
Tacit/ practical	Project design and management; Marketing; Knowledge of the changing trends in the society; Knowledge of the people's need for physical activity; Knowledge of health issues; Community life in general; Knowledge of welfare policies
Technical/theoretical	Capacity for applying knowledge in practice; Ability to make conclusions from research data; Ability to utilize big data; Research skills
Procedural	Sports related legislation; Crisis management; Risk Management; Stakeholder management
Contextual	The significance of sport and physical activity in the society. Basic general knowledge of sport management profession
Functional competence	**Corresponding competencies from NASME Project**
Occupation specific	Event leadership; Sponsorship management; Financial Management Customer relations management; Sales management; Organization of sports for all -events; Volunteer management; Elite sports event management; Sport facility management; Sport tourism; Physical activities for the disabled; Legacy Planning
Organization process	Organizational skills; Planning skills; Decision making skills; Strategic planning and development; Change management; Human resource management; Recruitment
Cerebral	IT-skills; Knowledge of a second language; Data management skills; Business intelligence in sport
Psychomotor	--------
Personal or behavioral competence	**Corresponding competencies from NASME Project**
Social/vocational	Capacity to adapt to new situations – Flexibility; Leadership skills; Ability to work autonomously; Social intelligence; Critical and self-critical abilities; Desire to succeed; Understanding of cultures and customs; Entrepreneurial spirit
Intra professional	Teamwork; Networking; Ability to work in an interdisciplinary team; Cooperation across different administration sectors; Ability to work in an international context
Values/ ethical competence	**Corresponding competencies from NASME Project**
Personal	Concern for quality enhancement; Ethical commitment; Environmental concern;
Professional	Management with focus on values, ethics and culture, Corporate social responsibility (CSR)

Figure 15.1 Competence Model for Sport Managers.

the link between the CPC topic areas and competencies that will be acquired as a result of the study is not available. The Program-Level Student Learning Outcomes matrix is required as well as the Basic Skills Development Program and the Personal Development Program and here we see room for improvement using the managerial competence model for sport managers that was suggested as a result of H_2.

Discussion

From the results of our study, a few questions emerged that should be reasonable to discuss further. First, worth discussing is the new meta-competency that has been revealed as the result of NASME project – digital competence. Communication as a meta-competency is referred to as the most important competence from early studies to recent studies and projects that deal with competencies of sport managers. As it has been shown by the NASME project results, current and future competencies are influenced significantly by the trends in society such as internationalization, commercialization, and digitalization. Thus, the so-called classical and long-term reoccurring competencies, traditionally bound to the managerial work and managerial roles (Mintzberg, 1975) that inevitably reflect the internationalization and commercialization trends, are enriched by the new competencies influenced by digitalization.

The classic IT skills represent in the digital era basic prerequisites for a new digital competence. This new competence is composed of a variety of sub-competencies – digital marketing, use of social media at work, use of virtual media/platforms at work – just to name those from the NASME project. They are all becoming vital for a sport manager's work and performance. This has been confirmed by the NASME project as the digital sub-competencies scored high as a competency that needs to be developed in the future – digital marketing (mean average 4.32) as well as the use of social media; use of virtual media/platforms at work (mean average 4.20), and IT skills (mean average 4.18).

Second, there is a need to explain the logic of our recommendation to include the suggested competence model for sport managers into existing most relevant and used accreditation frameworks (COSMA, QAA UK). They both have been analyzed concerning the competence model for sport managers that has been suggested based on the NASME data, using the new model of professional competence model suggested by Cheetham and Chivers (1996). To bridge the topic areas and competencies it is suggested to incorporate the competence models for sport managers into accreditations manuals to achieve the shift from an outcomes-based to competency-based curriculum design, although as has been proven by a literature source they are not mutually exclusive. The competence profiles of sport managers can create a vital part of the accreditation materials that would contain the competence/skillsets and thus they will form the frame for the contents of the Basic Skills Development Program and Personal Development Program. Thus, in the end, the assessors will be able to examine how the competences and skills will be acquired to fulfil the managerial competence profile of sport managers at different levels. This would also help to move from an outcomes-based study program design towards a competency-based education approach, the process that was described by Rivenbark and Jacobson (2014) earlier in this paper. The same recommendation is valid for QAA SBS. Developing CIMPSA standards for higher education in sport management can be useful as a point of departure in this process as well. At this point, worth repeating is the opinion presented by Mulder et al (2009) who warn that while formulating competencies in university education, over-generalization and over-specialization should both be avoided.

Third, in resolving the dilemma of shifting from a learning outcomes-based approach towards a competency-based approach, a proper understanding of the role and accurate utilization of Bloom's taxonomy could facilitate the whole process. Defining the level of competence/ skills and not the content of the competence is the viable way as confirmed by the CIMPSA standards, part of which might be seen as a competence model for sport managers as well. The inevitability of enriching the current accreditation standard in sport management and occupational standards that are in development (CIMPSA) regarding the new meta-competence – digital competence – can be confirmed by the fact that the digital sub-competencies achieved the highest difference between the current and future score (use of social media at work: 0.87; digital marketing: 1.2; and the use of virtual media/platforms at work: 0.99), see Appendix 15.1 , which indicates the need for their improvement, so they should be sufficiently covered in sport management curricula as well. Moreover, digital competence is crucial for other meta-competencies as well – communication (digital), creativity (the ability to develop new e-sport products and wise utilization of virtual reality), and even self-development, which is nowadays almost impossible without digital competence.

Conclusion

Our study identified the gap in sport management literature insofar as there is no coherent overview that would cover the development of the competence profile of sport managers and its link to the occupational as well as educational and accreditation standards in sport management. Therefore, we offer such an overview although it is not exhaustive and there is room for future research. Looking back can help foresee the factors that might influence the competencies of sport managers in the future and can enable updating the curricula accordingly. Thus, the mismatch between the sport management graduates' competency profiles and the real sport industry needs can be better balanced.

Our main proposition in terms of the curriculum design and changes in the accreditation standards in sport management studies is to utilize Wiggins and Mc-Tighe's (2005) Backward Instructional Design as it can, by looking at the skills and competencies that students need to achieve, help to introduce the competency-based education model. This model is not contradictory but complementary to the outcomes-based curriculum design required by the current accreditation manuals. The creation of competence models for sport managers as suggested in this paper can assist and guide that endeavour successfully. We do offer a different viewpoint on how to design curriculum for sport management education – taking into consideration existing competence frameworks, results of different competence and occupational studies as well as the result of the international EU projects over 13 years. The difference in our perspective lies in the fact that a single occupational or educational standard cannot capture the variety that exists in sport context (Byers et al., 2012, pp. 21–24).

We do see the competence models for the sport management profession as a viable way to bridge the perceptual gap between academia and sport practice when it comes to the expectation of the competences that should be acquired throughout the university studies by sport management students. The nature of the competency-based education described in six critical components (Van der Horst & McDonald, 1997) especially the first one – explicit learning outcomes for the required skills and concomitant proficiency (standards for assessment) – is of utmost importance in the whole process. In addressing the problem, our review makes a strong case insofar as it offers an overview of the existing approaches towards the setting of educational and occupational standards in the world and highlights the frameworks that can be adopted in the process of curriculum design for sport managers. Instead of focusing on a single competency or their previous clusters, we propose to adjust competency-based models from general business literature – to capture the very nature of the managerial job in sport regardless of the variety of sport context and setting. All this is supported by results regarding the future competencies for sport managers from NASME project. When it comes to the implications, they touch at least three target groups – sport management educators, accreditation bodies, and professionals in sport management.

The implication for sport management educators – they have to accept their responsibility in keeping the health of study programs and single modules wisely using academic freedom – not entirely relying on the result from previous studies and standards. Yiamouyiannis et al (2013) stated that the accreditation and accountability in sport management education are necessary to ensure academic rigor and can serve as vehicles by which sport management educators examine and enhance the academic quality of their programs. But at the same time, the values of US accreditation and recognition (CHEA, 2008) reflect the primary responsibility of higher education institutions in terms of academic quality. The institutional mission and autonomy are essential to judging, sustaining, and enhancing academic quality.

The implication for accreditation bodies – the body of knowledge for educational standards is developing so rapidly that it is not viable/workable to set a definite professional component that would be able to capture all complexities of management in the sport sectors. Therefore, the competence models for sport managers that would reflect the long-term competence needs of the sport labor market seem viable for accreditation purposes. Also, the proposed competency model can be used flexibly in setting accreditation standards and designing study programs for various managerial positions within the sports sectors and thus, create the reasonable core, elective, and compulsory elective subjects within the study programs that would reflect the required competence profile of respective sport management position.

The implication for professionals – they should be more aware of the fact that in the knowledge society and dynamic working environment of sport they cannot expect a graduate that would be able to tackle immediately the majority of the tasks, but they should expect flexible graduates equipped with meta-competencies. These graduates will be able to apply a creative approach and thus develop the nature of sport management work by exploiting the opportunities brought on by the digital era.

References

The Active Leisure Alliance. (2012). Retrieved from https://www.active-leisure-alliance.eu/about-ala

AEHESIS. (2006). Thematic network project aligning a European higher education structure in sport science. Report of the Third Year. Retrieved from http://eose.org/wp-content/uploads/2014/03/AEHESIS_report_3rd-year.pdf

Asumeng, M. (2014). Managerial competency models: A critical review and proposed holistic-domain model. *Journal of Management Research*, 6(4), 1–20.

Bloom, B. S. (1956). *Taxonomy of educational objectives - Handbook 1: Cognitive domain.* New York: McKay.

The Bologna Declaration. (1999). Joint declaration of the European Ministers of Education. Retrieved from https://www.eurashe.eu/library/bologna_1999_bologna-declaration-pdf/

Boyatzis, R. E. (1982). *The competent manager: A model for effective performance.* New York: Wiley.

Brassie, P. S. (1989). Guidelines for programs preparing undergraduate and graduate students for careers in sport management. *Journal of Sport Management*, 3, 158–164.

Byers, T., Slack, T., & Parent, M. (2012). *Key concepts in sport management.* London: Sage.

Chalip, L. (2006). Toward a distinctive sport management discipline. *Journal of Sport Management*, 20, 1–20.

The Chartered Institute for the Management of Sport and Physical Activity. (2020). Retrieved from https://www.workforce.org.uk/who

Cheetham, G., & Chivers, G. (1996). Towards a holistic model of professional competence. *Journal of European Industrial Training*, 20/5, 20–30.

Ciomaga, B. (2013). Sport management: A bibliometric study on central themes and trends. *European Sport Management Quarterly*, 13(5), 557–578.

COSMA Accreditation Manual. (2016). Retrieved from https://www.cosmaweb.org/accreditation-manuals.html

Council for Higher Education Accreditation CHEA. (2008). Accreditation and recognition in the United States. Retrieved August 22, 2019, from https://www.chea.org/sites/default/files/pdf/Principles_Papers_Complete_web.pdf

Cuskelly, G., & Auld, C. (1991). Perceived importance of selected job responsibilities of sport and recreation managers: An Australian perspective. *Journal of Sport Management*, 5, 34–36.

Danylchuk, K. E., & Boucher, R. L. (2003). The future of sport management as an academic discipline. *International Journal of Sport Management*, 4(4), 281–300.

Dick, W., & Carey, L. (2010). Instructional design model. Retrieved August 21, 2019, from http://www.instructionaldesign.org/models/dick_carey_model/

EASM Strategic Priorities 2018–2022. (2018). Retrieved from http://www.easm.net/general-information/

European Association of Sport Management. (2020). Retrieved from http://www.easm.net/

European Credit Transfer and Accumulation System. (2015). Retrieved from https://publications.europa.eu/en/publication-detail/-/publication/da7467e6-8450-11e5-b8b7-01aa75ed71a1

European Observatoire of Sport and Employment. (2020). Retrieved from http://eose.eu/

European Skills Competencies Qualifications and Occupations. (2020). Retrieved from https://ec.europa.eu/esco/portal/home

Hardy, S. (1987). Graduate curriculums in sport management: The need for a business orientation. *Quest*, 39, 207–216.

Hatfield, B. D., Wrenn, J. P., & Bretting, M. M. (1987). Comparison of job responsibilities of intercollegiate athletic directors and professional sport general managers. *Journal of Sport Management*, 1, 129–145.

Hogan, R., & Warrenfeltz, R. (2003). Educating the modern manager. *Academy of Management, Learning and Education*, 2(1), 74–84.

International Standard Classification of Occupations. (2020). ISCO-88. Retrieved from https://www.ilo.org/public/english/bureau/stat/isco/isco88/index.htm

Jamieson, L. M. (1987). Competency-based approaches to sport management. *Journal of Sport Management*, 1, 48–56.

Jones, D. F., Brooks, D. D., & Mak, J. Y. (2008). Examining sport management programs in the United States. *Sport Management Review*, 11(1), 77–91.

Kelley, D. R., Beitel, P. A., DeSensi, J. T., & Blanton, M. D. (1994). Undergraduate and graduate sport management curricular models: A perspective. *Journal of Sport Management*, 8, 93–101.

Kim, A. C. H. (2012). Knowledge structure in sport management: Bibliometric and social network analyses. Unpublished doctoral dissertation, The Ohio State University, Columbus, OH.

Kuhn, T. S. (1962). *The structure of scientific revolutions*. Chicago, IL: University of Chicago.

Lambrecht, K. W. (1987). An analysis of the competencies of sports and athletic club managers. *Journal of Sport Management*, 1, 116–128.

Le Deist, F. D., Delamare, F., & Winterton, J. (2005). What is competence? *Human Resource Development International*, 8(1), 27–46.

Li, M., Ammon, R., & Kanters, M. (2002). Internationalization of sport management curricula in the United States: A national faculty survey. *International Sports Journal*, 6(2), 178–191.

Malan, S. P. T. (2000). The 'new paradigm' of outcomes-based education in perspective. *Journal of Family Ecology and Consumer Sciences*, 28, 22–28.

Mathner, R. P., & Martin, C. L. (2012). Sport management graduate and undergraduate students' perceptions of career expectations in sport management. *Sport Management Education Journal*, 6, 21–31.

McClelland, D. C. (1973). Testing for competence rather than for "intelligence." *American Psychologist*, 28, 1–14.

Mintzberg, H. (1975). The manager's job: Folklore and fact. *Harvard Business Review*, 53, 49–61.

Miragaia, D. A. M., & Soares, J. A. P. (2017). Higher education in sport management: A systematic review of research topics and trends. *Journal of Hospitality, Leisure, Sport & Tourism Education*, 21, 101–116.

Mulder, M., Gulikers, J., Biemans, H., & Wesselink, R. (2009). The new competence concept in higher education: Error or enrichment? *Journal of European Industrial Training*, 33(8), 755–770.

NASPE-NASSM. (1993). Standards for curriculum and voluntary accreditation of sport management education programs. *Journal of Sport Management*, 7, 159–170.

National Association for Sport and Physical Education (NASPE). (2020). Retrieved from https://www.nassm.com/NASSM/Purpose

New Age of Sport Management. (2019). Retrieved from https://docs.wixstatic.com/ugd/dbfb00_072a07414679444f8f90cc2d22ba5b1e.pdf

New Age of Sport Management (NASME). (2020). Retrieved from https://www.nasme.eu/

North American Society for Sport Management (NASME). Retrieved from https://www.nassm.com/NASSM/Purpose

Parkhouse, B. L. (1987). Sport management curricula: Current status and design implications for future development. *Journal of Sport Management*, 1, 93–115.

Parkhouse, B. L., Ulrich, D., & Soucie, D. (1982). Research in sport management: A vital rung of this new corporate ladder. *Quest*, 34(2), 176–186.

Parks, J. B., & Quain, R. J. (1986). Sport management survey: Curriculum perspectives. *Journal of Physical Education, Recreation and Dance*, 57(4), 22–26.

Pitts, B. G., & Danylchuk, K. E. (2007). Examining the body of knowledge in sport management: A preliminary descriptive study of current sport management textbooks. *Sport management Education Journal*, 1, 40–52.

Pitts, B. G., & Pedersen, P. M. (2005). Examining the body of scholarship in sport management: A content analysis of the Journal of Sport Management. *The SMART Journal*, 2(1), 33–52.

The Quality Assurance Agency for Higher Education, QAA. (2016). UK subject benchmark statement: Events, hospitality, leisure, sport, and tourism. Retrieved from https://www.qaa.ac.uk/docs/qaa/subject-benchmark-statements/sbs-events-hospitality-leisure-sport-tourism-16.pdf?sfvrsn=159df781_10

Rivenbark, W. C., & Jacobson, W. S. (2014). Three Principles of competency-based learning: Mission, mission, mission. *Journal of Public Affairs Education*, 20(2), 181–192.

Ross, C. M., Jamieson, L. M., & Young, S. J. (1999). Professional preparation in sport management: An empirical study. SCHOLE: *A Journal of Leisure Studies and Recreation Education*, 14(1), 1–17.

Schwarz, E. C. (2010). The reciprocal and influential connection between sport marketing and management and the sport sciences. *International Journal of Sport Management and Marketing*, 7(1/2), 33–43.

Sector Skills Alliances. (2012). Sectoral social dialogue committee for professional football. Retrieved from https://eacea.ec.europa.eu/erasmus-plus/actions/key-action-2-cooperation-for-innovation-and-exchange-good-practices/sector-skills_en

Soucie, D., & Doherty, A. (1996). Past endeavours and future perspectives for sport management research. *QUEST*, 48, 486–500.

Tuning Methodology. (2000). Retrieved from http://tuningacademy.org/methodology/?lang=en

Van der Horst, H., & McDonald, R. (1997). *OBE: A teacher's manual.* Kagiso: Pretoria.

Wiggins, G., & McTighe, J. (2005). *2005 understanding by design.* Alexandria, VA: Association for Supervision & Curriculum Development.

White, R. W. (1959). Motivation reconsidered: the concept of competence. *Psychological Review, 66*(5), 297–333.

Yiamouyiannis, A., Bower, G. G., Williams, J., Gentile, D., & Alderman, H. (2013). Sport management education: Accreditation, accountability, and direct learning outcome assessments. *Sport Management Education Journal, 7,* 51–59.

Zaharia, N., Kaburakis, A., & Pierce, D. (2016). U.S. sport management programs in business schools: Trends and key issues. *Sport Management Education Journal, 10*(1), 13–28.

Appendix 15.1

NASME project results – Competencies mean average scores in descending order

NASME Competencies	Current (Mean Average)	Future (Mean Average)	Difference
Teamwork	4.21	4.49	0.28
Organizational skills	4.19	4.41	0.22
Planning skills	4.11	4.41	0.30
Oral communication	4.10	4.41	0.31
Decision making skills	3.98	4.41	0.43
Capacity to adapt to new situations (Flexibility)	4.13	4.40	0.27
Problem solving skills	4.07	4.40	0.33
Capacity for applying knowledge in practice	3.90	4.39	0.49
Strategic planning and development	3.81	4.38	0.57
Leadership skills	3.87	4.37	0.50
Communication skills and management	3.89	4.35	0.46
Networking	3.73	4.35	0.62
Capacity to learn	4.03	4.34	0.31
Ability to work autonomously	4.31	4.32	0.01
Use of social media in work	3.45	4.32	0.87
Digital marketing	3.12	4.32	1.20
Social intelligence	4.06	4.31	0.25
Written communication	3.94	4.28	0.34
Capacity to generate new ideas (Creativity)	3.84	4.28	0.44
Ability to work in an interdisciplinary team	3.97	4.26	0.29
Critical and self-critical abilities	3.83	4.26	0.43
Project design and management	3.75	4.25	0.50
Ability to communicate with experts in other fields	3.88	4.23	0.35
Marketing	3.39	4.21	0.82
Knowledge of the changing trends in the society	3.63	4.20	0.57
Use of virtual media/platforms in work	3.21	4.20	0.99
Concern for quality enhancement	3.88	4.19	0.31
Desire to succeed	4.19	4.18	−0.01
IT-skills	3.51	4.18	0.67

Event leadership	3.92	4.17	0.25
Service orientation	3.97	4.16	0.19
Sponsorship management	3.39	4.15	0.76
Ability to create new products or services	3.49	4.14	0.65
Financial management	3.42	4.14	0.72
Cooperation across different administration sectors	3.76	4.13	0.37
Knowledge of a second language	3.48	4.13	0.65
Customer relations management	3.45	4.12	0.67
Ethical commitment	3.88	4.10	0.22
Ability to work in an international context	3.56	4.08	0.52
Change management	3.51	4.08	0.57
Analyzing skills	3.59	4.07	0.48
The significance of sport and physical activity in the society	4.01	4.06	0.05
Management with focus on values, ethics, and culture	3.76	4.03	0.27
Interest to follow the development of the sport management field	3.69	4.03	0.34
Knowledge of the people's need for physical activity	3.88	4.02	0.14
Human resource management	3.58	4.02	0.44
Ability to make conclusions from research data	3.55	4.02	0.47
Sales management	3.18	4.00	0.82
Data management skills	3.46	3.99	0.53
Basic general knowledge of sport management profession	3.59	3.98	0.39
Understanding of cultures and customs	3.76	3.97	0.21
Organization of sports for all events	3.64	3.97	0.33
Business intelligence in sport	3.25	3.97	0.72
Entrepreneurial spirit	3.46	3.95	0.49
Volunteer management	3.54	3.94	0.40
Crisis management	3.43	3.93	0.50
Knowledge of health issues	3.55	3.91	0.36
Sports related legislation	3.22	3.89	0.67
Ability to utilize big data	3.11	3.89	0.78
Corporate social responsibility (CSR)	3.37	3.88	0.51
Environmental concern	3.49	3.87	0.38
Elite sports event management	3.46	3.86	0.40
Risk management	3.32	3.85	0.53
Community life in general	3.75	3.84	0.09
Recruitment	3.42	3.83	0.41
Stakeholder management	3.28	3.83	0.55
Sport facility management	3.32	3.81	0.49
Sport tourism	3.29	3.73	0.44
Knowledge of welfare policies	3.26	3.73	0.47
Physical activities for the disabled	3.04	3.64	0.60
Research skills	3.23	3.61	0.38
Legacy planning	3.01	3.56	0.55

Sources of data

9 National Reports in the NASME project: https://www.nasme.eu/

- Nová, J. (2019). *NASME report Czech Republic*. Brno: Masaryk University
- Nørgaard, M., & Sørensen, J. P. (2019). *The NASME report Denmark 2019*. University College Northern Denmark
- Puronaho, K., Laitila, O., & Puronaho, V. (2019). *NASME report Finland*. Helsinki: Haaga-Helia University of Applied Sciences
- Le Roux, N. (2019). *NASME report France*. Montpellier: University of Montpellier
- Wohlfart, O., Adam, S., Hovemann, G., & Kaden, M. (2019). *NASME report Germany*. Leipzig: Leipzig University
- Kosta, G., Tsitskari, E., Yfantidou, G., Matsouka, O., & Astrapellos, K. (2019). *NASME report Greece*. Komotini: Democritus University of Thrace
- Cingiene, V. (2019). *NASME report Lithuania*. Vilnius: Mykolas Romeris University
- Skirstad, B., Strittmatter, A.-M., & Grønkjær, A. B. (2019). *Sport management: Present and future trends in Norway*. Oslo: Norwegian School of Sport Sciences
- Gallardo, L., García-Unanue, J., Felipe, J. L., Sánchez-Sánchez, J., Cabello, D., & Colino, E. (2019). *NASME report Spain*. Toledo: Universidad de Castilla-La Mancha

Index

Note: **Bold** page numbers refer to tables; *italic* page numbers refer to figures.

Aaker, J. L. 212
Abramovich, Roman 104
Academy of Management Journal 85
The Active Leisure Alliance (ALA) 251
Advertising Value Equivalent (AVE) 119
Advisory Board model 14
Ahn, C. 86
Ahn, K. 87
Ali, Muhammad 214
Aligning a European Higher Educational Structure in Sport Science (AEHESIS) project 244, 250
Ali Sports 146, 148, 157, 158, 161
Al Nahyan, Sheikh Mansour bin Zayed 104
Alpha Romeo 121–122
Alpha Tauri 121–122
Al Sayed, Ahmad 104
Amabile, T. M. 87
Ancient Olympic Games 11
Anderson, Kenny 150
Andreff, W. 103–105, 107
Annuaire du Comité International Olympique 227
Antetokounmpo, Giannis 32
anticipatory principle, AI 18
Appreciative Inquiry (AI) 17; defined 17; as generative process *17*; principles 17–18
Arango, M. 133
Arellano, A. 27, 28, 34
Armstrong, D. A. 155
Arthur, M. B. 40

Association of National Olympic Committees (ANOC) 12
Association of Tennis Professionals (ATP) 193
Asumeng, M. 252, 253
athletic talents and team structure 165–178
ATP World Tour in Shanghai 193
Auld, C. 246
Avelino, J. 135

Baker, T. 154
Barghchi, M. 24
Baron, R. M. 93
Bavaria Munich 32
Bayle, E. 10–11
Beckham, David 3, 165, 166, 170
Beek, R. M. 106
behavior-focused strategies 83–84, 89
Beilein, John 215
Bergsgard, N. A. 22
Bevir, M. 1
Bianchi, Jules 116
bicultural-bilingual coaches: and communication 69; findings of research study 63–68; golf coaches 62–72; limitations 71; *vs.* monocultural-monolingual coaches 60–72; practical implications 70–71; research study 62–63; *see also* coaches
bicultural-bilinguals 61–62
biculturalism 61
"Big Count" study 103

270 Index

Big Ten Conference 153
Big Tourney.com 148
bilingualism 61–62
Bird, Larry 147
Blanchard, K. 86
Bloom, B. S. 254
Bobo, M. 135
Bologna Declaration 250
Bosman-Ruling 31–33
Boule, K. 34
Boyatzis, R. E. 252
'brain drain' phenomenon 31
branding and theory of awe 211–213
Brassie, P. S. 246
broadcast income 111
Bruce, R. A. 89
Byron, K. C. 22
Byun, J. 95

Canada, sport policy in 24, 26–27
Canadian Football League 154
career capital 40–41, 47–49
career success, and international
   experience 41–42, 49–51
Carey, L. 247
Carlson, B. D. 213
Cashman, J. F. 81
Caslavova, E. 107
CBS Sports 148
Certificate in Football Management
   (CFM) 45, 55
Chalip, L. 247
The Chartered Institute for the
   Management of Sport and Physical
   Activity (CIMSPA) 251; Higher
   Education Partnership Pilot scheme
   251; Professional Standards Matrix 251
Chartered Institute of Management 251
Cheetham, G., 252, 255–257, 259
Chepyator-Thomson, J. R. 23
Chiellini, Giorgio 136
Chinese Collegiate Athletic
   Association 162
Chinese Collegiate Athletic League
   161–162
Chinese collegiate sports 146–162; and
   CUBA Tournament 158
Chinese Super League (CSL) 5

Chinese University Basketball Association
   (CUBA): feasibility of Chinese
   Collegiate Athletic League 161–162;
   game design 156–157; game design
   and culture 150–151; limitations of
   CUBA League 151–153; management
   ideology 155–156; market development
   151; method 155; NCAA 153–155;
   organization structure 149–150;
   overview 146–147; restructuring
   146–162; review of literature 147–155;
   social participation 157–159; team
   management 159–160
Chinese University Basketball Super
   League (CUBS) 148
Chinese University Sports Association
   (CUSA) 146, 149–150
Chivers, G. 252, 255–257, 259
Choi, Y.-d. 25
Cleland, J. 231
coaches: bicultural-bilingual 62–63;
   bicultural-bilingual *vs.* monocultural-
   monolingual 60–72; communication in
   foreign languages 60
Code of Points 133, 136, 138, 141
Code of Punctuation 132
cognitive strategies 83–84
college football fans and Jordan Brand
   210–221
Collegiate Athletic League 162
Collegiate Licensing Company 154
commercial globalisation 106
commercial income 111–112
commercial revenue 104
The Commission on Sport Management
   Accreditation (COSMA) 245;
   accreditation manual 257; accreditation
   process 247, 254; accreditation
   standards 249
Commonwealth 231
Commonwealth Games 24, 232, 237
Commonwealth Games Federation
   (CGF) 232
Commonwealth of Nations 232
communal engagement 195, 199
competence, described 85
competence model, for sport managers
   254, 258

competencies for sport managers 245–248
competency-based education 253–254
competency-based training: competence models for sport managers 254, 258; competencies for sport managers 245–248; competency-based *vs.* outcomes-based education 253–254; curriculum model development 248–251; discussion 259–260; managerial competence models 251–253; method 255–256; overview 244–245; review of literature 245–254; of sport management personnel 244–262
Concacaf Champions League 168
constructionist principle, AI 17
constructive-thought-pattern strategies 89
Constructors' Championship 117, 118
Cooperative Governance model 14
corporate social responsibility (CSR) 28
Council of Europe 227
COVID-19 pandemic 15, 216
Crean, Tom 160
CUBA League *see* Chinese University Basketball Association (CUBA)
cultural diplomacy 192
cultural intermediary 195
curriculum model development 248–251
Cuskelly, G. 246

Dansereau, F. Jr. 79
Darby, P. 32
de Coubertin, Baron Pierre 225, 227
de D'Amico, López 135
DeFillippi, R. J. 40
Deloitte 111
designated player rule 166–167
destination image: cognitive dimension 193–194; defined 193; of event-hosting city 193–194
Dick, W. 247
Dienesch, R. M. 81, 82
digital globalisation 106
Ding 152
DJ Khaled 214
Donovan, D. T. 213
Downey, A. 27, 28, 34
Drivers' Championship 117
Drucker, P. F. 86–87

Duran, C. A. 82
Dyson, K. S. 60

Earth Summit 227
Ecclestone, Bernie 116
Edelman, M. 153
education: competency-based 253–254; outcomes-based 253–254
Emmert, Mark 149
empowerment 80, 84–85; and innovative behavior 86–87; and leader-member exchange 86; mediating effect of 93–95, **94**; research study method **88,** 88–93, **90–93**
English Football League (EFL) 3–4
English Premier League (EPL) 3, 5, 78
Erasmus Programme 39
Ernest, M. 106
Esmirna World Championship 2014 137
ESPN 148, 216
European Association of Sport Management (EASM) 250
European Credit Transfer and Accumulation System (ECTS) 250
European Network of Sport Science, Education and Employment (ENSSEE) 250
European Network of Sport Sciences in Higher Education 249
European Observatoire for Sport Employment (EOSE) 249
European professional football clubs: economic flows in 103–112; football globalisation of 105–107; models of economic flows in 108–111, *109*; professional sports finance *105*
European Skills Competencies Qualifications and Occupations (ESCO) 251
European Sports Charter 227
European Union (EU) 31, 32, 39, 249–252, 254–255, 261
event-hosting city, destination image of 193–194

Falcous, M. 33
FC Barcelona 32

Federation Internationale de Football Association (FIFA): "Big Count" study 103; doping scandal 9; laws of 29; World Cup 2014 132, 136
Fédération Internationale de l'Automobile (FIA) 116
Fehlmann, R. 196
Fernandez, S. 96
Ferrari 120–122, 127–128
Ferreira, M. 140
fiduciary approach, and sport governance 14
First Nation communities 33–34
Five Star Sports Television 158
football: globalisation of 105–107; goals of professional clubs 107–108; *see also* Federation Internationale de Football Association (FIFA)
football clubs: economic goals 107–108; goals of 107–108; social goals 108; sport goals 107; *see also* football
Force India 121; *see also* Racing Point
Formula One (F1) drivers 115–116, 129
Formula One Grand Prix 193
Formula One Group 116
Formula One (F1) racing: current landscape of 120–122, **120–122**; financial investment efficiency in 115–129; financial restrictions as incoming change 123–126, **124**; importance of winning in 118–120; overview and history of 116; payouts for teams for 2019 **118**; rule changes 123; and sponsorship 118–119; team-based structure of 117; and technology 119
Forsyth, J. 28
Fort, R. 107
Fort, R. D. 107
Fourth Industrial Revolution 16, 19
Fox Sports 148
Fredy, Pierre 12
Freitas, I. 141
Frick, B. 33

Gamarro, José 136
game design: CUBA 150–151, 156–157
Garber, Don 167
Garcia, B. 29

Gardam, K. 27, 33
GC2018 233, 235–236; LGBTIQ inclusion at 237; Reconciliation Action Plan (RAP) 236–237; Sustainable Goods and Services Guidelines 237
General Allocation Money (GAM) 167–168
General Association of International Sports Federations (GAISF) 12
generative approach, and sport governance 14
'Geneva Charter of the Rights of the Child in Sports' 227
geographical globalisation 106
German model 12–13
G-Force, defined 115
Ghemawat, P. 106
Ghosh, K. 79
Giles, A. 27
Giles, A. R. 28
globalisation: commercial 106; digital 106; of football 105–107; geographical 106
Global Mindset Project (GMP) 16
Global Reporting Initiative (GRI) 233, 240; Content Index integrated with SDGs **234–235**; reporting framework 226
GOLDOC 232, 237–239; SDG 11 achieved by **234–235**; Sustainability and Legacy Team 237
golf 60
golf coaches 62–72; bicultural-bilingual *vs.* monocultural-monolingual study 62–72; data analysis 63; findings 63–68; procedures 62–63; *see also* coaches
Gomez, S. 9
governance: contemporary view of 1; defined 1; overview 1–3; as "paradigm-generating concept" 10; in sport industry 3–4; of sport in globalized market place 4–6; traditional view of 1
Graen, G. 79, 80, 81
Graen, G. B. 80, 86
Grahlow, H. 196
Grands Prix 116
Gretzky, Wayne 214
Grix, J. 195–196
Grosjean, F. 61

Guangzhou Radio and TV Channel 158
Guardo, M. 141
Guillen, F. 133

Haas 121
Hackett, Jim 215
Haga, W. J. 79
Haidt, J. 211–212
Hamzeh, M. 30
Hanning, R. 34
Harris, Jordan 155, 160
Harrison, C. K. 215
Hayes, A. F. 94
Hayhurst, L. 27
Henghua International Group 148
Hilgers, D. 192
Hogan, R. 253
Hong, W. 87
Houghton, J. D. 86, 89
Houlihan, B. 195–196
Houston Rockets 4
Howell, R. D. 82
Huang, H. 193
Huh, J. 86
Hyundai 78

Ibrahimovic, Zlatan 3, 171, 173–174, 175, 177, **180–181, 189–191**
impact, and empowerment 85
Indiana State Sycamores 147
innovative behavior: and empowerment 86–87; and leader-member exchange 86; research study method **88**, 88–93, **90–93**
Instant Replay and Control System (IRCOS) 137
Intercollegiate Athletic Association of the United States (IAAUS) 161
International Basketball Federation (FIBA) 29–30
International Committee of Sports for the Deaf (ICSD) 12
international experience (IE): and career capital 40–41; and career success 41–42; defined 40; impact of 46–51; and research 42–43; and research methods 43–45, **44**; scale and forms of 45–46, 46

International Football Association Board (IFAB) 29
International Gymnastics Federation (FIG) 133, 135–138, 141–142
International Olympic Committee (IOC) 12, 30, 228; centenary congress 227; Commission for Sport and the Environment 227; Olympic Agenda 2020 229
International Organization for Standardization (ISO) 226
International Paralympic Committee (IPC) 12
International School Sport Federation (ISSF) 12
international sport events: endorsing public diplomacy through 192–204; engagement in 194–195; soft power and country reputation enhanced by 195–197
International University Sports Federation 12
IOC (International Olympic Committee) 225, 227–228, 229
ISO20121 226, 232

Jacobson, W. S. 254, 260
James, LeBron 214
Jamieson, L. M. 245
Jang, S. Y. 96
Japanese model 12–13
Jeong, W. 86
Jewell, R. T. 171
Johnson, Magic 147
Johnson, Trey 154
Johnson, T. W. 80
Jones, D. F. 247
Jordan, Michael 151, 210–221; fans and audiences of 213–216; review of literature 211–216
Jordan Brand: branding and theory of awe 211–213; collecting data in real time 216–219; and college football fans 210–221; fans and audiences of Michael Jordan 213–216; last dance phenomenon 216; overview 210–211; review of literature 211–216
'judgmental sampling' approach 62

274 Index

Kaka, Ricardo 3, 165, 171–173, 174, 175–176, 177, **182–184, 189–191**
Kang, M. 195
Kang, N. 86
Kase, K. 9
Kazan Action Plan 133, 229
Kelley, D. R. 246
Keltner, D. 211–212
Kenny, D. A. 93
Kent, M. L. 195
Kenya, sport policy in 23–24
Kim, C. S. 96
Kim, H. Y. 96
Kim, I. 87
Kim, K. S. 96
Kim, T. 86
Kim, W. C. 79
knowing-how, defined 40
knowing-whom capital 41, 54
knowing-why capabilities 40–41, 53
Ko, J. 95
Kohlberg, R. 134; moral development theory 134
Korea: hierarchical corporate culture 78; professional sports teams in 77–78
Korea Baseball Organization (KBO) 77
Kreitler, C. M. 60, 61
Kwak, M. 86
Kyoung, I. 86, 95

Ladies Professional Golf Association (LPGA) 4
La Liga 5–6
Lambrecht, K. W. 245
Lanfranchi, P. 32
The Last Dance 216
leader-member exchange (LMX) 79–80; attributes 81; dimensions **82**; and empowerment 86; and innovative behavior 86; overview 80; research study method **88**, 88–93, **90–93**; theorizing the process of **82**
Le Deist, F. D. 253
Lee, K. 87
Lee, M. 87
L'Etang, J. 195
Li, M. 246
Liden, R. C. 81, 89

Liga MX 166
Lim, J. 195
Liverpool FC 3
López, M. 133

Maennig, W. 192
Maguire, J. 33
Major League Baseball (MLB) 3, 6, 78, 165
Major League Collective Bargaining Agreement 168
Major League Soccer (MLS) 2, 3; beyond the pitch impact 175–176; data collection and analyses 172–173; designated player rule 166–167; founded in 166; general allocation money 167–168; history of 165–166; marquee player 171–172; overview 165; on the pitch impact 173–175; player statistics and attendance **180–191**; review of literature 170–172; rules comparing around the world 169; target allocation money 168–169
Malan, S. P. T. 253–254
Malaysia, sport policy in 24
Malem, J. 142
management cooperation 194
management ideology: of CUBA 155–156; of NCAA 155–156
Management Team model 14
managerial competence models 251–253
Manz, C. C. 83
March Madness 146–147, 150; *see also* NCAA Division I Men's Basketball Tournament
market development: CUBA 151; NCAA 151
marquee players: definition and background of 171–172; in Major League Soccer 165–178
Martin, C. L. 247
Martínez, M. 138
Maslow's theory of basic needs 134
Maslyn, J. M. 81
Mason, C. 33
Mason, C. W. 34
Mason, K. 212
matchday income 111

Index 275

Mathner, R. P. 247
Mauborgne, R. 79
McClelland, D. C. 252
McHugh, T. L. 33
McHugh, T. L. F. 34
McLaren 121
MCMMG (Media – Corporations –
  Merchandising – Markets – Global)
  104, 105, *105*
McSweeney, M. 27
McTighe, J. 247, 260
meaning, defined 85
measurement instruments 208–209
Meier, H. E. 29
Mercedes 120–122, 127–128
Michigan State Spartans 147
Millennium Development Goals
  (MDGs) 226
Millington, R. 27
Miragaia, D. A. M. 248
MLS Players Association 166
Moldogaziev, T. 96
monocultural-monolingual coaches: *vs.*
  bicultural-bilingual coaches 60–72;
  and communication 69–70; findings of
  research study 63–68; research study
  62–63
Montreal Olympic Games 136
Moon, Y. 86
morality 134
Mulder, M. 253, 260
Mullen, Dan 215
multilingual coaches 60
Muslimat 30

name, image, and likeness (NIL)
  compensation 3
narrative principle, AI 18
NASME project 244–245, 250, 255–259;
  competencies mean average scores in
  descending order 266–268; national
  reports in 268
National and European Qualification
  Frameworks 251
National Association for Sport and
  Physical Education (NASPE) 246, 248
National Association of Basketball
  Coaches (NABC) 147

National Basketball Association (NBA) 3,
  6, 32, 147, 165, 210
National Collegiate Athletic Association
  (NCAA) 2, 146–162; Board of
  Governors 149–150, 154; Committee
  156; game design 156–157; issues
  of 153–155; organization structure
  149–150; social participation 157–159;
  sponsorship 158; team management
  159–160; values and belief 156
National Collegiate Track and Field
  Championships 161
National Football League (NFL) 3, 165
national governing bodies
  (NGBs) 9–11
National Olympic Committee 23
National Sport Authority (NSA) 30
National Sport Federation of Ghana
  (NSF) 30
natural reward strategy 84, 89
NCAA Division I Men's Basketball
  Tournament 146; *see also* March
  Madness
Neck, C. P. 83, 89
Netflix 216
New Age of Sport Management
  (NASME) ERASMUS+ 244
Nicholls, S. 28
Nike 210, 214, 221
non-profit sport organizations 13
North American Society for Sport
  Management (NASSM) 246–248
Novak, T. 146
Nye, J. S. 196, 203

Obama, Barack 215
O'Bannon, Ed 154
Olajuwon, Hakeem 4
Olympic Agenda 2020 229
Olympic Charter 227
Olympic Movement 225, 227–229
Olympic Movement Agenda 21 228
Omar, D. 24
organization structure: CUBA 149–150;
  NCAA 149–150
Orris, J. B. 80
outcomes-based education 253–254;
  competency-based *vs.* 253–254

Paiva, C. 136
Palmer, C. 22
"paradigm-generating concept," governance as 10
Parkhouse, B. L. 246, 247
Passow, T. 196
Patron Governance model 14
Paul, Chris 214
Pay Drivers 119
Pedersen, P 104
Perez, Sergio 119
performance tolerance 194–195
personality 61; and acculturation 61; traits 61
Pfeffer, J. 79
Phillips, R. L. 82
Piña, J. 135
poetic principle, AI 17–18
Poland: applicability of international experience in the football context in 51–53; and football 42–43; and international experience research 41–45; results of international experience research 45–46
policy: defined 22; sport *see* sport policies
Policy Board model 14
Porsche, M. 192
positive principle, AI 18
Preacher, K. J. 94
professional football clubs *see* football clubs
professional preparation 244–262
Programme SOCRATES (Directorate General XXII) 249
Promoting Life-Skills in Aboriginal Youth (PLAY) program 27
prosocial behavior 194
Protestant Reformation 11
public diplomacy: destination image of event-hosting city 193–194; endorsing, through international sport events 192–204; implications 203–204; and international sport events 194–195; limitations 204; measurement 198–199; measurement model 199–200; overview 192–193; review of literature 193–197; sample and data collection procedure 197; soft power and country reputation 195–197; suggestions for future studies 204
public engagement, defined 195

The Quality Assurance Agency for Higher Education (QAA) UK Subject Benchmark Statements for Events, Hospitality, Leisure, Sport, and Tourism (EHLST) 249, 257
Quirk, J. 107

Racing Point 121, 128
Ramírez, J. 140
Real Madrid 32
Red Bull Racing 120–122, 127–128
Reese, B. 167
Renault 121
rhythmic gymnastics judging: discussion 141–144; method 138–139; overview 132–133; policy implications in 132–144; results 139–141; review of literature 133–138
Rivenbark, W. C. 254, 260
Robinson, L. 10–11
Roger Humanistic theory 134
Rooney, Wayne 171–172, 174–175, 176, 177, **187–188, 189–191**
Ross, C. M. 246
Ross, S. D. 170–171
Russian Olympic doping scandal 9
Ruth, Babe 214

Samsung 78
Sarbanes-Oxley Act (SOX) 12
Scandura, T. A. 86
Scelles, N. 107
school sport policy 23
Scott, S. G. 89
SDG 11: achieved By GOLDOC **234–235**; as urban SDG 230
SDG Compass Annex: Linking the SDGs and GRI Standards (GRI) 233
self-correcting feedback 84
self-determination 85
self-leadership 79, 83–84; dimensions 89; research study method **88,** 88–93, **90–93**

self-observation 84
self-reward 84
Senna, Ayrton 116
Sethna, C. 28
setting self-goals 84
Shanghai ATP Masters 1000 193, 204
Shanghai International Marathon 193
Shanghai Rolex Masters 197
Shao, Aifei 155
Sima, J. 107, 108
simultaneity principle, AI 18
Skinner, K. 34
Slim, Carlos 119
Slonaker, Mark 155, 157
Soares, J. A. P. 248
social participation: CUBA 157–159;
    NCAA 157–158
SOCRATES Programme of the European
    Commission 250
soft power and international sport events
    195–197
South Africa, sport policy in 23
Southeastern Conferences (SEC) 153
South Korea, sport policy in 24
Special Olympics International (SOI) 12
sponsorship, and Formula One (F1) racing
    118–119
sport fan engagement 192–204, 199;
    defined 194; in international sport
    events 194–195
sport for development (SFD) 26, 27
sport governance: challenges and
    opportunities 15–19, 17; at different
    levels 2; necessity of inquires into 6;
    systems of 10–15
sport industry: and globalization 4;
    governance in 3–4
sport judge or referee: assessment of 133;
    instrument for the judge's evaluation
    143; subjective value of 134
sport managers: competence model for
    254, 258; competencies for
    245–248
sport policies: in context of global sport
    bodies 29–30; defined 22; in diverse
    countries 23–26; future for development
    and implementation 33–35;
    glocalization-localization of 30–31;

implementation and challenges 27–33;
    in indigenous communities 26–27
sports: for advancement of social policy
    and development 22; defined 25;
    importance of 21; policies see sport
    policies; sector, sustainability in
    227–229
sport sustainability 227–229; Gold Coast
    2018 232–233; historical stages of 228
Spreitzer, G. M. 89
Staudohar, P. D. 103–105
Strachan, L. 33, 34
strategic approach, and sport
    governance 14
Stricklin, Scott 215
Stroll, Lance 119
Suarez, Luis 136
sustainability in sports sector see sport
    sustainability
Sustainable Development Goals (SDGs)
    16, 226, 229, 240; GRI Content Index
    integrated with **234–235**; urban 230
sustainable sport events: background
    and review of literature 230–233;
    future research 240; and impact on
    urban development 225–240; results
    and discussion 233–240; structuring
    225–240; sustainability in sports sector
    227–229; urban SDG 230
Suutari, V. 42
Swiss Agency for Development and
    Cooperation (SDC) 85
systematic random sampling 197

Tacon, R. 25
Target Allocation Money (TAM) Policy
    168–169
Taylor, M. 32, 195
team management: CUBA 159–160;
    NCAA 159–160
technology, and Formula One (F1)
    racing 119
theory of awe 211–213
Thomas, K. W. 80, 86
Thomson, M. 213
thought self-leadership (TSL) 84
Thunderbird School of Global
    Management 16

278 Index

Title IX 2
Toronto Raptors 32
transnational postcolonial feminist participatory action research study (TPFPAR) 27
Treaty of Rome 31
Tsuji, L. 34
Tuning methodology 250
2030 Agenda for Sustainable Development 229, 230–231

UK-US model 12–13
UN 2030 Agenda 226
UNCED (United Nations Conference on Environment and Development) Agenda 21 227–228
UNEP (United Nations Environment Programme) 228
UNESCO's International Charter of Physical Education and Sport 227
UN-Habitat 230
Union of European Football Association (UEFA) 3, 169; Certificate in Football Management (CFM) 45, 55; Financial Fair Play rule 104
United Kingdom, sport policy in 25
United Nations (UN) 231; International School Sport Federation (ISSF) 12
United Nations Environment Programme (UNEP) 228
United States Soccer Federation 165
urban development, and sustainable sport events 225–240
urban SDG 230
Urrutia, I. 9

Valdés, H. 140
Van Luijk, N. 27

Velthouse, B. A. 80
Venezuelan Gymnastics Federation (FVG) 136
Verschueren, J. 106
vertical dyad linkage (VDL) theory 80–81
Villa, David 171–173, 174, 176, 177, **184–187, 189–191**

Waldrep, Alvis Kent 155
Walters, G. 25
Wamsley, K. B. 28
Wang, H. T. 152
Wang, N. 157
Warren, C. J. 170–171
Warrenfeltz, R. 253
Weber, M. 212, 213
White, R. W. 251
Wiggins, G. 247, 260
Williamson, Zion 151
Williams Racing 122
Won, D. 86
Wooden, John 147
World Association for Sport Management (WASM) 7
World Economic Forum (WEF) 15
World Population Review 198
Wu, Q. 151

Yan, Z. 150
Yang, D. S. 96
Yiamouyiannis, A. 247, 261
Yoho, S. K. 86
Yoshida, M. 194, 199
Yun, I. 86

Zaharia, N. 248
Zhuang, W. 148

Printed in the USA
CPSIA information can be obtained
at www.ICGtesting.com
LVHW011141150324
774517LV00041B/1694